WHAT PEOPLE ARE SAYING ABOUT

THE TWILIGHT SYMBOLS

"*The Twilight Symbols* is very insightful. It enriched my understanding of the *Twilight* world. I can't wait to revamp *Twilight* with a keener eye!"
Angela Putnam, USA

"A fascinating expose of the hidden symbolism of the *Twilight* world".
Judith, Teacher (UK)

"Fantastic. These words about *Twilight* are perfect. They capture the true essence of the *Twilight* series".
Melanie ('soookee') South Carolina, USA

"Symbols represent ideas. The *Twilight* saga is a parable in which symbols express extremely complex ideas in an accessible way".
'scoundrel', UK

"This outstanding *Twilight* dictionary tells you things that you never knew about *Twilight*".
Lucas Hamilton, 12 years (Australia)

"This book inspires me so much. It really helps me to understand the *Twilight* world".
Katelyn Wescombe, 13 years (Australia)

"Enlightening for anyone interested in the Saga. You may never be able to see it in the same way again".
'briar', Australia

"A beautiful and magical analogy. It puts you in touch with your dreams, feelings, aspirations – and sends you back to nature and your childhood".
Vivienne Wright, Snr Social Worker (Westland NZ)

"Wow – Awesome... very interesting. I will be rereading this again. Author should tour".
Trish (Illinois, USA)

The Twilight Symbols

Motifs – Meanings – Messages

The Twilight Symbols

Motifs – Meanings – Messages

Dr JA Sykley

OUR STREET BOOKS

Winchester, UK
Washington, USA

First published by Our Street Books, 2012
Our Street Books is an imprint of John Hunt Publishing Ltd., Laurel House, Station Approach,
Alresford, Hants, SO24 9JH, UK
office1@jhpbooks.net
www.johnhuntpublishing.com
www.ourstreet-books.com

For distributor details and how to order please visit the 'Ordering' section on our website.

ISBN: 978 1 78099 435 2

A CIP catalogue record for this book is available from the British Library.

Design: Stuart Davies

Printed and bound in the USA by Edwards Brothers Malloy

This book is not authorized by or associated with any persons, publishers or producers of the Twilight Saga novels or films

CONTENTS

Acknowledgements

Thanks to John Hunt Publishing, John Hunt, Trevor Greenfield, Krystina Kellingley and Team for believing in my book. Life is nothing without dreams, and I hope that this book leads everyone to revisit their dreams with help from the world of symbols.

A sincere appreciation of Ms Stephenie Meyer – author, creator of the Twilight series, and dreamer.

Significant acknowledgement goes to Didier Colin's *Dictionary of Symbols, Myths and Legends* (2000; London: Hachette) for this book's expert guidance and explanation around symbols.

Many thanks to the people who read and reviewed this book!

Dedication

To TwilightMOMS – informative, inspiring, loving.

Twilight: A Saga of Symbols

> *"I love the symbolism in the story... I don't know if Stephenie Meyer did it intentionally, but there is a lot to be learned from Twilight, I think"* (IMHO, 2009).

Twilight Rules

The *Twilight Saga* is Stephenie Meyer's vampire story about forbidden love and a quest to fulfill one's true destiny. A famous four-book series, the novels *Twilight, New Moon, Eclipse* and *Breaking Dawn* have also become blockbuster movies. Whether you are a fan or not, whether you think the *Twilight* books are great literature or not, this Gothic thriller is a hit. Initially published in 2005, the first book "*Twilight* won tons of praise." The original novel was selected as an "Editor's Choice" by the *New York Times* and as 'book of the year' by *Publisher's Weekly*. *Twilight* is also ranked in the American Library Association's top ten "Books for Young Adults" and is one of Amazon's "Best Books of the Decade". According to USA Today's list of top 100 titles, Stephenie Meyer sold 22 million books in 2008 – the most of any author that year. All four *Twilight Saga* books were the top four best-sellers that year. *Twilight* even has a worldwide fan base. This covers teenagers to leading adult fan groups such as TwilightMOMS.com, with 50,000+ members. With a string of hit books and hit films, "*Twilight* has... become a full-fledged cultural phenomenon" (Shmoop, 2008). The *Twilight Saga* rules. But why? What makes this chilling vampire tale so hot?

Symbols Rule

A range of interesting theories help to explain the *Twilight Saga* effect. From the tale's romantic theme to sparkling vampires to the tackling of important psychological topics, compelling explanations abound as to why the *Twilight* tale ticks. Nevertheless, no matter which theory you follow, the *Twilight* books must still be doing something quite discernible to make their popular ideas stick. What could possibly make the characters, adventures, and settings so addictive? Is it the mystery? The fangs? Or some other key factor? According to some of the most enlightening analyses, if you really want to make a story impressive, inspiring and immortal, then all you need to do is tap into the oldest and most powerful language ever known to humankind – *symbols*.

What is a symbol? A symbol is an "idea, object or process that people can visualize that typifies, represents, or recalls something else" (Oxford Dictionary). As such, symbols are ideas, images, motifs, and metaphors that people can imagine, visualize, access quickly in their minds, and apply instantly. What's more, symbols *influence* people. A symbol is a sign or signal that possesses deep meaning or a clear message that an individual relates to instantly and finds really refreshing and uplifting. Symbols carry information, hide secrets, reveal knowledge, trigger insights, and inspire positive behavior. A motif, metaphor or symbol has the power to "inform, educate, teach values, discipline, build experience, facilitate problem-solving, change, and heal," says Australian psychologist Dr. George Burns.

This means that symbols, from the delightful to the frightful ones that hide inside the *Twilight* books, sell a story and make an incredibly huge impression on readers. Other literature reviewers agree:

> *"A powerful way to influence human behavior is to hand down symbolic stories which resonate powerfully in the subconscious mind... These stories have been adapted to the time and culture of the people they are told to, but the essence is always the same: a 'special' person with a great potential for heroic, liberating deeds"* (Andréa, 2009).

This means that the most gripping stories involve mighty motifs, meanings and messages that revolve around a main hero whose purpose is to free the inner hero in *you*.

The *Twilight Saga* is a world full of exciting symbols. From A to Z, these symbols can be clear or dear, strong or subtle, mighty or murky. Above all, we can use our favorite *Twilight* symbols to increase our own personal power in real life because the human mind absolutely loves symbols:

- Symbols inform, guide and inspire us
- Symbols are highly visual, meaningful, and emotional
- Symbols encourage behavior change and promote well-being
- Symbols connect to the deepest parts of the mind – our subconscious
- As infants, our pre-verbal minds understood the world only in terms of images and symbols
- Symbols can awaken our dead spiritual existence and make us feel truly alive

A picture paints a thousand words. But a symbol conveys pictures, words, visions, information, emotion, power, wonder and so much more.

Symbols Spotlight

The moment you enter the *Twilight* world, you also enter a whole new world filled dark, dreamy, beautiful, eerie and emotionally evocative symbols. Some symbols might have a moral and religious flavor. After all, Stephenie Meyer is a Mormon and member of the Church of Jesus Christ of the Latter-Day Saints. Her worldview would show through in her writing, even if her books did not mean to embrace such meanings and messages. "Mormon imagery runs deep" in the *Twilight* universe and involves Mormon ideas such as 'family', 'agency', and 'angels', says a university religion lecturer (Aleiss, 2010). A respect for Native American culture is also evident in the *Twilight* books. The Quileute people have special ideas about 'community', 'animals', 'nature', 'fire' and 'sacrifice', which Twilight scenes clearly affirm. Media study experts say that the *Twilight Saga's* use of images, ideas and popular culture definitely "deserve critical analysis… It is valid to ask what the story is about and why so many people are reading the books and seeing the films. It is probably more important, though, to talk together about what the movies mean" (Pacatte and Rupprecht, 2010). Spot on. The message behind a symbol, image or idea is what brings a story to life.

You may already be well acquainted with many symbols in the *Twilight* universe. An 'apple', for example, appears on the original cover of *Twilight*. The apple, as many *Twilight* fans would know, is a famous symbol of love, immortality, and temptation. And the *Twilight Saga* is exactly that – a tale about forbidden love. However, as this book will reveal, the *Twilight* apple is so much more, right down to its mystical core. Other *Twilight* symbols are not so easy to see or spot. For example, what do 'storms', 'deer' and 'cars' say about certain *Twilight* characters, situations, and themes? Already, your receptive human mind would adore and relate to some symbols much more than others. Symbols are a very personal affair. On top of this, it is likely that once you decode the meanings and messages of other symbols in the *Twilight* world that you didn't know about before, your reactions will range from: "That's *sooo* obvious" to "Aha! I thought so" to "Wow, I *never* knew that!" And you might love and learn from these new symbols too. Some symbols, like a 'bright full moon' will be fully entrancing. Other symbols, such as a 'gold sun' are bound to boost your happiness. As for more menacing symbols in the *Twilight* world, such as the Volturi vampire's 'underworld', they are sure to send a chill down your spine.

Symbols Hide

Symbols, like those that drive the *Twilight* books, are so powerful that people can be thinking, visualizing, dreaming, expressing, or writing about them – without even realizing it. This gives a book series such as the *Twilight Saga* extra thrills and spills because you never know what you could find. Authors themselves *may not be consciously aware* that they are communicating symbols in their writing nor know what their symbols may mean. It is possible that Stephenie Meyer included many different symbols in her books by sheer accident. After all, didn't Stephenie Meyer's first momentous idea for her book appear in a *dream*? As Ms. Meyer tells it, she started writing down a story without knowing why:

> *In my dream, two people were having an intense conversation in a meadow in the woods. One of these people was just your average girl. The other person was fantastically beautiful, sparkly, and a vampire... I don't know where it came from. I'm not a vampirey person... [I] sat down at the computer to write – something I hadn't done in so long that I wondered why I was bothering.*
> (Meyer, in Newkey-Burden, 2010)

Whether symbols in the *Twilight Saga* are crafted or covert, revised ideas or reinvented myths, mindful comments, or just complete random nonsense, one thing is for sure. You can't deny the fact that Stephenie Meyer's spellbinding story is a script-crypt packed with symbols.

Symbols Excite

If you really love the *Twilight Saga*, are captivated by the story, can't get enough, or you're simply getting curiouser and curiouser as to what all the freakin' fuss is about, do beware and do take care. Once you start reading *The Twilight Symbols*, you might get even more hooked by Ms. Meyer's books. Already, the *Twilight Saga* is written from the first-person point of view – an 'I' said, not 'you' or 'she/he' said perspective – which gets us involved in Bella's experiences as if they were our own. Add to this a bright new knowledge of the *Twilight* universe from a *symbolic* point of view, and it's *you* who could be having the deep, meaningful and transformative experience – not just Bella Swan or her friends. With guidance from this book, you will definitely become an expert in deciphering what symbols mean in the *Twilight* world and you may even be pleased to discover how you can use them in your own world. As one bright fan of the *Twilight* books says:

> *These books can be all things to all people who are willing. They can provide a light entertainment or, for those who love to delve beneath the surface of things, an ongoing study of connections and discovery.*
> (TwilightMOMS Post, Shimmerskin June 18, 2011)

Well then, see you on the other side. In the turning, burning, chilling, thrilling, beautiful, mysterious, daring and dazzling super-powerful world of *The Twilight Symbols*.

A

Apple

The *Twilight* Apple

In the *Twilight Saga,* the apple is perhaps the most famous, tempting, and talked-about graphic symbol of all. As many fans already know, a red apple appears on the original cover of *Twilight* – the first novel of Stephenie Meyer's four-book *Twilight* series. A pair of pale white arms of a young woman extend outwards, set against a jet black background. The hands, cupped together, are holding a ripe red apple. What's more, as some astute *Twilight* fans have noticed, the two outstretched arms happen to form a 'V' shape on the cover. Hey, that's 'V' for 'vampire', right?

The first time the apple is mentioned in the *Twilight* series is within the first 20 pages of book one, chapter one. During Bella's first day at Forks High School, a girl in the cafeteria walks past the main character Bella Swan with an "unbitten apple" on her tray (*Twilight,* p 17). We soon learn that this mysterious girl is Alice Cullen, a vampire with a gift to predict the future. Alice's apple may well be a symbolic gesture that foreshadows the great temptation ahead: Bella's attraction to Edward Cullen… a *vampire.*

The apple appears again in the school cafeteria in chapter ten of *Twilight*. Bella is sitting at a table across from Edward and is rolling an apple around in her hands. It is as if Bella is trying to decide whether to eat it or not. Bella remarks:

> "I'm curious," I said as I picked up an apple, turning it around in my hands, "what would you do if someone dared you to eat food?"
> (*Twilight,* p 181)

As you can see, Bella wonders what to do with her apple at the same time as she is wondering what to do about Edward. Who is Edward? Should Bella pursue this beautiful, but dangerous, young man? Or avoid him altogether? After all, Edward is a deadly predator, a vampire who thirsts for her blood. Bella's inner conflict, symbolized by the apple, is arguably the hottest symbol in the *Twilight Saga* and a constant source of psychological tension in the books. Clearly, Stephenie Meyer chooses to brand her Gothic fantasy using a striking visual symbol – a splash of bright red fruit.

Did you know that the apple has always been a strong and seductive symbol with mouth-watering meanings? Just as anyone can peel away the layers of a juicy red apple to taste the sweet, soft and pale flesh of the fruit hidden inside, the *Twilight Saga* has many alluring and inviting apple-like layers of meaning for hungry readers to peel away too. It is apt for Ms. Meyers to use an apple in a tasty tale of top-secret love. As a symbol, the apple is the most fascinating and forbidden fruit of all. Want to know more? Go on then… take another bite!

Forbidden Fruit

Apple-like temptation is a big theme in all four books of the *Twilight Saga*. *Twilight*, *New Moon*, *Eclipse*, and *Breaking Dawn* tell a tale about forbidden desire. As such, the apple fits. The main temptation in the *Twilight* books is the romantic relationship between Bella (a human girl) and Edward (a vampire). Their romance is a forbidden love because it is dangerous. You see, although Edward loves Bella, he also thirsts for her blood. Despite such danger, these ill-fated lovers crave each other's company from the very start. Although Edward is vampire and Bella is human, their passion is so strong that they will do anything to stay together. For this reason, their love for each other is symbolized by forbidden fruit – the apple.

Of course, the apple on the cover of *Twilight* is a *timeless* temptation symbol. In Genesis in the Bible, Adam and Eve lived in a paradise called the Garden of Eden. A sly serpent sweet-talked the new couple into eating fruit from a forbidden tree. In fact, many classical paintings and writings show Adam and Eve eating an apple, accompanied by a snake curled up in a nearby tree. According to Genesis, the fruit that Eve and Adam ate is "the knowledge of good and evil." Isn't this exactly what Bella gains? A working knowledge of the supernatural world? The latest gossip about nice and nasty vampires? Note that although apples *do* have a forbidding reputation, apples in the Garden of Eden are actually *never* mentioned, only that Adam and Eve wore fig leaves (Colin, 2000).

So why did the apple, like the *Twilight Saga* apple, come to symbolize forbidden desire? Since apples grow all around the world, the earliest writers promoted the apple tree as the tree of bliss. Later on, the early Christians came to view apples as sinful. This is because the fruit was so sweet and the trees were so abundant. As a popular and plentiful fruit, the poor old apple became linked to temptation and the tree of knowledge in Eden. In the *Twilight* world, Bella finds Edward irresistible – he is the tempting fruit she desires. Likewise, Edward is strongly attracted to Bella – she is the apple of his eye.

In one of the greatest literary works ever written in the English language, an epic verse called *Paradise Lost* describes just how tempting apples can be. John Milton is a 17th century English poet who wrote about a "goodly tree" loaded with "red and gold" apples in 1657. The fruit smelled so "sweet" that it was impossible for him to deny thirst and hunger:

To satisfy the sharp desire I had
Of tasting those fair apples, I resolved
Not to defer; hunger and thirst at once,
Powerful persuaders, quickened at the scent
Of that alluring fruit, urged me so keen.

In other words, the apples looked and smelled so good that Milton felt he had to eat them right away. Milton linked the fruit of this good tree to "knowledge of good bought dear by knowing ill." This symbolizes Bella and Edward's romantic appetite for each other perfectly. Both Bella and Edward are yummy lip-smacking apples to each other. Their attraction to each other, however, is 'ill' fated and dangerous.

In a piece called *A Song of Despair*, the Nobel Prize winning poet Pablo Neruda described apple power in the same way: "There was thirst and hunger, and you were the fruit." This is exactly what the apple in the *Twilight Saga* means. Since Bella and Edward are two young lovers with awakened romantic desires in their hearts, they both feel an undeniable lust and longing for each other. The *Twilight* apple is tempting.

It is noteworthy that despite the strong feelings of desire that Bella and Edward have for each other in the *Twilight Saga*, no sex is ever described directly in the story. Indeed, it's the young couple's lust struggle and abstinence from sex that spices up the *Twilight* tale. A *Washington Post* book review about the *Twilight Saga* books agreed that a "subtext of hunger and fasting as a metaphor for sex and abstinence. Yes, lust is the elephant in the room here, and it's what gives *Twilight* its decidedly grown-up bite" (cited in Shmoop, 2011). In symbolic terms, this means that the *Twilight* apple is red hot. The *Twilight* tale shows us a nice ripe apple that we never get to taste or bite, which makes us crave that juicy apple all the more.

Tempting Apples

The red apple, an ultimate symbol of temptation, does not just symbolize Bella and Edward's love in the *Twilight* world. Once you start peeling away more layers of meaning in the *Twilight Saga* (just like peeling an apple), other 'forbidden fruits' (temptation themes) emerge. Consider these other apple-flavored temptation themes.

Bella

From Bella's viewpoint, Edward is the obvious 'forbidden fruit' that comes to life in the *Twilight* world. She finds Edward absolutely fascinating and falls in love with him unconditionally and irrevocably, even though he is dangerous and wants to drink her blood.

Edward

Just as the apple symbolizes Bella's desire for Edward, Edward craves Bella. To Edward, Bella is the forbidden fruit – a human girl he loves. Although Edward loves Bella deeply, he must continually suppress his natural instinct to kill her. Not only is Edward a hard-wired predator designed to drink human blood, Bella's fragrance is so tempting that the pain he feels around her is excruciating. Edward must constantly struggle with his true nature as a vampire as soon as he meets Bella because she has the best-smelling blood he's ever sniffed. Due to Edward's vegetarian lifestyle, drinking Bella's blood is forbidden. Vampires hooking up with humans is also forbidden. One of the most important vampire laws is designed to keep the vampire race a secret. So, when Edward falls in love with Bella, he becomes an instant magnet for trouble.

Sex

In the *Twilight* world, sex is another 'forbidden fruit' that the apple symbolizes. Indeed, the apple is a classic symbol of sexual awakening because as soon as Adam and Eve ate fruit from the tree of knowledge, this caused a loss of innocence. They immediately became aware of their sexuality and tried to hide their nakedness in the Garden of Eden. In the *Twilight Saga,* the emotional and sexual desires between Bella and Edward also intensify in an Eden-like meadow in the forest.

The apple's link to sexual desire is relevant to today's teen relationships. In real life, many teenagers desire to have sex or may engage in unsafe sex. Young couples – mostly guys – can have difficulty controlling their emotions (especially with regards to sex and anger). These feelings can overwhelm them strongly and suddenly due to hormonal changes in the body.

In the *Twilight* world, however, Edward is a self-control star. He does not give in to forbidden and harmful urges. For example, Edward controls his thirst for Bella's blood, he does not prey on humans, he controls his anger around Jacob, and he controls his sexual desires. Edward's superlative self-control and his ability to resist temptation make him super-attractive. The fact that Edward doesn't use girls for sex, doesn't turn Bella into a vampire even though he can, and doesn't get into stupid fights with other guys are boyfriend plus factors.

A sexual twist in the *Twilight* series is that Bella pressures Edward to have sex. Edward's superhuman strength makes sex a 'forbidden fruit' because it could kill Bella if he lost control. So Edward declines to have sex with Bella, preferring to wait until Bella changes into a vampire so that it is safe for both of them. But Bella bribes him, saying she will stay human longer and attend university if he has sex with her when she is still a human. As a symbol, the apple's message is this. If you give in to strong primitive urges, such as unsafe sex or unprotected sex, this can be risky and dangerous. Bella's honeymoon bruises and perilous pregnancy support the idea that hasty, furious or impulsive behavior can have negative consequences. Whenever it comes to sex, it's best to take care.

Risk

Taking unthinkable risks is yet another 'forbidden apple' and temptation theme in the *Twilight* world. In *New Moon*, Edward decides it is far too dangerous to be around Bella so he breaks up with her and moves away. This plunges Bella into a deeply depressed state. Although she misses Edward, Bella spends time with Jacob and tries to distract herself. But her behavior gets more extreme. Bella increasingly engages in dangerous thrills and spills just to feel alive. When Bella leaps off a cliff – pretty drastic action – Edward believes she is dead. Edward then tries to kill himself in Italy by provoking the Volturi vampires. Bella saves him just in time. The apple's message? Although risks look tempting at the time, look before you leap. Think carefully about the effects of your actions. The consequences can be destructive, disastrous, or deadly.

Death

Perhaps the most 'forbidden fruit' of all in the *Twilight Saga* is Bella's wish to die. Her deepest, darkest, deadliest, and most destructive desire is to kill herself in order to become a vampire. In Freudian terms, Bella could be expressing a 'death drive'. In classical psychoanalytic theory, the death drive ('Todestrieb') is a drive towards death, self-destruction and a return to an inanimate state. Proposed in 1920 in *Beyond the Pleasure Principle,* Dr. Sigmund Freud describes the death drive as "an *instinct of destruction* directed against the external world." It is the opposite of the survival instinct – a natural human tendency to survive, seek pleasure, and express other creative, life-producing actions. Sometimes the death drive is referred to as 'Thanatos', a counter-intuitive force that opposes 'Eros' (our sexual drive) and the pleasure principle. Real life examples of the death drive might include soldiers who keep repeating or re-enacting traumatic war experiences. Or children whose games involve re-staging disappearances of people, especially themselves (Wiki, 2011).

In the *Twilight Saga,* Bella desires to die most strongly:

> I wanted to be fierce and deadly, someone no one would dare mess with… I wanted to be a vampire. The violent desire caught me off guard and knocked the wind out of me. It was the most forbidden of all wishes… the most painful.
> (*New Moon,* p 263)

As you can see, Bella's desire to be a vampire is shocking. She wants to die as a human, which contradicts nature's survival instinct to stay alive. A planned suicide is a drastic course of action that would devastate her family and friends. Bella's death wish may be the most gruesome idea of all, symbolized, of course, by the *Twilight* apple.

Snow White

The apple's lusty link with death appears elsewhere in celebrated literature. In the famous children's fairy tale *Snow White,* for example, the young heroine bites a poisoned red apple offered by a wicked witch. Snow White then falls into a long sleep, until a prince's kiss awakens her. In the same way, Bella feels like she is living in a dull, lifeless world until she meets Edward. He then awakens her emotional and sexual desires. The *Twilight Saga* even mentions the fairy tale *Snow White* and her apple. Bella describes her stone cottage in *Breaking Dawn* as "a place where anyone could believe magic existed. A place where you just expected Snow White to walk right in with her apple in hand" (*Breaking Dawn*, p 444).

Just one bite of the Snow White apple and you are frozen forever in a state of deep sleep, much like death. In the same way, it takes just one bite to become a vampire in the *Twilight* world. When Bella finally becomes a vampire in *Breaking Dawn*, her body also frozen in an unchanging, undead state of eternal life. Without a doubt, the apple symbolizes Bella's deathly desire… right down to the core.

Offspring

The creation of vampire children in the *Twilight Saga* is another forbidden fruit. After Bella and Edward marry and have sex, they end up having a biological child whom they name Renesmee. The ruling Volturi vampires plan to kill this child because they think that the Cullens have broken the most sacred vampire law of all

– creating an "immortal child" by means of a venomous vampire bite (*Breaking Dawn*, p 507). Vampires biting human babies is strictly forbidden. In the past, newly created infant vampires wreaked so much havoc attacking humans that they exposed the existence of vampires. This nearly destroyed the whole vampire race. Vampire babies are too immature to control their impulses and blood lust. So the Volturi banned child vampires altogether to protect their race.

As you can see, whether temptation themes in the *Twilight Saga* relate to love, sex, risk, death or other forbidden desires, the apple is certainly a symbol of choice. You can either surrender to your temptation or rise above it. Control your serious urges, or just cave in. In any case, dark desires add a delicious touch to the story's choice-making theme.

Why So Wicked?

Why are apples, like the ones in the *Twilight Saga*, so lust-packed in the first place? Want to know more about this wicked fruit? An important reason is that the idea of 'sin' derives from ancient health warnings. In early times, Mesopotamian physicians knew that certain illnesses could be picked up by poor hygiene, exposure to infected individuals, or sexual contact. In the hope of reducing disease and maximizing human health and survival, the Old Testament drew up a list of laws. "Any man or woman who kept these laws would know no evil, illness, or suffering" (Colin, 2000, p 412). Of course, well-behaved people with good hearts and pure intentions still got sick and suffered. So early societies had to find a logical reason for this. Hey presto! A symbolic story about 'original sin' using apples to justify the inexplicable and tormenting health problems of celibate people (Colin, 2000).

Fruit of Love

Although temptation is a main meaning of the apple, it is not the only one. Not just a 'forbidden fruit', apples have other meanings. Since antiquity, long before the emergence of Christianity and its idea of sin, the apple was a significant source of power. According to the oldest myths and legends in the world, the apple is the most mystical and magical of all fruits. It is a symbol of love, wisdom, prophecy and immortality. In Greek myths, the apple is the fruit of love. That is why, in early Greek history, the apple featured in courtship rituals as well as the rites of marriage. It was common for a happy couple in the seventh century BCE to share an apple as a symbol of their marriage and hopes of a fruitful union. What's more, the *Twilight* books seem to capture these romantic apple ideas.Hesperides Apples

The Greek god of wine, desire, and partying (Dionysus) is said to have created the first apple. Another Greek myth describes an orchard of golden apples growing in the Garden of Hesperides. This garden happened to be guarded by a very powerful and dangerous serpent. In fact, one of the twelve impossible tasks given to Hercules was to pick some apples from this garden. In any case, Amy Lowell's poem, *Apples of Hesperides*, describes the irresistible beauty of these apples quite well:

Glinting golden through the trees,
Apples of Hesperides!
Through the moon-pierced warp of night
Shoot pale shafts of yellow light,
Swaying to the kissing breeze
Swings the treasure, golden-gleaming,
Apples of Hesperides!

The *Twilight Saga* story surely echoes the same ideas of love and delight to apples as this poem does.

Paris' Apple

The plot that Bella and Edward fall in love resembles a famous

Greek legend called *Paris and the Apple*. According to this Greek myth, Eris (the goddess of discord) threw a golden apple from the garden of Hesperides into a wedding party, to cause trouble for not being invited. Zeus, the ruling god, gave this golden apple – marked "For the Fairest One" – to a mortal man named Paris. Then Paris had to present it to one of three goddesses in a beauty contest. What a tough choice! Well anyway, some erotic versions of this ancient tale say the goddesses stripped naked for the contest. This kind of partying behavior would definitely boost the apple's reputation as a symbol of love and desire, all right. What happened is that Paris ended up choosing Aphrodite as the most beautiful woman at the wedding. As such, he gave the apple to her. But the only reason why Aphrodite won the contest was because she bribed Paris by offering him Helen, the most beautiful human woman in all of Greece. In effect, this apple started a war. The Greeks' expedition to retrieve Helen from Paris in Troy is the mythological basis of the Trojan War (Wikisource, 2011). The exact same situation unfolds in the *Twilight Saga*. Edward gets Bella (the most beautiful and fascinating mortal woman in his eyes) and together they get married and have an unplanned child. This triggers the great Volturi war in *Breaking Dawn*. What trouble those apples cause!

Pomona's Apple

Just like Greeks, the Romans also believed that the apple symbolized love. The Roman fruit goddess and forest nymph Pomona was associated with love, beauty and fertility. Her name is from the Latin *pomum* for fruit. As a guardian spirit, Pomona's job is to protect orchards, gardens and groves that bear fruit and nuts and feed people (Barrette, in *Pomona's Day*, 2011). According to Roman folklore, the apple's color determines its meaning. Pink apples suggest friendship, yellow apples suggest prosperity, and green apples symbolize healing. Red apples, like those in the *Twilight Saga*, symbolize passion, energy and sexuality. In line with these Roman beliefs, it makes sense to use a red apple in *Twilight* to symbolize Bella and Edward's love.

Fruity Wisdom
Prophecy Power

The *Twilight* world also acknowledges that the apple is a symbol of knowledge, wisdom, and prophecy. As mentioned before, in the first novel *Twilight*, Alice walks past Bella in the school café with an apple on her tray at the start of the book. Since Alice can see the future and apples symbolize divinity, Alice's apple is probably a sign of Bella's future romance with Edward. This important scene from *Twilight* supports the apple's prophecy meanings.

To the ancient Celts 400 BCE, the apple symbolizes divination – foretelling the future. This ancient idea quickly spread through Western Europe. The mystical and powerful apple was used in magic rituals, to cast spells, and to reveal secrets. During Samhain (Halloween), a time of autumn and harvest, the apple had a big role in traditional rituals, celebrations, and divination in Celtic culture. Samhain, on November 1st, celebrates the passing of summer and the beginning of the dark season. An apple represents a customary offer to honor the spirit of Samhain from the autumn harvest just passed, at a magical time of year when the veil is thinnest between this world and the next (Galbreth, 2011).

To gain wisdom about the future, old Celtic practices included cutting away apple peel in one piece and tossing it to reveal one's future mate, cutting an apple in front of a mirror to see one's future beloved, and placing apple seeds on hot coals to read their reactions (seeds resting quietly predicted a happy relationship, seeds bursting predicted heartbreak). Other apple practices were related to death and banishing. To cure illness, settle squabbles, or break bad habits, apples were cut in half and buried. Apples were also thrown and hurled to drive away evil spirits, or left out to feed the spirits of the dead. All these ancient Celtic practices "draw on the apple's qualities as a magical fruit with power over the otherworld" (Barrette in *Pomona's Day*, 2011). Since the Celts roasted apples and nuts in bonfires, these practices inspired modern Halloween customs like 'bobbing for apples'. Alice's apple at the start of the *Twilight Saga* is a short and sweet pointer to the apple's prophecy power. So where did the idea of fruity wisdom come from in the first place? Take a deeper bite...

High Five

What makes an apple such a wise fruit? Firstly, as a sphere or *circle* shape, the apple symbolizes continuity, infinity, and eternity. The circle is a considered the most magical, protective and powerful shape of all. Then there are the apple seeds – the real source of the apple's wisdom and knowledge. If you cut an apple in half across its equator, the seed pattern inside looks like a perfect five-pointed star – an inner pentagram. The earliest wiccans (witches) observed that cutting an apple in half reveals a 'pentacle' at its core, marking it as a mystical fruit (Barrette, in *Pomona's Day*, 2011). This star symbol is so old and mathematically significant that it may have been discovered by astronomers as far back as 6000 years ago.

It was the Greek philosopher and mathematician Pythagoras who made the five-pointed star famous. He linked the pentagram (and therefore apples) to great wisdom for several reasons:

- The powerful Pythagorean mathematical formula known as the 'golden spiral' is based on the pentagram.
- Pythagoras believed that the number five was the 'human' number because people have five fingers and five toes.
- The world was seen to comprise five elements: earth, air, fire, water and the soul.
- The pentagram is the sign of the planet Venus (the

> dawn/evening star named after the Roman Goddess of love). This planet takes four years and one day to trace its course in the sky – which happens to be the shape of a pentagram. Venus is the only planet which traces this secret shape in the sky.

Due to the apple's seed pentagram, and supposed inner wisdom, people believed that eating apples would result in gaining profound wisdom.

In the *Twilight Saga,* when Bella bites the apple (gets to know Edward, that is) she also gains supernatural knowledge and wisdom. Edward reveals his secret identity to Bella, that he is a vampire. But knowing Bella is very dangerous because if Edward loses self-control he could not only kill her but expose his secret identity as a vampire. The Volturi vampires, who enforce the laws of secrecy, punish law-breakers by death. Maybe the need to find love (a part of Edward that had been suppressed for more than 100 years during his long, lonely life as a vampire) was awakened by Bella's unique scent and remarkable compassion, which compelled him to reveal hidden mystical knowledge.

In any case, maybe you doubt that Alice's apple at the very start of *Twilight* embraces ideas of wisdom by pointing to the future romance between Bella and Edward. Or maybe you doubt Alice's prophecy powers altogether. Well, you can interpret the apples in *Twilight* whatever way you want to, but I'm definitely betting on Alice and her apple!

Air

In the *Twilight Saga,* air is a crucial symbol. Air relates to spirits, life, breathing, the wind, scents and fragrances. One of four magical elements (air, water, earth, fire), air is a symbol that is often associated with spiritual themes and sky divinities. The *Twilight* books acknowledge this spiritual meaning of air.

As the *Twilight* world illustrates, air is essential for survival. Humans, like Bella Swan, need air to breathe. "The air we breathe keeps us alive. This makes it both vital and fatal, magical and ambiguous" (Colin, 2000, p 19). *Twilight*-style vampires like Edward Cullen, however, do not breathe air. Maybe it makes symbolic sense for supernatural vampires not to breathe air. The sky, after all, is already linked to supernatural forces. The sky is the home of great spirits all over the world. This includes ancient Greek gods like Zeus, the Christian God, and even strong Quileute spirit warriors according to *Eclipse*. Of course, the sky is where heavenly angels dwell as well. It is therefore worth noting that Edward is called an 'angel' a number of times in the *Twilight Saga* (e.g. *Twilight*, p 272).

Edward, a supernatural creature, does not need to breathe air in the *Twilight* world to survive. Detecting 'fragrances' in the air is how he discovers and relates to the physical world around him. In particular, Edward picks up on the fragrance in the air coming off Bella's skin straight away. To Edward, Bella had an irresistibly "mouth-watering" and "very floral" scent, like "lavender" or "freesia" (*Twilight*, p 267). According to symbols experts: "Air, whether it is breath or wind, is impregnated with the scents and smells, warmth and cold of the spaces it fills and within which it moves' (Colin, 2000, p 19). This makes air a magical medium. As a handbook on magic and folklore around the world reports, air fragrances can:

> *Awaken deep magical impulses within us. Burning oils in a special burner or lighting incense cones or sticks provides easy access to magical visions. Whether you meditate or just enjoy sitting quietly while your favorite incense or oil releases its fragrance into the air, the spontaneous impressions can offer insight beyond visual or aural senses.*
>
> (Eason 2002, p 20)

The fact that Edward can pick up on fragrances so well in the air around him strengthens his magical and supernatural nature.

Symbol experts see a clear difference between air and breath. "Air is the same for everyone, but breath is unique. When you inspire or inhale, you take in the air everyone else is breathing... but when you expire or exhale, you breathe out air that is unique to you, that has been filtered through your lungs" (Colin, 2000, p 21). It is therefore interesting that Bella's breath suddenly 'stops' or 'catches' in her chest whenever she is around Edward. Maybe this is a symbolic gesture that Bella will become a vampire. As the *Twilight Saga* shows, air is an invisible medium that captures and carries odors, both pleasant and foul. Air also vibrates with energy, sets the mood, and communicates a certain ambience. An atmosphere can be warm or cold, calm or tense, lively or deadly, especially in the supernatural *Twilight* world.

Angel

The first fabulous creature to be cited in the *Twilight Saga* is not a vampire nor a werewolf nor even a zombie. It is an angel. Bella describes Edward as a "destroying angel" (*Twilight*, p 56) who has a "grave angel's face" (*Twilight*, p 152). To Bella, Edward is something beautiful and wonderful, yet something menacing and melancholy at the same time. Angels are (usually invisible) creatures from the spiritual realm who often have positive meanings. Furthermore, people have believed in angels since the beginning of time. The first creatures to resemble angels appeared in the ancient Akkadian culture, dating back 2550 BC. Meanwhile, the word 'angel' comes from the Greek *angelos*, meaning 'messenger'.

The most unique feature of angels is their beautiful wings. These fluttering add-ons symbolize the angel's separation and transcendence from the earthly plane. While Edward may not have wings that sprout from his shoulders, his angelic appearance certainly awakens new aspirations in Bella and influences her earthly journey towards an unearthly existence. As a symbol, angels tend to be mediums or intermediaries between the heavenly realm and mortals on earth. They are God's messengers or agents. According to the Bible, angels form a 'heavenly host' and therefore they provide a protective function. For example, angels guarded the people of Israel when they crossed the Red Sea, they delivered individuals from blindness, and they watched over a religious character called Jacob (Colin, 2000, p 30).

In the *Twilight Saga*, Edward's character clearly reflects the protective role of angels. In particular, Edward saves Bella from death and danger a number of times. This includes protecting Bella in Port Angeles, which happens to mean 'port of the angel'. Edward rescues her from four violent thugs there. Later that evening, at the La Bella Italia restaurant, Bella uses angelic ideas to describe Edward. He is her "perpetual savior" (*Twilight*, p 144) and, later, her "archangel" (*Twilight*, p 272). An interesting possibility as to why angels appear in the *Twilight* series first and why Edward is described as so angelic is because the most important thing about an individual, whether it's in a novel or in real life, is not who that person is on the outside, but who that person is on the inside. In the *Twilight* world Edward may be a vampire, but he strives to do good things and harms no one. Deep down, where it really matters, Edward is an angel a vampire who symbolically possesses positive angel meanings. He is a beautiful, glorious, good-hearted, helpful, well-meaning – but not perfect – angel.

Animals

Twilight Saga characters, especially vampires, display behaviors that are often compared to animals. The word 'animal' is derived from the Latin *animalis*, which means "living, breathing" (Colin,

2000, p 31). In fact, the animal kingdom is full of life and magic. For thousands of years people believed that the human spirit could be reincarnated in the body of an animal. The belief that the human soul could inhabit the body of a sacred or deified animal (e.g. eagle or lion) was the ultimate sign of immortality of the soul and a great reward acquired by an individual during life on earth. Alchemists recorded a bewildering multiplicity of animal symbols in their important works – red lions, white eagles, stags, unicorns, winged dragons, snakes, birds, and more. These symbols have no fixed meanings. Rather, alchemists and others adjusted the meaning of animal symbols in ways that suited the mood, background, and goals of their works.

While Edward might deny the idea that he can change into a bat in the *Twilight* books, many stories *do* describe human beings who can transform themselves into animals. In TH White's tale *The Sword in the Stone*, the wizard Merlin, for example, changed himself into a 'field mouse', a 'cat' and even a 'gnat' to outmaneuver another shape-shifting sorceress. In the *Twilight* world, Jacob Black and his Quileute friends have the power to change themselves into wolves. In the *Twilight* books, animals and their symbolic meanings have a big and strong role.

Animal Attraction

The animal kingdom is incredibly diverse. As such, it offers an endless supply of living symbols and images that people and authors can use. The *Twilight* books contain a fair amount of animal symbolism and the symbolism of each animal species is described in this book. One thing worth noting about the *Twilight* world is that vampires tend to have acquired "beautiful" and "graceful" features while werewolves are described as "unattractive" or "uncivilized" at times. The metaphors of 'vampire' and 'werewolf' are themselves raw metaphors for 'beauty' and 'ugliness'. For example, Edward is "mesmerizing" (*Twilight*, p 148), Alice is "beautiful" (*New Moon*, p 382) and

Jasper is "charismatic" (*Eclipse*, p 360). Werewolf characters, however, are terrifying, grotesque, primitive, and "smelly" beasts (*New Moon*, p 387).

To this day, people are described in positive or negative animal-like ways. Some modern-day phrases that use animal qualities to describe people are these: 'sing like a bird', 'brave as a lion', 'blind as a bat', 'happy as a lark', 'sly as a fox', 'snake-tongued', 'eagle-eyed'. Given the strong impact that animals make and that animals are easy to visualize in the mind, it is no wonder the *Twilight Saga* mentions a whole variety of animals. These include birds (e.g. 'swan'), mammals (e.g. 'bear'), reptiles (e.g. 'snake') and fish (e.g. 'shark'). The incompatible relationship between *Twilight* vampires and humans is also described using animal symbolism. In particular, whenever humans and vampires appear together in a story, they are often described in terms of prey/predator animal pairs.

Prey/Predator Pairs

Many supernatural *Twilight* characters struggle with their natural instincts. It's natural for vampires to drink human blood, but the Cullens work hard to resist this urge. In particular, Edward and Bella's love for each other clashes with the laws of nature. As a vampire, Edward is a highly effective human hunter. By contrast, Bella is his natural food source (human blood). And yet Bella and Edward love each other and can't stand being apart. It makes sense to symbolize the Bella/Edward relationship in terms of prey/predator. The predator has the strengths, while the prey has vulnerabilities. These animal qualities help to show the differences between Bella and Edward's natures. For example, Edward is super strong and fast. By contrast, Bella has trouble walking across the room without tripping. Bella must eat, sleep, and breathe air to survive. Edward doesn't. Yet, Edward can be fragile too. He can only show himself in the sun when in he is with trustworthy company (because he sparkles). Bella can sun bake whenever she wants. Although the love between Bella and Edward is genuine and natural, they seem to live in two different worlds. Images and ideas that describe prey/predator animal pairs help to symbolize this. In the *Twilight Saga,* the main prey/predator animal pairs are these:

- Lamb/Lion
- Fish/Shark
- Seal/Whale
- Bird/Snake
- Mouse/Cat
- Eagle/Fish

Lamb/Lion

Perhaps the most popular prey/predator relationship in the *Twilight* universe that describes Bella and Edward together is the lamb/lion mix. Lamb qualities are used to symbolize Bella's character and lion qualities are used to symbolize Edward. The first mention of Bella's lamb-like qualities occurs well before the popular lamb/lion meadow scene. At school, Bella "smiled sheepishly" when she watched a movie in a darkened classroom with Edward (*Twilight,* p 192). Later on, Edward bravely declares his love for Bella during their visit to a meadow and says she is "the most important thing" of all to him (*Twilight,* p 240). However, because Edward thirsts for Bella's blood and is dangerous, she calls herself an "idiot" for being with him and he replies:

> "And so the lion fell in love with the lamb"…
> "What a stupid lamb," I sighed.
> "What a sick, masochistic lion."
> (*Twilight,* p 240)

Of course, it's pretty obvious that Edward means that he is the lion and Bella is the lamb in this strange situation. Most lions would love to eat a lamb for dinner, but in this case the lion (Edward) loves his lamb (Bella) and would not dream of hurting her.

Lamb

In the *Twilight Saga*, Bella is the 'lamb'. This animal has positive symbolic meanings. The lamb stands for innocence and purity, peace, the spiritual, gentleness, and agreement. Since lambs are born at the start of spring, lambs are therefore a symbol of spring, new hope and triumph over the dark, cold winter of adversity. In the *Twilight* world, Bella is certainly a character who promises new hopes and new beginnings. Some important examples:

- Bella suggests that two people from very different worlds and different backgrounds (such as a human and a vampire) can successfully love each other.
- Bella promotes a cooperative alliance between vampires and werewolves (who are traditional enemies).
- Bella maintains excellent self-control as a newborn vampire, not even feeding on nearby humans. Vampires, such as Jasper, are impressed by her ability to control her thirst for human blood.

As a symbol, the lamb also has an ill-fated meaning. It is a symbol of sacrifice. In ancient times, the first lamb of the season was often sacrificed to the gods. The sacrificial nature of the lamb features in Christian, Jewish, and Muslim faiths. Christ, the son of God, is like a lamb sacrificed and crucified on a cross to save humankind, and then resurrected by a caring and giving god.

In the *Twilight Saga*, Bella is not only directly referred to as a "lamb" in the text. Symbolically speaking, Bella is a sacrificial lamb. She is prepared to sacrifice her own life and mortal lifestyle just so she can be with Edward forever. Bella's personal sacrifices lead to peace and harmony because her love for Edward unites werewolves and the Cullen clan. In alchemy and religious scripture, the lamb and lion have often appeared together as a universal symbol of harmony and the balance of opposites. The phrase "And the Lion shall lie down with the Lamb" is supposed to suggest that the lamb is a person and the lion is god.

Lion

The lion is one of the most powerful creatures in the animal kingdom and has much symbolic meaning. This magnificent creature is traditionally associated with the sun and the zodiac sign of Leo. Totem animals of kings and emperors, lions have been linked to spiritual figures such as Krishna, Buddha, and Apollo. The male lion's shaggy mane looks like a halo that depicts male energy. However, the lioness is the skilled hunter and the fiercely protective parent. Since lions are so strong and ferocious, it is no wonder they have acquired protective meanings. This has led to the production of charms and amulets that feature lions.

In the *Twilight Saga*, Edward is clearly portrayed as a 'lion' in the meadow scene described above, while Bella is the vulnerable 'lamb'. Edward's big cat qualities are highlighted when he plays baseball during a thunderstorm. Bella observed that his "run was more aggressive", like "a cheetah" and that "he quickly overtook" the other Cullens in the game (*Twilight*, p 321). The first time Bella visits the Cullen house, Edward's body "shifted suddenly, half-crouched, tensed like a lion about to pounce" and "leap at me" (*Twilight*, p 301). Edward's brother Jasper is also described as "tall and leonine" (*Twilight*, p 283). Much later in the story, we meet Nahuel, a 150-year-old half-vampire who was named after a "jungle cat" (*Breaking Dawn*, p 682). On one occasion, Edward describes Bella as "brave as a lion" (*Twilight*, p 423) after she confronted a killer vampire. This suggests that animal meanings are not always fixed. As the *Twilight* world shows, sometimes the prey challenges the predator, and the predator yields to the prey.

A negative symbolic meaning of lions relates to their supposedly proud natures. A group of lions is called a 'pride', and the sin of pride is a weakness of Leo. Further, power can lead to corruption if there is no awareness of moral and ethical values. Although Edward and other vampires are often described in lion-like ways, Edward is not a completely arrogant character. Rather, Edward and the Cullens show lion-like independence. Although the lion is supposed to be "an effective killer, the lion is not a confrontational creature and generally prefers a peaceful life. When they hunt, they hunt together, symbolic not only of fellowship but strength and safety" (Nozedar, 2008, p 282). Not a bad description of the Cullens' lifestyle and hunting method. Just like lions, the Cullens keep to themselves, live peacefully with others, and hunt in remote places, far away from humans.

Of course, other animals help to symbolize Bella and Edward's prey/predator relationship further. These animal references emphasize that in the natural order of things (that is, if Bella and Edward weren't madly in love with each other) Bella would be the prey because Edward is the predator.

Fish/Shark

In *Twilight,* Edward explains to Bella that all animals have common origins, even vampires and humans. "Couldn't we have evolved in the same way as other species, predator and prey?" he proposes, from "the same force that created the delicate angelfish and the shark" (*Twilight,* p 269). As with the lamb/lion mix, this animal symbolism in the *Twilight* world suggests that Bella is the prey (angelfish) and Edward is the predator (shark). Although predator and prey groups are dangerous, it's also just part of nature. All creatures are just trying to coexist together in the same world.

Alice confirms the idea that vampires have sharp shark-like instincts when she tells Bella: "We're also like sharks in a way. Once we taste the blood, or even smell it for that matter, it becomes very hard to keep from feeding. Sometimes impossible. So you see, to actually bite someone, to taste the blood, it would begin the frenzy" (*Twilight*, p 362). So does the Quileute chief. Billy Black tells an ancient story at the bonfire, about a cold woman – a "Blood Drinker" – who "swam after [humans] like a shark" (*Eclipse*, p 228). An interesting comment in *New Moon*, which may not be a random red herring, is when Demetri (a human-blood drinker) says: "Nice fishing" to Heidi the vampire. She has just baited and reeled in a school of tourists for the shark-like Volturi vampires to feed on (p 483).

Even Charlie Swan's behavior is shark-like. When Charlie and Bella argue, Bella feels as if Edward "threw [her] to the sharks" (*Eclipse*, p 49). This may be a symbolic long shot, but maybe that's why Billy Black keeps bringing over "Harry Clearwater's homemade fish fry – Charlie's favorite" (*Twilight*, p 306). Fish is shark food. The idea that Charlie is a fish-eating shark could be an author's private little joke. In any case, sharks are always the predators and fish are the victims in the *Twilight* books.

Seal/Whale

The seal/whale relationship is another prey/predator mix in the *Twilight Saga*. In describing "the baby seal and the killer whale" (*Twilight*, p 268), the "seal" symbolizes Bella while Edward is clearly the "killer whale".

In the past, sailors often mistook seals, basking on rocky shores, as mermaids. So seals are linked to mermaid meanings, which seals the symbolic meaning of Bella's seal character even more. Apparently, a mermaid's love can "keep a man spellbound, plunging him into a sort of trance, a type of bewitchment. An irresistible and dangerous woman is therefore called a siren" (Colin, 2000, p 336). Since the *Twilight Saga* clearly refers to Bella as both a "seal" (*Twilight*, p 268) and a "siren" (*New Moon*, p 472) who fascinates Edward, this strongly suggests that Bella may have magical mermaid meanings. Bella lures Edward with her blood that 'sings' to him and is a not-so vulnerable young seal. Since a mermaid is a sea sorceress who bewitches people and can lead them astray, this captures Edward's fascination with Bella, a "magnet for *trouble*" (*Twilight*, p 151) perfectly.

Just as seal symbolism and mermaid metaphors suit Bella, whales may characterize vampires well. In the *Twilight* world, vampires are considered "monsters" and people once saw whales as marine monsters of the sea. These huge animals would swim into boats or ships sailing in the water, causing the vessels to capsize or sink and injuring or killing crew. The most ancient people viewed the whale to be a hostile and supernatural being, sent by the gods to punish mortals. Later on, people realized that whales provided a wealth of resources – oil, blubber, meat, whalebone, and cosmetic ingredients.

A very interesting whale tale is the biblical legend of Jonah being swallowed by a whale for three days and three nights (Jonah 1: 17; 2: 1, 10, in Colin, 2000). Jonah, however, didn't really get swallowed by a whale. This adventure simply symbolizes a rite of passage. It is a spiritual experience that involves being plunged into darkness (mystery) and then re-emerging enlightened (achieving insight). Bella seems to go through a dark and turbulent whale-like rite of passage herself after meeting Edward. Her very last rite is her transformation into a vampire, a dark and enclosed place of death for three days, as if a whale had swallowed her up. Just like Jonah's experience, Bella's change from human to vampire lasts three days and three nights.

Bird/Snake

In *Twilight*, when Bella first visits the meadow with Edward for the first time, she feels like "a bird locked in the eyes of a snake" (*Twilight*, p 232). This is yet another dangerous prey/predator relationship in the *Twilight* books. In folklore and in fact, birds and snakes are traditional animal counterparts.

As a symbol, birds are good creatures because their wings are believed to take them closer to the heavens. Snakes, which slither on or live below ground, allude to death and evil underworlds. So birds and snakes have always been traditional enemies, opposing each other throughout the ages. Folklore about magic birds depicts birds as snake-fighting creatures. Many famous tales describe birds and snakes fighting each other. A famous bird is the phoenix. The phoenix is as an eternal symbol of goodness that fights serpents, proving that good actions always triumph over evil. In *Harry Potter and the Chamber of Secrets*, a phoenix attacks a giant basilisk, pecking out its eyes (Rowling, 1998). In Indian myth, Nagas (snakes) rule rain and are in constant conflict with Garuda, a mighty sunbird.

As for birds in nature, the opposite is true in most cases. Snakes prey on birds. Unless, of course, you're a bird who insists of having the last laugh, like the snake-eating Australian kookaburra.

Mouse/Cat

A less obvious prey/predator pair in the *Twilight* world is the mouse/cat mix. Guess who is the mouse? Bella. And the cat? The vampire, of course. In one *New Moon* scene, Laurent tells Bella that he is going to kill her. And his voice sounded like a "seductive purr" (p 240). As soon as Laurent mentions Victoria, a vampire who wants to kill Bella, Bella "squeaked" just like a mouse (*New Moon*, p 240).

A quirky comment later in *New Moon* describes Bella's emotional scars (holes that Edward and Jacob have created inside Bella's chest, after they each rejected her). All these holes made Bella feel as if she was "now riddled through like Swiss cheese" (*New Moon*, p 273). A mousy metaphor, since cheese is something that a mouse would eat. As to whether this symbolic gesture is an author's crafty mousetrap or just a cheesy slip of the mind, one can only guess.

Eagle/Fish

An important prey/predator pair that helps to symbolize Bella/Edward's relationship is the eagle/fish. Sitting with Bella on the beach at La Push, Jacob points to "an eagle" diving into the sea from a great height, "its talons breaking the surface of the waves, just for an instant. Then it flapped away, its wings straining against the load of the huge fish it had snagged" (*Eclipse*, p 97). Jacob uses this animal metaphor to suggest that it is dangerous for Bella (a fish) to have a romantic relationship with Edward (an eagle), since eagles kill and eat fish. As Jacob tells Bella, this is "nature taking its course – hunter and prey, the endless cycle of life and death" (*Eclipse*, p 97). This is fate. Nature. The way things are meant to be. "You don't see the fish trying to plant a kiss on the eagle" (*Eclipse*, p 98), Jacob explains. In other words, Jacob is suggesting that it is risky to change the course of destiny, to make a choice that is unnatural, for the prey to romance the predator.

Eagle

As a symbol, the eagle is very powerful. This huge, diurnal bird of prey and its name are linked to the Latin noun *aquilo* (which means 'north wind'). This reflects the eagle's strength and velocity during flight. This carnivorous bird of prey has an impressive wingspan and sharp hooked talons that it uses to snatch up snakes, small mammals, and fish. Eagles mate for life and use the same nest each year to raise a small clutch of eggs. As such, although the eagle is a dangerous predator, it is also a loyal and territorial family-bird. In line with eagle symbolism, Jacob Black is loyal, hunts on Quileute land, fiercely protects his territory and believes he would makea good eagle-like mate for Bella.

In ancient times, the eagle was considered to be an equal of the sun, a symbol of royal and imperial power. Due to its acute vision, people considered it clairvoyant as it was the only creature that could look at the sun. Lord Tennyson's beautiful poem *The Eagle* captures the startling power and majesty of this feathered hunter:

He clasps the crag with crooked hands;
Close to the sun in lonely lands,
Ringed with the azure world, he stands.
The wrinkled sea beneath him crawls;
He watches from his mountain walls,
And like a thunderbolt he falls.

As a natural predator of the snake, the sun-loving eagle symbolizes the power of good over evil.

Meanwhile, those poor old snakes sure get a hard time symbolically, don't they?

Fish

The fish is the most prominent water symbol. Fish live in depths synonymous with the underworld, and have access to secret places forbidden to humankind. Since fish "have access to hidden depths, the fish is party to secret and sacred information" (Nozedar, 2008, p 272). Water is closely linked to the womb, and the idea of birth and rebirth, and so the fish takes on these meanings too. According to the Vedas, these scriptures were delivered by a fish acting as an avatar of Vishnu. For the Celts, the salmon was a symbol of hidden knowledge and wisdom. Early Christians, who kept their religion a secret to avoid execution, used a fish symbol called Ichthys to identify one another. Note that Bella (the fish) is a potential meal for both the shark (the animal that is like Edward) and the eagle (the animal linked to Jacob). That's a pretty precarious and fishy symbolic position to be in!

Shakespeare's View

Since the *Twilight Saga* cites William Shakespeare's *Romeo and Juliet,* and Bella and Edward's romance reproduce the star-crossed love theme, it may interest you to know that Shakespeare reveled in using animal symbols to describe the desirable/ dangerous relationship between Romeo and Juliet, which the love story between Edward and Bella echoes. In the following passage, Juliet's description of Romeo (the young man she is forbidden to love) is rich with animal symbols to help convey her taboo temptation. Juliet says:

O serpent heart, hid with a flowering face!
Did ever dragon keep so fair a cave?
Beautiful tyrant! fiend angelical!
Dove-feather'd raven! wolvish-ravening lamb!
Despised substance of divinest show!
Just opposite to what thou justly seem'st,
A damned saint, an honorable villain!
O nature, what hadst thou to do in hell,
When thou didst bower the spirit of a fiend
In moral paradise of such sweet flesh?

To highlight how torturous it is for Juliet to desire a beautiful but dangerous love like Romeo, Shakespeare describes Romeo as both a: serpent/flower, dove/raven, lamb/wolf, and saint/villain. This means Romeo has both positive and negative boyfriend qualities, symbolized by different animals.

Specific Animals

Bat

In the *Twilight Saga,* some specific animals are mentioned, such as bats. The *Twilight Saga* makes only one direct reference to bats.

When Edward offers to show Bella how he travels through the forest, Bella asks Edward, "Will you turn into a bat?" (*Twilight*, p 244). Cute. As an animal, the bat is a most unusual creature (part-mouse, part-bird) that has existed since the dawn of time. Its general appearance and habits – hanging upside down, sleeping during the day, and hunting by night has made it an unusual creature. The bat is the only mammal capable of true flight. And nothing beats a bat's power of detection. A bat's hearing is so sensitive that it can 'detect' an insect's footstep. A bat fires off sound waves from its throat, and then uses its own echo to navigate the night without error or effort.

While Edward may not change into a bat, he and his vampire family do show bat-like behaviors. Like bats, Edward and the Cullens:

- Have super-sensitive hearing
- Do not harm humans
- The Cullen mansion is like a bat cave where they hide out
- The Cullens have super-sharp senses and detection ability to get around in the dark

According to myth, the special powers and abilities of bats include:

- Navigation
- Detection
- Vigilance
- Unity
- Flight
- Rebirth
- Good fortune

The Cullen family seem to reflect these qualities:

Navigation and Detection – the superhuman senses of

Twilight vampires enable them to detect objects and navigate their way around the forest.

Vigilance – the Cullens are always highly vigilant. They take many precautions to keep their vampire identity a secret, such as keeping to themselves, avoiding humans on sunny days, and hunting long distances away.

Unity – the Cullens stick together as a family. Since the bat is the only flying mammal and suckles its young, the bat is considered most excellent parents.

Flight – the Cullens travel through the forest at super-fast speed, as if they were flying. Also, like the non-aggressive bat, they take 'flight' when disturbed, rather than attacking others. In *New Moon*, the whole family took flight from Forks to keep Bella safe.

Rebirth – Carlisle' actions to save individuals on the brink of mortal death, biting them and resurrecting them as vampires, strongly supports the rebirth theme in the books.

Good fortune – With all those cars, clothes, gadgets, centuries of saving and Alice's ability to predict the stock market, one cannot deny the Cullens' good material fortune. More importantly, with foster parents like the compassionate Carlisle and Esme, the Cullens are emotionally blessed also.

In particular, the bat's nocturnal nature and cave-dwelling habits strongly suggest that this creature symbolizes hidden knowledge and secret information, with the ability to detect things that daytime creatures cannot. Before echolocation was understood, the bat's ability to navigate its way through the darkness was a source of great intrigue, adding to its mystique. Just like bats, *Twilight*-style vampires must keep their vampire identities hidden and protect secret information. Otherwise, the Volturi vampires will execute them.

In China,, the peaceful bat is linked to happiness, faith, and persistence. It is a useful creature that eats mosquitoes and insect pests. The *Twilight* universe supports the bat as a positive animal symbol too. For example, Billy Black tells a legend about ancient spirit warriors. Their allies were bats and dogs. Once upon a time, the warriors "turned the dogs against their masters and then brought a mighty infestation of bats up from the cliff caverns" (*Eclipse*, p 218). With help from the screaming wind, the enemy tribe "scattered, calling our harbor a cursed place" (*Eclipse*, p 218). If vampires have bat qualities and the Quileute werewolves have canine qualities, then Bella has helped bats and dogs to be allies once again, as in this ancient myth.

As a creature of the night that gets tangled in long hair, and that can suck the blood of sleeping victims, many people are scared of bats. The nocturnal lifestyle of the bat, in particular, gives it some negative meanings. Symbolically, the bat is believed to swallow the light, and so it symbolizes the night devouring the day. Some Christians believe the bat is an incarnation of Satan. No wonder people fear vampires.

Bear

In the *Twilight* world, the Cullens hunt bears and Edward's 'big' brother Emmett looks like a bear.

As a symbol in North Europe, the bear is an earthly creature linked to ideas of world power and authority. The bear is associated with the moon too. Just as the moon disappears from the sky for a time, bears hibernate during winter. Shamans absorbed the spiritual energy of the bear by wearing bearskins. Meanwhile, brave warriors who fought in wore bear claws or teeth as magical amulets. The bearskin hats of the Guards at Buckingham Palace, still worn today, are remnants of these primitive times. According to the ancient Celts, 'bear' means 'warrior'. And the source of King Arthur's name is 'artos', which means 'bear-like'. The Greek Goddess of the Hunt, Artemis, also shares the bear's name and can shape-shift into a bear.

Given what bears mean, it is apt for Bella to consider Emmett as the ideal older brother. Emmett is strong, fierce, and protective. When Bella asks Edward why he goes hunting at Great Rocks on weekends, he answers "because of bears… Grizzly is Emmett's favorite" (*Twilight*, p 188). Other examples of *Twilight* text that links bears with characters like Emmett are these:

- "If you've ever seen a bear attack on television, you should be able to visualize Emmett hunting" (*Twilight*, p 189).
- "Emmett" was "Edward's playful bear of a brother" (*New Moon*, p 24), the kind of "big brother" Bella always wanted (*New Moon*, p 24).
- Emmett's fighting style when practicing with Jasper: "Emmett charged him like a bear" (*Eclipse*, p 350).
- Werewolves are also compared to bears. "Black bears don't get that big," says one male hiker in *New Moon* (p 121).
- Jacob crushes Bella with a friendly "bear hug" (*New Moon*, p 290).

As many Twilight fans know, Emmett joined the Cullen clan when he was nearly killed by a bear in the woods, but Rosalie rescued him. Now, Emmett's favorite food to hunt is bear.

Bee

The bee is *not* an obvious animal symbol in the *Twilight* world. But honey is an image that is repeatedly presented to the reader. What is the product of hard-working bees? Sweet, liquid gold honey. In the *Twilight* books, Edward's eyes look like honey. For example, they tend to glow "a deep, golden honey color" (*Twilight*, p 70).

According to symbol experts, "the bee or honeybee is a symbol of the soul, resurrection, work accomplished by communal effort, and self-fulfillment" (Colin, 2000, p 55). This describes the Cullens perfectly. They are productive, creative, industrious, work together as a team, pursue personal and social fulfillment, strive to grow spiritually, and their house is much like a cozy beehive. A bee in a dream is often a sign of death, rebirth, renewal. Or else it may mean that the dreamer is devoted to a higher cause, has a well-developed sense of community, or performs actions to protect or develop a community, clan or family. This kind of bee symbolism reflects the Cullens' way of life well.

When a bee stings you, it dies. This ultimate and painful sacrifice symbolizes a creative desire that is liberated under the effect of shocking or stinging circumstances. Edward is bee-like in that he falls in love with Bella, putting his own life at risk from the Volturi. The many references to Edward's honey-colored eyes and honey scent may therefore not be a random idea choice at all, but a sign of an author's symbolic mastery or rich unconscious creativity.

The famous Chilean poet, Pablo Neruda, wrote a love sonnet that mentions bees in a way that sounds Edward-like:

You – The One Who Puts Things in Order – you shimmer
through like a bee, probing spaces lost to the darkness;
conquering light, you with your white energy.

Just like this bee poem suggests, Edward shimmers in the sunlight, helps Bella to overcome loneliness, he has pale silver skin, and he gives out good energy. Just as the alchemy of bees turns flower pollen into sweet honey, Edward's inner goodness steadily inspires Bella to trust him and develop strong feelings of love for him, even if he does tell her to stay away from him at first.

In the *Twilight Saga*, the symbolic meaning of bees definitely helps to distinguish Edward and Jacob from each other as characters. Edward is a Byronic hero figure, sensitive and obsessive, sweet and thoughtful, who tends to brood, analyze, and think deeply about everything. Edward's mind would be a busy hive of thoughts and idealistic visions, interpreting the world in the best way possible and trying to reframe negative situations in a positive way, like bee alchemy. By contrast, Jacob is a direct, realistic, practical, and lively character, a doer not a thinker. Jacob would regard buzzing bee alchemy in his head very irritating. In fact, he does. As Jacob explains, his thoughts "bounced around inside my skull like a disoriented swarm of bees. Noisy. Now and again they stung, must be hornets" (*Breaking Dawn*, p 136). Not everyone tries to turn worry into honey in their minds; they prefer to solve problems in different ways. So, honey-eyed and sacrifice-centered Edward is bee-like, and Jacob is not. That's the main buzz.

Cat

An animal *Twilight*-style vampires strongly resemble is the cat. This includes big cats like lions, cheetahs and jaguars. For example:

- Edward's favorite food is "mountain lion" (*Twilight*, p 188) and he hunts "like a lion" too (*Twilight*, p 189).
- Edward displays lion-like behavior when he "growled", "half-crouched", and "tensed like a lion about to pounce" (*Twilight*, p 301).
- While playing baseball Edward "bounded off" with "grace and power" like a "cheetah" (*Twilight*, p 321).
- "Edward runs the fastest" Esme tells Bella during baseball (*Twilight*, p 323).
- "Alice was almost purring" (*Eclipse*, p 328), after the fantastic after-graduation party at the Cullens.
- Nahuel, a half-vampire character, is named after "the jungle cat" (*Breaking Dawn*, p 682).

Some bad vampires in the *Twilight* books also resemble cats:

- The way James and his nomad gang walked was "catlike, a gait that seemed constantly on the edge of shifting into a crouch" (*Twilight*, p 328) and Victoria's posture was "distinctly feline" (*Twilight*, p 329).
- Bella imagines Victoria's "brilliant hair blowing around her oddly feline face" (*Eclipse*, p 112).
- When Victoria finally finds Bella on top of the mountain: "There was a striking feline quality to the way she held her coiled body, a lioness waiting for an opening to spring" (p 480) and "her fingers were ready claws" (*Eclipse*, p 483).
- Victoria "showed her teeth and hissed" (*Eclipse*, p 484).
- When the fight between Edward and Victoria closed in "it was lion versus lioness" (*Eclipse*, p 486).

All these descriptions help to convey the idea that Edward, and other vampires, are strong, sleek and fast, just like big cats.

The cat-like descriptions of vampires in the *Twilight Saga* match cat facts and the symbolic meanings of cats:

- The 'big cats' include the lion, tiger, cheetah, leopard, snow leopard, and jaguar.
- Cats have strong teeth designed to tear and chew flesh. Their sharp and curved claws make excellent weapons for pouncing on prey. This describes the hunting style of *Twilight* vampires perfectly.
- Cat eyes appear to change color and glow in the dark. When light shines into a cat's eye, the retina reflects the light it has absorbed. Vampire eyes change color also, from red to black, and black to gold.
- Why does a cat land on its feet? Cats have a very flexible spine with numerous vertebrae. This enables the cat to twist and turn its body with ease. When Bella leaped out of the window as a newborn vampire, she landed steadily on her feet.

The magical and symbolic meanings of cats are said to be:

Perception
Cleverness
Communication
Independence
Immortality
Healing
Protection
Flight

Many people also believe that cats possess magic power and are supernatural messengers that communicate with spirits. The ancient Egyptians revered the cat as a deity. Cats were believed to carry the spirit of Isis. According to Egyptian priests, cats possessed the magnetic forces of nature which people could absorb if cats were around. Artemis, the Greek hunting goddess, has associations with the cat and could magically change herself into a cat, notorious for its hunting skills. When cats sleep, they curl themselves up into a circle (the head touches the tail). This links cats to circle ideas like immortality. In the Western world, cats acquired negative meanings and were considered to be companions of witches, especially black cats. According to medieval folklore, witches were said to ride on the back of black cats to feasts and festivals. Giddy-up, puss! And Bella does ride on Edward's back through the forest. Giddy-up Edward? Nevertheless, given these meaning of cats, it is apt for vampires to resemble cats. Both vampires and cats are powerful hunters and strong supernatural symbols.

Deer

The most significant deer scene in the *Twilight Saga* involves Dr. Carlisle Cullen. Carlisle hid after a vampire bit him and he was turning into a vampire. A compassionate man, Carlisle refused to drink human blood. One night, when Carlisle was perishing from starvation "a herd of deer passed his hiding place. He was so wild with thirst that he attacked without a thought" (*Twilight*, p 295). The deer helped Carlisle to realize that he could survive as a vampire without killing humans – he could drink animal blood instead. After the deer encounter, Carlisle began using his time productively to study art and science. For the first time as a vampire, Carlisle felt hopeful about the future. What's more, this important *Twilight* theme matches the positive symbolic meanings of deer.

According to folklore, the deer symbolizes meekness, gentleness, and swiftness. This creature is a magical messenger from the otherworld, belonging to the world of fairies and spirits. The deer is also a symbol of purity, healing, and life. Since the deer dwells in dark and shadowy forests, it is said to harbor hidden magic and secrets. This creature was revered in ancient times and during the Middle Ages, when it was exciting to visit dark forests and encounter a deer. "As a symbol of power, spiritual strength and material wealth, a deer appears in a dream as a guide and harbinger of good news, a messenger announcing a birth, a revelation or a realization" (Colin, 2000, p 145).

In line with these symbolic meanings, the deer in the *Twilight* world saves Carlisle's life, gives him strength, guides him spiritually, and helps Carlisle to value his own existence as a vampire who does not harm humans. Due to their tree-like antlers, deer were seen to be solar animals linked to the rays of the sun, the tree of life and the endless seasons of life. This may explain why the deer was considered such a sacred creature that acted as a guide for the soul on its journey to the afterlife. When Carlisle was still hiding, wondering about his future, it was a deer that showed Carlisle the spiritual way ahead and guided him towards a more peaceful afterlife as a vampire. The deer's role in spiritual freedom appears again, more subtly, in *Breaking Dawn*. On the brink of freedom, Jake, Seth, and Leah go hunting deep in the mountains. Jacob explains that, "We ran into a herd of black-tailed deer just as the sun was coming up, brightening the clouds a little bit behind us" (*Breaking Dawn*, p 287). When the deer appears in this morning scene, so does the dawn, the sun, and a glorious outlook – positive deer meanings.

In an old poem about a deer, Emily Dickinson paints a different atmosphere of mystery, sacrifice, and spirituality that reflects Bella's desire to die:

A wounded deer leaps highest,
I've heard the hunter tell;
'Tis but the ecstasy of death,
And then the brake is still.

Just like this deer, Bella also felt strangely satisfied about giving up her life for a higher cause. Namely, Bella was content – maybe even ecstatic – to die in order to save Edward, whom she truly, madly loves: "I imagined him by the shore, his skin sparkling like the sea… Despite all the horror and hopelessness, I was fleetingly happy" (*Twilight*, pp 384–385). Bella prepares for the horror of death by conjuring up the loveliest visions about Edward in her mind. When Bella meets James in the ballet studio so he can kill her, at the end of *Twilight*, she is a symbolic deer sacrificing herself to the hunter.

Dog

Compared to vampires who attract meanings associated with wild or dangerous animals, humans in the *Twilight* world tend to attract safe animal meanings. Mike, for example, is associated with dogs. Bella thinks of Mike as a friendly "golden retriever" because he likes to walk alongside Bella (*Twilight*, p 26) "wagging his tail" (*Twilight*, p 43). In other words, Mike likes to praise himself for being helpful. This description works well, because Mike is generally harmless, loyal, eager to please Bella, and always wants to attract her attention, just like a family dog. What's more, these canine qualities mentioned in the *Twilight Saga* fit with the positive meanings of dogs in folklore.

Every society in the world has dog myths. Dogs have kept company with humans for thousands of years, working and living together. The dog was the first wild animal to be domesticated by human beings, perhaps as far back as the 11th millennium BC in the Middle East. It is believed that the dog is a direct descendant of the wolf, a type of canine that is a mix of wolf, jackal and coyote (Colin, 2000). Dreaming about a dog might symbolize "the darkest, wildest, most impure, untamable and amoral side of our nature" but it can also signify "the most loyal, affectionate and submissive side" (Colin, 2000, p 151). In the *Twilight Saga,* Mike's personality surely seems to capture these loyal and affectionate dog meanings.

A dog's sense of smell is so keen that dogs are reputed to detect supernatural phenomena that humans cannot smell, hear or see. This helps to explain why dogs appear to mediate the seen and unseen worlds, seemingly gifted with psychic powers. To this day, people believe that dogs can see ghosts. Dogs are often associated with dark, obscure, and spiritual worlds, even death. In ancient Egypt, the dog-headed god Anubis guided souls of the dead to the next world. Maybe, if Mike concentrated harder, he could pick up some of the supernatural activity happening around Forks.

Of course, the werewolves of the *Twilight* world have also been called "dogs" a number of times, But this is meant to be insulting. For example, Alice calls Jacob a "dog" in *New Moon* (p 421). As traditional symbols, however, dogs do not tend to have any negative or degrading ideas.

Dolphin

> We watched the sunset from the rocky western cove. We swam with porpoises that played in the warm, shallow waters there. (*Breaking Dawn*, p 90)

In the *Twilight Saga,* the porpoise/dolphin is briefly mentioned when Bella and Edward are on their honeymoon on Isle Esme. The dolphin is described in a happy and positive way. How can these creatures not be? In nature, the dolphin is a highly benevolent, intelligent, playful and communicative creature. On a logical level, it certainly makes sense to have dolphins swimming at the beach on an island. Nothing strange or unusual about that… on the surface. However, the symbolism of dolphins and their link with Bella may actually run a bit deeper than what appears on the bright sunlit surface of the sea.

The name dolphin comes from the Greek word *delphinos,* which means 'womb'. The Delphic Oracle was once a temple dedicated to the sun god Apollo who visited Delphi as a dolphin. Over time, there have been many stories of dolphins that have saved humans from sharks or from drowning in the sea. This is why dolphins appear in Greek art and friezes, carrying the souls of the dead on their backs to the Isles of the Blest. As a saver of souls, the dolphin became associated with the Roman God Mithras, and later the Christian savior Jesus Christ.

It is on Isle Esme, swimming in the warm sea and spending time around the well of life, that Bella falls pregnant on her honeymoon. This establishes a curious little link between Bella and the dolphin, which is a symbolic source of life.

Of course, it could just be a coincidence that Stephenie Meyer chose a 'porpoise' instead of a 'sea slug', 'lobster', 'jellyfish' or some other sea creature swimming on the Isle Esme coast. But when you consider all the pieces of the *Twilight Saga* jigsaw puzzle together – such as Ms. Meyer's literature degree, her knowledge of Greek myth, and references to many other *Twilight Saga* symbols – the dolphin may be much more than just an accidental word in a sea of text.

Elk

Throughout history, the elk has been an animal hunted by

humans. As such, it makes sense that elks in the *Twilight* world are described as being the poor casualties of hunting. When Charlie takes Bella to *The Lodge* for a graduation dinner, Bella notices a "depressed-looking stuffed elk head" on the wall (*Eclipse*, p 319). Clearly, the elk is the victim. On another occasion, Charlie "bellowed" at Edward just like an elk after Edward and Bella returned to Forks from their Volterra ordeal (*New Moon*, p 498). Clearly, the elk-sounding Charlie is the tormented victim here. His daughter disappeared for three days which drove Charlie mad with worry.

Fish

The fish does not just appear in prey/predator animal pairs (fish/shark and fish/eagle) in the *Twilight* world. Stephenie Meyer puts fish on the literary menu in a number of other places in her books. Some good fishing spots, plot-wise, are these:

- Charlie likes to go fishing. The *Twilight* world therefore mentions fish in the context of sport, recreation and hunting.
- Bella does not like fishing or killing fish. Maybe this helps to foreshadow Bella's ability to excel as a vegetarian vampire. If she has empathy for fish as a human girl, then this foreshadows an ability to control her lust for human blood as a vampire, which she does.
- The Quileute people are a fishing tribe because, historically, their harbor has always been full of fish (*Eclipse*, p 217).
- There's also Billy's famous fish fry. Fish is a basic food that many societies eat.

Why does the *Twilight* world mention fish so often? Maybe the story is using 'fish' to highlight different qualities, values and coping styles of the characters. Some individuals, like Bella, seem to appreciate the fascinating abilities of fish. The fish is a creature that can swim underwater, navigate the marine depths, and negotiate the currents with ease, agility, and speed. For example, Bella is awed by the aquatic action in the rock pools at First Beach (*Twilight*, p 101). In other *Twilight* adventures, the fish brings out practical or social strengths in certain characters. For example, when Billy Black brings the famous fish fry around to Charlie's place, this custom or gesture is meant to promote peaceful and positive relationships.

As a symbol, fish have a number of spiritual and supernatural meanings. The fish's 'scale' has been used to symbolize the doorway to divine wisdom and the heavens. This is because the human eyelid resembles a protective fish scale. When an eye opens, or the eyelid recedes, people can then see things with their sensitive and mystical inner eye. As the encyclopedia of symbols puts it, people are like "fish, swimming in the ever-changing waters of their emotions, from which they draw inspiration and motivation" (Colin, 2000). In the *Twilight* world, Bella's transformation from human to vampire certainly fits with fish meanings. As Bella's human life recedes and falls away, this allows her psychic gifts to emerge. She also sees the world in totally a new way – with special vampire vision. Since fish live underwater in underworld-like depths, fish can enter secret places that are forbidden to humans. With this "access to hidden depths, the fish is party to secret and sacred information" (Nozedar, 2008, p 272). To the Celts, for example, the salmon was a symbol of hidden knowledge and wisdom. Other sacred scripture (known as the Vedas) was delivered by a fish acting as an avatar for the god Vishnu. In line with secret fish meanings, when Bella becomes a vampire, she gains access to a secret supernatural world of vampirism forbidden to humans.

Since water is closely linked to the womb and the idea of birth and rebirth, the fish takes on these meanings too. The first time Bella and Edward ever made love was in the warm tropical waters of Isle Esme, which most probably resulted in the creation of Renesmee. Maybe this is a procreative fish scene. In any case, with so many different fish references, there's something symbolically fishy about the *Twilight Saga*.

Gazelle

In the *Twilight Saga*, the gazelle is used to describe the way Alice Cullen moves around. This cute and tiny Cullen is likened to the nimble, buoyant and graceful gazelle. In *Twilight*, for example, Alice's movements were "graceful" (p 280), "graceful, almost danced" (p 302) as she "bounded up and to the door" (p 303). Later on, during a family baseball game, Alice clearly "ran like a gazelle" (*Twilight*, p 320). Even though Alice is a vampire, allocating features of the gentle and carefree gazelle to Alice helps to present this sweet Cullen family member as a gentle, fun-loving and loveable character, as is the endearing nature of gazelles.

Goat

The *Twilight Saga* scatters a few references to goats in the books, which can be tricky to spot. The word goat is first mentioned when Edward says he will go hiking in the Goat Rocks Wilderness (*Twilight*, p 93). Nothing too symbolically sinister there – just a vampire hunting haunt, that's all. In a later scene, another *Twilight* character is linked to the supple and sprightly goat. Jacob "leapt easily from rock to rock, not seeming to need his hands at all. His perfect balance reminded me of a mountain goat" (*Eclipse*, p 421). Adding to the hikes, hills and hopping, there may be a few more subtle goat references in the *Twilight* world.

With those hard little horns and all that shaggy hair, the goat is a powerful symbol of procreation, sexual virility, and lust. It may therefore be no coincidence that someone as masculine, athletic and sexy as Jacob gets goat virtues. The ancient

Egyptians worshipped the Goat of Mendes while Greek myths tell of half-man, half-goat creatures called satyrs. The God of Nature was a satyr named Pan who played music in the forest with his wooden pipes. Later, when Christians were keen to demonize pagan beliefs, they portrayed the goat as the Devil.

In some cultures, the goat is a symbol of fire and lightning. In ancient China and Tibet, for example, goats were believed to deliver messages and blessings from the heavenly gods. Meanwhile, the Norse God Thor rides a chariot drawn by two magical goats named Toothgnasher and Toothgrinder. This European myth certainly adds a thunderous element to the goat's storm and lightning image. Maybe the goat's ability to thrive high on mountains close to lightning storms, just like the Cullens and the Quileutes do, brings these harmless creatures closer to the heavens and explains their supernatural strengths.

The earliest people hunted wild goats for meat and hide, just to survive. Then, in 6000 BC, people domesticated goats for their milk and cheese. As a source of milk, the goat has links with the earth-goddess who cares for nature and nurtures humans. The goat therefore symbolizes ideas such as care, kindness and respect. When the Cullen vampires go hunting at Goat Rocks, this could be a symbolic tip to the traditional meaning of the goat because the Cullens only hunt animals to survive, not for sport or greed. The Cullens also respect the animals they hunt, are harmless to humans, and care about their impact on the environment, just as goat-friendly gods and goddesses would like.

Lizard

The lizard is a miniature dragon and one of the oldest creatures on earth. As such, ancient people feared and revered the primeval lizard. Assigning lizard-like features to the ancient Volturi-vampires seems apt. For example, when Bella first meets Caius in the Volturi underground, his half-closed eyes gave him a "heavy-lidded gaze of a lizard" (*New Moon*, p 481).

In the animal world, lizards are harmless creatures that do not deliberately attack humans. Lizards are not excessively aggressive or venomous like snakes. In *Breaking Dawn*, the Volturi leader Marcus looks too "tired" and "uncaring" to start a war, much like a lizard lazing on a rock in the sun. He desires no violence with the Cullens about Renesmee, choosing to "reevaluate later. Let us leave in peace" (*Breaking Dawn*, p 678). Meanwhile, Caius reveals the surprisingly brutal side of lizards in the final novel. In *Breaking Dawn*, Caius strikes out at innocent Irina for no rational reason, attacking and killing the female vampire in a fast lizard-like way in front of everyone (p 657). This scene is ever so symbolic of a motionless lizard that suddenly whips out its super-fast tongue to catch a naïve and unsuspecting fly. Symbolically, the lizard is generally a docile creature that is best left alone and not irritated.

Snake

The snake is used to describe *Twilight*-style vampires more often than any other creature. What's more, some snake qualities are linked to vampires in sneaky and subtle ways. Slithering on its underbelly, limbless, hairless and cold-blooded, the snake tends to have negative meanings as a symbol. A snake can hunt and feed on prey much larger than itself too, due to its super-flexible jaw. The snake-vampire connections are interesting and cover both good and evil vampires. Some examples of how snakes are used to allude to *Twilight*-style vampires are these:

- The trail during Bella's first forest hike "snaked around" at the same time she was thinking about a vampire she loves (*Twilight*, p 118). The forest path, which winds around just like a snake, surely suggests vampire danger to come.
- The forest "twisted, serpent-like" (*Twilight*, p 280) on the way to the Cullens' house. Another snakish hint of

vampire-danger.

- In *New Moon*, the driveway to the Cullen house was a "dark, serpentine lane" (p 44).
- Edward's eyes look like those of a "snake" (*Twilight*, p 232).
- Twilight-style vampires are venomous, just like snakes. As Alice explains to Bella "we're also venomous" (*Twilight*, p 361). If vampire venom is left to spread in a human body, it takes just a few days to become a vampire.
- Vampires in the *Twilight* world aren't just venomous like snakes, they move about like snakes. When Alice pitched at baseball, "her style seemed to be stealth" and just "like the strike of a cobra, her right hand flicked out" (*Twilight*, p 322).
- When the Cullens and the werewolves practice fighting in a forest clearing, Emmett and Jasper were "moving faster than cobra strikes" (*Eclipse*, p 381).
- When Alice told Bella that Edward plans to kill himself, "her gaze strangled the words in my throat" (*New Moon*, p 417). This resembles the way a snake strangles its prey.
- Aro "glided closer" to Bella, much like a snake (*New Moon*, p 473).
- When Edward tried to protect Bella from Jane, this evil vampire "hissed in frustration, leaning forward like she was preparing to spring" (*New Moon*, p 476). Jane sounded and moved just a snake preparing to strike its prey.

As you can see, the *Twilight Saga* vampires are not just linked to snakes because of their incapacitating venom, but they stare, slide, strangle and strike others in the same way that snakes do. This is exactly why snakes are such powerful and frightening symbols and such good vampire descriptors.

In all cultures, the snake symbolizes life, death, and regeneration. Some powerful examples are:

- The Egyptian Apophis, a symbol of primordial chaos, was depicted as a giant serpent.
- Many lethal monsters in Greek myth were part snake, e.g. Medusa's hair was made of writhing snakes.
- The Aboriginal Australian rainbow serpent created the world and everything in it during the Dreamtime.
- A snake tempted Eve to bite the forbidden fruit of knowledge in the original garden of paradise.

Since snakes bite, strike, squeeze, or poison their prey to death, they have developed a reputation for being deadly and aggressive. The *Twilight* vampires hunt and kill their prey in the same way as snakes do. They use venom (*Twilight*, p 396), crush their prey (*Eclipse*, p 349), and "hiss" just like snakes too (*Eclipse*, p 337). In fact, some of Bella's hisses and other snake-like behaviors may be foreshadowing the snake-like vampire she will become. For instance, Bella "hisses" at other people a number of times (e.g. *Twilight*, p 257; *New Moon*, pp 264, 281, 287). When Bella tells Jacob to leave her bedroom one night, she "hissed, putting as much venom into the whisper" as possible (*New Moon*, p 281). In an earlier adventure, Alice gives Bella a birthday gift and Bella gives Edward "a basilisk glare" (*New Moon*, p 28). As you can see, Bella hisses like a venomous snake/vampire.

Some the most famous snakes in myth and folklore are also suggested in the *Twilight Saga*. These mythical snakes help to describe certain vampire adventures:

Typhon – this fire-breathing snake could shoot flames out of its eyes. It symbolized the evil forces of the earth and was captured under a volcano in Sicily, which later erupted. In line with this myth, some *Twilight* vampires have fire-projecting gifts. The South American vampire Zafrina, for example, can produce fiery illusions.

Naga – this serpent from Indian myth can communicate between gods and humans. It can either be good or evil, just like

Twilight-style vampires can be.

Hydra – this nine-headed serpent from Greek myth lives in murky swamps and is a very difficult monster to fight. If you cut off one Hydra head, two new heads will grow. The Hydra is a snake symbol whose message is that life is full of obstacles that block the path to progress and truth. Do the nine snake-like permanent Volturi guards symbolize the terrible nine-headed Hydra? If you like, go to *Volturi* in this book now.

In all, snakes describe *Twilight*-style vampires well as aggressive, dangerous, deadly and magical.

Turtle

The *Twilight* world makes such a fleeting mention to turtles that it is easy to miss. During their honeymoon on Isle Esme, Edward lured Bella outdoors in the sun and in the sea to find *"sea turtles"* (*Breaking Dawn,* p 90). But sturdier turtle symbolism may hide elsewhere in the books. In particular, turtles are traditional metaphors for shyness. Their calm and easy-going pace is also highly regarded. Slow and steady progress, not rash and rushed action, leads to successful outcomes. At first, Bella presents as a shy turtle hiding inside her shell. But Bella makes stable and steady turtle progress in establishing knowledge, confidence, courage, and friendships. She takes turtle time to think about issues and solve problems, and just like a turtle, she is not aggressive. In the same way as a turtle moves across the ground slowly and carefully, Bella dislikes speed (driving too fast, fast-paced sports, athletics, smooth-talk) and she views herself as a thinker who is physically sluggish. Just as no one would expect a turtle to beat a hare in a race, no one would expect a shy peacekeeper like Bella to deflect the psychic gifts of evil vampires, win a Volturi war, and become a powerful vampire herself – all because of her protective turtle-like shell. Her mental 'shield', that is.

Wolf

Wolves are a mysterious and frightening symbol throughout Native American culture, symbolizing ferocity, skill, hunting prowess and death. In legends, the wolf is often seen as a god or a spiritual entity, working as both a protector and an antagonist to the human race. Whether for good or for bad, the mythology and folklore surrounding the wolf reflects the awe Native Americans hold for this powerful creature.

There is no doubt that the wolf plays a big role in the *Twilight Saga*. Above all, Jacob and his friends are werewolves, or shape-shifting wolves, to be precise (*Breaking Dawn*, p 654). Not only do Native American people in the *Twilight* world respect wolves and shape-shift into huge, furry wolves, the Quileute characters have picked up other wolvish meanings.

Loner

The wolf is usually a loner, a lone hunter, and a symbol of male power, energy and sexuality. This isolative behavior is depicted clearly in the *Twilight Saga* and shows how animal metaphors illustrate a certain character's approach to life. Jacob, for example, runs away in *Breaking Dawn* and disappears from La Push for a while because he is so upset that Bella plans to become a vampire. Jacob retreats into his wolf-form for a while, which suggests that he prefers to cope alone and get in touch with his most primitive animal instincts. This enables Jacob to explore his deeper emotions and resolve inner turmoil. As Seth explains, "He's trying not to think *human*, you know. Just going with his instincts" (*Breaking Dawn*, p 9). A wolf's long and eerie howl under a full moon epitomizes the idea of the lone wolf. It is one of the most mournful calls of the wild. When Bella and Edward finally marry and embark on their honeymoon, they can hear Jacob's "piercing, heartbroken howling" far in the forest behind them (*Breaking Dawn*, p 68).

Guide

In Western culture, wolves often have evil meanings. The wolf in *Little Red Riding Hood* is a symbol of evil and predatory behavior. But in Native American culture, the wolf is a magnificent guide, teacher, and source of sacred wisdom – it has positive meanings. The *Twilight* world definitely embraces the positive symbolic meanings of wolves. For example, Bella once dreamed that a "great russet wolf… gigantic, monstrous" was "trying to convey something vital with his intelligent eyes" (*New Moon*, p 292). With its "intelligent eyes", this wolf acts more like a messenger than a monster. In fact, the wolvish guide in this dream helps Bella to recall the Quileute wolf legend. In the *Twilight* world, Bella makes allies with a powerful pack of Quileute werewolves. She is increasingly accompanied, guided and guarded by these loyal wolves. In Greek myth, the Goddess Artemis was always guided by a pack of hounds during her hunt. This reinforces the symbolic support role of wild dogs and adds extra mythical mystique to Bella's character.

Guardian

One of the most fascinating meanings of wolves is that they protect the spirits of dead people. In point of fact, all dogs guard souls in the spirit world. In ancient Egypt and in Greece, people thought that the wolf escorted the souls of the dead into the afterlife, making sure that people's spirits crossed over safely to the other side. Anubis, the greatest of all the conductors of souls in Egypt, had the head of a wolf, jackal, or other wild dog. It is most noteworthy that of all the characters in the *Twilight Saga*, Jacob is the character asked to accompany Bella's journey to the world of the dead, as she lay dying on a hospital bed in the Cullen house and when she begins to change into a supernatural creature. A true spiritual guardian, Jacob attends Bella's transition to the next world. In particular, Jacob kicks and fights Rosalie out of the way when she is exposed to Bella's blood loss and loses control. Except for Edward, Jacob is the only character in the Cullen house powerful enough to guard Bella and not hurt her because he does not crave her human blood.

See also *Werewolf*.

Archetypes

What is an archetype? Archetypes are a type of feature or a typical feature that is found in an:

- Idea
- Image
- Theme
- Symbol
- Character type
- Plot pattern

A number of archetypes can appear in myths, legends, stories and the human personality (www.scribd.com, 2011). For example, two 'character archetypes' or familiar types of characters in a story are the 'hero' (a good character) and the 'villain' (an evil character). A list of archetypes that indicate a certain type of character is presented below, along with important information from the *Twilight* world to illustrate each one.

Character Archetypes

The Hero – Every story has a central character who struggles against evil. Bella is the good and brave hero in the *Twilight* world. She risks her own life and undergoes significant changes to achieve peace and happiness for her and others.Mentor – Carlisle is an excellent example of a mentor. He guides his own family, heals people as a doctor, and helps to prepare Bella for her transition to vampire life.Mentor-Pupil Relationship – Carlisle-

Bella, Carlisle-Edward, and Billy-Jacob are good examples of characters who have mentor-pupil roles.Hunting Group of Companions – Bella's hunting companions would be the Cullen family as well as the wolf pack.Friendly Beast – Both Edward (vampire) and Jacob (werewolf) are 'beasts' who befriend Bella.The Shadow – Negative (destructive) shadow characters in the *Twilight* books include James, Victoria, and the Volturi. As for Bella's personality, her dark or shadow side might be her depressive tendencies or her lack of self-confidence at times.Damsel in Distress – If Bella is the main hero character in the *Twilight* tale, it would not make sense to classify her as a damsel in distress, although she might seem like that at times. Perhaps Bella's mother fits the distressed damsel archetype – she is described as flighty and anxious. Also, Leah is a lone female werewolf with a broken heart, after her partner Sam fell in love with Emily. Leah may have become the distressed damsel.

It may interest you to know that each character archetypes can be sub-typed further. For example, consider the Heroic Archetype. There are several types of hero that a character can become. These include *Hero as Warrior, Hero as Lover,* and the *Romantic/Gothic Hero*. Using Edward as an example, Edward has qualities that fit with all three hero sub-types. Edward could be a 'Warrior Hero' (because he battles evil forces such as Victoria's newborn army and the Volturi), a 'Lover Hero' (Edward loves Bella and will do anything to be with her), and a 'Gothic Hero' (Edward has a dark side – he lusts Bella's blood).

Literary Archetypes

As for literary archetypes, most stories have several types. Each fictional character has an important role or personality style that helps to drive the story. Consider these archetypes in literature:

Hero – born under unusual circumstances, marked for greatness, exiled, and must prove him/herself through test/trial. *Twilight Saga: Bella was born at a time when her young parents were* *not ready to marry. She is marked for greatness in that she is super-intuitive, pale-skinned, and no one can penetrate her mind. This foreshadows her future as a vampire. Bella chooses to exile herself in Forks in an attempt to make her mother happy. Her social anxiety exiles her from others. Bella proves she is a good and brave person because she stays friends with Edward and Jacob (supernatural creatures) and risks her own life to keep others safe (e.g. Bella meets James alone at the ballet studio).*

Helper – usually has special abilities, but lacks traits of being a hero on his/her own. *Twilight Saga: Jacob is always helping Bella, as well as his disabled father. Jacob has social strengths and practical skills. He comforts Bella when Edward leaves, introduces her to the Quileute community, fixes up old motorbikes, rescues Bella from blood-thirsty vampires, and protects Bella and her unborn child. But for some time Jacob seriously lacks confidence to lead the wolf pack as their true Alpha.*

Mentor – 'Wise old man'. *Twilight Saga: Dr. Carlisle (a physician who is more than 300 years old) and Quileute chief Billy Black are wise male archetypes in the tale.*

Femme Fatale – seeks to destroy the hero. *Twilight Saga: A few evil females seek to fully destroy Bella. The main vampire characters are Victoria, Jane, and Irina.*

Good/Earth Mother – possesses all the positive aspects of life (warm, nurturing, protection). *Twilight Saga: As the vampire mother hen who loves children and cares deeply for others, Esme fits this role well.*

Father Figure – represents all that the hero is trying to attain or find; may have a secret that affects hero's destiny. *Twilight Saga: Bella really likes Carlisle, who reveals Edward's dark secret. The reason why Edward refuses to change Bella into a vampire is because he thinks he has no soul, and so he does not wish to destroy Bella's soul by turning her into a vampire.*

Trickster – causes problems or messes things up, may be accidental or on purpose. *Twilight Saga: Rosalie is a fitting trickster* *because she is hostile towards Bella at first (bitter that her human life was stolen from her, resentful that Edward likes Bella, jealous that Bella is can have children). Rosalie really messes things up when she incorrectly tells Edward that Bella has committed suicide, which launches Edward into suicide mode.*

Nemesis – hero's sworn enemy, usually evenly matched in ability. *Twilight Saga: As a human, Bella's friend Jessica appears to be a schoolyard archenemy. But as a vampire, not even the supernatural gifts of Aro, Jane or other Volturi vampires penetrate Bella's incredibly powerful shield.*Damsel in Distress – needs a hero to save her fragile being in harm's way. *Twilight Saga: If a hero and damsel could appear in one character, then Bella may be a good example. Bella is good and brave but she is also clumsy, a risk-taker and a real 'magnet for trouble'.*

Situational Archetypes

Adding to character and literary archetypes, certain situations, circumstances, events or plans may seem pretty familiar, typical or archetypal in many stories and legends too. Here are the main situational archetypes that appear in a story, illustrated with examples from the *Twilight* books from Bella's point of view:

The Quest – Bella is clearly on a quest to find love, happiness, and her true inner self.

The Task – Bella must use her human skills, strengths and wit to survive her relationship with Edward.

The Journey – Bella is on a journey of self-discovery and personal empowerment.

Death and Rebirth – Bella lives a dead emotional life as a human. When Bella almost dies giving birth to her daughter, she is reborn as a vampire, and finds her new supernatural experience exhilarating.

Battle between Good and Evil – In the *Twilight* world, good vampires and good werewolves continually battle Volturi forces and other evil vampires.

The Unhealable Wound – When Edward breaks up with Bella in *New Moon* and moves away, he creates a painful and permanent emotional scar – a huge hole inside Bella's chest.

Arrowhead

An arrowhead is a type of triangle, often narrow, that does not have sides of equal length. The most prominent arrowhead appears in the *Twilight* world when Bella, Jacob and Renesmee hunt together for the first time. They go hunting in a clearing that looks like the head of an arrow. It is very cold. And snow has just started to fall. Even so, the snowflakes melted before they could "stick to the yellowed grass in the long arrowhead-shaped meadow" (*Breaking Dawn*, p 495). At that moment, a vampire named Irina spots the trio hunting from a distance. After noticing Renesmee (a child vampire), Irina races off to inform the Volturi. Adding to the arrow effect, Irina has just fired a symbolic arrow in that she has set off the *Breaking Dawn* war.

As a symbol, an arrowhead suggests flight, penetration, and direction. As a weapon, the arrow is a symbol of power, along with the bow. As a symbol in myth, the arrow is the sacred attribute of the Goddess of the Hunt, Artemis/Diana, as well as Eros, who uses his arrows to pierce human hearts with love. The decaying meadow in the scene above, with its dead yellowed grass, is shaped like a menacing arrowhead. This symbolically supports the destructive mood and intent of this hunting scene. Irina is angry and bitter because Bella's werewolf friends killed her vampire boyfriend Laurent. At this time, Irina is a dangerous weapon, just like the arrowhead meadow place in which she appears.

Another meaning of the arrow is that it stands for swiftness and sureness. An arrow can only travel in a sure and straight line. As such, the arrow is a symbol of intuition, directedness and quick wit. The astrological sign of Sagittarius shoots an arrow from his bow. The word arrow and this creature's name derive from the Latin verb *sagire*, which means to 'perceive keenly or quickly'. Although Bella does act quickly to alert the Cullens about Irina's visit, it is too late. Irina disappears into the forest in a piercing flash of vengeance; much like a poisoned arrow might fly. As you can see, the *Twilight Saga's* arrow-shaped meadow suggests choice, strong-mindedness, and death.

Ashes

Ashes feature prominently whenever the Volturi vampires are around. This tends to give ashes in the *Twilight* books negative meanings. In *Breaking Dawn*, for example, a ruling vampire burns a vampire named Irina down into a smoldering "pyre". This surely makes an announcement that "death was coming with fierce, unstoppable speed" (p 657).

As a symbol, ashes are a by-product that follows the combustion of inflammable materials. Since ashes are all that remain of fire, they are associated with the idea of death. It is this meaning that the Volturi promote. Volturi vampires kill and burn their own kind.

Another meaning of ashes is a spiritual one. Early cultures used to cremate the dead and the ashes of dead people assumed a magical and sacred quality. They were regarded as the physical remainders of the deceased and their soul. As such, ashes scattered by wind across the lands had the power to haunt the places that they reached. An important symbolic meaning of ashes is that "death is not an end, but a transition, a transformation, and that the soul of the person who was so dearly loved and respected on earth is eternal" (Colin, 2000, p 38). The Volturi vampires, who commit evil acts and behave like the 'soulless monsters' they claim to be, are far removed from this uplifting spiritual meaning of ashes.

In the *Twilight Saga*, Bella dreams about ash piles sometimes.

Scattered mounds of "smoking heaps" and "smoldering pyres" that were the remains of executed vampires (*Breaking Dawn*, p 33). To dream about ash or ashes, as Bella does, may mean that it is time to consider aspects, experiences and events in your life on another higher spiritual level. That is, to detach yourself from certain material concerns to help yourself feel lighter, less burdened, and more free (Colin, 2000).

Axis

All four *Twilight* books mention the four cardinal directions – north, east, west and south. The first letter of each direction spells the word 'news'. Depending on where a *Twilight* adventure takes place, that event may be extra important. The north direction, for example, tends to play a big part in relation to the Cullen family. The location of the Cullen House is "northward" (*Twilight*, p 280) and this direction is repeated. For example, "Edward drove north through Forks" to the Cullen house (*New Moon*, p 23). In another *Twilight* scene, an important decision about the immediate future is about to be made to the north. "Edward will be under the clock tower, to the north of the square" (*New Moon*, p 445). At this point in this scene, Edward's mind is directed to his immediate future, imminent death by suicide, unless something happens to change it.

As a symbol, the north is the gateway to progress, the future, and new possibilities. Facing north is supposed to symbolize adaptation, innovation, and moving forwards in life. The Cullen vampires not only support this meaning, their lifestyle epitomizes evolution. The Cullens are golden-eyed vegetarian vampires who have moved on from primitive food sources. Unlike the ancient and stagnant Volturi vampires, the Cullens have tried to expand their minds and adapt to their world. They strive to form productive bonds with humans, look after the environment, and fulfill a higher moral purpose. The Cullens are future-oriented – they value education, modern ideas (e.g.

clothes, cars) and Alice can foresee the future. As a result, the vegetarian Cullens have become more loving, more empathic, more social, more spiritual, and less driven by physical needs. Vampires who have stuck to a traditional diet of human blood, however, still travel alone, in pairs, or covens no larger than three *(New Moon*, p 429). Their contributions to making the world a better place for vampires and others is zilch.

In contrast to the Cullen vampires who live in the north and look to the future, the Quileutes live in the south, in the opposite direction. The south suggests a commitment to the past and respect for tradition. And the Quileutes are past-oriented and value tradition. Just as the symbolic meanings of a southerly direction suggest, the Quileute value their ancient legends and laws, their folklore and history, their elders, the spirits of their ancestors, and they maintain their original spiritual relationship with the land.

A path that descends south can also symbolize moving backwards, relapse and decline. Certain barriers and weaknesses can hold people back. The Volturi vampires appear to embrace this meaning. They do not use past wisdom to adapt to the present environment. Their laws are archaic, their hunting styles primeval, and their methods of execution hark back to the Dark Ages.

Some aspects of the Cullen family are also south-oriented. For example, Edward's room on the top floor of the Cullen house has a window that faces south. A glass window the size of the wall, provided a view of "the winding Sol Duc River" and "the untouched forest to the Olympic Mountains range" (*Twilight*, p 300). A window facing south could be a symbolic nod to Edward's preference for the past, his preference for Victorian traditions and nineteenth century courtship customs.

A westerly direction is also mentioned in the *Twilight* series. West is the direction of the setting sun, a place of dreams, inner visions and journeys, the gateway to the emotions. The west also alludes to ideas of dying and death because the sun sets or dies in the west every day. The deathly meaning is suggested whenever *Twilight* scenes manifest in the west. For example, Bella's bedroom faces west over the front yard (*Twilight*, p 8). Is this the first secret symbolic clue in the *Twilight* series that Bella is destined to die as a human? Maybe. Also, Bella has dreams and nightmares, embarks on a significant inner journey after she meets Edward, which is also consistent with the meanings of the west..

In another westward scene, Carlisle's office is described as having a "high ceiling", plenty of "towering bookshelves", and a "west-facing window" (*Twilight*, p 292). It may be a meaningless coincidence that Carlisle's view of the world faces west. It may also be a meaningful acknowledgement that Carlisle and his family have risen from the dead and of Carlisle's serious contemplation of the after-life.

Some *Twilight* events out west seem to be more sinister. This certainly seems to be the case in *Twilight* when Bella arranges to meet a murderous vampire named James. At the ballet studio, Bella faces James to die. She observes that "the west dance floor was dark, I could see through the open viewing window. The east dance floor, the bigger room, was lit. But the blinds were closed on the window" (*Twilight*, p 387). The dance floor was dark to the west – which is the direction where suns set, where days die, and the direction of death. This may well be a symbolic clue set up to point to Bella's death.

Other adventures in the *Twilight* books highlight the east. The east is where the sun rises and dawn appears. As such, the east is the gateway to rebirth, new beginnings and where clear thinking takes place. In the *Twilight Saga,* a meaningful reference to east appears during Bella and Edward's honeymoon trip. This involves plane travel to Rio, then a short boat cruise over "the night-blackened water" and heading "due east into the open ocean" (*Breaking Dawn*, p 70). This easterly direction may be foreshadowing the start of Bella's new immortal life with Edward.

Another eastern adventure involves Bella's window. It

actually faces west, so when Edward visits her and greets her outside the window, he must face east. The sun rises in the east so when Edward visits Bella, her appearance at the window alludes to a famous easterly Shakespeare love metaphor: "What light in yonder window breaks? It is the East and Juliet [in this case, Bella] is the sun." To Native American people, the east represents Gathering, Preparation, Resolving Issues, and Accepting Unresolvable Issues (Eason, 2002).

B

Bathe

Bathing symbolizes life and rebirth. The *Twilight Saga* has two significant bathing adventures that embrace these meanings:

1 Rebirth adventure – Bella dives off a cliff, and almost dies under the water. But Jacob jumps in and saves her (*New Moon*).
2 Birth/Life adventure – Bella and Edward make love in the water during their honeymoon. This is their first sexual experience together and results in the birth of their daughter Renesmee (*Breaking Dawn*).

Both these adventures involve bathing or immersing oneself in water. And both these adventures fit with the powerful symbolic meanings of bathing.

According to symbol experts, "bathing is a symbol of purification and regression, since it is often symbolically associated with life in the womb" (Colin, 200, pp 52–53). So, both literally and figuratively, taking a bath means to cleanse and purify yourself, to gather your strength, and revive and renew your vitality and energy. Bathing also symbolizes a return to one's source, to the waters of the womb or the primordial waters from which all life emerged, especially since water is the original source of all plant and animal life on earth.

When Bella dives off the cliff in *New Moon*, this is not necessarily stupid teenage behavior. Symbolically, Bella is reborn as a more confident young person. It was in the water that she got in touch with her unconscious mind, her deep desires, and the truth that Edward really does love her. After Bella gets in touch with her true inner self, she makes some clear and powerful decisions. For example, she chooses to save Edward in Italy in *New Moon*, despite all the danger and Jacob's pleas not to go.

In *Breaking Dawn*, Bella bathes in the warm tropical waters of Isle Esme. By bathing in these waters, Bella returns to the source of life (water). Bella also becomes a mother because she gives birth to a baby daughter. This happens after Bella baths in the waters of an island named after the most prominent mother figure in the *Twilight Saga* – Esme Cullen. As you can see, that midnight skinny dip is linked to a number of symbolic birth meanings.

Birds

Birds are a very special group of animals, symbolically and spiritually. The *Twilight Saga* alludes to a number of birds in the most enchanting and intriguing ways. As you will see, Bella is linked to *eleven* bird species. Her friend Jacob is linked to three. Edward has no links with birds. As a symbol, birds are linked to the heavens, the soul, and spiritual power. As winged creatures of the sky, birds are close to heaven. Wings symbolize flying and freedom, an ability to rise above gravity and the material world. Wings express the sublime, and a desire to transcend everyday reality. The bird, which symbolizes the soul flying across the sky towards heaven, is often thought to be a spiritual messenger or guide. In particular, the bird has a "privileged position that gives it a superior and panoramic view of reality, an overview" (Colin, 2000, p 446). This is why feathers are linked with clairvoyance or divinity and why shamans and healers wore feathers. A bird's-eye view sees all. For these reasons, the bird has a strong bond with the spirit world as a deity or messenger between earth and heaven.

To alchemists, the most important thing about birds is that almost all of them fly. As such, their element is air. Birds mediate and communicate between the earth and the heavens. "The alchemist in observing the flight of birds recognized in them a picture of the human soul undergoing spiritual development" and the soul "aspiring upwards, flying free of the restraints of the earthbound body seeking the heavenly light" (*Birds in Alchemy*, 2008). So, in alchemy, birds symbolize the soul's experience. Indeed, alchemists used certain birds to describe certain stages of inner alchemy or spiritual development. Some important birds used in alchemy include: "The Black Crow – White Swan – Peacock – Pelican – Phoenix". This alchemy sequence (bird chain) is supposed to symbolize a person's spiritual journey. The White Swan stage, for example, describes an early bright white light-filled stage (true illumination) when a person first encounters the spiritual realm. Just as a swan swims gracefully on the surface of water, the White Swan stage signifies the soul's contact with the upper reaches of the sky – the soul's interface with the physical surface of the heavens.

All *Twilight Saga* bird references hint at spiritual experiences. Some bird references are quite cryptic or hard to spot. For example:

- The first creature to appear in the *Twilight Saga* is a bird. At La Push Beach Bella sees "pelicans", "seagulls" and an "eagle" (*Twilight*, p 99). At the end of this scene, Bella leaves La Push with a newfound knowledge about supernatural activity and the cold ones.
- Bella calls herself a "bird" (*Twilight*, p 232). This supports Bella's connection to bird symbolism and her supernatural experience to come.
- Just before Bella finds her special meadow, she notices that the forest was "full of life" and she heard "birds chirping" (*New Moon*, p 233).
- After a snowstorm ends, Bella wakes up to a sunny dawn after spending the night with Jacob in a sleeping bag. She

hears "morning birdsong" and "nothing else" far away (*Eclipse*, p 453).

- Covert references to birds: Bella thinks that "flying doesn't bother me" (*Twilight*, p 10). To Bella, the cloudy Forks sky looked like "a cage" (*Twilight*, p 11). During Bella's 'flight' from Volterra, a "huge, ancient portcullis above was like a cage door" threatening to "lock us in" like birds in a cage (*New Moon*, p 492).
- At end of *Breaking Dawn*, symbolically speaking, Bella is as happy and free as a bird.

What's more, Bella's symbolic links with eleven specific bird species is especially fascinating and inspiring.

Eagle

The first creatures Bella notices in the *Twilight Saga* at La Push Beach are three birds. One of these is an "eagle" (*Twilight*, p 99), an important symbol worldwide. As the 'King of the Birds', 'Lion of the Skies', and a strong solar symbol, eagles surely suggest power, authority, majesty, and truth. In Greek, the word *aigle* (eagle) means 'ray of light'. Due to their sharp eyesight, which surpasses that of humans, eagles symbolize truth. The high-flying ability of eagles strongly suggests that they can see the 'big picture' from above. Because eagles fly so high, many people thought that eagles were the only creatures on earth that could look directly into the sun. As such, eagles suggest clairvoyance, and mental and spiritual enlightenment. Only those of pure heart can face the bright light of the gods without fear.

In the *Twilight* world, the eagle's symbolic meanings link in with the Bella-Edward-Jacob love triangle. Edward has lion-like features (he hunts lions and moves like a lion) and so does Jacob (*Twilight's* sun – this links him to eagles and makes him the lion of the sky). Symbolically speaking, it's an even match between Edward and Jacob – 'lion versus lion' fighting it out for Bella's love. Eagles also hunt and kill snakes. In the *Twilight* series, Bella befriends Jacob (her sun/eagle) and she also falls in love with Edward (a snake-like vampire – cold-blooded, venomous, deadly). This eagle and snake symbolism highlights the rivalry between Jacob and Edward, two powerful characters in the *Twilight* world.

Hummingbird

The tiny hummingbird is another bird with which Bella has bonds. Sitting with Edward in the Cullen house, alone, she gets anxious and blushes when she plans to ask him to have sex with her: "Listen to your heart fly," he murmured. "It's fluttering like a hummingbird's wings" (*Eclipse*, p 390). Later in this scene, Edward gives Bella an engagement ring. She "flutters her fingers" in a bird-like gesture, which pleases Edward incredibly (*Eclipse*, p 407). Bella then agrees to marry Edward.

When you explore the significance of hummingbirds, an even stronger link emerges between Bella and these little birds. You see, hummingbirds come from South America and their main meanings come from there. In the Andes, this bird is a symbol of death and resurrection. It loses much heat at night (in order to conserve energy) and may look dead if it is found at night. In the morning, the heat of the sun revives it. Hummingbirds are so "skilled in hovering and flying backwards" that Native American Indians regarded this bird as belonging to the gods and used hummingbird feathers in magic (Eason, 2002). Since hummingbird wings beat super-fast (300 times per second), this flying feathered jewel must consume loads of nectar to stay alive. This makes hummingbirds fierce and competitive feeders in nature. They are teensy and aggressive nectar-sucking vampires, and a vampire is what Bella becomes.

In ancient South America, Aztec awe for the hummingbird was profound. The cloaks and wands of great shamans were decorated with hummingbird feathers. In Cherokee myth, a shaman once shape-shifted into a hummingbird to find lost tobacco, which when burnt created a smoky pillar to the heavens. It is also noteworthy that hummingbirds originate from South America and Edward travelled alone to South America to contemplate life without Bella (*New Moon*, p 399). Why would a vampire who sparkles in the sun risk visiting such a sunny place? Bella's link with hummingbirds, perhaps. As for Bella and Edward's honeymoon destination, this also happens to be near 'Rio de Janeiro' in South America, the hummingbird's native country (*Breaking Dawn*, p 69). Rio is where Bella makes plans for Jacob and Renesmee to escape to also. The hummingbird's native home is a place of safety and survival (*Breaking Dawn*, p 625). Is Bella's bond with the hummingbird a clever choice or just crazy coincidence? It may prove wise not to dismiss Bella's symbolic link with hummingbirds too quickly. At the very least, there are enough symbolic clues in the *Twilight* books to make your heart flutter.

Jaybird

The jay appears twice in the *Twilight* books. After researching vampires, Bella walks through the damp and green forest alone and hears "the sudden cries of jays" (*Twilight*, p 118). This is the moment Bella decides that she really "wants" Edward (*Twilight*, p 121). In *New Moon*, a pack of werewolves chase Laurent away from Edward's meadow. Suddenly Bella hears "the quiet whisper of unseen things moving in the leaves" and the "call of a jaybird" (*New Moon*, p 246). It is as if Bella can sense the unseen magic of the forest – Edward's forest. In this sense, the jay heralds Edward's lingering spiritual or supernatural presence. This establishes a symbolic bond between Bella and the jay.

Lark

This small brown bird likes to nest in meadows where it feeds on insects. Larks are best known for their melodious singing, which greatly moves those who hear it. A lark can sing while flying as high as 400 m in the sky (that's 1,300 feet)! Lark-song epitomizes a joyous and happy life, which makes the lark a very positive and sacred symbol. At the end of their first night at the cottage, after Bella and Edward make love for the first time as vampires, Bella hears a lark singing at dawn. "The sky began to lighten. The tiny ocean outside turned from black to gray, and a lark started to sing somewhere very close by" (*Breaking Dawn*, p 447). A bird that evokes emotions singing right after a romantic night is surely significant. A symbolic bird voice or just a random bird-choice? Given that these small birds arouse big feelings and that writers have revered this little songbird for centuries, I suspect that the *Twilight* lark is meaningfully linked with Bella.

A few lines from a verse by the great English novelist George Meredith capture the shimmering magic of lark-song:

He rises and begins to round,
He drops the silver chain of sound
Of many links without a break,
In chirrup, whistle, slur and shake.
Without a break, without a fall,
Sweet-silvery, sheer lyrical,
Perennial, quavering up the chord
Like myriad dews of sunny sward.

With its happy news and sweet, sunny, and sparkling song, it is no wonder Bella noticed a lark during one her most joyful *Twilight* moments.

Parrot

In the *Twilight* series, parrots are mentioned when Bella and Edward travel to Isle Esme. They "visited the parrots that lived in the canopy on the south end of the island (*Breaking Dawn*, p 90). While this reference is brief, it is nevertheless apt. The parrot, an exotic island bird, probably derives its name from the French *Perrot*, from the old French word *perorele*, which means a 'frivolous conversation'. Bella and Edward really enjoy their island visit at first and their constant and casual dialogue definitely resembles cheerful parrot-like chatter.

Parrots are appealing, affectionate, colorful and expressive birds. There are more than 300 species of parrot in the world, mainly in Africa, China, India, the Middle East, South America and Australia. The ancient Greeks, Romans and pirates really liked these birds. To Native American people, colorful parrot feathers depicted the brightness of the sun. For Brahmins, the parrot is a sacred bird that must never be harmed. This because the parrot is bestowed to Kama, the Indian God of Love. Just like parrots, people in love often imitate one another's body language and speech patterns. Images of parrots are hung in temples where weddings take place. Symbolically speaking, don't Bella and Edward look like a striking pair of parrots in love?

Pelican

The pelican is the first creature mentioned in the *Twilight Saga* at La Push Beach (*Twilight*, p 99). The white pelican is a nomadic, migratory bird. It tends to live near large lakes, lagoons, rivers and the seashores because it likes to eat fish. What's more, the pelican is reputed to sacrifice itself in order to save its young. This links the pelican to ideas like charity and resurrection. Well then, it is rather interesting that Bella sacrifices herself to save others in a pelican-like way. In the *Twilight* world, a moving moment of sacrifice is when Bella prepares to save Renesmee. She gives her daughter a small golden locket with the words "*more than my own life*" inscribed in French on the back (*Breaking Dawn*, p 605) along with a new passport and tickets to flee the murderous Volturi. In accordance with pelican legend, Bella sacrifices herself to save her own young.

Phoenix

The phoenix is one of two mythical birds that have links with Bella. To start with, Bella comes from Phoenix, a place that has the same name as the mythical phoenix. According to legend, the phoenix is a fabulous creature, most famous for its immortality. Every 500 years, this bird is reborn from a nest of fire. Besides eternal life, however, the phoenix also symbolizes goodness. Blessed with positive powers, the phoenix only carries out good actions in the world and does not harbor evil intentions. A good heart and a transition to immortality are clearly Bella qualities. It is also worth noting that when Bella dies as a mortal, she "burns" from vampire venom to arise as a newborn vampire. So, not only does Bella come from Phoenix, her rebirth in the *Twilight* world resembles the fiery rebirth process of a magical phoenix.

Seagull

Along with pelicans and eagles, Bella notices "seagulls" at La Push Beach (*Twilight*, p 99). Bella also notices seagulls in a much later scene. Sitting at the beach with Jacob, listening to the waves, Bella hears "the cry of gulls high overhead. It was very peaceful" (*Eclipse*, p 113).

Of course, the seagull is the best known of all coastal birds. It is found mainly in North America and along Atlantic coasts. In 1923, Ernest Ingersoll, wrote that gulls are "foolish". This may have led to the word "gullible" although other sources say that the similarity of these two words is just a coincidence. Although seagulls eat fish, they also eat eggs, hunt other young birds, eat carrion and food scraps on the beach, screech loudly, and compete aggressively with each other for food. This gives them a sinister side.

Seagulls are most famous for their wheeling, whirling flight as they weave through the air currents above the sea. The gull's knack of mingling with turbulent air currents, flying through stormy seas, and reaching the open sea led sailors to believe that seagulls symbolized the spirits of dead mariners. "According to ancient legend, the seagull represents the soul of a mariner who died or was lost at sea" (Colin, 2000, p 212). To this day, it is considered taboo to kill a gull.

Seagulls appear in many legends and lore around the world. Old stories of seagulls are found in British folklore, Native American myth, and the northern hemisphere where seagulls are common. Native North American people view the gull as a 'trickster' who can outsmart other creatures. Many people still watch gulls along coastlines to predict the weather. Gulls wheeling high in the sky, for example, forecast a looming storm. Bella, who is highly intuitive, has an innate knack for picking up emotional storms ahead, just as a seagull is in tune with the weather.

Siren

Another magical bird mentioned in the *Twilight Saga* that is linked to Bella is the beautiful and lyrical siren. It is Aro who refers to Bella as a bird-woman creature from Greek myth. He is surprised to learn that Edward can restrain himself from drinking Bella's blood, especially when it "calls" and "sings" to him so strongly. Aro did not know that "such strength was possible. To inure yourself against such a siren call, not just once but again and again" (*New Moon*, p 472). Clearly, Bella is Edward's songbird.

In myth, the beautiful and seductive qualities of sirens disguise their monstrous intent. Sirens are supposed to have the heads and breasts of lovely women and the bodies and wings of birds. Perched upon rocky shores and cliffs, sirens use their pretty faces and sweet voices to lure sailors toward them, whom they later kill and eat. As such, sirens symbolize danger and death itself. A siren is a warning of what can happen when one gives in to lust and desire. That is why Edward must always remain vigilant around his siren to maintain safe self-control of his urges.

Sparrow

Bella has a cute little link with sparrows. Bella becomes sparrow-aware after her daughter tells her about "the sparrows that had hopped closer and closer when Jacob had held her". However, "the birds wouldn't come close to Rosalie" (*Breaking Dawn*, p 433).

As birds, all sparrows are valuable because they eat insects. In fact, this small brown bird was a household spirit and a widespread symbol of protection in Roman times. The most common sparrow species are the tree sparrow (which prefers the green countryside) and the house sparrow (which thrives in cities).

Since the sparrow is a prolific breeder, this bird became an important fertility symbol. Maybe this is why Bella has a positive link with sparrows (she is a mother) and why Rosalie does not have a strong bond with sparrows (she has been jealous and bitter about being infertile). For thousands of years the sparrow symbolized domestic bliss. It is a bird able to live with lots of people that is happy to share the surrounding landscape. Getting on well with everyone is something Bella always strives to do, even after she becomes a vampire. Rosalie, however, does not trust humans well and was very wary of Bella at first. Maybe that is why the homely little sparrows like Renesmee but fear Rosalie.

Swan

The swan is a powerful symbol. Symbol experts say that a swan's "pure white color, its strength, and its beauty make it a symbol of light, both of the direct light of the Sun and the reflected light of the Moon" (Nozedar, 2008, p 338). Thus, Bella "Swan" is aptly named, for the *Twilight Saga* plot places her at the center of a love triangle between Edward (whose silver colors link him to the moon) and Jacob (a sun symbol). An otherworldly creature, the swan is said to float gracefully upon the calm waters that resemble the spirit world.

In ancient Greece, the swan was an attribute of the Muses and symbolized Apollo, a god of poetry and song. Apollo could shape-shift into the form of a swan, and when he was born, it is said that seven swans flew around the island of his birth, seven times. The "immaculate whiteness of its plumage" makes the swan a key "symbol of purity and perfection" (Colin, 2000, p 482).

Of all birds mentioned in the *Twilight Saga,* Bella "Swan" is most closely linked to the swan:

Swans symbolize purity and power – Bella's personality is also pure (she accepts vampires, believes Edward is good and says he has a soul) and powerful (Bella has the strength to save others and is determined to follow her heart).

Swans have attractive S-shaped necks – Bella Swan's neck is attractive to thirsty vampires.

Swans are symbols of love – the name "Swan" may be a tip to Bella and Edward's love for each other. Swans are also believed to mate for life, which resembles Bella's loyal and eternal commitment to Edward.

Swans suggest William Shakespeare – and the *Twilight* books reflect and mentioned the medieval works of Shakespeare. For example, Edward and Bella's love story echoes the play *Romeo and Juliet*. And just as Bella is a 'Swan', Shakespeare is the 'Swan of Avon', named after the river that runs through his birth-place.

***Swan Lake* is a Russian ballet** – Bella used to do ballet as a young girl and the climax of the *Twilight* novel occurs in a ballet studio.

Swans are gentle creatures – swans are sweet peace-loving birds. This accurately reflects Bella's personality – she often tries to please or protect others, and harms no humans when she becomes a vampire.

The swan's death-song – the swan is believed to be silent until the moment of death. In folklore, the phrase 'swan song' is the song that a dying swan sings. Since Bella wants to die so she can be with Edward forever, her deadly plan is much like a dying swan song.

Swans are beautiful – in the fairy tale of the *Ugly Duckling*, a plain baby duckling grows into a beautiful swan, a symbol of the swan's transformative powers. In Italian, *bella* means 'beautiful' and in the *Twilight* series it is "Bella" who eventually becomes a '*beautiful* Swan'.

Feathers?

The *Breaking Dawn* honeymoon scene is a famous and funny scene among *Twilight* fans. Bella is immersed in "fluffy white snow" and "a cascade of white" drifting in her hair – she is completely "covered in feathers" (*Breaking Dawn*, p 81). During an intimate honeymoon encounter between Bella and Edward on Isle Esme, Edward accidentally chews the pillows, causing feathers to go everywhere. Whether the feathers are a firm reference to the Bella-bird bond or just a symbolic slip of an author's mind, this scene is definitely a feathery favorite.

From being initially trapped in a "cage" (*Twilight*, p 10), that is surely her lonely human existence, to finding a place so true and meaningful in her world (her loving relationship with Edward) that it makes her "laugh" and "sing" (*Breaking Dawn*, p 485), there is no symbolic doubt that Bella is the *Twilight Saga* bird who finally escapes misery and flies free. Whether you think the symbolic link between Bella and birds is strong or weak, there is definitely a Bella-bird bond. After all, Bella is a dreamer and so is author Stephenie Meyers. According to legend, it is said that dreams are carried on the wings of birds.

Bird Power

So now you know *where* bird references have been made in the *Twilight* books. You also know *which* birds are linked with Bella. But *why* might this be important? How could Bella's bird meanings help her to survive and thrive in a supernatural world? According to the symbolic role of birds, these feathery creatures are believed to have power in supernatural underground worlds. In the *Twilight* world, this would be the Volturi's lair in Volterra, Italy. A gloomy and deadly place, this subterranean vampire chamber is frightfully similar to a Greek underworld of the dead known as Hades. A main reason why Bella survives her journey to an underground vampire world and back may well be her symbolic bond with birds. For more information on Bella's bonds with birds, see *Volturi*, where all will be revealed.

Jacob's Birds

In the *Twilight* world, Jacob has important links with three birds. It is interesting to note that these three birds (eagle, owl, goose) also appear on the Native American Medicine Wheel, which strengthens Jacob's symbolic bond with these birds even more. This circle of power features certain animals, describes natural seasons and cosmic cycles together, and is central to Native American magic (Eason, 2002).

Eagle

In the *Twilight Saga*, Jacob is linked to the eagle because he is Bella's "sun" (*New Moon*, p 145) and the eagle is a mighty sunbird. In an important beach scene, it is Jacob who points out a sea eagle to Bella in *Eclipse* (p 97). Jacob is also eagle-eyed. He reveals his sharp vision when he is able to see which members of Sam's gang are jumping from the cliffs at a distance. In *New Moon*, Bella notices that Jacob has excellent eyesight because he can make out who is cliff-diving from a great distance. Bella was "surprised that he could tell who it was from this distance" (p 172).

According to Native American folklore, the eagle suggests a need to stick to principles and have a clear vision of the future. The eagle encourages people to focus their energy, take action, and draw on inner strength to reach important goals. The eagle's message is positive and inspiring: "If we heal our fear of standing alone and can outface the disapproval of others, then we can soar like the Eagle" (Eason, 2002, p 352). Jacob's choice to leave the wolf pack in *Breaking Dawn* stands by these eagle meanings. Jacob stood up for important principles (not to kill innocent people), was prepared to take action alone (he left the wolf pack), and he overcame the disapproval of others (disobeyed Sam's order to kill Bella and her child). Jacob aimed high and true and achieved results that exceeded his expectations, soaring like an eagle on the wind.

Owl

The owl is mentioned just once in the *Twilight* series, when Jacob runs through the forest as a wolf. At the *Eclipse* epilogue, Jacob's wolvish hearing is so acute that he hears "the matted leaves beneath my toenails, the whisper of an owl's wings above me, the ocean – far, far in the west" (*Eclipse,* p 558). Since Jacob is travelling at night and his attention is drawn to the west (where the sun 'dies' every evening), it is fitting for an owl to appear. Owls are creatures that hunt at night and hide by day, which links them to darkness, sadness, solitude, and death. In ancient times, this nocturnal bird was associated with the moon. The owl is an important symbol of clairvoyance and divination due to its supposed ability to see through darkness and deception. With its wise and protective role, the owl can guard mortals from demons or warn people of evil threats.

According to Native American folklore the owl is "Chief of the Night and a sacred protector of all who must travel or work in darkness" (Eason, 2002, p 357). This makes the *Twilight* owl an apt symbol to accompany Jacob, whose supernatural role is to protect people from demonic vampires. Jacob's owl flying overhead may well symbolize auxiliary protection to help him defend others.

Goose

A grand goose scene in the *Twilight* world is when several wolves form a V-pattern in *New Moon* to protect Bella. In exactly the same way, geese form this shape whenever they are flying together. They do this to support, direct and protect each other. The protective role of Jacob and the werewolves corresponds with these goose ideas. In nature, there are many varieties of goose such as the snow goose in North America and Greenland, the multi-colored Egyptian goose, and the loyal graylag goose that mates for life (Colin, 2000). Geese like to nest and live close to ponds, lakes, and rivers where they can feed on grass and seeds. In ancient Egypt, a goose symbolizes the soul of a god who once ruled Thebes. This enhances the image of the goose as "a type of angel, a messenger between heaven and earth, gods and mortals" (Colin, 2000, p 211). The Roman Goddess Juno Moneta (also known as 'she who warns') was an oracular goddess, a prophetess who was often consulted and gave advice and warnings. Juno had sacred geese whose cackling warned the Roman soldiers of an invasion in 390 BC, known as the Legend of the Capitoline Geese. Just like a flock of protective geese, Jacob and other wolves team up to protect their territory in battles.

According to Native American folklore, the Snow Goose appears on the Medicine Wheel. This ties the significance of geese even more closely to Jacob, a Quileute Indian. To Native American people, the arrival and departure of snow geese during migration is "a reminder that all things have a time and season and that winter, whether the season or a frozen period in your life, will pass. When the time is right, the ice will melt and you can move forward" (Eason, 2002, p 357). The Snow Goose message is: "Wait and withdraw from reality if you need to, but only for a while." This is exactly how Jacob coped when he found out Bella planned to become a vampire. He shape-shifted into a wolf but did not remain in that form for too long. As soon as Jacob saw Bella's daughter, his loving feelings, his warm loyalty, and his sunny personality strengths melted away the ice-cold feelings of bitterness and loneliness in his heart.

Black

In the *Twilight Saga,* the color black appears in positive, neutral and negative ways. For example, at the end of Bella's wedding day on the way to their honeymoon destination Bella and Edward "turned onto the black highway and Edward hit the accelerator" (*Breaking Dawn,* p 68). This "black" path seems neither positive nor negative. It suggests that Bella and Edward are heading towards a new unknown future together. Nothing sinister about that, just a touch of mystery.

As a symbol, black has attracted more negative meanings such as evil and death because it is the color of night and the absence of light. That is why many black animals are viewed badly. For example, a black cat is unlucky, a black raven is evil, and a black dog is an omen of death. In the West, black is the color of death, funerals, and mourning – the denial of life. Black tends to evoke sad, gloomy, wicked and disturbing thoughts and ideas (but not always). Black is also seen to be an empty space – primeval chaos, a deep abyss, the black void. Technically, black is not a color but the actual absence of any color. When Bella described her experience of dying, death was like a dark abyss. "I held the blackness of nonexistence at bay by inches" (*Breaking Dawn,* p 346). In the *Twilight Saga,* black acquires evil meanings whenever it is linked to the Volturi vampires. For example, when the Volturi army appeared, Bella noticed that "The outer perimeter was gray; the color darkened with each line of bodies until the heart of the formation was deepened black. Every face was cowled, shadowed" (*Breaking Dawn,* p 631). In this scene, the meaning and mood of black is very negative.

Black also has some positive meanings. Black suggests maturity, wisdom, authority, perfection and purity, especially in

Eastern cultures. In Japan, black is the color of wisdom and experience. A person who holds a black belt in martial arts, for example, is considered to be at the pinnacle of his/her abilities. It is therefore quite interesting when Edward tells Bella that with time, her eyes will "darken up in a few months" (*Breaking Dawn*, p 372). Darker eyes points to maturity and experience as a vampire. Another reason why black can be positive is because you can only see light in profound darkness. When Bella was alone in the "dim" and "darkening forest" forest in the middle of the day, she reached mental enlightenment about Edward (*Twilight*, p 121).

In the *Twilight* series, Bella's psychological journey is dark and difficult – black. When people are overwhelmed by problems in life, the path ahead can look like a 'black tunnel' with 'no light' at the end. The only way to dispel the darkness is to look within for bright ideas and solutions. Bella must look deep inside her mind and heart – the darkness within the darkness – to resolve her personal doubts and despair. Then Bella can dissolve her black uncertainty with the white light of hope and clarity. In the *nigredo* or black phase of alchemy, the alchemist must sacrifice everything and give up all worldly attachments in order to be reborn as a more powerful being. Bella does exactly this, it seems.

Blood

Life Force

Just as blood means life or death in the *Twilight Saga*, these are the two main symbolic meanings of blood. In the *Twilight* books, Bella offers her blood and sacrifices herself to save the lives of others. The vampires who drink human blood, however, take life away from their victims. Others must die, so that they may live. Sometimes bad vampires kill others simply for power or greed.

As a symbol, blood is life, a flowing medium for the soul.

Blood flowing in our veins is the life force in motion. As such, blood stands for life, energy, vitality and passion. In ancient times, blood was credited with regenerative and purifying properties. The *Twilight* books provide plenty of evidence to suggest the idea that blood is life:

- Bella can detect the smell of "rust" and "salt" in human blood (*Twilight*, 86).
- Bella faints at the sight of blood (*Twilight*, 84), hates needles (*Twilight*, 402) and worries about becoming a blood-sucking monster once she changes into a vampire (*Eclipse*, p 396). If loss of blood means loss of life, then Bella's disdain for blood loss suggests she values life.
- Since blood is said to carry the soul, blood suggests the flow of life to Bella who says that "time passes… like the pulse of blood behind a bruise" (*New Moon*, p 93).
- The sweet scent of Bella's blood brings Edward's feelings to life, which have been dormant for more than a century.
- The vampire Marcus notes that Bella and Edward feel surprisingly "intense" about each other and then Aro suggests that Bella's blood "sings" to Edward (*New Moon*, p 471).
- On her wedding day, Bella was so anxious that "blood flooded [her] cheeks", clearly making her a "blushing bride" (*Breaking Dawn*, p 44). Being flushed with blood suggests the flow of life. To be hot blooded suggests a fiery and passionate person, whereas a cold-blooded person is evil, lifeless, a killer.

Magic Power

As well as being a symbol for life, blood is said to have magical power. This is why people spill blood at rituals or use blood as ink in magical rites, to charge certain words or messages with power and energy. The clearest example of this in the *Twilight* series is the Quileute people who view themselves as possessing "magic in their blood" (*Eclipse,* p 217). This magic enables individuals to pass on their shape-shifting powers from generation to generation. Blood transmits substances and contains unique genetic material that children inherit from their parents. Blood symbolizes magical transference, kinship or the 'blood line'.

The Quileute people in the *Twilight* world acknowledge blood magic through blood sacrifices. According to an important Quileute legend, a chief's "third wife" and soul mate distracted a "cold woman" (vampire) by stabbing herself with a knife. "Blood spurted through the third wife's fingers and splashed against the Cold Woman" (*Eclipse,* p 229). Since the vampire-woman was distracted by the scent of fresh blood, the chief was able to kill her. This human woman saved a whole tribe. Bella sacrifices her blood in a similar way in the *Twilight* books. She leaves traces of her blood on rocks and trees to prepare for an oncoming vampire attack. The scent of her blood will make the newborn vampires crazy with thirst (*Eclipse,* pp 417–418). At the height of the vampire battle, Bella thinks: "If I had to bleed to save them, I would do it. I would die" (*Eclipse,* p 478). So she grabs a sharp rock to stab herself with so as to distract the evil vampires (*Eclipse,* p 487).

Blood Loss

As a symbol, blood can have negative meanings. An excessive blood loss can lead to death, which links blood with death and danger. Cutting yourself with a piece of paper and broken glass at the Cullen house is not a good idea unless you want to look into the "fevered eyes" of several extremely "ravenous vampires" (*New Moon,* p 29). Another example that supports the idea that blood means danger involves Edward. At first, Edward finds it really difficult to control his need to drink Bella's blood: "I knew that the scent of my blood – so much sweeter to him than any other person's blood... caused him actual pain from the burning thirst" (*Eclipse*, p 15). Should Edward lose control, even for a moment, the consequences for Bella would prove fatal.

As you can see, life, death, and magic are important symbolic aspects of blood, all of which appear in the *Twilight* books.

Blue

The *Twilight Saga* has a bit of a 'blue theme' that begins in Port Angeles. Sitting in a local restaurant, Edward tells Bella: "That color blue looks lovely with your skin" (*Twilight*, p 148). Alice picks up on this and the blue theme evolves from there. Is blue simply Edward's favorite color? Or could blue mean other things in the *Twilight Saga*? A close study of the text reveals that blue appears in a number of interesting ways. Some of the most important references to blue are these:

- The very first color mentioned in the *Twilight Saga* is blue. The sky in Phoenix was a "perfect, cloudless blue" (*Twilight*, p 3).
- Bella's bedroom walls in Forks are "light blue" (*Twilight*, p 9).
- The first fire Bella ever sees is "blue" (*Twilight*, p 100), caused by sea salt absorbed by washed up driftwood.
- The first time Bella visits Port Angeles, she wears a "deep blue V-neck blouse" (*Twilight*, p 130). Is that blue for honesty and "V" for vampire?
- Edward tells Bella that "blue looks lovely with your skin" (*Twilight*, p 148). This is the trigger that makes blue a hit color.
- Alice dressed Bella in a "deep blue, frilly" dress for a school dance (*Twilight*, p 420).
- Alice picks a "blue" sweater and skirt outfit for Bella to wear at her graduation party (*Eclipse*, p 309).

- Bella's honeymoon outfit was a "deep blue" top and skirt ensemble (*Breaking Dawn*, p 66).
- The first item of clothing Bella wears as a vampire is an "ice-blue silk" dress (*Breaking Dawn*, p 377).
- The house on Isle Esme has a "blue room" with dark walls and "blue silk" fittings (*Breaking Dawn*, p 91).

In fact, Bella seems to wear blue whenever a significant change occurs in her life, e.g. first visit to Cullen house, first trip to Port Angeles, graduation party.As the color of the sky and sea, blue suggests peace, purity, truth, heaven, the soul, calm contemplation, and the eternal and infinite (Colin, 2000; Nozedar, 2008). This makes blue a calming color of relaxation, harmony, and sentiment. A cool and detached color, blue is said to calm fever, passions and tensions, ward off fate, and absorb evil. Blue is therefore a highly beneficial color. As the coolest color, blue's cool vibration encourages easy and peaceful communication.A pure blue is the color of inspiration, sincerity and spirituality. Dark blue is the color of truth. Blue is linked to consciousness and intellect. People who wear light blue are said to be analytical and have a practical approach to life. People who wear dark blue are intelligent and self-reliant and take on a great deal of responsibility. Bella wears various shades of blue, which suggests an open-minded and versatile approach to life.

Blue is also seen to be a cool or cold color and it may therefore be a hint that Bella will herself become a 'cold one'. Since blue has a calming effect, it is a relaxing color to wear on a first date with Edward or first visit to the Cullen house. Blue is also associated with winning a prize, coming in first place – the blue ribbon. We know that Edward views Bella's love as the ultimate prize. In personality tests, blue signifies a person who likes to make others happy and this definitely applies to Bella.

A few more musings on blue:

- Edward is out-of-this-world and comes out-of-the-blue. Who would have suspected Bella to find a vampire boyfriend?
- Bella's love for Edward is sincere or true-blue.
- Bella becomes very depressed or 'blue' after Edward leaves her
- Once she becomes immortal, Bella sets off into the blue, her Fairy Tale world and the unknowable future.

(Source: TwilightMOMS Post by LynnL, February 3, 2009)

Boat

A brief boat scene is described in the *Twilight Saga* when Edward takes Bella to Isle Esme by boat. "Edward sped forward while the lights of Rio faded… the boat plunged through the waves and I was showered with sea spray" (*Breaking Dawn*, p 70). The meaning of boats makes the boat appropriate in this adventure. The boat symbolizes destiny and the path of life, while the oars signify free will. In a way, when Edward takes Bella to that island, Bella sails off into a life of marriage and is on the last (sea) leg of her journey to becoming a vampire. What's more, Bella has made a conscious choice to be with Edward and go down this path (oars, wheel). In ancient times, the boat symbolized a vessel that transported dead people to the afterlife. A boat therefore corresponds to both birth and death especially as it resembles a cradle or coffin. In line with spiritual boat meanings, Bella is on the brink of death and she has almost reached her afterlife as a supernatural creature.

Book

Since books symbolize knowledge, wisdom and freedom, it is most intriguing that two of the wisest leaders in the *Twilight Saga* make their first appearance alongside books. The French word *liber* (as in the word *library*) means 'to free or liberate'. As such, information and knowledge from books can liberate people from poverty or ignorance. A book also exposes ideas that can set you free yourself from some kind of invisible or self-inflicted chains that hold you captive. In tarot cards, the High Priestess holds a book or scroll. "The book symbolizes knowledge and hidden secrets… and the very Universe itself" (Nozedar, 2008, p 28). The book also relates the Tree of Life. Just as a tree has leaves, so does a book. Each individual leaf contains ideas, information, and inspiration. A closed book conceals secrets, which is why people who are guarded or 'hard to read' are called 'closed books'. A person who is prepared to share information is an 'open book'.

What makes books meaningful symbols in the *Twilight Saga* is that they appear when readers first meet Carlisle Cullen and Billy Black, two of the oldest and wisest characters in Forks.

Dr. Carlisle Cullen – his office had "towering bookshelves" filled with more books than a library. When Bella first meets Carlisle, he was sitting in a leather chair behind a big wooden desk "placing a bookmark in the pages of the thick volume he held" (*Twilight*, p 292).

Chief Billy Black – during Bella's first visit to the Black House, she noticed that Billy was in "a tiny square living room, a book in his hands" (*New Moon*, p 132). Just like Carlisle, Billy is also associated with books – a symbol of knowledge. This makes sense because Billy Black is a Quileute Elder and chief.

Breath

Invisible and ethereal, yet essential, breath symbolizes the soul, spirit and life. Inspiration, the act of taking a breath, also means that an idea has come to mind from a divine source. Expiration or breathing out, however, suggests death. And taking someone's breath away causes physical death. The Druids believed that the breath carried magical properties. So breathing or blowing onto something became an important magical practice. The act of breathing in and out is a complete cycle of respiration and the recurring rhythm of life. For humans and animals, breathing is a "spontaneous, instinctive and vital action" that enables us to "live and move" (Colin, 2000, p 20).

Twilight vampires don't breathe but they still inhale scents. For them, scent replaces breath, molecules of fragrance replace oxygen molecules. As Bella explains as a vampire: "I could taste an almost-honey-lilac-and-sun-flavored scent" (*Breaking Dawn*, p 358). This sunny, honey, yummy smell was Edward's scent.

Perhaps the most symbolic breath adventures in the *Twilight* world involve Bella's breathing stopping whenever she is around Edward. For example: "I couldn't breathe" (*New Moon*, p 351). She cannot breathe, just as *Twilight* vampires cannot breathe. Is this a vampire omen, foreshadowing Bella's future as a vampire? Of course, Bella does become a vampire the moment her heart stops beating: "My heart stuttered twice, and then thudded quietly again just once more" (*Breaking Dawn*, p 356). In other words, when Bella exhales her final breath she dies as a human and is reborn as a vampire.

A Ukrainian poet from the 19th Century described a Bella-like breath-stopping moment in a famous poem. Writing about his beloved, Hryhoriy Chubai recalls that:

When I am half a breath from you,
When I am half a step from your lips —
You whisper something spellbound and quiet,
That blue whisper is cutting my soul.
And I am forgetting that I know how to breathe.

Love is a powerful breath-stopper, symbolically speaking.

Bridge

The bridge is a crossing point, a link between two banks, sides or worlds, between earth and heaven, earthly life and supernatural life, the visible world and the invisible world, between humans and gods, and even life and death (Colin, 2000, p 73) Crossing a bridge is also the mark of an archetypal hero. It is one of the core challenges heroes must face during a journey. This makes sense because you can't be a hero until you get across some kind of gap, obstacle, or challenge.

In the *Twilight Saga*, Bella crosses several important bridges/bodies of water. Some crossings are much easier to spot than others:

- The road to La Push was fringed with "dense green forests" and "the wide Quillayute River snaking beneath it twice" (*Twilight*, p 99).
- When Bella first visits the Cullen house, she travels "over the bridge at the Calawah River" (*Twilight*, p 280).
- When escaping an evil vampire (James), Edward drives Bella across "the bridge" over the river at night (*Twilight*, p 347).
- Outside a Port Angeles bar, Bella decides to talk to some men in a bar, which triggers Edward's voice in her mind. "I stepped carefully over the gutter, running with water that was black in the darkness" (*New Moon*, p 114). Not a bridge? Well then, why water and not rubbish? You see, when Bella steps over the streaming gutter, she takes a risk, the mark of a hero.
- Bella travels by plane to Rome, and then crosses the sea again to return to Forks (*New Moon*, p 494).
- Bella leaps over a "river" in "one long bound" on her first hunt as a vampire (*Breaking Dawn*, p 380).
- To find her surprise gift from the Cullens (a small cottage

in the woods) Bella must leap over the river (*Breaking Dawn*, p 439).

What about bridges in your life? Whenever a bridge appears strongly in a dream, it often suggests that the dreamer is in a state of transition, either physically or personally with regard to inner and spiritual development. He or she may be on the point of taking an important step, of entering a new phase of life, just as people cross a bridge to get from one side of a river or world to another.

Brown

Although the *Twilight* books do not mention the color brown often, it does get mentioned in a positive and pleasant way. The main symbolic meanings of brown relate to ideas of poverty, humility, and practicality. Brown is the main color of the earth, soil, and trees before they get covered in green. The Latin word for earth is *humus,* which forms the word humility. Like its meaning suggests, brown gets several humble mentions in the *Twilight* books:

- The sick bay at school had a brown, vinyl mattress (*Twilight*, p 84).
- Bella chose to wear a "brown" sweater" (*Twilight*, p 198) because it was her favorite color that day.
- Bella describes brown as "warm" and the color of "tree trunks, rocks, dirt" (*Twilight*, p 200).
- Just after Bella tells Edward her favorite color is brown, he wears a "tan sweater" the next time he sees her (*Twilight*, p 221).

Burning Experience

Burn Baby, Burn

The warmth beside my heart got more and more real, warmer and warmer. Hotter… Too hot. Much, much too hot…

The burning grew – rose and peaked and rose again until it surpassed anything I'd ever felt.

I felt the pulse behind the fire raging now in my chest…

The fire blazed hotter and I wanted to scream…

Flames… were chewing their way out from my heart now, spreading with impossible pain through my shoulders and stomach, scalding their way up my throat, licking at my face.

The endless fire burn raged on.

(*Breaking Dawn*, pp 347–349)

Bella's transformation into a vampire happens to reflect a powerful burning experience in alchemy. Alchemy is an ancient practice that mixes science, medicine, and magic in an attempt to turn metal into gold. What this really means for the *Twilight Saga* is that Bella is turning from a mortal physical being (metal) into an immortal divine being (gold). She is connecting to perfect happiness, freedom and the highest spiritual power. This living alchemy possesses profound psychological wisdom (Andréa, 2009; *Alchemy Dictionary*, 2009).

The werewolves in the *Twilight* world undergo a divine burning experience also, which transforms them from mortal humans into supernatural wolves. When transforming into a wolf, Jacob describes the feeling as fiery: "the fire trembled down my spine, throwing tight spasms out along my arms and legs. It only took a second. The heat flooded through me, and I felt the silent shimmer that made me something else" (*Breaking Dawn*, p 143).

By connecting with spiritual (supernatural) power, the burnt and transformed individual attains a new consciousness. This means a union with higher spiritual forces, and therefore freedom from time, suffering, evil, and death. A mortal individual has turned their personal experiences of lead and metal into the great gold of insight, wisdom, love and eternal spiritual power.

Living Alchemy

In the living alchemy process, "the New Soul, which is born in the heart, slowly spreads like a fire through the whole body – if the alchemist surrenders... making it the most important thing in his or her life. It's a purifying fire that cleanses and purifies the alchemist. This is a process called 'transmutation'. It spreads through the blood, the autonomic nervous system, and the hormones of the endocrine glands. It builds up a new 'tree of life' in the spinal cord (Andréa, 2009).

Bella is born as a vampire after a fire of unearthly and intolerable power has burned in her heart. This fire is from another world and its light and heat are of a higher vibration than anything found in this world. Human life (Bella's blackness) is overpowered by red (rubedo – alchemy's higher phase, linked to the Philosopher's Stone). This helps her to achieve spiritual gold linked to the birth of a new and more aware soul. By following her heart's deepest desire and becoming a vampire, Bella finds her 'true place' in the world and achieves inner gold.

In fact, Bella's mortal dying is described as a red and black experience. The black suggests death and the red alludes to a divine rubedo alchemy phase:

> The pain was bewildering...
> Non-reality was black, and it didn't hurt so much.
> Reality was red, and it felt like I was being sawed in half, hit by a bus, punched by a prize fighter, trampled by bulls, and submerged in acid.
> (*Breaking Dawn*, p 341)

Bella's Liberation

According to alchemy, Bella achieves liberation in life. Freedom from death, suffering, illness, and evil, that is. But how? Throughout the *Twilight* series, Bella has performed important actions that will free her from the chains that bind her to the seven planes of human existence. In alchemy, the human personality comprises seven parts, each one at a certain energy level in the universe. All seven planes vibrate at different rates but only the physical plane is visible and valid according to science. To be spiritually free of all planes, Bella must take certain actions at each level.

7 Steps to Divine Power

Since about the 14th century, the Path of Liberation has been passed down in alchemy in symbolic stories. A famous one is the 1616 work *The Alchemical Wedding of Christian Rosycross*, reviewed by Jan van Rijkenborgh. This mystical tale is a road map to spiritual power, eternal life, and perfect happiness. This 'spiritual diary' presents picture-symbol-soul-events that reveal the secrets to spiritual enlightenment. The actual work of the alchemical processes in *The Alchemical Wedding* is carried out in the Tower of Olympus. So it is interesting that the *Twilight Saga* setting just happens to be the Olympic Peninsula. This tower has seven levels, symbolizing the seven planes of existence in the fallen world. Here is how Bella's actions fit with each of the seven levels and how she liberates herself from each level:

7 – Physical: Bella is not a material girl. She is detached from physical beauty and monetary wealth. Bella prefers sentimental gifts and tries to make others happy. These choices and behaviors free Bella from the physical plane.

6 – Etheric: In terms of atmosphere and surroundings, Bella gives up her earthly and environmental comforts to make her mother happy. She moves from sunny Phoenix to cold and rainy Forks.

5 – Astral: Instead of making friends with humans, Bella befriends spiritual and supernatural creatures – werewolves and vampires.

4 – Mental: Bella makes a choice to love Edward and to be with him forever, a sign of astonishing willpower over fate.

3 – Mental Ego: Rather than being selfish or 'I'-centered, Bella's empathy for others enables her to save them. Ultimately, Bella develops an all-powerful psychic shield.

2 – Emotional Ego: Bella gives Renesmee a locket when she thinks she is going to die. This symbolizes Bella giving her heart to another. It is an act of unselfish unrequited love. Bella expects nothing emotionally in return.

1 – Consciousness Ego: Since Bella is so considerate towards others, she easily conquers her desire to kill humans and drink their blood as soon as she becomes a vampire. Bella also avoids bloodshed in the final *Breaking Dawn* war because her desire to protect others, symbolized by her red "shield" of light, is far stronger than her urge to hurt others.

Each step of liberation at each plane is a major advancement towards the light. It takes courage, commitment, and time. Just imagine how it would feel to complete the first step – a detachment from material wealth! You would never feel greedy or care about possessions, nor would you wish to be immortal because you know that you and your loved ones are together forever in your hearts (Andréa, 2009). This is exactly John Lennon's idea in his timeless song *Imagine*: "Imagine no religion, no possessions too." Once you master your emotions, no outside force can ever steal your happiness or make you feel angry or depressed. Breaking free from the last consciousness plane (a sense of isolated individuality) would involve feeling part of the great universe and merging with the higher forces that created life and everything. This would give you an inextinguishable feeling of joy and love for all of creation. As Bella helps to show, this can give you incredible feelings of love and ecstasy forever and forever.

As a vampire, Bella grows in beauty and power. She has resurrected herself as an imperishable and indestructible body of glorious majesty. Bella became a supernatural being because she sacrificed her human life to give birth to Renesmee. She devotes her life to the new soul-fire burning in her heart. Bella does not try to kill Aro and the Volturi vampires. The divine soul does not fight. It radiates love, symbolized by Bella's shield, which stops conflict and evil. Bella's compassion for others is what saves others as well as her own soul. This is the key to understanding the *Twilight* plot and Bella's liberation from finite consciousness to a state of divine perfection.

When we are willing to sacrifice ourselves to help others, and surrender ourselves to higher forces, as Bella does, then we too can burn in a divine and spiritual way and achieve superhuman strength, grace, wisdom, immortality and peace. Bella Swan symbolizes the divine, immortal and perfect being hidden inside every person.

C

Car

The car is a big theme and important symbol in the *Twilight Saga*. Symbols are not just ideas or images from a distant past. As the encyclopedia of symbols reports, "the history of symbols is still being written" (Colin, 2000, p 45). Maybe the automobile is a fairly new human invention, but it still conveys useful information. Car ideas are also associated with older symbols such as the cart or chariot.

In the *Twilight* books, a range of cars is mentioned. In symbolic ways, the *Twilight* cars reveal special information about their owners or drivers. Humans in the *Twilight* world tend to drive average vehicles, while the Cullens own new and expensive cars. Here's a quick rundown of some key *Twilight* characters and who drives what:

Bella – old red 1953 Chevrolet Pickup Truck (*Twilight*, p 5)
Charlie – Police Chief Cruiser (*Twilight*, p 5)
Jacob – red classic 1986 Volkswagen Rabbit (*New Moon*, p 133)
Edward – glossy silver Volvo S60R (*Twilight*, pp 66–67)
Carlisle – black Mercedes S55 AMG (*New Moon*, p 378)
Rosalie – red BMW M3 Convertible (*Twilight*, p 195)
Emmett – huge jeep, with four spotlights and a red hardtop (*Twilight*, p 314)

It is not clear if Stephenie Meyer chose each character's car for symbolic reasons or whether each character was assigned a certain vehicle randomly. Nevertheless, each car does seem to reflect the personality of its owner and each car happens to have some personality of its own.

The Mind Drives

The basic symbolism of cars is that they comprise a 'mind' and a 'body'. The 'driver' is the 'mind' and car's physical form stands for the 'body'. Someone driving a car – as well as what kind of car they choose to drive, how fast, and where – signifies the mind directing one's body and behavior on the highway of life. In fact, a car's engine or 'motor' is a word derived from the Latin verb *movere* ('to move'), which is also the source of the word motivate.

The driver symbolizes an individual in control of his/her thoughts and desires, directing himself/herself, and travelling from place to place down the road of life or destiny. The car also evokes ideas of mobility and making headway.

Bella's Car

In relation to Bella's truck in the *Twilight* series, it is a vintage classic. An oldie but a goodie. It sticks out from other cars because of its personality. It may look as if it has been a bit neglected and would benefit from some TLC (tender loving care) but for now it seems to be surviving just fine. Kind of like its owner (Schmoop, 2008).

Just like her car, Bella is not a modern material girl who craves the latest clothes, gizmos, boys and other teen accessories. She likes classic literature, classic objects and old-fashioned values – she likes books, she does not get bored on her own, she does not need TV to survive, and she likes sentimental gifts. What's more, Bella "likes" this old, downbeat car just as she is not into the latest fashions and gossip with other girls at school. Just as Bella's red truck is a survivor, Bella is a survivor as an only child who has not been raised by overly attentive parents.

Bella's engagement car, a black Mercedes Guardian has "missile proof glass" and hefty "body armor" that is usually reserved for "Middle East diplomats, arms dealers, and drug lords" (*Breaking Dawn*, p 6). Very protective, just like Bella's *shield*. With the "engine snarling like a hunting panther"

(*Breaking Dawn*, p 3), this fast and sleek car sounds like a vampire. A hint to Bella's future as a vampire, perhaps? Since Edward chose this car for Bella, perhaps it is more of a reflection of *his* protective, defensive and cautious personality. Later on, when Edward gives Bella a red Ferrari as a wedding gift, Bella chooses to drive Edward's safe and secure silver Volvo instead of going for the beauty, flamboyance, speed, and material luxury of the Ferrari.

Edward's Car

The silver Volvo Edward drives is supposed to be a safe and reliable car. Such a vehicle accurately reflects Edward's protective, watchful and fastidious manner, especially towards Bella. Not only does Edward protect Bella's human life, he strives to keep her soul safe too. The color silver really suits Edward because he likes to stare at the moon and Bella is the silver moon to him. Silver is also sophisticated and stylish, not too outrageous as a color, just how Edward tries to present himself. In the *Twilight Saga*, Edward is the main vampire character and in the sunlight, *Twilight* vampires sparkle in a silvery way, silver is the color of their venom, and it also alludes to the pale-white color of vampire skin.

Jacob's Car

Jacob fixes up his red Rabbit Volkswagen and builds it "himself out of scraps" (*Eclipse*, p 209).

Since Jacob does not come from a wealthy background and has suffered hardship (his mother died, his father is wheelchair bound), he has learned to adapt and be resourceful. The car is red just as Jacob is red-skinned. Red is also associated with the sun and fire, Jacob's elements. Jacob's car has more personality than the average automobile. It's economical, practical, and friendly (red is a warm color) – just like Jacob.

The most outstanding feature of the Rabbit is that it is an old classic, a sign of respect for the past. Native American people like Jacob respect their elders and strongly value tradition and legends from the past. Even though Jacob needs a master cylinder, tries to repair his car for some time, and is developing mechanical ability, the Rabbit does not run for a while. In the same way, Jacob is trying to form a relationship with Bella, he experiences steady personal growth as a teen wolf, and he learns more and more about his shape-shifting heritage.

Baby, You Can Drive My Car… Unless You're a Volturi

The Cullens and cars are inextricably linked. After all, the Cullens are mobile, progressive, and innovative. Their best example of innovation is that they are vegetarian vampires who do not feast on traditional food – human blood. The Volturi vampires, in curious contrast, do not drive cars. In fact, these "ancient ones" live in a historical city and almost never venture out of their underground lair at all. Nor do they roam their local surroundings to seek prey. Rather, their meals are delivered to them (*New Moon*, p 483). The Volturi are pedestrians who "march" together on foot (*Breaking Dawn*, p 631) at a "slow but deliberate" pace (*Breaking Dawn*, p 632). Symbolically, the Volturi's lifestyle and lack of fast cars strongly suggests that their outlook is also immobile, inert, out-of-touch, and stagnant. The Volturi are not steering themselves in a way that helps them to get along with others and adapt to the modern world because they repeat the same old behavior patterns as they have done for "millennia" (*Breaking Dawn*, p 631). Another way to put it is that the Volturi have dreadfully little creative innovative spark or fuel ('mental driving forces').

Character Names

What's in a Name?

A name can say a lot about a person and that person's character.

Many names have some sort of psychological, historical, or symbolic meaning behind them. In the *Twilight* books, the name game is especially interesting and meaningful. As such, a list of character names and what they mean is presented here. (Main Source: www.behindthename.com; Wikisource, 2011.)

Bella 'Isabella' Swan

Bella

Bella means 'beautiful' in Italian and is short for Isabella. Bella's full name 'Isabella' means devoted to God and is a Latinate form of *Isabel*. This name implies a person who is held in high esteem. In the *Twilight* series, Edward holds Bella above everything else and believes she is beautiful. Since Bella insists being called Bella instead of Isabella (e.g. *Twilight*, p 14), this presents her as a choice-maker, not a fate-follower. A notable bearer of this name was the powerful ruling Queen Isabella of Castile, who sponsored the explorations of Christopher Columbus. Isabel is a Medieval Provençal form of Elizabeth, which happens to be the name of Edward's mother. The name spread throughout Spain, Portugal and France, becoming common among the royalty by the 12th century. It grew popular in England in the 13th century after Isabella of Angoulême married the English king John, and became even trendier when Isabella of France married Edward II the following century.

Swan

Bella's surname Swan refers to a graceful aquatic bird, the swan. The surname *Swan* boosts the importance of Bella as a central character because she expresses the manner and symbolism of swans. Both Bella and swans are similar in that they are pure, powerful, have neck appeal, suggest love/romance, are linked with William Shakespeare (the Swan of Avon), possess gentle natures, and start life off as 'ugly ducklings'. (See *Swan*, under *Birds*, for details).

Edward Cullen

Edward

The name Edward means wealthy protector and is derived from the Old English 'rich, blessed' and 'guard'. Saint Edward the Confessor was a king of England known to be a just ruler. Because of his popularity this name remained. In the *Twilight* series, Edward is financially wealthy and protects Bella. Moreover, Edward is the first name of several heroes from Victorian novels such as Edward Rochester from Charlotte Bronte's novel *Jane Eyre*. On choosing the name Edward, Stephenie Myers said:

> *I decided to use a name that had once been considered romantic, but had fallen out of popularity for decades. Charlotte Bronte's Mr. [Edward] Rochester and Jane Austen's Mr. [Edward] Ferrars were the characters that led me to the name Edward. I tried it on for size, and found that it fit well.*
> (Meyer, 2005)

Cullen

Cullen is a surname derived from an Old French form of Cologne, the name of a city in Germany.

The dictionary definition of 'cull' is defined as: "1. to select from a group; to choose; 2. to reduce or control the size of (as a herd) by removal (as by hunting) of especially weaker animals." (Oxford). In this light, the name Cull-en seems to hint at Edward's romantic and vampiric behavior. Edward "selects from a group" by choosing Bella to be his true love. On the other hand, Edward wants to hunt her down like he would an animal. The Cull-ens tend to hunt or cull animals involved in population explosions. They are morally fussy hunters. Whether the name Cullen was symbolically intentional or not, Meyer picked the perfect word on which to base Edward's last name.

The name Cullen could also be a version of the term "cold

one". Jacob Black's ancestors may have first called them "The Cold Ones", which may have been interpreted as "Cold 'Uns" and then "Cullens". Language can evolve that way (TwilightMOMS post, Maria, May 9, 2008).

Another theory is that ancient Irish myth may be a source of Cullen. It is an Anglicized version of the Celtic name *Culann*. In Ireland, all children learn a famous fable about a child called Setanta who killed Culann's hound in self-defense and offered to take the dog's place as Culann's wolfhound.

Jacob Black

Jacob

The name Jacob is from the Latin *Iacobus*, based on the Greek *Iakobos*, which comes from the Hebrew *Ya'aqov*. In the Old Testament, Jacob (later called Israel) was the father of the twelve founders of the twelve tribes of Israel. In the *Twilight Saga*, Jacob is a Native American character, a member of the Quileute community at La Push reservation, and the son of a chief. A friendly, protective, social, and sunny character, Jacob becomes Bella's best friend and turns into a teenage werewolf (*Twilight*, pp 103, 104, 109, 110). Born holding onto his twin brother's heel, Jacob's name means 'holder of the heel' or 'supplanter' (to take the place of another). Other theories suggest that this name derived from a hypothetical name like 'may God protect'. In *Breaking Dawn*, Jacob does form his own tribe as the true Alpha and supplants (replaces) Sam. Jacob also supplants the place of Edward in *New Moon* as Bella's boy friend (but not true boyfriend).

Black

This family name refers to color black, which has a range of compelling meanings. For more symbolic gossip, see *Black*.

Cullens

Carlisle – this name means strong one and is the name of a city in northern England. The Romans originally called this city *Luguvalium,* which means 'stronghold of Lugus'. As his name suggests, Carlisle is the strength behind the family. This old name suits Carlisle as the oldest member of the family.

Esme – means 'esteemed' or 'loved' in Old French. It was first recorded in Scotland in the 16th Century. Like her name, Esme is esteemed as a loving and caring mother by her family.

Alice – from the Old French name *Aalis,* which a short form of the Germanic name *Adalheidis* ('noble' and 'kind sort'). Just like her name, Alice is noble in that she sees the true future. Alice is also very kind – she comforts war-torn Jasper and tries to make Bella happy. This popular 12th century name was made more popular by Lewis Carroll's *Alice's Adventures in Wonderland* (1865), a story that features another bright and clever Alice. This Alice was so optimistic and imaginative, just like *Twilight's* Alice, that one of her most famous sayings was: "Why, sometimes I've believed as many as six impossible things before breakfast" (Carroll, 1865).

Jasper – means 'treasurer' in Persian. This name was given to one of the wise men (also known as the Magi, or three kings) who visited the newborn Jesus. The name can also refer to the gemstone jasper. As an emotionally intelligent person and a military mastermind, Jasper is definitely a wise man and precious gem in the Cullen family.

Rosalie – is based on the Latin *rosa,* named after the flower (rose). A rose is beautiful, as is Rosalie. The surname Lee belonged to Robert E. Lee, a commander of the Confederate forces during the American Civil War, which happens to match Jasper's war history. A *lee* is also a shelter from the storm. Rosalie had a 'stormy' human life and a traumatic death, but has now found shelter with the Cullens.

Emmett – the male version of *Emma,* a Germanic name that means strong, whole or universal, strong, powerful, hard worker. With his physical build, strength of a bear, and teamwork attitude, Emmett's name certainly suits him.

Renesmee – is a combination of *Renée* (the name of Bella's mother) and *Esme* (the name of Edward's foster mother). In a way, the name Renesmee has unique *Twilight Saga* symbolism. This is because Renesmee merges names from two different worlds: the human one and the vampire one. As such, Renesmee suggests the idea that different groups can co-exist together in peace. Of course, Jacob nicknames Renesmee "Nessie", which catches on very fast. Bella, however, is not so pleased that her baby has the name of a sea serpent: "You nicknamed my daughter after the *Loch Ness Monster?*" (*Breaking Dawn*, p 417). The Loch Ness Monster is a famous lake creature that is said to inhabit Loch Ness in the Scottish Highlands. It was brought to the world's attention in 1933, although evidence of its existence is minimal and photographic material and sonar readings are controversial. The most popular theory about the Loch Ness Monster is that this harmless creature is a plesiosaurus, a water-dwelling dinosaur. Though the scientific community regards the Loch Ness Monster, affectionately nicknamed 'Nessie' since the 1950s, as a modern-day myth, this creature remains one of the most famous examples of cryptozoology ('the study of hidden animals'). Just as the Scottish Nessie is considered unique, impossible, and harmless, so is the existence of *Twilight's* Nessie.

Volturi

Aro – this name has unclear origins. Its source may be Greek: *are* ('bane, ruin') or *arsen* ('male'). In ancient Greek myth, Ares was a bloodthirsty god of war, the son of Zeus and Hera, who were rulers. However, Aro is also a god of judgment of the West African Odinani faith. In the *Twilight Saga*, Aro matches these meanings in that he is a ruler, prefers violence, tries to start a war, and claims to be a law-enforcer.

Marcus – is believed to be a derivative of Mars, the Roman God of War. In Shakespeare's play *Julius Caesar,* two characters happen to be named Marcus. In fact, it was Caesar's friend Marcus Brutus who assassinated Caesar in the Senate – not for greed, envy or political power – but for the good of Rome. Caesar was an arrogant leader who wanted to become king. When Brutus committed suicide later, his enemy Mark Antony (Marcus Antonius) described him as "the noblest Roman". In *Breaking Dawn,* Marcus the Volturi leader considers the good of all, just as the Roman leader Marcus Brutus did. He tried to avoid violence and bloodshed by voting against making war.

Caius – is a Roman first name, of Etruscan origin, whose meaning is unknown. The most famous bearer of this common Roman name was Caius Julius Caesar, the great leader of the Roman Republic. This name was held by many of the Caesars, including the corrupt Caligula. According to Roman history, a senator named Caius Ligarius conspired to assassinate Caesar. This Caius didn't like Julius after Julius embarrassed Caius for saying good things about Pompey, another Roman leader.

Jane – is a Medieval English form of *Jehanne,* an Old French feminine form of *Iohannes* (or John). The name derives from a Hebrew name *(Yochanan, Yahweh),* which means 'gracious'. This name owes its popularity to two highly revered saints from the New Testament. One was John the Baptist, a Jewish ascetic who was considered the forerunner of Jesus Christ. In the *Twilight Saga,* however, Jane is an evil figure whose personality contrasts the good and gracious meanings of her name. Maybe Stephenie Meyer named an evil Volturi guard Jane as a tribute to classic writers like *Jane Eyre* or *Jane Austen.* Or maybe the name is random. In any case, Jane does rhyme with 'pain' – Jane's top talent.

Alec – is short for Alexander, a Latinized form of the Greek name *Alexandros.* This name means 'defending men' from the Greek *words alexo* ('to defend, help') and *aner* ('man'). In Greek myth, Alexander was another name of the hero Paris (who gets mentioned in the *Twilight Saga*) and it belongs to several figures in the New Testament. The most famous person to bear this name was Alexander the Great, King of Macedon. In the 4th century BC he built a huge empire out of Greece, Egypt, Persia, and India. A key Volturi guard, the name Alec may also point to the three Furies of Roman mythology, one of whom was named *Alecto*.

Demetri – is based on an old Slavic name *Dmitrei*, a derived form of the Greek name *Demetrios*, which derives from *Demeter*, a Greek earth goddess. Her name means 'earth mother' (a merging of the Greek words *(de)* 'earth' and *(meter)* 'mother') and she was the goddess of agriculture. In the *Twilight* world, Demetri is a gifted tracker who will relentlessly roam the earth to find his target. According to *Breaking Dawn*, Demetri is "the best tracker in the world" (p 535). Just how closely or cryptically Demetri's character fits with the meaning of his name is something yet to be discovered.

Felix – a Roman phrase meaning 'lucky, successful' in Latin. It was acquired as a nickname by the 1st century BC Roman general Sulla. It also appears in the New Testament belonging to the governor of Judea who imprisoned Saint Paul. Due to its favorable meaning, Felix became a popular name among early Christians.

Quileutes

Billy – is a short form of William, from the Germanic name *Willahelm*, which merges the elements 'will, desire' and *helm* 'helmet, protection'. As such, William means a will to protect others. The name was common among Normans, and it became extremely popular in England after William the Conqueror was recognized as the first Norman king of England. Since Billy Black is a Native American Elder, a Quileute chief, has a magical heritage, and his role is to protect his tribe, the name Billy is a powerful and appropriate choice.

Sam – is short for *Samson* and *Samuel*. The name Samson is from the Hebrew name *Shimshon* and probably means 'sun'. Samson was an Old Testament hero of exceptional strength. His uncut hair was the secret source of his power, but his mistress Delilah betrayed him and cut it. Thus Samson was captured by the Philistines, blinded, and brought to their temple. However, in a final act of strength, he pulled down the pillars of the temple upon himself and his captors. In comparison, Samuel is from the Hebrew name *Shemu'el* which means 'name of God' or 'God has heard'. Samuel was the last of the ruling judges in the Old Testament. As an Alpha wolf who leads a tribe of shape-shifting wolves, the name Sam matches Sam's strong, brave, loyal, and protective character.

Emily – In the *Twilight Saga,* Bella notices the relationship between Emily and Sam and how much they adore each other. Despite everything, including Sam's wolvish streak, Emily seems to admire him. The name Emily is a feminine form of the Roman name *Aemilia,* possibly derived from the Latin word *aemulus,* which means 'rival'. Emily is an extremely popular name in English-speaking countries. Due to the famous poet Emily Dickinson, the name Emily has also acquired literary associations, evoking images of a beautiful and smart woman.

Leah – as a *Twilight* character, Leah is a rather melancholy individual. After Sam fell in love with Emily and broke up with Leah, Leah became lonely and bitter. Leah is the only female wolf in the *Twilight Saga,* which surely reinforces her loneliness. This name may derive from the Hebrew word *le'ah,* which means 'weary'. Leah may also come from a name that means 'mistress' or 'ruler' in Akkadian. In the Old Testament, Leah is the first wife of Jacob and the mother of seven of his children. Although Jews used this name in the Middle Ages, it did not become a typical English Christian name until much later. In the *Twilight Saga,* Leah the she-wolf has been worn out by her experiences of heartbreak and rules with supernatural powers as a female shape-shifter.

Seth – is a young shape-shifter and a very decent character in the *Twilight Saga*. As a name, Seth means 'placed' or 'appointed' in Hebrew. In the Old Testament he is the third named son of Adam and Eve. In England this name was used after the Protestant Reformation. In *Breaking Dawn*, Seth is the first wolf to join Jacob, the true Alpha. He therefore receives the highest ranking place at Jacob's side.

Some *Twilight* fans believe that Stephenie Meyer's Mormon background may have had a religious influence on choosing Quileute names like Jacob, Seth, Samuel, and Leah.

Other *Twilight* Characters
Bella's Parents

Renée – a female form of the French *René*, from the Latin *Renatus*, which means 'born again'. In the *Twilight* books, Renée is reborn again when she remarries and tries to regain a lost sense of freedom from the past. Bella and her mother Renée are similar in that they are dreamers, independent, worry about others, and feel emotionally close to each other. They are both absent-minded professors. Bella is a physical klutz who is highly intelligent. Renée overlooks daily routine but is musically trained and talented. Renée differs to her daughter Bella in that she seems much more social, spontaneous, talkative, and emotionally expressive.

Charlie – this name is a version of *Charles*, based on the name *Karl*, which is a Germanic word meaning 'man'. The fame of Charles the Great (742–814) made this name popular. *Twilight's* Charlie is definitely manly: he fishes, drinks beer, deals with thugs, carries a gun, and is career-driven. Perhaps Charlie's masculine personality contributes to the emotionally distant and awkward emotional relationship between him and his daughter Bella.

Forks High Boys

Mike – is short for *Michael,* derived from the Hebrew name *Mikha'el* (which means 'who is like God?'), implying no person is like God. Saint Michael was an archangel in Hebrew culture and the only archangel in the Bible who lead heaven's armies. While Mike at Forks High may be an active member of the high school crowd and a social high-flier at school (*Twilight,* p 26), Mike is no authentic god-like character in the *Twilight* books.

Eric – from the Old Norse name *Eiríkr,* which combines *ei* 'ever' and *ríkr* 'ruler'. Several early kings of Sweden, Denmark and Norway had this name. In the *Twilight Saga,* Eric is the first student at Forks High who introduces himself to Bella and offers to show her the way around school. Bella finds this black-haired boy "over-helpful" and missing a "sense of humor" (*Twilight,* pp 14–15) as some traditional royal rulers may be.

Tyler – is an old English surname meaning 'tiler of roofs'. In *Twilight,* Tyler would have crushed Bella with his van if Edward had not used his super strength and speed to save her. After this car accident, Tyler made numerous attempts to 'patch up' his relationship with Bella and 'cover' and 'veneer' his mistake, just like a tiler lays out tiles to create a new overlay.

Forks High Girls

Jessica – this name was first used by Shakespeare in *The Merchant of Venice* (1596), and is probably based on the biblical name Iscah (*Jescha*). This name derived from the Hebrew *Yiskah,* which means 'to behold'. As a bubbly, enthusiastic, and sociable character who places importance on her looks (*Twilight,* p 125), Jessica certainly does try hard to be noticed. Maybe Jessica makes efforts to look pretty and get boys to behold her physical beauty because she lacks depth under the surface.

Angela – a version of the Latin male name *Angelus,* which derives from *angelos,* the Greek word for 'messenger'. Angela is a bit of angel in Bella's eyes because she is pleasant to Bella, does not pry like the other girls at school, and works hard, like taking time to prepare hundreds of party invitations.

Lauren – this name derives from the Latin *laurus* 'laurel'. Saint Laurence was a 3rd century deacon and martyr from Rome. According to legend, Laurel was roasted alive because when he was ordered to hand over the church's treasures, he gave all of it to the sick and poor instead. In *Twilight,* Lauren is described as "standoffish" (p 67) and "insolent" (p 106), the kind of student who likes to roast others alive with scorching verbal criticism.

More Vampires!
The Tracker's Gang

James – a New Testament Greek form of the Hebrew name *Ya'aqov* (Jacob), which relates to the word "supplant". As *Twilight's* most evil vampire, James tries to supplant (replace, overthrow, remove) Bella and Edward, by taking action to hunt, torture, and kill them. As Edward explains, James is a passionate and obsessive tracker who is unstoppable "once he commits to a hunt" (*Twilight,* p 335). Even after James lures Bella alone to the ballet studio, he hopes to 'supplant' Bella by baiting Edward to come over (his most-wanted target). What a wicked trap!

Victoria – this name is from the Latin *Victoria* meaning 'victory'. In the *Twilight* world, Victoria's 'gift' for evasion certainly makes her a victorious winner – because no one can catch her. Unfortunately, Victoria used her gifts for no good, so she did not stay victorious for very long.

Laurent – means crowned with laurel (a plant). Laurel is a plant and there are several derivations of it. It can be used in cooking and medicine. "It makes me think of the outdoors and how Laurent lives. I think of him living as a nomad in the woods until he meets James and Victoria" (TwilightMOMS post, sheacox January 1, 2009).

The Denali Clan

Eleazar – from a Hebrew name meaning 'my God has helped' *(El'azar)*. The first male known as Eleazar was the son of a High Priest of Israel. In the *Twilight* books, Eleazar's supernatural ability is that he has an "instinctive feel for the gifts of others" (*Breaking Dawn*, p 537). He is described as a gentle and compassionate person who used to enforce the law as a good Volturi soldier.

Carmen – a Medieval Spanish form of *Carmel* influenced by the Latin word *carmen* 'song'. *Karmel* (meaning 'garden' in Hebrew) is a mountain in Israel that is mentioned in the Old Testament. It was the site of several early Christian monasteries. In *Breaking Dawn*, it is Carmen who first supported Renesmee and convinced other vampires to listen to the young child's story (pp 544–555).

Tanya – is a Russian diminutive of *Tatiana*, the female form of the Roman name *Tatianus*, and a version of the Roman name *Tatius*. But this Roman family name has no known meaning. In the *Twilight* world, Tanya considers that "grave danger" abounds, but she is not clear as to which side to support (*Breaking Dawn*, p 546).

Kate – this name is short for *Katherine*, used in England since the Middle Ages. It derives from the Greek name *Aikaterine*, which can either derive from the Greek word *hekateros* ('each of the two') or *aikia* ('torture'). As a Denali clan vampire, Kate is aptly named given that her 'gift' is the offensive ability is to torture others by delivering painful electric shocks (*Breaking Dawn*, p 556).

Irina – is a version of *Irene* from the Greek *Eirene*, derived from a word meaning 'peace'. A Greek goddess of peace was named Irene as well as some Christian saints. In the *Twilight* series, the meaning behind Irina's name (peace) is inverted because Irina starts a war. Irina is also a fractured version of 'Iris' in Greek myth (a rainbow goddess who brings good news) because *Twilight's* Irina is a vampire who delivers bad news in the form of betrayal, violence, and war.

American Nomads

Garrett – an English surname derived from the given name *Gerald* or *Gerard*. Based on a Germanic name meaning 'rule of the spear', this word merges the elements *ger* 'spear' and *wald* 'rule'. The meaning of Garrett's name suits this vampire's leading role in the *Breaking Dawn* war as a crusader for liberty who exposes the Volturi's true goals: power (p 666).

Mary – an English form of Maria, the Latin form of the New Testament Greek names *Mariam* and *Maria,* and based the Hebrew name *Miryam*. The meaning of the word is unclear, but some possibilities are 'sea of bitterness', 'rebelliousness', and 'wished for child'. A likely source is an Egyptian name, perhaps derived in part from my 'beloved' or my 'love'. This name was used for several New Testament characters. Most importantly, Mary is the virgin mother of Jesus, and another important figure is Mary Magdalene. Due to the Virgin Mary this name has been very popular in the Christian world. An American nomad vampire in *Breaking Dawn,* Mary travels alone to be a witness for the Cullens, making friends easily with others along the way (p 566).

Peter – this name is derived from the Greek word *Petros,* which means 'stone'. This is a translation of the name Cephas in the *New Testament,* which means 'stone' in Aramaic. As soon as Peter the vampire hears Renesmee's story in *Breaking Dawn,* his "commitment" to support her is as strong as stone (p 564).

Charlotte – a French feminine form of *Charles*. It was introduced to Britain in the 17th century. A notable bearer was Charlotte Bronte (1816–1855), the eldest of the three Bronte sisters and the author of the classic novel *Jane Eyre*. In *Breaking Dawn,* Charlotte is Peter's vampire wife. Her open mind and curiosity motivates her to help Renesmee (p 564).

Randall – from an English surname which was derived from the medieval given name *Randel,* a medieval diminutive of *Randolf* and other names beginning with the Germanic element rand meaning 'rim (of a shield)'. In line with the meaning of his name, the nomadic American vampire Randall chooses to "stand with" with the Cullens against the Volturi, which strengthens their growing defense or shield (*Breaking Dawn,* p 567).

Irish Vampires

Maggie – is short for *Margaret,* derived from the Latin name *Margarita,* which was from the Greek word *margarites* ('pearl'). Saint Margaret, the patron of expectant mothers, was martyred at Antioch in the 4th century. Later legends told of Margaret's escape from a dragon, with which she was often depicted in medieval art. The saint was popular during the Middle Ages, and her name has been widely used in the Christian world. In *Breaking Dawn,* Maggie has curly red hair and a gift for detecting the truth. Her red color and strong inner instincts suggest dragon-like qualities.

Siobhan – is an Irish form of *Jehanne,* which is a Norman French variant of *Jeanne.* In *Breaking Dawn,* the vampire Siobhan leads the Irish clan and is described as being "a woman of immense presence" who was both beautiful and mesmerizing (p 564).

Liam – is a short Irish form of *William,* which is from the Germanic *Willahelm* and a name which merges the elements 'will, desire' and helm 'helmet, protection'. The most famous figure that bears this name is William the Conqueror of England and later on other rulers of England, Scotland, Sicily, the Netherlands and Prussia bore this name. Liam in *Breaking Dawn* is the "hard-faced" Irish vampire husband of Siobhan.

Romanian Vampires

Stefan – is a form of *Stephen,* from the Greek name *Stephanos,* which means 'crown'. Saint Stephen was a deacon stoned to death, as told in the New Testament, and is the first true Christian martyr. Due to him, the name became common in the Christian world. It was popularized in England by the Normans. This was the name of kings who ruled England, Serbia, and Poland, as well as ten popes. In *Breaking Dawn*, Stefan is described as having dark hair, clear burgundy eyes, and wearing classic black clothes (p 581). This Romanian vampire clearly declares his willingness to "fight" the Volturi (*Breaking Dawn*, p 612).

Vladimir – this name means 'to rule with greatness', derived from the Slavic element *volod* ('rule') combined with the Slavic word *mer* ('great') or *mir* ('peace'). This was the name of an 11th century Grand Prince of Kiev, venerated as a saint because of his efforts to Christianize Russia. Vladimir was the name of a notorious and bloodthirsty Slavic ruler too, who used to impale his victims on spikes. Gruesome! Some vampire myths were inspired by Vladimir's blood lust and horrific wanton violence. In *Breaking Dawn*, the ashy blond-haired Vladimir is the keenest "fighter" of the two Romanian vampires. He is sick of the Volturi's corrupt rule (p 611).

When Jacob calls Vladimir and Stefan "Dracula One and Dracula Two" and says they are "creep-tacular", he is right on the mark when it comes to the macabre reputation of Romanian vampires and violent leaders of the past (*Breaking Dawn*, p 586).

Egyptian Vampires

Amun – the name *Ammon* is the Greek form of the Egyptian *Ymn* (reconstructed as *Yamanu*) and it means 'the hidden one'. In early Egyptian mythology Amun was a god of the air, creativity and fertility, whose spirit ruled the city of Thebes. In *Breaking Dawn*, the Egyptian vampire Amun is domineering and refused to touch Renesmee when he arrived at the Cullen house (p 565). With a name that means 'hidden one', Amun is certainly keeping his true feelings 'hidden' in the *Twilight* world.

Kebi – there is no clear meaning for this name. But *Kuba* is a Polish form of *Jakub*, which is a Polish, Czech and Slovak form of *Jacob* (or *James*). As the Egyptian vampire wife of Amun, Kebi tends to play a quiet and passive role in *Breaking Dawn* (p 565).

Benjamin – a Hebrew name (Binyamin) that means 'son of the south' or 'son of the right hand'. Benjamin in the Old Testament was the twelfth and youngest son of Jacob and he founded a southern Hebrew tribe. His original name (Ben-'oniy) means 'son of my sorrow' as his mother Rachel died shortly after childbirth. In the *Twilight* series, the Egyptian vampire Benjamin has a gift for manipulating the natural elements – air, water, earth, fire (*Breaking Dawn*, p 566). This may be a symbolic nod to Benjamin Franklin, who flew kites and learned to manipulate lightning.

Tia – is a short form of names ending with *tia*. It has been suggested that this name became fashionable since the 1950s as a result of the brand name for the coffee liqueur Tia Maria. It also means 'aunt' in Spanish or Portuguese. In the *Twilight* world, Tia was a quiet vampire who made a huge impression when she chose to speak (*Breaking Dawn*, p 565).

Amazon Vampires

Zafrina – In the *Twilight* series, Zafrina is a vocal and powerful South American vampire. She is a tall, lean, dark-haired woman dressed in animal skin vest and pants. The "eccentric clothes", "restless crimson eyes" and "sudden darting movements" made her seem wilder (*Breaking Dawn*, p 568). Zafrina is a supreme illusionist – her supernatural gift is to make people see what she wants them to see (*Breaking Dawn*, p 569). She can produce visions such as a fire or a forest, or make people believe that they are completely blind. A very dangerous offensive weapon, indeed. The name Zafrina may be a variant of the Arabic name *Zafira*, a variant spelling of the name *Sapphira*, which means 'Sapphire' in Greek. The name Sapphira was popularized by the movie *Eragon* in 2006.

Senna – is an Amazon vampire who has a close relationship with Zafrina. While Zafrina is an active spokesperson for the pair, Senna does not speak at all. Nevertheless, Senna moves with Zafrina as if they were "two limbs of the same organism" (*Breaking Dawn*, p 569). Silent, but deadly, just like her South American sister, no doubt. The name Senna does not have any recorded history or meaning, although there are many names that sound similar to Senna.

Kachiri – is a vampire who separated from Zafrina and Senna in order to assist Alice and Jasper. As such, Kachiri arrives in the snowy battlefield in the middle of a war, just after the Volturi vote to kill Bella and Edward's child. The name Kachiri does not have any recorded history or meaning, although many other names do sound similar to Kachiri.

European Nomads

Alistair – In *Breaking Dawn*, Alistair is a brooding English vampire and a loner. He does not trust authority and he has a supernatural gift for getting what he seeks (*Breaking Dawn*, p 567). The name Alistair is an Anglicized form of *Alasdair*, a Scottish form of *Alexander*, which is the Latinized form of the Greek name *Alexandros*. The Greek word *alexo* means 'to help and defend' and *aner* means 'man'. The most famous bearer of this name was Alexander the Great, King of Macedon, who built a great empire from Greece, Egypt, Persia, and India. Due to his fame, and stories about him, the name Alexander became popular in Europe and was used by kings, emperors, and popes.

Charles – *Charles* is based on *Karl*, a Germanic name that means 'man'. This nomadic European vampire in *Breaking Dawn* does not stay to challenge the Volturi, although he is deemed to possess some kind of quantifiable supernatural gift (p 702).

Makenna – this name is a version of *McKenna*. It derives from the Gaelic surname *Mac Cionnaith*, which means 'son of *Cionaodh*', a modern Irish form of *Cináed,* which means 'born of fire' in Gaelic. This was the name of the first king of the Scots (9th century). In *Breaking Dawn,* Makenna is a nomadic European vampire and Charles (above) is her mate. In front of witnesses, she accuses Aro of blackmail: "Are those are only choices… agree with you, or fight?" (*Breaking Dawn,* p 668). In the end, however, Makenna and Charles prefer not to stay and fight.

Dodgy Downtowner

Jenks – this name is based on the Hungarian name *Jancsi,* a version of *Janos,* which is Hungarian for *John* – a name that means 'gracious'.

In the *Twilight Saga,* Jenks is extremely gracious as far as wheeling, dealing, and cajoling business is concerned. An independent and offbeat character who is not part of a team, Jenks is rather odd and a bit of a loner, much like a joker in a pack of cards. As a clever lawyer who runs his own business, Jenks does not need others to survive. The name Jenks does also sound a bit like 'jinx' and Jenks does like to jinx others. How? He inflicts faults in the truth and devastates accurate information by creating fraudulent identities or 'junk' files. So the 'joke' is on 'others' because they are deceived and do not know the real truth. The activities of Jenks in the *Twilight* world as well as his name aptly point to frivolous and fraudulent dynamics.

Chess/Choice

Chess Means Choice

> Edward and Alice playing chess was one of the funniest things I'd ever seen… [as] Alice foresaw the moves he should make and he [using his mind-reading ability] picked up the moves she would make in return out of her head.
> (*Eclipse,* p 51)

The chess scene above is the only time this game is ever mentioned directly in the books. A big theme in the *Twilight Saga* is choice, which is often symbolized by chess. Overall, people's experiences in life are a combination of choice and change, free will and fate. In other words, life is a result of external factors (things outside our control) and internal factors (things we can personally control). The field of psychology clearly shows that the happiest, healthiest and most satisfied people in life are those who feel they have a fair amount of personal influence over their lives. This makes the *Twilight Saga* extra helpful to readers because it is a story where Bella, in particular, makes choices, follows her heart, and takes effective action to attain personal success and fulfillment. We cannot control all events, but we can choose our reactions to those events – our thoughts, feelings and behaviors. As a chess game suggests, we cannot control the board or the pieces, but we do control how to make our moves.

The importance of choice is clearly suggested on the original cover of *Breaking Dawn*. The red pawn represents Bella before her transformation to immortality. As a human, Bella is arguably the weakest piece in the game, colored red perhaps to symbolize the blood that runs through her veins. The white queen represents Bella after she becomes a vampire. In chess, the queen is the most powerful and versatile piece in the whole game. The *Twilight* queen is white, most probably to symbolize the pure and powerful state Bella has reached or perhaps to suggest her pale vampire skin. It is worth noting that the actual *Breaking Dawn* battle scene that occurs between the so-called good vampires and bad vampires takes place outdoors on a white snow-covered ground, after the solid black triangle (the Volturi army) arrives. Hence, we get a black and white backdrop – classic chess colors.

Speaking to an interviewer about the *Breaking Dawn* battle scene, Stephenie Meyer reveals that:

> It was always for me more like a courtroom drama, which is

> one of my few TV addictions, rather than a battle scene. It was always about outmaneuvering someone mentally; I knew that if it turned into a physical battle, there was never going to be a winner. That was the ending that really felt true to the characters to me – because it was a mental game.
> (*Time Magazine*, 2008)

In other words, choice, strategy, plans, and smart moves influence events. No matter what life deals you – whether you're born with a silver spoon in your mouth or you just have 32 possessions on a 64 square block, it's the personal choices that move you forward and produce success. Life is the biggest chess game ever.

Did you know that chess is itself a secret symbol? This game, which originated in India, is played on a checkered board. The playing field "is symbolic of the world that we understand, that is composed of opposing forces. Also, the black and white colors of the symmetrically arranged squares stand for male/female, light/dark, positive/negative, good/evil" (Nozedar, 2008, p 37). This unique pattern is a constant reminder of harmony and tension between opposites, an idea that the black and white playing pieces reinforce. The square shape of the board symbolizes the stability of the earth. Meanwhile, the four corners symbolize the four natural elements and the four directions. Each side of a chessboard has eight squares (the number of judgment and infinity). Success at chess is based on making calculated judgments, choices based on strategy, sacrifice, and surprise, as well as chance. As such, this game symbolizes fate and free will. Chess is plainly connected with war strategy, and the ability to surprise an opponent. A good player knows how important it is to sacrifice pieces in order to gain an ever-increasing advantage.

In the *Twilight* world, Bella *chooses* to become a vampire so that she can be with Edward forever. Despite the playing pieces life deals you and the playing field before you, it's the choices and moves that you make that make the difference between winning and losing, happiness and misery. As a result of her choices, Bella is no longer a 'pawn' whose life is controlled by fate and outside influences such as her parents' separation, the gloomy Forks weather, and the threat of evil vampires. Each choice Bella makes moves her forward and transforms her into a confident young woman who is in control of her life. Eventually, Bella becomes the powerful queen who uses personal strengths like her "shield" to protect loved ones, defy the Volturi vampires, and find authentic happiness.

Mental Games

"Now," he said significantly, "it's your turn."
(*Twilight*, p 155)

When Bella and Edward take turns learning about each other and asking one another questions, Edward makes it sound like a chess game. In the *Twilight* series, the chess game starts early, symbolically speaking. Whether Edward should or should not make a move on Bella, whether or not Bella should hang on to the dangerous but beautiful Edward. Of course, their dialogue is continually competitive, a chess-like banter. "'Oh, Bella?' he called after me, his voice more even. He leaned toward the open window with a faint smile on his lips. 'Yes?' 'Tomorrow it's my turn'" (*Twilight*, p 197). Both Bella and Edward are inquisitive, smart, and strategic players. At other times, the mental chess Bella and Edward play highlight their strong wills. With dialogue such as: "' I'm not negotiating this, Bella.' 'Neither am I'" – this clearly suggests a stalemate (*Eclipse*, p 127).

As the relationship between Bella and Edward deepens, the choices they have to make get bigger and more serious. In *Eclipse*, for example, Bella gives Edward a choice. Either Edward does not fight the newborns, or else Bella fights with them. "Either way, as long as we're together" (*Eclipse*, p 374). Choices have consequences that impact on others. And like chess, the best choices are those that plan several steps ahead or consider several different scenarios. Bella has chosen to be with Edward as a vampire (*Eclipse*, p 386). As a result, the whole Cullen family and the wolves are fighting Victoria's army of newborn vampires to protect Bella. In *Breaking Dawn*, close teamwork of the Cullens, the wolves and their allies lead to more complex chess-like planning strategies – such as discussing Jane's vampire gift (to impose pain on others) and the ability of her twin brother Alec (to numb the senses of many people simultaneously). So what's the game plan? Best to kill Alec first (as he can overpower many), then Jane (who can only incapacitate one person at a time) (*Breaking Dawn*, p 535). Chess is a war game, as life can be a battle sometimes.

Jacob's Choice

When Jacob chooses not to kill Bella, the wolf pack drives him away. Jacob's choice has created a crisis and a chance for change. As Jacob explains: *"I won't follow you, Sam. Not for something so wrong"* (*Breaking Dawn*, p 193). This crucial *Twilight* adventure shows that choice means freedom, but it also means taking responsibility because of consequences. As Jacob's confrontation with Sam demonstrates, important choices can isolate you, and even good choices can produce enemies. Jacob becomes "homeless" and needs to wear clothes offered by the Cullens (*Breaking Dawn*, p 247). But Jacob's choice was worth it for the greater good. His choice changes the course of destiny and makes the *Twilight* world a better place because everyone on the good side bands together to beat the Volturi.

The Cinema Scene

Everyone wants to be happy. Fortunately, psychology research shows that happiness is largely determined by choice. You can't choose many things that happen but you can choose your reaction to those things. Sometimes, happiness-boosting ideas hide in the weirdest places, like inside the movie theatre at Port Angeles. In *New Moon*, Bella, Jacob and Mike go to the cinema to watch the zombie movie *Crosshairs*.

This *New Moon* choice scene reveals three different interpretations about the same movie situation. Mike – is a pessimist who has a negative view: "his face stiff as he glared" at the screen (*New Moon*, p 209). As a result, Mike does not enjoy himself at the cinema. Jacob – well, he sees the funny side of the movie. For example, how "the blood squirted twenty feet" and how "fake" the horror looks (*New Moon*, p 210). His light-hearted approach helps him to enjoy the movie so he has a good time. Bella – views the movie in a neutral and abstract way, just watching the "colors and the movement on the screen" (*New Moon*, p 209). But Bella is open-minded and willing to *flex* her interpretation to watch the movie from Jacob's angle. This helps Bella to "laugh", enjoy herself more, and see the positive and funny side of the film too. Same situation, three different people, three different reactions. And it all depends on how you choose to look at it. This unique little 'Meyer movie metaphor' shows that choices have emotional consequences. You can't choose the way the movie unfolds, but, depending on how you look at it, you can influence how much you enjoy yourself in a social situation. The best news of all is that everyone can learn skills to develop a positive and optimistic attitude, like Jacob's, and weaken negative thinking styles that strengthen feelings of depression, anxiety, anger and other mood states. We all have the choice to shape our life experiences.

Circle

> The whole universe is based on rhythms. Everything happens in circles, in spirals.
> – John Hartford, American folk musician

The circle is an important shape that seems to appear in *Twilight Saga* adventures where its symbolic meaning truly counts. Why is the circle so special? What does it mean? Ancient people once believed that the earth was flat, a land suspended inside a circle, a great celestial globe. The oldest known circles in nature are the sun and moon. Since the sun, moon, stars and planets follow circular paths in the sky and days, nights and seasons rotate after each other, the circle came to symbolize the world, celestial forces, the everlasting spirit, and the mighty cosmos itself. As such, the circle acquired the most protective, magical and sacred meanings because being 'inside the circle' meant being inside life, being part of the world. The world was also considered to be the center of the universe, around which the planets, elements and celestial forces circled or revolved. This is why ancient leaders and chieftains, such as Billy Black the Quileute chief in the *Twilight* books, were considered to be the center of the community.

The circle is a powerful architectural pattern. A strong and protective structure, a circular igloo or a round lighthouse can withstand freezing blizzards and raging storms. As an unbroken line, the circle suggests spiritual strength – no start, no end, just an eternal flow. This is why circles are used in magic. In spell casting "the magic circle creates a fortress of psychic protection, a physical and spiritual safe haven where unwanted or uninvited entities cannot enter" (Nozedar, 2008, p 4).

As a symbol, the circle suggests a number of important ideas which the world of *Twilight* embraces. These include:

Inclusion
Unity
Nurturing
Safety
Wholeness
Completion

RevolutionInfinity
Eternity

Important circles that appear in the *Twilight* world are deep and diverse.

The Meadow

A sacred, secret, and perfect circle in the *Twilight Saga* is the meadow where Bella and Edward spend intimate time together, share feelings, and reveal secrets. In the *Twilight* world, "the meadow was small, perfectly round" (*Twilight*, p 227). This shape of this meadow must be symbolically significant because the subsequent novel highlights it again. The meadow was "perfectly round as if someone had intentionally created the flawless circle… beautiful and serene" (*New Moon*, p 234).

Why would Bella and Edward's special meadow be a circle? The couple feel safe and comfortable there, which reflects traditional symbolic meanings that a circle is magical and protective. Inside the circle of the meadow (inside this sacred symbolic place), Bella and Edward can nurture each other and feel complete. As social outsiders who have kept to themselves until meeting each other, Bella and Edward would feel a sense of belonging, symbolized by the enclosure of their grassy circle. Most importantly, Bella and Edward declare their everlasting love for each other, which ties in perfectly with the idea that a circle is a continuous, endless and eternal shape.

The Bracelet

At Alice's graduation party, Jacob gives Bella a special gift – a bracelet. It is a "silver bracelet" with a hand-made "tiny wooden carving" of a "miniature wolf" made from "red-brown" wood (*Eclipse*, p 332). As a circle shape, the bracelet surrounds Bella's wrist. Of course, this pretty bracelet is packed with symbolic meanings.

This bracelet (which forms a circle when it fits around Bella's wrist) symbolizes a circle of friendship – an eternal and unbreakable bond between Bella and Jacob. It is a circle (eternity), hand-made (a sentimental non-material gift), has a wolf charm (symbol of loyalty) that is made of red-brown wood (the color of Jacob's skin). Wood also suggests earthly values and closeness to nature. As such, this bracelet suggests that Jacob has endless ability and enthusiasm to love others and appreciate nature, just as a circle is a constant and unending line.

The Ring

Another important circle in the *Twilight Saga* is Bella's engagement ring. Edward gives Bella a beautiful ring that once belonged to his mother. It "sparkled in the dim light. The face was long and oval, set with slanting rows of glittering round stones. The band was gold – delicate and narrow" (*Eclipse*, p 406). Needless to say, a circle-shaped ring is a traditional symbol of eternal love. It suggests a powerful emotional bond that can never be broken.

The Locket

As the *Breaking Dawn* battle scene draws near, Bella buys Renesmee a gift from an antique store. It was a "little golden locket... It was round with a slender vine border carved around the outside edge of the circle" (*Breaking Dawn*, p 604). Inside the locket was some space for a small picture.

Indeed, a circle-shaped locket is a symbolically meaningful item within which to put one's love for safekeeping. The triple symbolism of the locket makes it an especially powerful, magical, and spiritual amulet. The locket is 1) gold (which suggests positive power); 2) it is etched with vine leaves (which suggests inter-woven links, nature's cycle, evergreen plants); and 3) the locket is a circle shape (which suggests inclusion, protection and eternity).

The Shield

The psychic shield Bella uses to protect others is another powerful circle in the *Twilight Saga*. This all-powerful circle-shaped shield surrounds and protects the entire "good side" against the destructive power of the Volturi vampires. In *Breaking Dawn,* Bella projects her supernatural shield. "I inspected my shield; it felt just as impenetrable as before. I flexed it now into a low, wide dome that arced over our company" (p 652). Since Bella's shield is a circle that protects others, it matches the magical and protective meanings of circles perfectly.

Social Circles

Social circles include family, friendship, and community circles. And the *Twilight Saga* mentions a few of them. The first *indirect* circle ever mentioned in the *Twilight Saga* (indirectly) is extremely well hidden. It is a *secret social circle* that you can see more clearly when you visualize Venn diagrams. When Bella first meets Edward at Forks High School and ponders his beauty, she considers her life and his life to be worlds apart: "I pictured his perfect face. I was well aware that my league and his league were spheres that did not touch" (*Twilight,* p 46). Two separate spheres of life. Two unlinked circles. Two separate circles, not intersecting or overlapping each other as if drawn as a mathematical Venn diagram.

The first circle *directly* mentioned in the *Twilight Saga* happens to be a social circle also. It is the "driftwood circle" at La Push (*Twilight,* p 101). Bella first meets Jacob here (*Twilight,* p 102). In a later scene at a Quileute bonfire, Bella hears the story about the Third Wife's Sacrifice. Here, everyone is sitting in a "circle" around the bonfire (*Eclipse,* p 214)

Edward's supportive and romantic body language tends to be circular, which matches the protective and nurturing meanings of circles. For example: "His arms encircled me" (*Eclipse,* p 165). In other scenes: "Edward's arms wound around me" (*Twilight,* p

429) and "Edward pulled me into the circle of his arm" (*Eclipse*, p 233). These repeating gestures fit with the nurturing and protective meanings of the circle.

Edward also refers to social circles when he says, "we've come full circle" (*Twilight*, p 298). In this scene, Edward tells Bella the background story to Carlisle's life and how Carlisle changed Edward into a vampire when he was on the verge of death from Spanish influenza.

In fact, family circles are an especially important theme in the *Twilight Saga*. A variety of family circles are referred to:

- Bella and her parents
- Edward and the Cullens, none of whom are biologically related
- Jacob and his father Billy Black
- The Uleys
- The Clearwaters
- Various vampire covens such as the Denali

Bella is accepted as being part of the Cullen family circle from the start. In *Twilight*, Carlisle gestures to his foster family and Bella and says, "This is my family" (p 329). When Bella and Edward fall in love with each other, and marry, they complete a circle – two soul mates, two halves of a circle, merge as one. Bella and Edward are now joined for eternity (a circle) and Bella formally completes the Cullen family circle too. With the birth of Renesmee, a new family circle is formed (Bella, Edward, Renesmee), embraced and encompassed by the larger Cullen family circle.

Much later, when Jacob imprints on Nessie, the Quileute community is drawn in to the Cullens' social circle. The wolf pack suggests social circles interlinked with other social circles. So we get interlocking circles and circles that nest inside each other. When Bella is transformed, the circle of her shield protects all the family circles, from the small nuclear family circle that comprises Renesmee to the wider social spheres of vampires and werewolves. The circles within circles become complete. The Battle Circle

While the Volturi form an angular or triangular shape, spreading out like a dark fan, the Cullens' side looks more circular and embraces protective circle shapes:

The Bella Circle – during the Volturi battle in *Breaking Dawn*, in the very center of all the circles, you have the innermost circle. The three key positions within it are: Bella, Edward, and Renesmee (who sits astride Jacob). Symbolically speaking, three points (when joined by imaginary arcs) make up a circle. Being the most deeply embedded circle, Bella's position is symbolical and central. Not only is she the 'center' of all the action and a 'womb' that has given birth to a new species (Renesmee, a vampire-human hybrid), she is also the centralized starting point of a new future (TwilightMOMS post, Ava1989, December 30, 2009).

The Cullen Circle – Bella's inner circle is enclosed by the Cullen family circle who "surround" Bella with their love, support, and a desire to fight for freedom. It may be worth noting that Jasper is part of this protective Cullen circle too and that in Egypt it was believed that magic rings of jasper could be worn for success in battle.

The Werewolf/Witness Circle – At the battle, the Cullen circle is enclosed by another wider circle, which comprises werewolves and witnesses, all standing unified against the Volturi. In previous adventures, when wolves met up with each other, they assembled together in a circle (*Breaking Dawn*, p 147). Other creatures form circles in nature too, such as rabbits and hares. This linked the power and magic of the circle to nature and to certain animals.

The Round Shield – from the center of these three circles the outermost circle of all is projected – Bella's supernatural shield. When everyone faces the Volturi at the *Breaking Dawn* battle, they would appear, from above, as being arranged in a pattern of *four concentric circles*. That is, circles within circles. The TwilightMOMS post by Ava1981 (2009) is to be credited for sharing this insightful observation.

In stark contrast to the cohesive Cullen-related circles, the Volturi's solid black form ends up being a broken circle. They and their witnesses are unable to stand unified and their circle is broken, leaving them weak.

Cliffs

Tall, rocky, windy and barren, cliffs are striking symbols. Cliffs are often associated with negative ideas – risk, fear, danger, and death. But cliffs suggest positive ideas too – opportunity, excitement, challenge, and vitality. Some of the most fabulous creatures from myth have perched themselves high on cliff tops, guarding secrets, knowledge, and magic. Symbolically speaking, to stand on top of a cliff means a chance to 'leap' into life, be on the 'edge' of discovery, on the 'cusp' of change, on the 'threshold' of a new experience. Positive or negative, the meaning of cliffs is always exhilarating, never boring.

Staggering rocky cliffs by the sea appear in several scenes in the *Twilight Saga*. In *New Moon*, Bella sees four Quileute boys cliff diving the very first time she visits the cliffs, south of La Push, when Jacob takes Bella motorbiking near there (*New Moon*, p 170). Since cliffs symbolize risk, it is a symbolically suitable spot to ride motorbikes – itself a risky activity. After Bella watches the teenage boys jump off the cliffs into the sea, Jacob says that he has done cliff diving himself. He describes the experience "a little scary, kind of a rush" (*New Moon*, p 171). As you can see, it's pretty hard for cliffs to be dreary and boring. It is no wonder

Bella goes cliff diving herself.

One of Bella's wildest experiences in the *Twilight Saga* is the cliff dive in *New Moon*. Standing on top of the tall rocky cliffs at the "half-moon" point of the beach (*New Moon*, pp 351–352), this scene also symbolizes the idea that Bella is at a brink or 'halfway' point in her decision-making process. She is at a point at which her choice will either fall one way, or the other. In that scene, Bella looks for the path that will leads her "out on the ledge" of the high, rocky cliffs (*New Moon*, p 357). In other words, Bella wants to choose a path in life – and the cliffs symbolize making a choice.

In *New Moon*, "the cliffs were a black knife edge against the livid sky" (p 356). Here, the cliffs seem to split the sky into two, like a black weapon. All that worrying has lead to a sharp and clear decision point that will split into two possible fates. Standing on top of the cliffs reminds Bella about the idea that cliff diving is an experience that could make her feel free. A moment of danger would surely trigger Edward's voice inside Bella's mind, another idea that makes her feelings flare with excitement. On the edge of the cliffs, Bella is symbolically on the brink of making a decision (whether to jump or not, whether to choose Edward or not).

- She is out on the edge
- She is reaching out for something
- She is stretching her mind for a solution
- She is on the cusp of something
- She is at the point of change
- She is about to fall, she is on the 'brink' of making a decision
- As Bella hangs off the cliff's edge, this scene is an emotional cliff-hanger

Standing on a cliff top might give Bella a great sea view, but it also symbolizes a choice that will move her towards one destiny or the other. So when Bella's toes hug "the edge of the rock" at the cliff's edge (*New Moon*, p 358), symbolically Bella is teetering on the edge of an important decision-making moment. The moment Bella definitely decides to leap off the cliff, that's the moment when she also decides that Edward really loves her: "Edward's voice is only seconds away" (*New Moon*, p 358). Bella flings herself off the cliff, screaming and spinning as she falls down, her body finally cutting into the icy cold water. While Bella's big leap off the ledge might look like stupid and reckless teenage behavior on the surface, this cliff adventure symbolizes Bella's choice – she chooses to be with Edward.

Another cliff adventure in *Eclipse* also captures the idea that cliff jumping symbolizes choice making. Bella thinks about becoming a vampire. As Bella considers the possibility of losing all her human connections, she panics. While Bella is contemplating her choice to "trade mortality for immortality", she thinks about her big decision in cliff-like ways: "The future beyond that was a big, dark abyss that I couldn't know until I leaped into it" (*Eclipse*, p 239). Exactly! Making big choices in life is just like leaping off a big cliff. You don't always know how your choices will work out or where your decisions will take you. But for people who are brave and adventurous at heart, like Bella, this is precisely what makes decision-making so thrilling and invigorating.

Clouds

In the *Twilight Saga*, clouds help to give Forks and the forest a mysterious, menacing and melancholy atmosphere. But clouds also help to symbolize or foreshadow other things. In particular, Edward's presence. The *Twilight* vampires can only venture outside if the sky is cloudy. Their skin sparkles in the sunlight, which is harmful and dangerous because it exposes them as vampires. On sunny days, vampires must keep well away from humans.

Some important cloud-covered scenes in the *Twilight* world are these:

- On Bella's first day of school "the clouds were dense and opaque" (*Twilight*, p 25). This is also the day that Bella first encounters Edward, and becomes infatuated with him forever more.
- As soon as Bella meets Jacob at La Push Beach, the "clouds" advanced, creating "shadows across the beach", and blackening the waves (*Twilight*, p 102). The clouds eventually covered the whole sky, which caused "the sea to darken" and the "temperature" to drop (*Twilight*, p 105). It is as if Edward's presence is intensifying, trying to move in on Bella and Jacob's meeting. It is as if Edward is trying to cast a cloudy gloom over Jacob's sunny presence.
- When Bella looks out of her bedroom window, she sees "a thick, cottony layer of clouds veiled the sky" (*Twilight*, p 221). This means great Edward weather, a great time with Edward ahead.
- Edward picks Bella up for the afternoon school graduation ceremony. "Edward looked up at the clouds, his face thoughtful" (*Eclipse*, p 312). Another cloudy day, another big Edward occasion coming up.

Other cloudy *Twilight* adventures suggest deeper cloud meanings. What do clouds suggest? Symbol experts say that "a cloud is first of all something that conceals or obscures the daylight, darkening day and making night seem blacker" (Colin, 2000, p 103). It blots out the sun and moon that light up the sky, and darkens the earth below. When the sky is filled with heavy black clouds, this usually points to bad omens, threatening forces, and imminent danger. Angry gods are notorious for hurling thunder and lightning at people and releasing torrential rains from dark, heavy, menacing clouds. Of course, plump clouds also bring rain – helping plants to grow and animals to thrive, and bringing the land to life. On a lighter note, clouds can also suggest a fluffy substance or light process, something dreamy, ethereal or unreal, as in the phrase 'to have your head in the clouds'. Forks weather, however, tends to have heavier cloud cover. This may explain the lack of comical ambience and hilarious vampires frolicking about.

Since clouds, made from billions of water particles, float across the sky and change their shape and structure constantly, they are the supreme symbol of ambiguity. The ancient Celts loved using the changing and undefined state of clouds for divination to predict the future. Just like a veil, clouds obscure things from view, protect or block your vision, or make you oblivious to the cares of the world around you. An important scene from *Breaking Dawn* uses clouds to symbolize ambiguity and mystery. On the verge of the Volturi battle, the weather was very cloudy. The "clouds rolled in, diffusing the light so that it could have been morning or afternoon. Edward's eyes tightened as he scrutinized the view" (*Breaking Dawn*, pp 629–630). This thick cloud-cover suggests an unclear outcome and a "very gray" and vague future. Anything could happen in a fight with Volturi vampires.

Color

Colors are proven to have a profound effect on the human psyche and on our moods. They resonate with elements, directions, seasons, and the planets. The most prominent colors in the *Twilight Saga* appear to be: *Black, White, Red,* and *Gold*. These are the colors of alchemy, magic, and Slavic sorcery. Of course, the *Twilight* world has noteworthy streaks and splashes of other colors too.

Crescent

The crescent is a unique geometrical shape that is almost always linked to the moon. Whenever the moon is about to grow or disappear, it appears as a thin crescent in the sky. Since the crescent of the moon is visible at the start and the end of the lunar cycle, the crescent is linked to both life and death. In the *Twilight Saga*, the crescent is an important symbol of transformation that crops up in a range of places.

- Bella acquires a "crescent-shaped" scar on her hand from a vampire bite (*New Moon*, p 19).
- The lake near forks is a "crescent lake" (*New Moon*, p 257).
- Bella was "wandering the beach, pacing the length of the rocky crescent back and forth, again and again" (*New Moon*, p 350). As with the crescent moon, Bella's walk on a crescent-shaped beach symbolizes new beginnings and upcoming endings. Whatever choices Bella makes, her life will develop and unfold, wax and wane – just like the moon that starts and ends as a crescent – in the direction of her choices.
- First Beach, where Bella spends time with Jacob (but not Edward) is a "crescent" shape (*Eclipse*, p 234).
- When Edward removes Bella's baby from her body, the baby leaves a "tiny double- crescent bite mark just over her left breast" (*Breaking Dawn*, p 324). So Bella receives a crescent-shaped bite mark during the birth process. Get it? Crescents – mean birth. Renesmee – is born. *And* Bella is about to be reborn as a vampire. The crescent bite occurred over Bella's heart too, which may be a hint to Bella's love for her vampire partner and half-vampire daughter. Symbolic or what?

A crescent is not a full circle. This symbolizes the love between

Jacob and Bella, which will never be fully realized. Since Bella and Jacob spend a lot of time together on a crescent-shaped beach, this may be symbolic tip that Bella and Jacob's relationship will never be 'fully' romantic, like a full moon. Rather, their romance is 'cut short'. In fact, the scythe and sickle (a small scythe) are agricultural tools with crescent-shaped blades that are used to cut down ripe harvest. The most famous scythe, a symbol of death, belongs to the Grim Reaper. Hooded and cloaked, this sinister black figure swings the scythe in his bony hands to reap his harvest of souls. The 13th card in the Major Arcana of the tarot shows a grisly image of a skeleton holding a scythe, standing in a field littered with skulls. Macabre! But don't be too terrified. Encountering scythe symbols or dreaming about death does not always mean that someone will die. Death can symbolize a sudden, significant or radical change in one's life. Is that typical of life or what? In Bella's case, the death of a romantic future with Jacob must occur (cut off by a crescent-shaped scythe) if a loving relationship with Edward is to be fully realized. A symbolic death is necessary in one place so that Bella can achieve personal development elsewhere. A sickle always points to the idea that "we reap what we sow and that, depending on the nature of our actions, the harvest will be either good or bad" (Colin, 2000, p 456).

Cross

The most obvious cross to appear in the *Twilight Saga* is Carlisle's cross that hangs on the wall inside the Cullen house. At the top of the stairs at the end of the hall hung "a large wooden cross… early sixteen thirties" that once "belonged to Carlisle's father" (*Twilight*, p 288). Carlisle's father was a 17th Century pastor who led a brutal campaign to hunt and kill witches, werewolves, vampires and people of Catholic faith. He led hunts for all of these creatures, as did his son. So why does Carlisle decorate the wall outside his office with a 370 year old cross? It probably inspires Carlisle to achieve higher spiritual power. Maybe it motivates Carlisle to resist his urge to kill others, the way his bitter father did. Certainly, Carlisle's cross helps to remind Carlisle that not all bad myths about vampires are true. Crosses don't hurt *Twilight*-style vampires. This means not all vampires must necessarily be evil creatures. In this sense, Carlisle's cross symbolizes hope.

Carlisle's use of the cross to inspire himself spiritually certainly fits with some of the earliest meanings of the cross. The cross is one of humanity's most beautiful and ancient symbols. It symbolizes the union between heaven and earth, between two opposite forces (represented by the vertical line crisscrossing the horizontal line). The line that links north and south represents the tree of life, while the east to west line symbolizes the horizon. The cross shape was one of the first popular magical and mystical signs used by people, long before it was used by Christians. The oldest cross comes from Crete and dates back further than fifteen centuries BC. This ancient symbol has many meanings. For example, it symbolizes the union of material and spiritual. As a geometric tool, a cross inside a circle divides a circle into four equal parts. Having four cardinal points, the cross represents the elements (fire, air, earth, water) and the directions (north, east, south, west). All over the world, the cross is a symbol of protection (Colin, 2000).

The cross is also the crossing of paths, a point of convergence, a meeting point, a crossroad is where four roads meet and, as such, a crossroad is a magical place, a crossing place, a doorway and a threshold. The Greek goddess Hecate, who had the power to grant wishes and satisfy the desires of those who believed in her – was worshipped at crossroads, which are regarded as magical places.

Cullens

The Cullens may be "pale", "chalky", have "purplish" shadows under their eyes and be social "outsiders" (*Twilight*, pp 16, 19). Nevertheless, you can't always judge vampires by their cover… of darkness. You see, the Cullens are a friendly bunch of vampires and more. Good, vegetarian, ethical, and industrious, each Cullen character has special symbolic qualities that make him or her extra interesting.

Edward

Edward Cullen is a protagonist vampire who falls in love with the story's narrator, Bella. While Bella describes Edward as an angel, he also has a dark side. In the beginning, Edward warns Bella that he may be dangerous: "What if I'm not a superhero? What if I'm the bad guy?" (*Twilight*, p 79). Although Bella thinks Edward could be "dangerous", she does not believe he is "bad" (*Twilight*, p 80). Much of the *Twilight Saga's* tension is the result of Edward being a vampire. By nature, he hunts people and drinks human blood. However, Edward is fascinated by Bella and falls madly in love with her. Even though Edward craves Bella's blood and it tortures him, he admits that he could not live with himself if he ever hurt her.

Edward's allure is probably due to many different factors. As a character, Edward is super-strong, polite, attractive and talented (this stimulates reader affinity), mysterious (this stimulates reader curiosity), and moody on the outside but hurt on the inside (this attracts reader sympathy). This certainly suggests a Byronic Hero, a compelling character type who is lonely or in great inner pain somehow. Examples of Byronic heroes from literature similar to Edward include:

- Edward Rochester from *Jane Eyre*. This Edward is a bossy, jealous intimidating man whom the character Jane, a young governess, falls in love with. This Edward also falls in love with Jane even though he is married and keeps his mad wife locked up in the attic. Alas, it's hard to resist love when you've been lonely for so long.

- Heathcliff from *Wuthering Heights* is an angry, aggressive young man raised in the same household as his true love Catherine. She is the only person who can bring out his humanity. When she chooses to marry another man for money and social status, Heathcliff becomes jealous and does his best to get revenge.
- The beast from the fairy tale *Beauty and the Beast* is a terrifying monster. Yet, a young woman named Belle falls in love with him, and her love breaks a curse that transforms him back into a human.
- In William Shakespeare's *Romeo and Juliet,* both young lovers must die in order to be together.

Psychologically speaking, perhaps people are infatuated with Byronic heroes because the human mind is geared to notice incongruent information. The mind is compelled to figure things out like:

- How can two ill-fated lovers live happy ever after?
- How can we soften rough and gruff characters?
- How can we make opposites coexist together in peace?
- How can this problem be solved?

In addition to being a *Byronic Hero,* the *Twilight* books relate Edward to heroes from Greek myth. For example, Bella considers that Edward makes a "Herculean effort" to control his thirst for her blood (*Eclipse,* p 15). This suggests that Edward is a hero, just like Hercules. As for Edward's physical appearance, he is likened to the Greek figure Adonis (*Twilight,* p 277). Edward is also linked to angels – good spiritual creatures. Bella thinks Edward looks like an angel and describes him as her "destroying angel" when he rescues her from a car crash. Edward also makes a flashy, silver angel's entry at Port Angeles to rescue Bella from four thugs (*Twilight*, p 140). Edward's symbolic heroic features surely make him a mighty and memorable character.

Carlisle

In the *Twilight Saga*, Carlisle is a handsome, charming, intelligent, and conscientious character. Not only is he the patriarch of the Cullen clan, he is a medical doctor, a humanitarian, and pioneer of the vegetarian vampire diet.

Born in the 17th century, Carlisle was the son of a zealous witch-hunter and vampire-killer. While helping his father, a vampire bit Carlisle – and Carlisle himself turned into a vampire. Horrified at what he had become, he tried for years to kill himself, but nothing seemed to harm him. Eventually, Carlisle found peace when he figured out he could survive on animal blood. He travelled to America to start a new life.

Just as Carlisle has rules about his diet, he also has a set of rules regarding creating new vampires: he will only transform people who are about to die and have no other option. When the human Edward was about to die of Spanish influenza, Carlisle bit Edward and transformed him.

Carlisle is linked to a number of fascinating mythical and literary figures which may help to explain his charismatic character.

Zeus – is the principal god of the Greek pantheon, ruler of the heavens, the father of gods and mortal heroes, and the supreme ruler of Mount Olympus. As the god of the sky and weather, the ancient Greeks gave Zeus many titles such as Lord of the Sky, the Cloud-gatherer, the Rain-god and Zeus the Thunderer, all of which suggest power over nature. Zeus is more powerful than any other god or even all the other gods combined. As a ruling god, Zeus was usually associated with mighty symbols such as sun, the eagle, the bull and the oak tree. Zeus was noble, glorious, awesome and wise, and he did not participate in daily arguments and petty schemes of other gods. Zeus also protected political order and peace. His breastplate was so glorious that no human could see Zeus in all his splendor and survive. His weapon is, of course, the thunderbolt which he hurled at whoever displeased him. Although Zeus was a great ruler, he had his personal weaknesses. Others could oppose, deceive or trick Zeus. He could not control the Fates or Destiny. And he could feel pleasure, pain, anger, grief and love. Zeus was anything but a faithful husband to his wife Hera and had countless love affairs with other women (Zeus Publications, 2011).

In the same way as Zeus, Carlisle is the head of the Cullen family, father to five fostered children, and is one of seven wonderful vampires. Carlisle is noble and wise, avoids petty quarrels, protects mortals, and is a medical doctor who devotes his life to saving human lives. Just like Zeus, Carlisle is a powerful vampire with superhuman strength and a great capacity to love. But Carlisle is not impervious to painful emotional experiences. Unlike Zeus, however, Carlisle is a loyal and loving husband.

Prometheus – Carlisle resembles the mythical Greek character Prometheus too. Prometheus was a Titan who, at Zeus' request, created mankind from clay. Prometheus grew very fond of humans, just as Carlisle has done. Since the world was cold and dark at that time, Prometheus stole fire from the gods on Mount Olympus and gave it to humans. As punishment, Zeus tied him to a rock and every day an eagle (or vulture) would attack him and eat his liver. The liver would grow back every night and the torture was repeated. Just like Prometheus, Carlisle has chosen to help humans in his role as a medical doctor. His gift to people is health, rather than fire. Just as Prometheus endured daily physical pain from the eagle/vulture, Carlisle endures the smell of human blood every day and must remain constantly vigilant in case the Volturi ever choose to attack the Cullen clan. Both Prometheus and Carlisle face great hardships as a result of their desire to help and better humans. Both Prometheus and Carlisle have committed selfless acts, trying to help humanity. In the Greek myth, birds of prey attack the liver and the liver's main role is to make food useful to the human body. In the same way, Carlisle transforms his new vampire existence into a productive and useful life by helping humans, promoting a vegetarian diet, and building a social and cooperative family (TwilightMOMS post, perkysue 2010).

Frankenstein – Both Dr. Carlisle Cullen and Dr. Victor Frankenstein from Mary Shelley's *Frankenstein* create 'monsters', but they differ in the way they treat their creations. Dr. Frankenstein is horrified by the monster he's made and he rejects it. Carlisle, on the other hand, treats his creations as family. In fact, Edward reveals it is unethical to abandon a vampire you have created. Dr. Frankenstein abandoned his monster and rejected him emotionally, and the monster did become a 'total savage'. In complete contrast, Carlisle would never dream of abandoning his beautiful wife Esme and his much-loved foster children.

Esme

Esme is Carlisle's wife and the mother figure of the Cullen family. Esme describes herself as having strong "mothering instincts" (*Twilight*, p 321). She joined the family after she jumped off a cliff to attempt suicide. Despite tragedy in her human life (losing a baby), Esme presents as a calm, kind, caring and loving foster mother and a generous and considerate host who opens her heart and home to the vulnerable and anyone who needs it. She excels at providing a warm family atmosphere and has other people's interests at heart. Esme, the vampire mother hen, who stuck a pillow under Jacob Black's head to make him more comfortable in *Breaking Dawn*, has other important roles too. She referees baseball games and sibling quarrels. She therefore has a judicial role. Esme is also artistic. She decorated Bella and Edward's stone cottage in *Breaking Dawn*.

With her maternal instincts and as second in charge of the Cullen family, Esme may resemble Hera in Greek myth, the wife of Zeus. Hera was a very beautiful Greek goddess and was one of three contestants in the beauty contest which led to the Trojan War. In the same way as Esme is a gracious and noble mother, Hera was the goddess of marriage, guarded married women, and was a noble and gracious protector of heroes. Exactly like Esme, one of Hera's most outstanding qualities is emotional empathy. When Zeus changed himself into an injured bird to lure Hera to him, she felt sorry for it and held it to her breast to warm it. Hera's chariot, throne and shoes were made of pure gold (Zeus Publications, 2011). It may therefore make sound symbolic sense for Esme to have beautiful golden-yellow eyes.

Alice

Alice is Edward's adoptive sister and is very supportive of Edward's relationship with Bella. This is probably because Alice knows how lonely he has been and how well things will work out, given her gift of seeing the future. When Bella sees Alice for the first time, she describes her as "pixie-like", "thin" and as having "wild, pointy black hair (*Twilight*, p 16). As a small-framed individual, Alice tends to skip, hop and dance around like a happy sprite or some small agile animal.

Unlike other Cullens, Alice does not remember her human life at all. She finds out that she suffered as a human child because she was abandoned by her parents, locked up in an asylum and given shock treatments because of her "visions". Alice was the only human who did not get caught by James, an evil vampire. An old vampire transformed Alice into a vampire to keep her safe, but James killed him, leaving Alice to learn about vampire life alone. The Cullens met Alice after she was transformed into a vampire. Alice was unique in that she developed a strong sense of morality on her own. Despite having no guidance, Alice decided not to hunt humans. As a vampire, Alice has a special power: she can see the future. But as soon as someone's plans change, so does her vision of the future.

Despite her tragic past, Alice has an extremely happy nature. The Enneagram, a personality model, may help to explain this important tendency. According to the Enneagram, people have one of nine personality types. Everyone is born with a dominant type. This determines how people develop and adapt to their world from early childhood. While everyone may have some qualities from all nine types, one personality style will stand out as your main personality. Very briefly, the basic personality types are:

Type One – controlled, perfectionistic
Type Two – demonstrative, people-pleasing
Type Three – adaptable, ambitious
Type Four – dramatic, self-absorbed
Type Five – innovative, secretive
Type Six – responsible, anxious
Type Seven – spontaneous, versatile
Type Eight – willful, confrontational
Type Nine – receptive, relaxed
(Enneagram Institute, 1998–2011)

Alice appears to have a Type Seven personality –happy and cheerful. This personality type often develops in people who have suffered great emotional deprivation and despair. To minimize suffering and pain, people become pleasure-seeking 'enthusiasts' who hope to experience as much happiness as possible and take care of others to compensate for insufficient pleasure in their own past (Enneagram Institute). Strong evidence of Alice's enthusiastic Enneagram profile is, for example, that:

- Alice bonds with Jasper, a wounded war veteran
- Alice treats Bella like a sister straight away.
- Alice tries to make Bella look beautiful by dressing Bella in stylish clothes
- Alice puts on parties to make everyone happy

Alice Cullen's perpetual optimism, desire to have fun, and bright, warm, and supportive presence makes her a strong symbol of happiness.

Jasper

Jasper, just like the semi-precious stone jasper, is definitely a family treasure. He is Alice's loving partner and the family's military strategist. Jasper's supernatural gift is the ability to manipulate mood and "control the emotional atmosphere" around him (*Eclipse*, p 263). He can soothe and settle emotional tension and help others to feel calm and relaxed. Jasper certainly has a conscience as he developed a vegetarian feeing style all by himself before joining the Cullens. In fact, Jasper is still mastering his self-control around human blood, which isn't easy for him at times. Due to his extensive military experience, training and fighting newborn vampires, these aspects of Jasper's character may symbolize Mars, the Roman God of War. However, since Jasper prefers peace to war and to soothe conflict rather than cause it, his character suggests more of a 'helper' archetype.

Rosalie

Rosalie is a member of the Cullen clan, and Edward's adoptive sister. According to Bella, Rosalie is a golden-haired beauty who should grace the cover of magazines (*Twilight*, p 16). Though Carlisle originally intended for Rosalie to be Edward's companion, neither were romantically interested in each other. Rosalie found Emmett in a forest and bonded with him. Every couple of years Rosalie and Emmett go on holiday and celebrate their marriage. Towards Bella, however, Rosalie was cold, distant and unfriendly at first until Bella saved Edward from committing suicide. Later, Rosalie became Bella's best ally and "tenacious" to a "T". She provided a gutsy patrol of Charlie's house in *Eclipse,* to make sure no harm came to Bella from enemy vampires. And in *Breaking Dawn* Rosalie became a resolute and determined protector of Bella and her unborn child. A rose is a good visual way to describe Rosalie –beautiful, but thorny.

Emmett

Emmett is the most recent addition to the Cullen clan. Physically, he is the biggest and strongest vampire. In fact, Bella describes him as "big – muscled like a serious weight lifter" (*Twilight,* p 16). Emmett joined the Cullen family after Rosalie rescued him in the forest. He had been mauled by a bear, was badly wounded and almost dead. Rosalie carried Emmett to Carlisle to change him into a vampire. Emmett then became romantically involved with Rosalie. In general, Emmett enjoys a good challenge. He likes to hunt bears, fight evil vampires, arm wrestle Bella and, above all, tease Bella with his cheeky attitude. In the Cullen family, Emmett symbolizes strength and confidence.

D

Dance

> When the music started, Edward pulled me into his arms for the customary first dance.
> (*Breaking Dawn*, p 51)

At the heights of happiness on Bella and Edward's wedding day, a dancing scene enhances the joyous mood of this lovely moment.

The *Twilight* books introduce readers to a number of dance themes and scenes. For example:

- When Bella was a young child, she learned ballet.
- Bella doesn't like going to proms, parties and dances.
- Immersed in a private dance with Edward in *Twilight* at a school prom, Bella finds the experience pleasant, relaxing and "effortless", after all (*Twilight*, p 425).
- Alice, the tiniest vampire in the Cullen family, moves so gracefully, it looks as if she is dancing on air all the time.

The wedding waltz in *Breaking Dawn* is one of the most important romantic scenes of all. This scene clearly shows that dance produces feelings of joy and dispels fear and worry. In fact, as a type of behavior therapy, psychology research shows that dancing is one of the most powerful happiness-boosters of all, more effective than the gym, walking or sport (Hanna, 1995; Koch, Morlinghaus and Fuchs, 2007; Sandel, Judge, Landry, Faria, Ouellette and Majczak, 2005). The power of dance appears in courtship rituals in the animal kingdom and throughout all stages of human history, in every culture around the world.

As a form of wordless communication, dance is a powerful

symbol. Since dance involves body movements, graceful gestures, rules, rhythms, and behavior patterns, dance is a dynamic non-verbal language. In ancient times, people danced to copy, follow and bond with nature. Dancers would imitate the forms and movements of the earth, sun, moon, stars, mountains, valleys, rivers, oceans, trees, flowers, animals and more. By bringing people together in spirit and by expressing emotions, dance became a very special and sacred practice. To this day, many Indigenous cultures dance to invoke rain, healing, fertility and to tap into the magic and power of nature.

As the *Twilight* school dance and the *Breaking Dawn* wedding dance help to show, dancing is a joyous and uplifting metaphor. Dance is a happy activity that celebrates life, expresses feelings, and symbolizes the rhythm of nature. Consider the motion of windy eddies, spiraling smoke, watery whirlpools, twisting tornados, spinning planets and the great swirling galaxies in space. Wheeling waltzes, Polish polkas, whirling dervishes, wild Ukrainian Cossack dance, not to mention the technical twirling of today's rap dancing, can produce strong feelings of excitement and ecstasy. The rhythm and repetition of dancing allows dancers to forget themselves, merge with the music, and disappear into a state of trance.

While dancing seems to suggest complete spontaneity and abandonment, good dancing involves a great deal of effort, skill, technique-tuning, discipline, and practice. This important dance issue is definitely suggested in the *Twilight Saga*. During her entire human life, Bella has always thought of herself as a graceless klutz. Once Bella changes into a vampire, she is surprised to find that she moves easily, effortlessly, and elegantly in *Breaking Dawn*. However, all those years of ballet practice combined with the joy she feels about her shiny new life is probably helping Bella to be an authentic dance diva, much more graceful than even the Cullens expected, even if Bella is not fully aware of it herself.

Darkness

"I like the night. Without the dark, we'd never see the stars." (*Twilight*, p 204)

Many people are afraid of the dark and often associate darkness with bad and evil things. As a symbol, darkness also stands for mystery, the mind, and the unknown. Somewhere in our inner darkness, people possess personal powers that can shed bright light on all important matters. The only way to find the light is to face the darkness.

In the *Twilight Saga*, darkness occurs in a number of adventures:

- The sea (e.g. *Twilight*, p 102)
- The forest (e.g. *Twilight*, p 121; *Eclipse*, p 160)
- In Bella's dreams (e.g. *Twilight*, p 58)

Bella's very first dream about Edward, for example, is "very dark" (*Twilight*, p 58). But this dream is not a scary one. As such, Bella's dark dream can mean various things – feeling baffled, an unknowable adventure, an uncertain future at this time, unseen possibilities, or some unresolved conflict about Edward deep in Bella's mind.

Darkness and shadows are inextricably linked. And shadows are associated with "all that is hidden, dark, mysterious or gloomy" (Colin, 2000, p 451). For example, the only reason why the waves "blackened" on the choppy surface of the sea at La Push was because advancing clouds had "cast long shadows across the beach" (*Twilight*, p 102). A Latin phrase *In tenebris lucidior* means 'The brightest in darkness'. This suggests that darkness reveals the light. Dark and difficult times compel people to see bright ideas and brilliant solutions, which can surely help Bella and her friends to succeed.

See also *Forests*.

Dawn

In the last book of the *Twilight Saga, Breaking Dawn*, Bella finally becomes a vampire. She breaks free from human misery and breaks through to an inner dawn. Just as a new day is born at every dawn, Bella also remarks: "I had been born to be a vampire" in *Breaking Dawn* (p 485). As a symbol, dawn stands for "the triumph of light over dark, and consequently, of good over evil" (Nozedar, 2008, p 252). Dawn is a happy a joyful start to a new day.

Other adventures in the *Twilight* world herald new and important things to come, especially at dawn. For example, just as dawn in nature heralds a new day, Bella's wedding day begins at dawn. "The sky outside my window turned gray and then pale pink" (*Breaking Dawn*, p 35). On a poignant occasion, Bella gives a gold locket to her daughter "at dawn" (*Breaking Dawn*, p 607). But perhaps the most powerful dawn scene is at the very end of *Breaking Dawn*. Bella feels so happy being with Edward: "I'd opened my eyes to my new life, to the endless dawn of immortality" (*Breaking Dawn*, p 698).

In a more sinister scene on New Year's Eve day, at dawn, the Volturi arrived to make war "by the time the sun rose" (*Breaking Dawn*, p 627). Since dawn tends to have good meanings, why is this dawn scene so menacing? An extra symbol is hidden here, one that seems to be overshadowing the positive power of dawn. You see, it is New Year's Eve, the eve of 'January'. The two-faced god Janus from Greek myth rules this month and its meaning. While the month of January does symbolize a new start and a new year to look forward to, it also marks the end of an old year to look back on, including bad memories and past horrors to reflect upon. Janus, with his two faces, can see forwards into the future, but he can also look backwards and create a negative atmosphere by drawing power from bad times, sad times, dark times, and subsequently luring the terrible Volturi to Forks.

At the end of the first night at the cottage, after Bella and Edward make love for the first time as vampires, Bella hears a bird singing just as "the sky began to lighten" (*Breaking Dawn*, p 447) and the little pool in the garden "turned pearl-colored with the sunrise" (*Breaking Dawn*, p 448). That's right on dawn. Shortly after this, Bella and Edward head "west" to the Cullen house (*Breaking Dawn*, p 450). This means that Bella and Edward's cottage, itself a symbol of a new life together, must be in an easterly direction – where the sun rises. Another secret but significant reference to dawn? A white or golden dawn is supposed to symbolize beautiful ideas – light, purity, perfection, happiness, hope and peace. It marks the end of evil or despair, the birth of new ideas and bright insight, and the grand power of light. In the *Twilight* world, Bella finally finds peace in a light and bright dawn, in her new and everlasting life with Edward.

Diamond

The diamond is a brilliant stone and the hardest of all minerals. Beautiful and rare, the diamond is one of the most costly gemstones. The Greek word for diamond is *adamas*, which means 'hard' and 'untamable'. The diamond is certainly a beautiful symbol in the *Twilight* books. In the sun, Edward's white skin "sparkled, like a thousand tiny diamonds were embedded in the surface… smooth like marble, glittering like crystal… shimmering" (*Twilight*, pp 228–229). In fact, Edward looks as if he was "made of diamond" (*New Moon*, p 4). Maybe that's why Bella doodled a "row of diamonds" in *New Moon* (p 262). Edward must be sparkling in her mind. But are the diamonds Bella gets really "a girl's best friend" as movie legend Marilyn Monroe suggests? This is a fair question because in the *Twilight Saga*, Bella does receive three diamond gifts:

1 A Diamond Charm
2 A Diamond Ring
3 A Diamond Necklace

The Charm

In *Eclipse,* Edward gives Bella a "brilliant heart-shaped crystal" charm for her bracelet (p 389). It is a graduation gift and a jewel that belonged to his mother. Bella learns, after talking with Alice, that this cold rock is "five carats or something crazy like that" (*Eclipse,* p 422). It's not a crystal, but a diamond. It is a symbolic gift because the diamond is a traditional protective talisman. Knights and warriors once placed diamonds in their shields and sword hilts for this reason.

The Ring

Edward gives Bella a diamond engagement ring in *Eclipse* that once belonged to his mother. It "sparkled in the dim light. The face was long and oval, set with slanting rows of glittering round stones." Bella had "never seen anything like it" (*Eclipse,* p 406). The presentation of a diamond engagement ring is a romantic and classic custom that is consistent with the traditional meanings of the diamond as a symbol of love and commitment. Since a diamond is hard enough to engrave glass, "scribbling rings" were all the rage during the reign of Queen Elizabeth I. People wore rings set with sharp pointed diamonds to scribble and etch secret love notes on glass windows. How romantic.

The Necklace

The last and most controversial diamond gift that Bella receives is a necklace from Aro, an imperial Italian vampire who rules over all vampires. "The necklace was simple – gold woven into a thick rope of a chain, almost scaled, like a smooth snake that would curl close around the throat. One jewel hung suspended from the rope: a white diamond the size of a golf ball" (*Breaking*

Dawn, p 492).

According to legend, diamonds can absorb both good and bad energy. As a result, diamonds were viewed as suspicious stones. Magnificent diamonds throughout history have caused envy, greed, and even bloodshed, and are therefore believed to be cursed. But in *Breaking Dawn*, just before the Volturi war, Bella puts Aro's necklace on in the hope that it has a positive effect:

> I couldn't hope that the coming confrontation would be resolved peacefully…
> I must have had some hope left after all – blind, senseless hope – because I'd scaled the shelves and retrieved Aro's wedding present to me.
> Now I fastened the thick gold rope around my neck and felt the weight of the enormous diamond nestle into the hollow of my throat.
> (*Breaking Dawn*, p 628)

It is very clear that Bella wears Aro's big diamond to bring hope. Indeed, hope arrives. A happy result in *Breaking Dawn* is that a bloody battle does not take place, thanks to smart mental strategies. Could this link between 'hope and diamonds' be a quirky hint to the famous Hope Diamond? The most notorious diamond in the world? If so, then Stephenie Meyer may be having fun fracturing the legend of this great gemstone. While Aro's diamond of hope does bring some luck, the cursed Hope Diamond has brought disaster and death to anyone who touched it (www.diamonds-are-forever; www.diamond-legend.info).

The Hope Diamond

It is interesting that the *Twilight Saga* makes a connection between diamonds, evil, and hope in *Breaking Dawn*. One of the most cursed stones in history is the Hope Diamond. This big blue diamond fluoresces a reddish color under ultraviolet light, measures about two centimeters across, and weighs almost 46 carats. According to a gem catalogue in 1839, the Curse of the Hope Diamond foretells:

> *Bad luck and death not only for the owner of the diamond but for all who touched it.*

Just as Aro and the Volturi guard execute and burn vampires, the Hope Diamond has left a trail of death and ruin over centuries and across continents. The history and lives of the owners of the Hope Diamond are filled with tragedy, illness, debts and death. According to legend, it all started when the diamond was stolen from a statue in India. The sacred stone was said to have a curse that brought bad luck and death to anyone who touched it. The original thief was reputed to have been torn apart by wolves. Over time, the Hope Diamond passed through different owners. In 1653, the gem was acquired, possibly stolen, by a French gem merchant who took the diamond from India to Europe.

- The diamond was sold to King Louis XIV of France in 1668, who died from illness along with almost all his family.
- When Marie Antoinette and King Louis XVI came to possess the diamond, both were beheaded.
- Stolen during the French Revolution of 1792, the diamond was acquired by King George IV of England who acquired huge debts shortly after.
- Later, the diamond turned up in London in 1830 where the wealthy Henry Philip Hope bought it. All his family died in poverty, giving the stone a gruesome reputation for bad luck.
- In 1911 a wealthy American woman named Evalyn McLean bought the stone. Both of her children died freak deaths (car accident and suicide) and she lost her entire

fortune.

- In 1949, Harry Winston bought it and donated it to Smithsonian Institution in Washington in 1958, where it has remained government property ever since.

If Aro's diamond necklace(Bella's diamond of hope) had the alleged power of the cursed 'Hope Diamond'when she wore it to the Volturi battle, the consequences could have been disastrous. Maybe Bella's hope and loving energy shone through along with her shield, helping her to beat the Volturi army that fateful day. To this day, people believe that hope and diamonds are a dangerous mix.

Disabilities

> There was the old man in the wheelchair with the lined face and the white smile that everyone else saw. And then there was the direct descendant of a long line of powerful, magical chieftains, cloaked in the authority he'd been born with. Though the magic had – in the absence of a catalyst – skipped his generation, Billy was still a part of the power and the legend. It flowed straight through him..
> (*Breaking Dawn*, p 48)

In the *Twilight Saga*, Billy Black is an important figure in more than one way. Not only is Billy a Quileute elder, he has magic in his blood. This enables him to pass on shape-shifting powers to his family. His son Jacob, for example, can transform into a huge wolf. What's more, Billy has another powerful symbolic side to him.

It is obvious that Billy Black has a physical disability, as he is "wheelchair" bound, and cannot walk at all (*New Moon*, p 132). At a symbolic level, however, people with physical disabilities, such as lame or blind people, are believed to be gifted with powerful talents or supernatural abilities. A blind person, for example, may have lost or sacrificed the ability to see the outside world in favor of developing strong or supernatural inner sight. A person who can see with their eyes may be 'blind to the truth'. A person who can walk on two legs may be a 'lame person' psychologically because they are emotionally irresponsible or spiritually corrupt. Yet someone who is blind physically can be wise, deeply spiritual, detect the hidden meanings of things, and easily see what is going on underneath the surface of something or someone. A blind person deals with the world by letting the light of truth and wisdom guide their insight.

Symbolically, a person who does not have the ability to walk may discover a great sense of spiritual freedom – walking through fire (problems and challenges), running through their unlimited imagination or soaring with happiness in their hearts. A life without barriers.

This sounds just like Billy Black and his dual nature. Yes, Billy has a physical disability. But as an individual and a symbol, Billy is a great leader, storyteller, and tribal elder. Yes, physically disabled. But super-abled in other ways. That's what Bella sees underneath Billy's reddish-bronze Native American skin and the lost mobility of his legs – a great spiritual warrior. As a symbol, disabilities suggest that it's the inner magic that counts.

Ancient legends value people with disabilities such as Quileute Elder Billy Black. Many old stories suggest that individuals with physical disabilities have been "touched by a divine grace", enabling them to acquire "the supernatural gift of knowledge, awareness, and understanding usually reserved for the gods" (Colin, 2000, p 312). A very famous disabled figure from Greek myth was Hephaestus, the god of fire and metalwork. He became physically disabled after his father Zeus flung him out of heaven for siding with his mother Hera during a quarrel. At a symbolic level, the tale of Hephaestus suggests that a disabled person is like an apprentice, a newcomer who must learn knowledge and skills to fulfill a powerful quest. These views gave rise to the idea that meeting a lame man heralds great wisdom or realization to come, a test or trial to undertake, an obstacle to be overcome, a conflict or difficulty from which one will emerge victorious but which will leave its mark. It will also generate great moral, psychological or spiritual growth. This sounds exactly like the kind of magic Billy Black's stories about spirit warriors and brave sacrifices involve.

Door

The doorway is a pretty familiar everyday object. In the *Twilight Saga,* when recalling scenes that involve doors or doorways, some fans might enjoy reflecting on Edward's 19th century behavior. He is a real gentleman, forever courteous, who always seems to be opening doors for Bella. On Bella's first visit to the Cullen residence, for example, Edward "opened the door for me" (*Twilight,* p 280). However, beyond Edward's well-meaning old-fashioned courtesy, symbolically speaking, sometimes a door is much more than just a door.

Doorways symbolize a crossing point between two worlds. Or else a door can suggest two different views or approaches to reality. A doorway symbolizes travel from one place to another. And the threshold of a doorway is seen as a place where two worlds merge and meet. Among the most famous doors are those that lead to death, heaven and paradise. Even Heaven and Hell lie beyond great gates or doorways. In the *Twilight* world, Edward opened the front door of his house for Bella when she arrived for a graduation party (*Eclipse,* p 325). And when Bella reached Edward's bedroom door for the first time, Edward was "opening it and pulling me through" (*Twilight,* p 300). While opening doors for others is definitely good manners, there may be deeper meanings in such *Twilight* scenes. Symbolically, doorway scenes in the *Twilight* world suggest the idea that

Edward is opening up his hidden supernatural world to Bella. Edward is choosing to open up a whole new world of magic and immortality to his human girlfriend, drawing Bella further and further in.

On their wedding day, Edward stood before an "an arch" overflowing with "flowers and gossamer" (*Breaking Dawn*, p 44). Another important door symbol. This doorway suggests the transition from single life to married life, from childhood innocence to adult responsibilities, and heralds a new experience on the other side. This traditional meaning occurs again when Edward lifts Bella over the "threshold" of their new home as newlyweds, through the entrance of a small stone cottage in the woods (*Breaking Dawn*, p 443). In this scene, Edward "led the way to the little rounded door" (*Breaking Dawn*, p 442) of the cottage, after Bella opens the door with her key. In such situations, stepping through a doorway such as this one can symbolize a desire for adventure, increasing independence, stepping into the unknown, or leaving the past behind in order to experience a new way of life. Otherwise, why would you want to go in? According to symbol experts "to dream that you are inside a house, on the point of opening a door, but are unsure whether to turn the handle, reveals excitement or fear of the unknown" (Colin, 2000, p 153).

Just as a door can be open or closed, so can someone's mind, heart, or personality. Since Edward invites Bella to cross the threshold of his home and opens up to her about his background as a vampire – these scenes suggest he has an open personality, which is symbolized by opening doors. A dream or a social situation can reveal valuable information about your situation as well as any people you are with. For example, are you left standing in front of a door or behind one? Are you inside a room or house, or were you left outside? When a door is shut to someone in a dream, myth or story, this can suggest cold, closed-minded or uncaring behavior, depending on the situation.

Driftwood Tree

The *Twilight Saga* sure has some magical places. One of these is the 'driftwood tree' that Bella and Jacob always visit at La Push Beach. Many things happen there – beauty is spotted, secrets are revealed, stories are shared, lessons are learned, and feelings are expressed. The symbolism of driftwood tree is positive and negative, exquisite and deep.

Positive Meanings

Pretty

The *Twilight* world reminds us that the world is a rich, diverse and beautiful place. The first driftwood pile Bella encounters is a bonfire of driftwood at La Push Beach. The fire burns beautiful, unusual and surreal colors – green fire, because the wood has absorbed the sea salt.

When Bella chats with Jacob at one driftwood tree they prefer to sit on, there is always something magical or beautiful to see. Although the sea and clouds are gray at the beach, when Bella is with Jacob at the driftwood tree she notices color everywhere. For example, when they walked slowly towards their driftwood bench, Bella spots the "rainbow-colored pebbles" (*Eclipse*, p 101).

The small, pretty things in nature like a driftwood tree, along with Jacob's happy and magical presence perhaps, help us to appreciate nature's beauty.

Lively

The unusual beauty of the driftwood tree and the surrounding beach remind us that nature is alive. It may contain spiritual or magical activity. After all, the *Twilight Saga* is a supernatural story and the Quileute land is a sacred and magical place. It therefore makes sense not to underestimate the magical power of nature. Unseen spirits and sprites often like to express themselves through natural objects – in wind currents, the colors of flowers, the chatter of streams, and in rocks, sand and trees. According to European folklore, signs of fey or the fair folk of the earth can be found in peculiar colors, shapes and forms, in:

> The color-coded messages of autumn leaves… curious colored clovers to oddly unfamiliar toadstools… Elf Cup – a stone hollowed out from dripping water; Elfstone – a pocket-size stone with a hole in it that is rumored to have mystical connections to magic things; Elf-twisted – a deformed or curiously gnarly branch, tree or form of vegetation.

The beauty of a curled and twisted driftwood tree suggests that spiritual energy flows through nature and that magical activity hides in the delights of nature. The pretty patterns and exquisite texture of La Push driftwood provide delightful evidence of lively magic in nature.

Happy

Another positive meaning that the driftwood tree in the *Twilight* world suggests is health and happiness. The natural beauty of the tree and its outdoor setting encourages us to bond with nature and experience the power of nature for ourselves.

To increase happiness, people don't always have to take big, bold, or grand action. If you can appreciate and notice nature, even if it is just visiting a pretty piece of driftwood on the beach, like Bella and Jacob do, then you are much more likely to boost your feelings of well-being in these ways:

- Increase your feelings of inner calm
- Worry less and settle troubled emotions
- Heal inner hurt
- Focus on pleasant and peaceful ideas
- Refresh your mind, body, and soul
- Feel less lonely, more connected to the world around you

- Deepen your bonds with nature

Bella and Jacob's driftwood tree certainly seems to have a positive effect on their mood. For example, their first talk at the twisted, spider-like driftwood tree involved "smiling", "laughter", "taunting" and "flirting", even though Bella hears a story about the "cold ones" (*New Moon*, pp 106–110). By observing nature carefully and spending time around delightful and beautiful things, you can increase your powers to watch, listen, reach a deeply relaxed state of trance, and connect to the positive forces of the world around you.

Negative Meanings

As well as having positive meanings, the driftwood tree at La Push Beach also suggests some negative ideas. In particular, the driftwood tree reminds us that there are forces beyond our personal control and sometimes these forces can be a bit firm, scary or harsh.

Sticky

In *Twilight*, Jacob wandered to the uprooted driftwood tree on the beach that had "its roots sticking out like the attenuated legs of a huge, pale spider" (p 107). Clearly, the tree has been washed up by wind and sea, by the powerful forces of nature. It is stuck in the sand, which suggests that anyone can be made to stick to a certain path, to follow a certain destiny. With its spider-like structure and numerous tentacles reaching out, the tree itself is a trap. The driftwood tree suggests that Bella could become entangled in the sticky network of fate, in a world that does not accept vampires, as in the web of the spider or getting trapped in the tentacles of a sea creature. If Bella were to succumb to the lure of Jacob's charm and pursue a relationship with Jacob, this path would trap both her and Jacob, consuming their rightful *true* paths, which the plot reveals much later. However, the legs of the spider and sea creature are weak and brittle. They do not hold the strength to fight against fate. Bella's choice to be with Edward is too strong and determined.

Spooky

On Bella's first visit to the driftwood tree, Jacob tells Bella a scary story about the "cold ones" (*Twilight*, p 106). According to this ancient legend, the Quileute people were once great spirit warriors who descended from wolves. As Jacob explains, "the cold ones are the natural enemies of the wolf… wolves that turn into men, like our ancestors. You would call them werewolves" (*Twilight*, p 107). In the *Twilight* world, the Cullens are cold ones, and cold ones are "blood drinkers" or "vampires" (*Twilight*, p 109).

Since this driftwood tree is twisted, bleached, uprooted, and washed up on a lonely, gloomy beach, this creates a perfect setting for a scary story. The driftwood's prickly qualities and the wild, desolate scenery enhance the spooky atmosphere for Jacob's cold tale. Symbolically, the 'twisted' branches suggest that some earthly and unearthly beings could be twisted, distorted, or corrupted in some way. All thoughts, feelings, and forms of power can become broken and bitter, just like Jacob's driftwood tree.

Spiky

> I found what I was looking for before I realized I was looking for it. It materialized out of the gloom when it was just a few feet away: a long bone-white driftwood tree stranded deep on the rocks. The roots twisted up at the seaward end, like a hundred brittle tentacles. (*New Moon*, p 303)

The stiff and stranded driftwood tree, washed up in Quileute territory where Jacob lives, helps to symbolize Jacob's predetermined approach to life. Jacob strongly believes that chance, fate, and nature rule. Not choice, free will or nurture. His view suggests that no matter what you learn or what you do, you cannot change the future. You are doomed to follow destiny.

The brittle roots of the driftwood tree trapped in the sand suggest that fate has fixed and inflexible pathways. Since the spiky driftwood tree is stuck on the beach, this helps to symbolize the power of nature further as suggested by the mighty and primordial force of the sea, the ever-present movement of the tides, and the relentless booming, roaring, crashing and rolling motion of the waves. Even Bella gets swept up by fate in this scene without realizing it. As Bella explains, she "found" something without actively "looking" for it. "It materialized out of the gloom" (*New Moon*, p 303). What materialized? The spiky driftwood tree and, symbolically, the dark truth (a prickly realization) that even she could be doomed to follow fate. It is horrible, but possible, that Bella's true love Edward may never return to her in Forks.

"Our Tree"
Dreams and Destiny

In particular, the driftwood tree symbolizes Bella and Jacob's relationship. As Bella views it, the driftwood tree was "our tree" (*Eclipse*, pp 92, 101). It marks Bella and Jacob's special and private place. The driftwood tree definitely suggests a beautiful friendship, like the beautiful sea, sky and sand that surround that tree. But the driftwood tree also suggests that any serious romantic relationship possibilities between Bella and Jacob's relationship would be unstable and volatile – much like the shifting sands that the tree itself is trapped in. What's more, the driftwood tree is uprooted, just as the idea of Bella and Jacob romancing each other is uprooted and absurd because Bella loves Edward. Bella provides irrefutable evidence to support this theory when she uses a Shakespeare motif to explain that: "Juliet gets dumped [by Romeo] and ends up with Paris would never be a hit" (*New Moon*, p 371). In *Twilight* terms, this means: "Bella getting dumped by Edward, and ending up with Jacob, would never work out."

A big reason why a romance between Bella and Jacob would never work out is suggested by the driftwood tree. Jacob has fixed ideas about the future, he firmly believes in fate. Bella has the opposite view. She is a stargazer, trail-blazer, choice-maker, and rule-breaker – someone who dares to dream and will do anything to achieve her truest and deepest desires.

Rainbows and Diamonds

The driftwood tree helps to highlight important differences between Edward and Jacob. For example, at First Beach at the driftwood tree with Jacob, Bella can see more than just the gray sea and gloomy sky. Whenever Bella is with Jacob at the beach, she also notices "colorful rainbows" – the sand, pebbles, and sea life. At the meadow with Edward, Bella can see more than just green grass and wildflowers. Whenever Bella is with Edward deep in the forest, she notices "diamond sparkles" – Edward sparkles just like diamonds in the sunlight. Both Edward (diamonds) and Jacob (rainbows) are different beauties who bring out the magic of nature in very different ways.

E

Earth

The four magical elements in nature are fire, water, air and earth. As a symbol, the earth is certainly a living element that nourishes life, whether the land is wild or cultivated. Everything comes from the earth and returns to it. The earth, primordial matter, generates all forms of life. It can be kind and nurture, provide a variety of food sources such as fruit, nuts, vegetables and animals. Or cruel – in the form of fires, earthquakes, droughts and floods (Colin, 2000). In Greek myth, Gaia, the great earth goddess, was the second deity to appear, just after Chaos created night and day. As the book *Life Magic* asserts: "the ways of the Goddess are there in every puff of wind, ripple of water, crackle of fire and clod of soil" (Bowes, 1999, p 6).

Since earth is a primeval source of power, earth magic is evident in a number of ways around the world. For example, according to magic and folklore in Europe, gnomes guard the earth and its hidden treasures. This suggests that the earth is a place of physical manifestation and that the earth symbolizes abundance, fertility and prosperity of the natural world (Bowes, 1999). Megaliths are great stones on earth. A ring of huge megaliths is Stonehenge in England. These bluestones, with their supposed magic healing powers, have excited the imagination of generations. Standing stones are said to be doorways to other worlds and people have detected lights glowing above Stonehenge and have heard music coming from them. The earth is said to have 'ley lines' too. These are energy lines running underneath the ground. They form crisscross patterns that posses "psychic and/or physical" energy (Eason, 2002, p 159). Ley energy is especially strong in places of natural earthly power such as crossroads, standing stone circles, or cairns on hills. A great number of spirits appear around such sites, near woods and water, where ley energy is strong.

In the *Twilight* world, prominent supernatural adventures occur in places that are consistent with earth magic and folklore.

- Bella and Edward romance each other in a meadow clearing, in the center of a green forest maze.
- Bella and Jacob meet at a driftwood tree, on wild and windswept beach.
- The Cullens live in a meadow on the banks of the river, and Bella and Edward get married there.
- The Cullens hunt animals at Goat Rocks.
- Bella jumps off a cliff in *New Moon*
- The magic of the Quileute people is revealed in stories on a cliff top around a fire.

Eclipse

A Bad Omen

An eclipse is a powerful cosmic junction. When the light from the sun or moon is masked by another planet, this produces a loss of light, brilliance or splendor. *Eclipse* is also the third novel of the *Twilight* series, which describes a symbolic eclipse. It is Jacob who utters: "I would have been the air, the sun... But I can't fight with an eclipse" *(Eclipse,* p 531). What Jacob means is that he is like a sun whose love is overshadowed by Edward's love for Bella. This masks Bella's ability to see Jacob's love. Edward's place in Bella's heart blocks out any chance for her to love sunny Jacob. The love that Bella and Edward share eclipses Jacob's chances of being with Bella. In other words, Jacob's love is truly eclipsed.

A solar eclipse is said to symbolize bad things – a loss, disappointment, confusion, misfortune, depression, and dark, depressing thoughts. "An eclipse of the sun was always a negative sign... since they regarded it a voluntary interruption of divine light. It was therefore an ominous sign or bad omen" (Colin, 2000, p 167). To eclipse another means to outshine, surpass or block something or someone. Sometimes, when the sun (the conscious self) and the moon (unconscious self) unite, this suggests a psychological union (the coming together of two unlike personal forces). But a full solar eclipse, which causes complete darkness, means a total 'eclipse' of reason by emotion.

A heart eclipsed by love is a popular symbol in literature and music. Bonnie Tyler's song, *Total Eclipse of the Heart,* was a huge hit in its day:

> *Once upon a time there was light in my life, but now there's only love in the dark*
> *Nothing I can do, a total eclipse of the heart.*

Love for a long lost lover casts a constant shadow over her, causing a total eclipse of the heart. This is exactly what happens to Jacob in the *Twilight* world.

Diamond Ring Effect

An insightful *Twilight* fan has pointed out a fascinating visual effect that occurs at the *start* and at the *end* of a full solar eclipse (TwilightMOMS post, Ava1981, 2009). The first or final burst of sunlight that appears in an eclipse (known as Baily's beads of light) creates a visual result known as 'the diamond ring effect'. This is when a thin circle of light surrounding the black disc that covers the sun briefly forms a patch of light bursting out of the dark circle. This makes the solar eclipse (a glowing ring of light) look like a diamond ring in the sky (the burst of light looks like a big diamond). And in the novel *Eclipse,* Edward gives Bella a beautiful diamond engagement ring and proposes marriage. This beautiful diamond engagement ring as well as the diamond ring that occurs during an eclipse *definitely* eclipses any chances of

Jacob getting together with Bella. What an interesting symbolic observation.

Eclipse Rising

Well before Jacob's famous eclipse phrase in *Eclipse*, symbolic hints hidden in the *Twilight* world already foreshadow an oncoming eclipse. In an early scene, Bella's first meeting with Jacob occurs at La Push Beach. She notices that: "The clouds started to advance, sinking across the blue sky, darting in front of the sun momentarily, casting long shadows across the beach, and blackening the waves" (*Twilight*, p 102). This scenery surely suggests an oncoming eclipse – Edward's gloomy presence and love for Bella starting to eclipse Jacob's sunny love for her. In this covert eclipse scene, the clouds (which are linked to Edward, as he can only venture out safely in overcast weather) are already overshadowing the sun (the sun is linked to Jacob). Is Edward's attraction to Bella already masking and shrouding Jacob's attempts to get to know her? Prelude to an eclipse? It seems so. Eventually, these clouds cover the whole sky, which causes "the sea to darken" and the "temperature" to drop (*Twilight*, p 105). This symbolizes the idea that Edward is casting his dark and cold influence over Jacob's bright and warm sunny presence.

In another symbolic eclipse scene, Bella gets a chance to hang out with Jacob at La Push. She observes that "the sun had set" and notices a "cloud-obscured sun" (*Eclipse*, p 213). Clouds mask the sun, again. It is as if Edward is extinguishing Jacob's sunny presence with his cloudy presence. Edward's gloom eclipses Jacob's sun. Another prelude to an eclipse? Maybe so. As you can see, visual interplays between sun and clouds in the *Twilight* world suggest an eclipse on the rise.

Egg

I cooked this morning, frying up some eggs – too hungry to

> do anything more elaborate… "Since when do you eat eggs sunny-side up?" he asked. "Since now." "Do you know how many eggs you've gone through in the last week?"
> (*Breaking Dawn*, p 101)

Why does Bella eat loads of eggs in *Breaking Dawn?* Hungry? Favorite food? Pregnant already? Maybe. But another theory is a symbolic one. And it's a pretty plausible one given Bella is going to have a baby.

Eggs are a powerful symbol, a potent life force. All over the world, from the ancient Celts to the Hindus to the Egyptians to the Greeks, all cultures believe that the egg symbolizes 'the cosmic egg' or life from which the universe itself hatched. According to traditional folklore, eggs were regarded as "fertility tokens. They have been connected with life, birth and hope from early times" (Eason, 2002, p 242).

In alchemy, the Philosopher's Egg stands for the seed of spiritual life, and depicts the place wherein a great transformation takes place. Chocolate eggs at Easter represent the resurrection of Christ, and the emergence of new hope and life. The egg is therefore a symbol of new life. Since Bella is going to have a baby, Bella eating eggs for breakfast may be a symbolic nod to the idea that she will give birth to a child. In addition, Bella herself will be reborn as a vampire.

An egg can also symbolize immortality. "The egg is the symbol of perpetual rebirth, therefore a symbolic symbol of resurrection" (Colin, 2000, p 165). In ancient burial sites of Ukraine and Russia, archaeologists have found very old clay eggs. This supports the old belief that eggs suggest eternal life. Since Bella is going to become an immortal vampire, Bella eating eggs for breakfast may by an amusing symbolic nod to the immortality theme.

In Greek myth, Night was seduced by the Wind, and then laid the primordial egg. This egg, a symbol of perfect unity and wholeness, cracked open to give birth to Eros (the god of love). The egg, cracking into two halves, formed heaven and earth. This split created duality in the world – pairs of opposites like good and bad, life and death, male and female (Colin, 2000). Since Bella and Edward are a male and female who have fallen in love (the work of Eros, no doubt), and Bella plans to die in order to live, Bella eating eggs for breakfast may also be a symbolic nod to the duality idea.

In any case, the eggs in *Breaking Dawn* do egg on a few good egg theories!

Eyes

The eyes, it is said, are windows to the soul. And although *Twilight* characters like Edward think they are headed for eternal damnation, Bella shows that she can see much more: "His golden eyes were so deep that I imagined I could see all the way into his soul" (*Breaking Dawn*, p 22). As a symbol, the eyes relate to ideas of light and the spirit, and are often called the mirror of the soul. Eyes also symbolize powerful insight. A spiritual or supernatural inner eye or third eye is sometimes pictured as appearing in the middle of the forehead. The All Seeing Eye, an eye inside a triangle surrounded by rays of light, symbolizes inner vision and spiritual insight. Sometimes small fishing boats paint an eye symbol on both sides of the vessel to protect it from the evil eye at sea. That is why ancient Egyptians painted eyes on coffins. What about the *Twilight Saga*? Edward's eye-talk certainly suggests a sinister streak. "When he finally looked up, his eyes were different, harder – like the liquid gold had frozen solid" (*New Moon*, p 69). This probably reflects traditional evil eye symbolism, which has been around for more than 3000 years. There is an idea that "some people can curse an object (or a person) simply by the act of looking, as though the eye itself can direct a malevolent thought" (Nozedar, 2008, p 557). In other words, looks can kill.

So, just how important is eye-symbolism and eye-talk in the *Twilight Saga*?

Eye Stats

In *Twilight,* Edward uses his eyes to communicate 335 times altogether (see the Appendix for a full list). Statistically speaking, Edward's most communicative feature in *Twilight* is his eyes. Edward uses his eyes slightly more than his voice, and eye references are nearly twice of his crooked smile. Numerically, the *Twilight* novel mentions:

Eyes: 335 times
Voice: 330 times
Smile: 174 times

This suggests that Edward's, golden, blazing eyes may be his most distinguishing feature. Edward's hypnotic eyes will have definitely played a big role in luring readers into the story and getting readers to love this charming vampire character in the first place.

Eye Contact

Bella and Edward didn't bump into each other in the school corridor, call or text each other, or meet on Facebook. The first time they encountered each other was when they made eye contact in the school cafeteria (a place where people 'feed', by the way). When Bella looks at Edward for the first time, she notices that "his dark eyes flickered" towards hers (*Twilight*, p 17). In the game of love, catching another person's eye can mean game over – you're in love. Eye contact rules!

Eye Power

Edward's vampire eyes are incredibly powerful. Indeed, they are designed to influence and mesmerize others. There's one scene where Edward tries to persuade Bella to agree with him. How? Not with his speaking voice nor his debating skills. Rather, "he unleashed the full, devastating power of his eyes on me" (*Twilight*, p 49).

When two people are in love, like Bella and Edward are, the couple's passion is usually described using eye symbolism. Some popular phrases are:

- they caught each other's eye
- they have an eye for each other
- starry-eyed lovers
- blinded by love

That's certainly powerful eye-talk.

Eye Color

Another expressive feature of *Twilight*-vampire eyes is eye color and the fact that vampire eyes can change in appearance. Bella notices that the color of Edward's eyes is an accurate gauge for his hunger and inner mood state. For example, Edward's eyes were "coal black" in their first biology class together (*Twilight*, p 20), which means that he was desperately hungry for food. In a later scene, Bella notices that Edward's eyes were "a completely different color: a strange ocher, darker than butterscotch, but with the same golden tone" (*Twilight*, p 39). This means Edward is not hungry. Rather, he is relaxed and content.

Gold/Red Eyes

The most important feature of vampire eyes in the *Twilight Saga* is their color. Good vegetarian vampires who don't drink human blood have golden eyes, which are black sometimes when the vampires are hungry. Edward, for example, has:

- "dark gold eyes" (*Twilight*, p 41)
- "the gold in his eyes blazed" (*Twilight*, p 49)
- "burning gold eyes" (*Twilight*, p 93)
- "deep, golden honey color" eyes (*Twilight*, p 70)
- "golden butterscotch" eyes (*Twilight*, p 148)
- "liquid topaz eyes" (*New Moon*, p 9)
- eyes "warm with liquid gold" (*Eclipse*, p 15)
- "buttery, burning gold" eyes at the wedding altar (*Breaking Dawn*, p 44)

All the Cullens have gold eyes – a "golden tint" and a "tawny" touch (*New Moon*, p 8). All vampires identify the Cullen clan by their "strange yellow eyes" (*Eclipse*, p 509).

The bad vampires in the *Twilight Saga*, the ones who kill people and drink human blood, have red eyes. For example:

- When Bella met James, Victoria and Laurent "their eyes were different", being "a deep burgundy color that was disturbing and sinister" (*Twilight*, p 329).
- James had "dark red eyes" and his "irises were nearly black, just a hint of ruby around the edges. Thirsty" (*Twilight*, p 388).
- Laurent had "dark red eyes" (*New Moon*, p 237) and "his red eyes flickered" (*New Moon*, p 239).
- The irises of the Volturi guard were "deep crimson around the edges, darkening until they were black around the pupil" (*New Moon*, p 463).
- The newborn vampire Riley had "vivid red" eyes (*Eclipse*, p 480) with "brilliant crimson irises" (*Eclipse*, p 481).

These examples clearly show that the *Twilight* world has two distinct types of vampires – golden-eyed and red-eyed ones, animal-blood drinkers and human-blood drinkers, good and bad. While the gold eyes of vegetarian vampires are especially beautiful, there is a deeper symbolic meaning about gold than meets the eye.

Eye Alchemy

Gold, as a color and a metal, is linked to power, fire, the heavens, and the sun. Gold does not tarnish, corrode, or lose its color and luster if melted. Due to its "physical incorruptibility" gold has become a symbol of spiritual purity and power (Nozedar, 2008).

Alchemists use gold to symbolize the soul. Turning lead into gold is what alchemists have been trying to do all these centuries. However, the search for the Philosopher's Stone (which can change metal into gold) has nothing to do with finding a precious gemstone. The real work of alchemy (a mix of science and mysticism) involves turning leaden human experiences into the spiritual gold of insight and enlightenment (Bennett-Goleman, 2001). The alchemists were looking for ways to purify the spirit and achieve positive personal power – one's *inner gold*. In alchemy, gold symbolizes the highest possible spiritual state and a yellowing phase in alchemy is known as *citrinitas* or xanthosis (Wiki, 2011).

In the *Twilight Saga,* it makes excellent symbolic sense for Carlisle, the Cullen vampires, and the Denali coven to have golden eyes. These vampires choose a higher way of life, to be vegetarian. They drink animal blood, do not harm humans, and strive to live in peace. Basically, they are as good as gold on the inside and try to be the best vampires they can be. Since Carlisle and the Cullens seek higher personal meaning and have soul-searching backgrounds, their golden vampire eyes symbolize the process of spiritual alchemy.

Consider the different spiritual journey of the two types of vampires in the *Twilight Saga*. The golden-eyed (animal-drinking) vampires value love, peace, happiness, bliss, and spiritual power. By contrast, the red-eyed (human-drinking) vampires value lust, war, greed, brutality, fleshly pleasures, and material/social power (marriana mirinda, 2011). Vampires with dark red eyes have not evolved in higher or better ways like the vampires with bright gold eyes. Rather, the red-eyed Volturi vampires have deliberately prolonged a brutal and bloodthirsty lifestyle for centuries. This has blocked them from reaching their glittering inner gold, which would show in their eyes. In view of what gold/red eye colors means, it is easy to see that Dr. Cullen is *Twilight's* top alchemist. This scientist-philosopher-alchemist-father figure has always pursued and promoted peace, happiness, and the true gold of insight.

Clear/Cloudy Eyes

As well as color, another eye-opening aspect of *Twilight* vampire eyes is their clarity. The good vampires tend to have bright and clear eyes. For example, Bella notices that Edward's eyes were "topaz, clear and deep" (*New Moon*, p 70). Clarity suggests ideas like transparency, sincerity, honesty, and truth. Other evil vampire characters tend to have milky, muddy or murky eyes. The best example is the Volturi

leader, Aro. Although his eyes were "red", Bella also observes that they were "filmy", "misty", and that their "color was clouded, milky; I wondered if his vision was affected by the haze" (*New Moon*, pp 463, 464, 467). As a Volturi leader, Aro's vision of the world would surely be clouded, tainted, corrupted.

Even Aro's favorite guard Jane, who has the supernatural power to inflict pain, has "dull crimson irises" (*New Moon*, p 456). What does this mean? A trip to the optometrist? Does Aro need glasses?

Symbolically speaking, Aro's milky eyes and clouded vision means that Aro's ideas and ideals are corrupt. Cloudy eyes suggest dishonesty (the truth is veiled) and immoral behavior. This fits the Volturi lifestyle well – they kill people, drink human blood, and cheat in battle. As the encyclopedia of symbols suggests, a veil is a thin piece of fabric that that obscures, distorts and corrupts a person's vision. As such, veils are associated with lying, concealment, a refusal to see something, as in the expressions 'to draw a veil over' or 'cloud an issue' which mean to conceal something from the knowledge of others, as a veil conceals a person's face (Colin, 2000). Cloudy eyes mean clouded issues, truth shrouded, and a filmy web of lies and deceit. In *Twilight* terms, Aro will try to milk everyone of their freedom, happiness, and power, for sure.

F

Family

Family is an important theme in the *Twilight* world. What the story helps to highlight is that a successful family structure does not necessarily have to be linked by blood or biology. A happy family can also be formed by the power of love (vampire foster families) and spiritual influences (Quileute culture, bonds in a werewolf pack, werewolf imprinting). This is a very empowering message. It gives people in the real world hope that if they do not have blood-related kin to count on, they can find care, comfort and company with others. Those individuals who have lost biological family, have no such family, have been abandoned by their family, or who may come from an abusive family, are not doomed to be alone. This is exactly what Bella thinks. As she leaves her wedding party, Bella notices "so many different kinds of love, harmonious in this one moment. It seemed a very hopeful picture to me" (*Breaking Dawn*, p 68). Another good example in the *Twilight* world is Alice Cullen. She was abandoned by her natural parents at an orphanage. Despite her childhood hardship, Alice is a happy, healthy and much-loved member of the Cullen family. Ultimately, the family is a symbol of love, harmony, and belonging – not genetic links.

Human Family

In the *Twilight* world, Bella does not have the happiest family background. Her parents Renée and Charlie are divorced and they live a long way from each other. When Bella lives with one parent, she is geographically distant to the other and cannot access that parent's support as much. Throughout her childhood, Bella has grown up emotionally supporting her mother, with whom she has a close relationship. When her mother remarries, Bella chooses to move to Forks to live with her emotionally distant and career-driven father. As you can see, Bella's human family features divorce, emotional and geographical distance, and suggests family hardship in a number of ways. When Bella eventually meets the Cullens, it makes sense that she is drawn to this caring and close-knit family.

Vampire Family

The Cullen clan is top example of family strength in the *Twilight Saga*. None of the Cullen family members are related biologically or genetically. A higher purpose brought the Cullen clan together and keeps them together. A compassionate man, Carlisle created several members of his family by turning them into vampires when they were on the brink of mortal death. Each Cullen has experienced tragedy in their life, and this seems to compel Carlisle to care about them. For example, Edward became orphaned after his parents died from disease and he was on the brink of death. So Carlisle turned him into a vampire. Then, Carlisle saved Esme after she jumped off a cliff to kill herself. Carlisle also rescued Rosalie from death after she was brutally attacked by her fiancé, a group of drunken men, and left to die in the gutter. The last person Carlisle changed into a vampire was Emmett. He had been mauled to near-death by a grizzly bear. Carlisle then adopted loners Alice and Jasper to join the clan.

Since getting together, the Cullens continue to stick together because they share a similar lifestyle, values and 'diet'. The Cullen clan strives to live peacefully with others and are vegetarian vampires who do not feed on humans. What's more, the Cullen family comprises three happy and committed long-term marriages – Carlisle and Esme, Rosalie and Emmett, and Alice and Jasper. And when I say long-term, I mean for more than a century. As the Cullen family shows, love keeps people together… forever. "Though none of them are blood-related, the

Cullens understand each other like no humans can, and have genuine affection for each other" (Schmoop, 2008). Even Bella concludes that "real families" are "relationships based on love" (*Breaking Dawn*, p 656). As a positive family symbol, it's not the fact that the Cullens are *vampires* that make their family outstanding. It's their extraordinary *love* for each other.

In a dark family moment, Bella once doubted the bond between the Cullen clan members. Alice and Jasper left Forks when the Volturi planned to visit. Bella assumed that their family bond was insincere and that Alice and Jasper did not want to stand by their kin. Bella assumed that Alice and Jasper abandoned the Cullens completely. One of her theories was that neither Alice nor Jasper is linked to the other Cullens biologically. Nor are Alice and Jasper linked to the Cullens by venom – Carlisle did not create them with a vampire bite. As such, Bella incorrectly thought that Alice and Jasper did not feel strongly attached to their family (*Breaking Dawn*, p 550). How can they feel love if they choose to leave? However, as the end of *Breaking Dawn* reveals, it is not bloodline or bite-source that defines family, it *is* love. A desire and devotion to care for another in sickness and in health, through thick and thin. In a triumphant and touching scene, Alice and Jasper return to Forks with an answer that averts the Volturi war and deters mass destruction (*Breaking Dawn*, p 680).

Werewolf Family

Another good family model is the Quileute people. These descendants of spirit warriors have the power to shape-shift into wolves. Quileutes form strong family links in a number of ways:

- As Native American people, the Quileutes traditionally value family, community, and culture.
- The Black family (Jacob and his father Billy) are strongly bonded. Jacob and Billy live together in a small house, help

each other (e.g. Jacob drives his dad around), and are emotionally close even though Billy is a chief, in a wheelchair, and despite the sad loss of Jacob's mother.

- Emily and Sam's cottage is an open house to all the Quileutes and their friends. Sometimes a whole 'pack' of friends visit at one time.
- The werewolves are always watching out for each other. Despite having a leader, an Alpha wolf, they work closely as a team. The pack hunts together, sticks together, and plays together.
- Since a number of Quileute community members have the power to shape-shift into wolves and can read each other's minds, this magical experience is a *shared* experience that would bind members together even more closely.
- Once a Quileute shape-shifter imprints on his soul mate, that all-powerful spiritual bond can never be broken, no matter what.

These positive examples of werewolf bonding in the *Twilight* world support the view that family is a symbol of divine love.

Fire

In the *Twilight* series, fire is everywhere. It blazes on cliff tops, ignites passion, and burns throats. As a symbol, fire has several positive meanings – creation, birth, light, joy, and divine power. Across the ages, people have used fire to survive. It is a source of light, heat, a means to cook and make tools. But fire can also be a destructive force. This is because it burns and consumes everything in its path, leaving only a pile of ashes behind. Lightning bolts strike down trees and rivers of lava fire flow from volcanoes. Fiery events were once believed to be punishment inflicted by angry gods. Although fire is a symbol of "life, revelation, illumination and purification" and "passion", it also means "destruction. Fire shines in paradise but burns in hell. It gives life but also takes it and transforms it into ashes" (Colin, 2000, pp 186–187). From peaceful bonfire gatherings to scorching Volturi anger, the *Twilight* world illustrates both the good and evil meanings of fire.

Positive Fire

Some important adventures in the *Twilight Saga* describe fire in positive ways.

Magic

The very first fire mentioned in the *Twilight Saga* has a magical atmosphere. It is a "fire circle" at La Push Beach. A student called Mike throws a log on the fire. The salt in the driftwood log causes the fire to look "pretty" and "blue" (*Twilight*, pp 99–100). The unusual color of the flames creates a magical atmosphere for this scene. As Bella explains: "I watched the strange blue and green flames crackle toward the sky" (*Twilight*, p 100). After all, it is at the driftwood campfire that Bella first learns the Cullens' supernatural secret, that they are the "cold ones" according to old Indian folklore.

In another adventure, the Quileute council members have a meeting at La Push. This involves the elders and others sitting around a bonfire, listening to stories and legends about magic. Jacob invites Bella to this "bonfire party". The Quileutes light a beautiful bonfire on a cliff top. "The fire crackled, settling low toward the sand. Sparks blew up in a sudden puff of brilliant orange against the black sky" (*Eclipse*, p 213). What a magical vision. This fire definitely enhances a sense of mystery and magic on the night. Just as wild eagles perch high on cliff tops, the proud Quileute meeting takes place around a cliff top fire that reaches higher still, as flames and smoke extend towards the stars and sky. What a magical vision. In fact, when you think about it, this warm, bright scene is so unlike encounters with the Volturi vampires who live in cold, dark underground tunnels beneath an old stone city. When Billy Black is ready to tell the legend about the Quileute spirit warriors the fire crackles again, "sending another explosion of sparks glittering up against the sky" (*Eclipse,* p 216). The magic of the fire enhances the magic mood of the night and reinforces the magic of important Quileute folklore.

Passion

Another positive symbolic meaning of fire is that it stands for emotion, especially passion and desire. The *Twilight Saga* definitely incorporates this meaning. Who can forget the kiss between Bella and Edward as vampires, just after the Cullens and their supporters deterred a full-scale war. That victorious kiss was so passionate Bella thought it would "set the forest on fire" *(Breaking Dawn,* p 687).

When Bella hears Edward speak in her dream at the start of *New Moon,* her passion is so strong that Bella makes an admission. She declares that she would be willing to "walk though fire" just to "respond" to this voice (*New Moon,* p 4). That's another example of fiery passion.

The fire of Bella's passion burns especially hot on her honeymoon night. Moments before Bella and Edward consummate their marriage in the water, the fire of sexual passion is ablaze: "The fire... was slow and deep now; it smoldered away all my awkwardness, my shy uncertainty. I slipped the towel off without hesitation" (*Breaking Dawn,* p 77). This passionate scene almost sets the page on fire.

Transformation

Another positive meaning of fire is its supposed ability to transform things magically. The phoenix is perhaps the most famous example from myth. This magical bird dies and then resurrects itself from a nest of fire. The same process occurs in

Bella's conversion from a human into a vampire. As Edward's silver vampire venom surges through Bella's body just after she gives birth to Renesmee in *Breaking Dawn,* she burns for three days. Her human body is purified and magically transformed into a supernatural state. Just as a phoenix rises from the ashes of fire, Bella is reborn from the burnt remains of her mortal body into a divine and supernatural vampire.

In the *Twilight Saga,* the link between fire and magical transformation also applies to Quileute werewolves. Just before Jacob and his associates turn into wolves, they bodies become really hot. Before Jacob transformed into a wolf for the first time in *New Moon,* he developed a burning fever and felt sick. What does it feel like to shape-shift into a wolf? It is a fiery experience, according to Jacob:

> I started shifting. The fire trembled down my spine, throwing tight spasms along my arms and legs. It only took a second. The heat flooded through me, and I felt the silent shimmer that made me something else.
>
> (*Breaking Dawn,* p 143)

Again, the fire in this scene symbolizes magical transformation. Namely, the transformation of a human body into a super-powerful wolf body.

As you can see, the positive symbolism of fire is expressed in several ways in the *Twilight Saga.* Fire can be magical (e.g. the Quileute fire), passionate (e.g. fire in a kiss), and transformative (e.g. vampire conversion, shape-shifting).

Destructive Fire

Of course, fire symbolism is not just limited to positive meanings. Symbolically, fire can also be destructive.

Anger

As a symbol, fire relates to anger – hot tempers, scorching fury, burning and explosive anger. A great example of how the *Twilight Saga* uses fire to symbolize anger is when Jacob finds out that Bella is pregnant and may die. This makes Jacob furious with Edward. When Jacob observes Edward touching Bella's face: "This made the room turn red, made me see fire – that after all he'd done to her, he was still allowed to touch her that way" (*Breaking Dawn*, p 161).

Another good scene that features fiery anger involves the character Victoria, a vampire hell-bent on killing Bella. Victoria's flaming red hair is an incredibly hot omen of horror to come. In one adventure, when Victoria finally finds Bella:

> Victoria was staring at me. Her orange hair was brighter than I'd remembered, more like a flame… the fire around her face seemed to shimmer slightly, as if it were alive.
> (*Eclipse*, p 480)

Victoria's fiery presentation captures her scorching anger well. This use of fire to symbolize Victoria's terrible anger is confirmed in the critical scenes that follow. For example, as Bella describes it: "I could see the burning desire to kill" (*Eclipse*, p 484). Victoria's head was a "fiery tangle of hair" with "shivering orange waves" (*Eclipse*, p 490). Victoria's fiery hair helps to enhance her fiery anger.

Death

As a symbol, fire is inextricably linked to death and destruction – its most negative meaning. A blazing out-of-control fire can kill and destroy all life, and death by fire would be extremely painful. In the *Twilight* world, the only way to kill a vampire is to "tear him to shreds and then burn the pieces" (*Twilight*, p 348). The Volturi vampires like to execute other vampires using fire. In a cruel act, the Volturi leader Caius murders Irina and burns her, a ploy to start a war (*Breaking Dawn*, pp 657–658). When Caius murders Irina by fire, he himself symbolizes a destructive "spark" that seeks to trigger the "fire" of a brutal battle in *Breaking Dawn*.

In another destructive fire scene, Alice burns the ballet studio down to make Bella's hospitalization look like an accident, after James brutally attacks Bella (*Twilight*, p 408). Although Alice's fire does *destroy* a building, it is a pretty *creative* cover-up idea!

Flowers

From bunches to bouquets, from vases to fields, the *Twilight Saga* features fabulous and fragrant flower power. In fact, the original cover of *New Moon* shows a wilted white flower spattered with red. The white flower symbolizes Bella. The flower's wilting state represents decline and depression in Bella's life after Edward breaks up with her; her life is nothing without Edward. The wilted flower is spattered with red to symbolize the blood that Bella shed on her 18th birthday at the Cullen House. Just as roses symbolize love, the flower bleached of color could also symbolize the demise of Bella and Edward's love. Their lives are meaningless without each other, and they each die and decay in their own ways. A 12 year old *Twilight* fan from Australia, Lucas Hamilton has his own theory about the flower on the cover of *New Moon*. Lucas says: "When Edward leaves, Jacob (who is red because he has red skin and he loves Bella) starts to take over Edward (who is white because he has white vampire skin). Jacob's red love starts to spread over the white part (the Edward part) of the flower (Bella)" (10/11/2011). Thanks Lucas, that's so cool.

Flower Scenes

According to symbol experts, "the flower is the symbol of the soul, but a happy, fulfilled soul, detached from material possessions and free from the passions that can disturb and distort it. Each flower has its own particular symbolism. We still give flowers as a sign of affection, gratitude, remembrance, joy and happiness" (Colin, 2000). The most prominent flower adventures in the *Twilight Saga* occur in these places:

The Meadow – the lovely, round meadow in the sunshine was "filled with wildflowers – violet, yellow, and soft white" (*Twilight*, p 226).

Bella's 18th Birthday Party – Alice surrounded the Cullen house with "big bowls of flowers – pink roses" and packed the inside of the house with "crystal bowls filled with hundreds of roses" (*New Moon*, p 25).

Emily's house – A window box underneath a narrow window of Emily's gray house "was filled with bright orange and yellow marigolds" (*New Moon*, p 331). Not only do these bright flowers enhance the happy home atmosphere, the traditional symbolic meanings of flowers suggest that Emily strives to develop inner strength and spiritual power, not just material wealth.

Wedding Day – On the day of Bella's wedding, Alice decorates the house with "orange blossoms", "lilac", "freesia" and "roses", which give out an overwhelming and intoxicating fragrance (*Breaking Dawn*, p 38). Bella's white bridal bouquet comprised: "the scent of roses and orange blossom and freesia enveloped me in a soft mist" (*Breaking Dawn*, p 43). Bella's wedding dress makes her look like an upside-down lily. In *Breaking Dawn*, "the narrow sheath of the shimmering white dress flared out subtly at the train almost like an inverted calla lily" (p 52).

Stone Cottage – Bella and Edward's stone cottage, nestled in the forest, is overgrown with beautiful flowers. In particular, climbing honeysuckle and roses (*Breaking Dawn*, p 440). These flowers that surround the cottage suggest or symbolize the idea that Bella and Edward's new life together and new home is filled with love. The back wall of Bella and Edward's cottage had "big glass doors that opened into a little hidden garden" with "climbing roses" (*Breaking Dawn*, p 445). Climbing roses may mean love aspiring.

Flower Meanings

The traditional meanings and messages of different flowers in the *Twilight Saga* are these:

Daisy – innocence, purity, beauty, love. "You are my first true love."

Violet – trust, faithfulness, love. "I will not betray your love."

Orange Blossom – innocence, eternal love. "I seek a permanent commitment."

Lilac – first feelings of love. "You have awakened new emotions in me (purple)."

Freesia – innocence, trust.

Honeysuckle – commitment. "Accept this token of my love."

Lily – purity. "My love for you is spiritual." The lily was dedicated to all maiden goddesses, especially the moon goddess Artemis.

Rose – love. A red rose means: "I love you with all my heart."

Twilight's Most Famous Flower

The rose is the most famous and magical flower symbol of all in many cultures around the world. Maybe this not surprising, since fossilized roses from 35 million years ago have been found, and wreaths made of roses have been found in the most ancient tombs. As the ultimate flower of love, roses are ingredients of love potions and dedicated to the Goddess of Love, Aphrodite. In this light, it is symbolically meaningful that Rosalie is named after the rose and that she is also described as having the beauty of Aphrodite, whose flower is the rose.

A beautiful, pure and hallowed symbol, the rose is the most mystical flower in the West, popular in Greece and native to Asia.

Rose oil was one of the most highly prized perfumes in Arabia. Many species of rose were introduced to Europe in the 12th century by the crusaders, who brought rose bushes back with them. As far back as the first century BC, Greek physicians such as Theophrastus and Dioscorides cultivated roses not only for their beauty and fragrance, but for their medicinal properties. Rose water is supposed to tone and clean the skin, giving the rose youth-giving powers.

(Source of flower meanings: Colin, 2000; Eason, 2002; Nozedar, 2008)

Fog

Foggy Weather

Not only is Forks a cold and wet place in the *Twilight Saga,* it gets really foggy too. Bella describes Forks as a place that has "gloomy, omnipresent shade" (*Twilight,* p 3). This certainly suggests overcast weather. On the morning of her first day at Forks High School "thick fog was all I could see out my window in the morning" (*Twilight,* p 10). This is also the morning of the day that Bella first meets Edward. In a later scene, when Bella confesses that she loves a vampire, it started to get "foggy and dark outside my window, absolutely perfect… unusually foggy; the air was almost smoky" (*Twilight,* p 172). Can you see the pattern? Fog is linked to Edward – an idea that fits well with his mysterious nature.

Edward is a character clouded and shrouded in mystery and so fog helps to symbolize his obscure presence or influence. For example, the first time Edward picks Bella up for school "the mist was ice cold" and then out of the "thick fog" Bella realizes that Edward's car is waiting for her at her house. The "fog" appears again when Bella has a nice day with Edward at school and although "the day was still dark with low, oppressing clouds. I smiled up at the sky" (*Twilight,* p 177). Why does a girl who loves the Phoenix sun smile about Forks fog? Because it symbolizes Edward, of course. This link is confirmed in another foggy weather moment. When Edward takes Bella home to meet his vampire family, they drive through the "misty forest" (*Twilight*, p 280).

In nature, fog is a form of low-level cloud. It is caused by droplets of condensed water vapor suspended in the air. The best known effect of fog is that it reduces visibility considerably. Mist is similar except that it is less dense than fog, so it does not reduce visibility as much. While fog does not appear that often in the *Twilight* world, it is a very powerful symbol:

> Fog represents everything that is undifferentiated, undefined, indistinct and indeterminate. It can also apply to a state of mental obscurity, confusion (in such phrases as 'fogging the issue') and uncertainty. Dreaming about a fog can be a sign of inner confusion, a period of turmoil, discord and conflict with those around you. Mist has similar connotations of haziness and lack of clarity – for example in the expression 'misty past' – but the symbolism is much less intense.
> (Colin, 2000, p 195)

So fog suggests chaos and a lack of order. This is because you can't see where you're going or what is happening when it is foggy. Fog can also be an omen of an important event, creation, birth or something new that is about to happen in your life. Do you suddenly recall that foggy morning the day Bella met Edward? Then all those nice foggy days spent with Edward. Ding! That's fog symbolism – symbolic Forks news that you're about to encounter a vampire.

Alec's Mist

The symbolism of fog can be good or bad depending on other information in the scene. When foggy Forks weather involves

Edward, fog has positive meanings. Fog means that Edward can spend time safely outdoors with Bella, it signals Edward's presence, or it alludes to Edward's mystery that consumes Bella. In complete contrast, fog becomes a negative symbol once it involves the Volturi. For example, Bella has a bad dream about the Volturi: "The line of black advanced on me through the shroud-like mist. I could see their dark ruby eyes glinting with desire, lusting for the kill" (*Breaking Dawn*, p 107). Bella's dream suggests that mist can be menacing. In particular, one of the most powerful and mist-ifying Volturi guards is Alec. This vampire has a gift so powerful that he can numb the senses completely, cutting off an individual's ability to see, hear, smell, taste and touch. In effect, Alec's weapon renders its victims blind, deaf, and completely powerless. In *Breaking Dawn*, Alec shows how he projects his mist to numb everyone's senses:

> The mist approached us. The wind shrieked louder but didn't change the course of the mist…
>
> The mist curled upward, seeking a breach, a weakness. It found none. The fingers of searching haze twisted upward and around, trying to find a way in.
>
> (*Breaking Dawn*, p 676)

Alec's supernatural gift fogs, blankets, and smothers all the senses, a total and terrifying sensory deprivation.

Bella's Fog

Perhaps the most hidden and heartfelt fog symbolism in the *Twilight* world is one that occurs in *Breaking Dawn*. When Bella considers the possibility that the Volturi army cannot be beaten: "All my hope faded like fog in the sunshine" (*Breaking Dawn*, p 599). The fog inside Bella's heart symbolizes positive ideas and feelings – all things Edward. Traditionally, sunshine is the happy weather symbol. But here, Bella's feelings of hope are symbolized by fog, since fog is Edward-related. In *Breaking Dawn*, on the verge of a terrible battle, the Volturi vampires dissolve Bella's inner fog as easily as they can make a vampire vanish in a puff of smoke.

Forest

The Dark Forest

Set in the Olympic Peninsula, forest scenery abounds in the *Twilight Saga*. The main thing Bella notices about the forest is its dark beauty. The deep green forest surrounding Forks is often described as dark and black. For example:

- Bella notices the "gray-green light of a cloudy day in the forest" (*Twilight*, p 45).
- When Bella was "alone in the darkening forest… the rain made it dim as twilight under the canopy" (*Twilight*, p 59).
- Bella loses sight of the sky in the forest and notices its "murky and ominous" atmosphere (*Twilight*, p 101, p 105).
- During Bella's first big hike alone in the forest, it is "overcast" (*Twilight*, p 118).
- The forest is "dark" (*Twilight*, p 105).
- The forest was "a black wall" (*Twilight*, p 158).
- Edward "stared into the dark forest" (*Twilight*, p 224).
- Edward "stared into the shadowy forest" (*Twilight*, p 240).
- The "shadows of the forest" grew stronger (*Twilight*, p 244).
- Bella's first trip into the forest, after Edward leaves her, is black. Cold, alone, distressed, she trips and falls onto the wet forest ground – a pool of "black" (*New Moon*, p 73).
- The "tips of the treetops" were "almost black against the light gray of the sky" (*Eclipse*, p 546).

The dark side of forests fits well with lore and legend. It seems that forests are powerful places because of their darkness. Trees thrive in forests, blocking out the sunlight. The forest canopy is a thick organic curtain of darkness, which casts shade below. Since many people believed that darkness was evil and that it opposed the powers of light and the sun, people's fear of shade, shadows and the dark have enhanced the forest's forbidding image. Dark and wild, forests come across as unsettling, unpredictable, and dynamic places. (See also *Darkness*).As you can see, the *Twilight* forest backdrop is deep, dark and shadowy. Wild forests are especially mysterious and powerful. Pure and pristine, free from human intrusion and interference, forest power is not yet spoiled or damaged by people. As a result, these special places in nature remain magical and powerful to this day. Anyone who strives to help nature and not hurt nature is bound to experience forest power.

The Inner Self

The *Twilight* forest adventures allude to Bella's personal experiences. According to the famous psychoanalyst Dr. Carl Jung, the "dark forests" that people think, dream or write about symbolize the dark and unknown territory of the human mind. In other words, forest forces represent psychological forces – a person's hidden thoughts, forgotten ideas, private secrets, wishes, fears, and desires. In line with this symbolism of forests, Bella often thinks of useful ideas, makes important choices, or resolves some kind of conflict deep in her mind when she is somewhere deep in the forest. In many myths, legends, and fairy tales, finding hidden treasure somewhere in a forest (e.g. gold, magical objects, creatures that grant wishes), means that someone has found some kind of inner treasure (e.g. insight, personal strengths, good solutions).

A number of important forest scenes in the *Twilight* books reflect Bella's thoughts, feelings, and personal experiences. For example:

- Bella realizes that she really does love Edward and wanted "nothing more than to be with him" after walking in the rain into the "darkening forest" that was a "dripping green maze" (*Twilight*, p 121).

- After hearing Jacob's scary story about the "cold ones" and researching "vampires" on the Internet, Bella takes a walk in the forest. When Bella reaches a deep, dim, darkening place in the forest (looks deep inside her heart, that is), where no one can "see her" (secret desires), she makes a choice that changes her life forever. She chooses Edward, no matter how dangerous this might be (*Twilight*, p 119).

As you can see, the dark forest symbolizes Bella's inner self. The message? If you want to be truly happy, look within and follow your heart's deepest desires.

Edward's Forest

The forest tends to symbolize Edward, while the beach at La Push symbolizes Jacob. In particular, Bella spends only spends special time with Edward in the forest, not the beach. Slowly and steadily, as Bella gets to know Edward, she views the forest in a less menacing way. As Bella herself explains, the forest "didn't seem sinister like it used to" and if she left Forks now she expects she would miss "the green, the timelessness, the mystery of the woods" (*New Moon*, p 63). The more Bella likes Edward, the more she likes the forest. Some of the most important scenes with Edward occur inside the forest – in the dark shadows, in the cool shade, or in a secret sunlit clearing somewhere in the woods.

So why are dark forests linked to Edward? Maybe it is because he is a dark and mysterious figure. Another good theory points to the legends of the vampire. The most popular myths about vampires evolved in the dark forests of Eastern Europe. Traditionally, vampires like to roam in wide and wild woodland that teem with brown bears, wolves, and lynxes – namely, the forbidding Carpathian Mountains that traverse Ukraine,

Romania, and Transylvania (Wiki, 2011). Whatever the reason that makes Edward's bond with the forest so strong, not even Jacob's personal sunshine can infiltrate Edward's dark and gloomy forest. When Jacob hikes with Bella deep into the forest, he cannot help her to find Edward's magic meadow nor brighten the forest's "natural gloom" (*New Moon*, p 199). The forest belongs to Edward.

Forks

The *Twilight Saga* is set in Forks, Washington. Forks is a city in Clallam County, Washington, United States. It's a small town with a small population, located in the Olympic Peninsula with one of the rainiest weather conditions in the United States. It is named after the 'forks' in the nearby Quillayute, Bogachiel, Calawah, and Sol Duc rivers.

For many years, Forks was the "logging capital of the world". The city's economy was fuelled by the local timber industry. With recent declines in the industry, however, Forks has relied on the nearby Clallam Bay Corrections Center and Olympic Corrections Center as a source of jobs. Forks is a popular destination for sport fishers who fish for salmon and rainbow trout in nearby rivers. It is also supported by visitors to Olympic National Park. In recent years, the city has gained popularity for being the main setting in Stephenie Meyer's *Twilight* series.

In the *Twilight Saga*, the fictional chief of police at Forks is Charlie Swan. There is a high school called Forks High School, a small public library, and a number of stores, including Newton's Olympic Outfitters, where Bella once worked part-time. A restaurant known as The Lodge is Charlie Swan's favorite. Forks also has a hospital, Forks Hospital, where Dr. Carlisle Cullen works.

Of course, a 'fork' can also mean a split, divide, branch or junction. A 'fork in the road' suggests two different pathways. So a fork symbolizes personal choice, which plays a big part of all the action in the *Twilight* world. A famous Robert Frost poem captures choice power when he arrives at a fork in a road:

Two roads diverged in a wood, and
I – I took the one less traveled by,
And that has made all the difference.

As these lines suggest, choice clearly has consequences.

The fact that the name Forks in the *Twilight* world suggests choice could be a complete coincidence. However, Bella and her friends do make an awful lot of critical choices. In particular:

- Bella meets Edward, a beautiful but dangerous vampire. Should Bella get together with him?
- Edward loves Bella, but he also thirsts for her blood. Should he woo her or shoo her?
- By virtue of being human, Bella attracts an evil vampire tracker. This puts Edward's life in danger. Should Bella die for him? Is this the best thing to do?
- The only way for Bella to be with Edward forever is to become a vampire. Could she? Should she? Would she? If Bella becomes a vampire, will she kill people? Will she lose her soul?

In particular, choice is the defining feature of the Cullen family. It's their choices that make them good, great and emotionally fulfilled vampires. The Cullens *choose* to suppress their natural desire for human blood by only drinking animal blood. They *choose* to live as a family and make their bonds unbeatable, even though they're not biologically related. They *choose* to live peacefully with others – people, werewolves and other vampires as well as the environment. Dr. Cullen *chooses* to be the best vampire he can be – healing the sick and saving human lives. It's the

Cullen clan's choices to do good things and support moral standards that explain why so many people love them.

G

Games/Sport

Games and sports say a lot about characters in the *Twilight Saga*. They suggest and symbolize attitudes, personality, and more. Games, sports, and related activities are watched, discussed and played by a range of different characters in the *Twilight* series. Not only does do games/sports symbolize challenge and victory, they sure say a lot about the player. Games and playing involve either winning or losing. The results are influenced by strength, skill, strategy or maybe just chance. The potential to win a game and the power to influence it is what makes games so exciting.

In ancient times, games were deadly serious. They symbolized a player's ability to master dangerous challenges and defy lethal odds. "Games-playing was originally a matter of life and death, in other words, it was a way of winning the right to hold on to life, to be in control of it, to wrest it from the gods. Winning a game was like a second birth" (Colin, 2000, p 203). Warriors fighting each other or with wild animals such as bulls or lions in a Roman amphitheatre was once a huge and gruesome spectacle. "If a player won, if he passed all the tests set for him during an initiation, he saved his soul, to become the master of his own fate" (Colin, 2000, p 203).

These days, however, game playing is not so disastrous. These days, people have free time to play games for enjoyment. The goal of games is have fun or maybe to win money if the game is a gamble – a bet against chance or fate. Many people who play lotteries hope and dream to become filthy rich overnight, even if the chance of winning is a long shot. However, the best and most sophisticated games are the ones that have some sort of social, emotional, educational or other health reward such as positive feelings and relaxation. Games that do not involve relying completely on chance are more engaging, enjoyable and empowering. Chess and many other games, for example, boost memory, planning, problem-solving, and other mental abilities. That is why it is so much fun 'betting on Alice'; she unleashes her mental powers fully when playing a game or choosing her next move.

In the *Twilight Saga*, chess is the main (non-sport) game that features. Once, Edward and Alice were playing chess with each other, which was extra exhilarating because both vampires have supernatural powers that would help them to trick and trap each other (*Eclipse*, p 51). The big *Breaking Dawn* war between two sides (the Volturi, and the Cullens and their allies) also resembles a chess game. It is described with striking imagery – "black" and "white" are the two colors that dominate the battlefield. The Volturi vampires' black cloaks are set against the fresh white snow. This creates a black and white chessboard visual. Meanwhile, important chess pieces include kings and queens (e.g. the Volturi rulers and their wives), royal guards with special gifts (e.g. gifted vampires, guardian werewolves) and pawn-like pieces (e.g. fighters, spectators). Anyone for chess? Of course, chess symbolizes choice (see *Chess/Choice* for details). In particular, the *Twilight* tale follows Bella's series of choices to be with a vampire – and become one. The original cover of *Breaking Dawn* shows a red pawn and white queen. This symbolizes Bella's chess-like journey from innocence to power.

Twilight Sports
Baseball

Lightning? Thunder? Storm ahead? Well then, let's play ball! Vampire-style baseball, that is. It is a favorite American sport, after all. And when the super-strong and mega-fast Cullens play, they sure do make a racket! In the *Twilight* world, the Cullens play it, Esme referees it, and Charlie and Billy watch it on TV.

Using skill, speed, bats, gloves, and 'wicked curve balls', it's a pretty exciting game. As a symbol, however, what does baseball mean? And what does it reveal about the Cullens?

The big symbolic thing about baseball is that it is a social and cooperative game, despite its competitive streak. Friends, family, colleagues and communities can come together for a game of baseball. As such, baseball is a game that unites everyone, encourages people to join in and fit in, and above all, requires teamwork. It is not surprising that the good Cullen vampires prefer to play a game that is prosocial, emotionally healthy, and physically healthy, just like they are. Baseball may be an average American pastime, but it is a supreme symbol of social harmony.

Ballet

Another artistic sport form suggested in the *Twilight* books is ballet. Bella went to ballet school as a child. So what does ballet say about Bella? And what does this organized leisure activity symbolize? Although ballet has some social features just like baseball (e.g. attending ballet classes, dancing with others on a stage) it has some unique features too.

It requires aspiration, commitment, discipline, technique, solitary practice, and a drive to be perfect and precise. These qualities reflect Bella's personality – she is an idealist, loner, high achiever, and perfectionist. The meanings of ballet fit with Bella very well. And although Bella thinks that only Alice moves like a graceful ballerina, Bella's early ballet lessons would have instilled Bella's positive work ethics and empowered her to become the super-graceful vampire that she eventually becomes.

Fishing

Who wants to go fishing? Charlie does! Why? Because Charlie is easy-going, practical, and down-to-earth, well suited for an outdoor sport like fishing. Fishing is a relaxing leisure activity. It involves practical skills and, who knows, it might even produce a free dinner. As an outdoor sport, fishing is a fairly casual affair that is not mentally taxing, it fosters contact with the outside world (rather than the inner world of ideas and the imagination), you can go fishing alone or with others, it demands little emotional expression, and it even requires a tough touch (killing/filleting fish to eat). Who does that remind you of? Charlie, of course – earthly, manly, emotionally reserved, interacts with the outside world, and looks forward to relaxing outdoors on weekends.

Tracking

In the *Twilight Saga*, tracking is a 'blood sport' of the worst kind possible. A 'tracker' is a vampire who hunts human prey. Not just to feed on, but for the thrill of making and watching the victim suffer and squirm with fear. As a symbol, tracking has sinister meanings. It is antisocial, exploitative, cruel, and hostile. It is virtually a solitary game – the lone hunter's prize is to seize prey and terrorize it. Tracking is the perfect 'game' for James, a ruthless, obsessive and evil vampire. The tracker symbolizes the psychopathic personality – someone who is callous and socially deviant.

Garden

A garden is a place of creation and regeneration, a paradise, a place of peace. In nature, a garden is a magical and sacred place, a heaven on earth. It is a source of emotional nourishment, fulfillment and wonder. People have always loved and longed for nature, so they need gardens. After the noise, fast pace, and tough pressures of city life, a setting that has grass, plants, trees and flowers helps people to recharge their batteries, providing both physical and spiritual nourishment.

According to one source, the Garden of Eden was "a place that was perilous for the soul, not a place of refuge. As such, they believed it was to be avoided at all costs… In calling Eden dangerous, the cabbalists meant that it represented the comfortable, stable condition into which mankind, by nature, tends to settle and which causes them to stagnate, preventing or destroying any potential for self-development" (Colin, 2000, p 205). Symbolically speaking, maybe the Volturi have entered such a garden – because they reject innovation and creativity, and remain stagnant. They also resist progress and change – such as adopting vegetarian lifestyles or being open-minded about half-vampires like little Renesmee. The Garden of Eden also suggests that a garden can symbolize one's inner state, the emotional world within. "Everyone has an inner garden that they can visit to find their true self, recharge their batteries and grow" (Colin, 2000, p 204).

Garnet

The garnet is a gemstone mentioned in the *Twilight Saga*. It was Bella's favorite gem for a long time. As Bella explains, "My favorite gemstone was garnet" (*Twilight*, p 201).

As a gem, the garnet can be clear, brown, ultraviolet, green, yellow and orange. But it's best known color is blood red. Since its rich, dark liquid-looking color resembles blood, the garnet was believed to have therapeutic powers. For example, the blood-red garnet has the supposed power to treat bleeding wounds, blood disorders, and hemorrhaging. As a healing stone, it is considered to revive the body and spirit, improve heart function, encourage healthy emotions, promote passion, and cure depression. Since Bella has experienced bleeding and feelings of depression to a considerable degree, and is trying to sort out her romantic feelings for Edward, the garnet may well be a very useful stone for Bella to like and possess.

Gold

Gold is sacred to all sun deities and signifies pure power, success, courage and confidence. Due to its yellow tint and solar gleam, gold metal is considered protective. Gold, which over the centuries has been regarded as a precious metal all over the world, is linked to things beautiful, rare and valuable. Gold conjures up thoughts of riches, treasure and wealth. As a symbol, gold also refers to inner riches – one's finest and most precious personal assets. This includes qualities such as bravery, honesty, kindness and a loving heart. Since gold is a valuable metal, it is also a symbol of power and an object of greed and desire.

In the *Twilight Saga*, Edward has some special links to gold. The gold in Edward's eyes is mentioned *sixteen* times in *Twilight*. Given what gold means, Edward's eyes suggest that he is a good vampire on the inside – gentle, generous, and loving.

Gold is the lion's color and Edward has links with lions. He moves like one and his favorite food is mountain lion (*Twilight*, p 188). In art, lions are often colored gold, just like Edward's eyes. In particular, gold is intimately linked with the sun and divine power. It symbolizes wealth, royalty and success.The meaning of gold is illumination, wisdom, and wealth. Gold represents the warmth of the sun. To Bella, Edward is better than winning the "lottery", that's first prize, the gold prize, the jackpot (*Twilight*, p 415).

It may be worth noting Edward's bedroom décor. The color scheme is gold and black, the colors of positive power and the dark unknown. Edward's bedroom includes a black wrought iron bed frame, a gold comforter set, and gold-colored carpeting and curtains. Not only does this color choice match Edward's eyes (which change from black to golden butterscotch), but it sums up Edward's personality. Black – for mystery. Gold – for positivity. A color-code that symbolizes a Byronic Hero.

Gothic Fiction

The *Twilight Saga* is a 'Gothic fiction' series. Gothic fiction, or Gothic horror, is a genre or style of literature that merges horror and romance together. The English author Horace Walpole is credited with inventing Gothicism with his 1764 novel *The Castle of Otranto*, subtitled "A Gothic Story". This work is considered to be the first ever Gothic novel. Gothic literature alludes to emotional extremes from awe to ecstasy to blood-curdling terror, and above all, a quest for atmosphere.

The ruins of Gothic architecture in English landscapes and remote places evoke strong feelings. This is because old crumbling buildings symbolize the doom and decay of human society. English Gothic writers linked medieval buildings with ideas of darkness and horror, and a macabre and mysterious past.

According to Gothic fiction experts, this literary style incorporates such elements as "terror (both psychological and physical), mystery, the supernatural, ghosts, haunted houses and Gothic architecture, castles, darkness, death, decay, doubles, madness, transgression, excess, secrets, and hereditary curses." Typical Gothic fiction characters include: "tyrants, villains, bandits, maniacs, Byronic heroes, persecuted maidens, femmes fatales, monks, nuns, madwomen, magicians, vampires, werewolves, monsters, demons, dragons, angels, fallen angels, revenants, ghosts, perambulating skeletons, wanderers and the Devil" (www.slideshare.net, 2011).

In the *Twilight Saga*, Gothic fiction symbols come alive. A few brief examples from the *Twilight* books are these:

Byronic Hero – Edward

Persecuted Maiden – Bella

Mystery themes – Who is Edward? What does Bella's 'glitch' mean? Is the Forks forest safe? How will Bella and Edward's forbidden love work out? Will he bite her? The *Twilight* world has many more mystery themes.

Supernatural themes – vampire gifts, werewolf shape-shifting, werewolf imprinting, the afterlife

Secrets – vampires must keep their true identities top secret, werewolf shape-shifting magic is sacred and secret

Death – hunting human prey, drinking human blood, the wish to die to save others, suicidal feelings, executions, immortal life requires mortal death. The *Twilight* world abounds with death themes.

Gothic Archetypes

In the Gothic genre, characters can be sorted according to different archetypes (that is, their classic type – the kind of character they typically are). The main types, with examples from the *Twilight* world, are these:

Gothic Hero – is the main character (protagonist) who tends to be an isolated figure. For example, Edward keeps to himself at Forks, has never had a romantic relationship before Bella, is a loner, and is considered a social outsider at school.

The Villain – is the main enemy (antagonist) who tends to suggest ultimate evil and malice. For example, James, Victoria and the Volturi vampires are supreme villains.

The Wanderer – is an isolated, self-exiled traveler, who suffers some kind of divine punishment. For example, Carlisle has wandered the lands, has exiled himself and nearly starved to death, he drinks animal blood to avoid human blood, and he works tirelessly to save human lives to atone himself for becoming a blood-drinking monster.

Other classic character types (or archetypes) include:

Hero – a good, honest and brave character who confronts the tyrant, e.g. Bella is the main hero of the story.

Tyrant – an evil oppressor, e.g. the ruling Volturi vampires.

Virginal Maiden – a young, beautiful, innocent, and caring female figure, who has a mysterious past, e.g. Alice is a lovely young vampire who knows nothing about her human life.

Older Foolish Woman – a silly, gullible, or passive character, e.g. Bella's carefree mother may fit this role.

Stupid Servant – a comical figure who informs, jokes around, and entertains with hilarious antics, to move the plot forward and to lighten the mood, e.g. Jacob might fit the comical criterion of this role, but he is not stupid.

Clown – provides comic relief to break the tension, e.g. Emmett sure jokes a lot.

Banditti – gangsters, thugs, rough characters, e.g. the human thugs that try to attack Bella, James the evil vampire and his gang.

Clergy – weak and evil ministerial figures, e.g. the Volturi

(Source: David De Vore, Gothic Fiction: Byronic Hero)

Dark Settings

In Gothic fiction, a 'dark setting' is the most important feature. It's all about atmosphere, atmosphere, atmosphere. The plot often features Gothic architecture such as an old castle, an abbey, or some other secretive place. This gloomy, scary and haunting scenery is what sets up the whole novel. According to literature expects:

> *Without a dark and imposing backdrop, the Gothic Novel would not exist… The setting is essential in Gothic novels, to promote an atmosphere of terror and dread, and to suggest deterioration of its world. The crumbling, decaying, ruined scenery of a castle or a deserted landscape implies that at one time there was a thriving world.*

In the *Twilight Saga,* the forest around Forks is dark, dense, gloomy, and black. It ain't no fluoro-green firecracker. As for ruined buildings and melancholy landscape, the *Twilight* world has some outstanding examples. There was a time when Bella visited the Cullen mansion after the Cullens left town and found the place to empty, dreary, and lifeless – a Gothic ruin. "The emptiness screamed from the blank windows. It was creepy… a fitting haunt for vampires" (*New Moon*, p 161). When the Cullens left Forks in *New Moon*, the house became cold and sinister because the Cullens, despite the fact that they are cold creatures, didn't live there anymore. Although the house itself had not changed, the soul and heart of the house went missing. This sent the house's homely presence into decay.

Another time Bella returned to the magic meadow she and Edward once shared together. Except there was no magic this time. With Edward gone, the meadow was "empty of atmosphere, empty of everything" (*New Moon*, p 234). Without Edward, the meadow loses it's warm and loving atmosphere and it was "the wrong season for wildflowers" and "the ground was thick with tall grass" (*New Moon*, p 234). This meadow surely symbolizes emotional suffering and decline, in line with Gothic prose in art, poetry, and graveyard poets. As Bella confirms, "there was nothing special about this place without him" (*New Moon*, p 234). So now you know a bit about Gothic fiction. As you can see, it's quite amusing trying to figure out who fits there, and what goes where.

Gray

As a color, gray is a midway point between black and white. Similarly, as a symbol, gray is usually a midway point between two extreme viewpoints or opposite sides. As such, a 'gray area' is an area that is baffling, uncertain, or undecided. As a plain and placid color, gray certainly blends into the background.

The color gray in the *Twilight Saga* is used a lot to describe the Forks weather or the cloudy sky. For example:

- The water around La Push at First Beach is "dark gray, even in the sunlight, white- capped and heaving to the gray, rocking shore" (*Twilight*, p 99).

- Bella visits Port Angeles, where she notices the sky "graying, shot through with streaks of pink and orange" (*Twilight*, p 137).
- Bella awakens to a "pearl gray morning" and feels "cheerful" when she meets up with Edward waiting for her (*Twilight*, p 211). As their romance blossoms, this neutral color seems to looking more and more attractive to Bella.

What's more, the *Twilight Saga* has some superb symbolic scenes involving gray. For example:

- Bella says: "I am a neutral country. I am Switzerland" (*Twilight*, p 128). This gray as gray scene suggests that Bella is not taking sides with vampires or werewolves. She is neither anti-this nor pro-that, not black nor white – just a calm, steady, and peaceable gray.
- On the first day of *New Moon*, Bella wakes up to a "dull gray light" and an "overcast morning", which happens to be her 18th birthday (*New Moon*, p 6). This scene is not just talking about Forks weather. Symbolically, this gray morning also means that Bella's future is unclear and uncertain from this moment on. Will Bella's life unfold in a good way or a bad way? No one knows. The symbolic weather is way too gray.
- Bella had a dream that she was holding an ancient and silver knife, after she heard the tale of the Third Wife's Sacrifice. The next day, the morning "dawned pearl gray and still" (*Eclipse*, p 235). Well, today is the day that the newborn vampires have their picnic in the woods, so to speak, so they can kill everyone. At this stage, the symbolic forecast is a hazy, indeterminate gray. Anything can happen involving a fight against a newborn army of vampires.

Green

Green is the color of grass, leaves, the countryside and nature. It is a relaxing and refreshing color. Perhaps the best description of nature in the *Twilight Saga*, which captures the cool, calm beauty of green is when Bella first comes to Forks:

> It was beautiful... Everything was green: the trees, their trunks covered with moss, their branches hanging with a canopy of it, the ground covered with ferns. Even the air filtered down greenly through the leaves. It was too green."
> (*Twilight*, p 7)

Other exquisite references to green include these:

- The forest and ferns were "deep green" (*Twilight*, p 119). To Bella, the forest suggested a place where "myths and legends" could dwell (*Twilight*, p 119).
- The forest was a "dripping green maze" (*Twilight*, p 121).
- When the sunlight streamed through the leaves above, it was if "the canopy transformed, the murky olive tone shifting to a brighter jade" (*Twilight*, p 226).
- Edward's mother had "green eyes" that looked just "like emeralds" (*New Moon*, p 40). What this scene might really mean is yet to be discovered.

Since all plant life renews itself in spring, the color green has also become a symbol of hope, new life, renewal, strength, and environmental awareness. Green also has spiritual and supernatural meanings. In pagan times, for example, the Green Man was a leafy nature spirit who protected the forests and woods. Later on in the Middle Ages, in an attempt to wipe out pagan beliefs, green became associated with the Devil. To this day, the stained glass window of the Chartres Cathedral depicts a devil with green eyes and green skin. In a beautiful, magical and spiritual place like Forks, it might be nice to think twice about green.

H

Hair

Other than hair-raising adventures, just how important is a 'good hair day' in the *Twilight* world? People's hair can be described in terms of color, length, thickness and curliness. But hair has some deeper meanings too and the *Twilight* series taps into these hairy meanings.

Hair Psychology

As the *Twilight Saga* helps to show, the appearance of someone's hair can say a lot about characters and their personalities. A neat and tidy head of hair, for example, often suggests that the person underneath has a settled and organized approach to life. Nits, knots, and hot pink spikes sticking out, however, send a message that harks back to the rebellious punk rock era like: "I am an anarchist!" These ideas fit with folklore and history.

According to symbol experts, "to have unruly hair is to indicate a separation from conventional society, a sign of someone who flouts the rules, whose ideas are different from the norm and whose long hair is a symbol of freedom from the constraints of society" (Nozedar, 2008, p 561). Long and messy hair is not just limited to peace-loving hippies of the 1960s or other cultures. Traditionally, witches and wizards had long, unruly, and disheveled hair and they lived in remote places, far away from society. There's also the 'mad professor' look – a super-smart but insane scientist whose hair sticks out everywhere. To a brilliant mind, the pursuit of knowledge is far more important combing a head of hair.

This kind of hair symbolism definitely applies to Bella:

- She has long hair
- She has messy hair
- She does not spend much hair-care time.
- She is smart and excels at school.
- Bella's "hair looks like a haystack" (*Twilight*, p 273)

Other characters such as Alice are constantly helping to groom Bella's hair.

At a symbolic level, Bella's hair suggests that she is deep thinker, a teen philosopher, and a budding intellectual. This hair theory is backed up by *Twilight* world evidence that Bella is smart. For example, Bella is an abstract thinker and a high academic achiever who gets accepted by the university of her choice.

Hair Power

Did you know that hair is supposed to possess magic, power and its own life force? Hair stands for energy, power and sensuality, an extension of the personality and human identity. Men's hair tends to symbolize "strength" and "masculinity" while women's hair symbolizes "femininity", "immortality", "wisdom", and "love" (Colin, 2000, p 214).

To remove someone's hair means removing an important part of what makes them unique. That is why a strand of hair is such an important ingredient in magic spells to gain power over someone. In Victorian times, elaborate jewelry containing the locks of the departed was very popular. Hair is associated with romance to this day. A hairy example is the first time Bella and Edward visit their stone cottage in the forest. As Bella tells it, Edward was "twisting my fingers into his hair and pulling my face closer to his" (*Breaking Dawn*, p 445).

Hair Cuts

In the beginning, Jacob Black has lovely, long, sleek black hair.

But in *New Moon*, he cuts it all off and gets a tattoo, too (*New Moon*, p 262). While this could mean a hairstyle fashion craze among young wolves at La Push, there is probably a more meaningful symbolic explanation. You see, shamans, sages, monks, mystics, priests, priestesses and others would cut (or shave off) their hair as a sign of spiritual devotion. An 'extreme' haircut means that the person is rejecting material life in favor of embracing a new spiritual one. Jacob, who once considered his father's werewolf stories "superstitious" now fully acknowledges his magical heritage.

As a growing teen wolf, Jacob takes on more spiritual responsibilities. His role is to learn the spiritual ropes from the leader Sam Uley and to protect innocent humans from the cold ones. It makes sound symbolic sense for Jacob to reject Bella in *New Moon* when he tells her, "Go home, Bella. I can't hang out with you anymore" (*New Moon*, p 270). While Jacob may look as if he has obtained an extreme haircut away for "practical" reasons, he is at an important ritualistic shape-shifting, pack-bonding, scent-tracking and haircutting stage of his life right now. When Jacob cuts his hair short and gets a tattoo, this symbolizes a critical rite of passage. Jacob's short hair says: "I am on an important spiritual quest!"

Hand

Hand gestures are a main form of body language and a vital way people express themselves. In a cold climate like Forks, only the face and hands are unclothed and even then people wear gloves or mittens outside. All around the world, the hand is one of the most visible and expressive parts of the human body. People shake hands to greet each other. People use hands to communicate messages or warnings. Hand actions also convey feelings. Basically, people talk with their hands. Beyond the psychological value of hand-talk, hands also have metaphoric meanings.

Symbolically speaking, "hands, as an extension of the will and of the intention, carry a great power" (Nozedar, 2008, p 563).

Some symbolic hand signals are steeped in tradition as the *Twilight* world shows. Marriage ceremonies are among the most famous example. At the altar on Bella's wedding day, for example, "Charlie took my hand and, in a symbol as old as the world, placed it in Edward's" (*Breaking Dawn*, p 45). Hand signals also conveyed interpersonal feelings just before the Volturi appeared on the snow-covered ground. All emotion was spoken without sight or sound, all through a single hand gesture. For example, "Without risking a glance behind, Edward reached back to me. I stretched my arm forward so that I could grip his hand. He squeezed my fingers" (*Breaking Dawn*, p 630).

In the *Twilight Saga*, some of the most important and emotional information is communicated by hands only. Hand-talk, especially between Bella and Edward, reveals how deeply they love each other. There's the first ice-cold touch in biology class which evokes mystery (*Twilight*, p 38), the hesitant hand stroking in the meadow that evokes love (*Twilight*, p 229), Bella kissing the palm of Edward's hand (*Eclipse*, p 396), and Bella's open-handed peace signal to Irina (*Breaking Dawn*, p 497). In such scenes, the hands convey great feeling and more. This is without help from the eyes, the voice or other body-talk.

Back when people had sacred and spiritual bonds with nature, they expressed their respect for nature through magic rituals and ancient practices. In pagan times, certain hand gestures were special forms of communication to certain nature divinities and spiritual forces. In Bella and Edward's honeymoon scene, Edward enters the sea at midnight under the moonlight with his palms facing upwards. "He was motionless, his hands resting palms down against the water" (*Breaking Dawn*, p 77). This hand-gesture may be a sign of devotion to the moon from pagan times. The fact that Edward goes skinny-dipping at night adds extra symbolic significance. It is as if he is cleansing himself spiritually in the water. Bella is his "moon", after all. Edward's life was a "moonless night" before he met her.

An especially powerful hand gesture is when Alice returns with new friends at the brink of the *Breaking Dawn* battle scene. "I reached out to touch her arm, and so did Edward, Esme, Carlisle. There wasn't time for any other welcome" (*Breaking Dawn*, p 680). Just one brief touch by hand says it all. A picture may paint a thousand words, but a loving touch must surely convey a thousand feelings.

Hero

As a Gothic fiction series (romance and horror genre), the *Twilight Saga* definitely features heroes. As you may already know, the hero is a certain symbol, archetype or type of character who usually has the biggest role in a story. In fact, the word hero comes from the word Heracles, who is better known as Hercules – a good, strong and brave figure from Greek myth. Since the books are written in the 'first person' (Bella narrates or tells the story from her point of view), this makes Bella the main character in the *Twilight Saga*. Bella clearly aspires to be a hero from the very beginning. As she tells Edward: "I want to be Superman, too" (*Twilight*, p 413).

It may seem strange to classify Bella as a 'hero' when she describes herself as physically uncoordinated, uninteresting, lacking in social skills (*Twilight*, pp 9, 67) and "absolutely ordinary" (*Twilight*, p 184). She is a normal everyday teenage girl who does not have remarkable looks or abilities, with a tendency to be clumsy, a bit anxious and accident-prone. Stephenie Meyer views Bella as: "*An everygirl. She's not a hero*" (Meyer, in Kirschling, 2008). What this means is that anyone can relate to Bella. It also helps the story to highlight how an average person can perform heroic feats like those Bella achieves. To be a hero doesn't require great looks, cool clothes or the strength of a supernatural creature. Rather, a true hero is someone who uses their smart mind, good heart and inner courage to overcome obstacles and challenges in their life.

All good characters in the *Twilight* world have heroic qualities. In fact, every single person on the planet is on a heroic quest of some kind, striving to be happy and successful. But as always, stories tend to have a starring character, or maybe two to three main characters, such as Bella, Edward and Jacob in the *Twilight Saga*. In particular, Bella fits well with the 'classic hero' features. Meanwhile, Edward's character reflects the 'Byronic hero' in the Gothic genre. What qualities and meanings do these two types of hero symbolize? Why not let Bella and Edward show you themselves. To start with, here are the most important markers of Bella's character, the things that make a classic hero.

The Classic Hero: Bella
Good and Brave

What makes a hero? A hero usually possesses these characteristics and experiences these things on the course of their heroic adventure:

Features of the Classic Hero

The hero is naïve and inexperienced:

Bella has lived with her mother throughout her childhood, but then chooses to live with her father in Forks. Bella starts high school in her junior year, graduates, and makes plans to go to college. She also experiences her first deep romantic relationship with Edward, and deals with increasingly difficult supernatural challenges. From being a quiet and solitary teenager, love and other adventures change Bella into a mother and a vampire warrior.

The hero meets monsters or monstrous men:

When Bella moves to Forks, she meets both good and bad vampires and the local werewolf pack. Later on, she meets the

Volturi vampires in Italy.

The hero has a strange, wise being as a mentor:

Edward (as well as Carlisle and Alice) explain the vampire world to Bella.

Jacob (and his father Billy) mentor Bella about Quileute spirit legends and the werewolf world.

The hero yearns for the beautiful individual who is sometimes his guide or inspiration:

Bella is guided by Edward, a young vampire with good looks, lots of life experience, and smoldering eyes.

The hero must go on a journey, learn a lesson, change in some way, and return home:

Geographically, Bella moves to rainy Forks to live, travels to the ballet studio in Phoenix, visits the Volturi chambers in Italy, and meets secretly with Jenks in Seattle. Psychologically and philosophically, Bella learns that death is not important – protecting and loving others is much more important. Bella encourages everyone to get along, experiences many different kinds of families, and learns to appreciate everyone – vampires, werewolves, humans and half-vampires.

The hero often crosses a body of water or travels on a bridge:

Bella crosses bridges and travels over water a number of times in the *Twilight Saga*. Important crossings include driving over the river to La Push (*Twilight*, p 99), crossing a bridge near the Cullen house (*Twilight*, p 280), driving over a bridge at night (*Twilight*, p 347), stepping over a gutter with running water (*New Moon*, p 114), and leaping over a river as a vampire (*Breaking Dawn*, p 380).

The hero is born and raised in a rural setting away from cities:

Bella was born in Forks, a rainy town in the rural Washington state. She moves to Phoenix in the desert after her parents separate, and then returns to her original rural setting.

The origin of the hero is mysterious or the hero losses his/her parents at a young age, being raised by animals or a wise guardian:

Bella's parents separate when Bella is a young child and she seems to raise herself. In fact, Bella is quite responsible for her age and does many things to please and support others (*Twilight*, p 129). She helps her mother to manage the household and pay the bills on time. She also cares, cooks, and cleans for her dad, clearly taking on a parent role (*Twilight*, p 130). As a result of raising herself to a large degree, Bella describes herself as responsible, cautious, and thoughtful (*Eclipse*, p 40). Once Bella moves to Forks, wise members of the Cullen family guide her as do the magical Quileute werewolves.

The hero returns to the land of his/her birth in disguise or as an unknown:

Bella has "ivory", "sallow", "pallid" skin (*Twilight*, p 9) – opening omens that Bella was destined to be a vampire. Then Bella returns to Forks as a vampire, her red eyes are disguised by wearing brown contact lenses.

The hero is special, one of a kind. He/she might represent a whole nation or culture:

The *Twilight Saga* introduces Bella as a shy, invisible and solitary individual – a weirdo and a loner. Bella is introduced as a "new girl… a curiosity, a freak" (*Twilight*, p 9), who cannot "relate well to people" (*Twilight*, p 9) and who views the world differently to others, due to the "glitch" in her brain (*Twilight*, p 10). When Bella moves to Forks, she dodges the romantic advances of several high school boys and does not get enmeshed with the high school girls or the usual social scene either.

At Forks High, Edward thinks Bella is really special:

- "You are the opposite of ordinary" (*Twilight*, p 184).
- "You fascinate me" (*Twilight*, p 214).
- "You are *exactly* my brand of heroin" (*Twilight*, p 235).

- "You were too interesting, I found myself caught up in your expressions" and your "scent would stun me" (*Twilight*, p 238).
- Jacob describes Bella as "a little strange" (*New Moon*, p 172).
- Alice tells Bella "you are so bizarre, even for a human" (*New Moon*, p 437).

The hero struggles for something valuable and important:

Bella strives for love, happiness, and equality.

Bella figures out that engaging in risky, dangerous behavior triggers Edward's voices inside her mind (*New Moon*, p 185).

Bella takes risks to prove that Edward's love exists. For example, approaching men in a Port Angeles bar was an exciting, adrenaline-pumping experience (*New Moon*, p 110).

The hero has help from divine or supernatural forces:

Bella receives help from the Cullen vampires, the Quileute werewolves, and, much later, her own new supernatural gift – her psychic shield.

The hero has a guide or guides:

Bella receives advice and guidance from her mother, Edward, Carlisle, Alice, Jacob and Billy Black. Just before Bella gets married, her mother gives her some best-ever advice – follow your heart, only you know what is best for you.

The hero goes through a rite of passage or initiation, an event that marks a change from an immature to a more mature understanding of the world:

As a human, Bella's parents' separating and Edward abandoning her makes her more mature.

After nearly losing Edward, Bella gains increased knowledge about the soul, spirituality, and Edward's inner pain (he thinks he has no soul, and does not want Bella to become a vampire in order to protect her soul).

The hero undergoes some type of ritual or ceremony after his/her initiation:

Bella attends a school prom after being bitten by an evil vampire, James (*Twilight*).

Bella calls a Cullen family vote after Jasper tries to kill her and the Cullens move away from Forks for a while (*New Moon*).

After Bella emulates the third wife sacrifice during the battle against newborn vampires, Edward proposes to Bella and gives her an engagement ring (*Eclipse*).

After marrying Edward and having an island honeymoon, Bella becomes pregnant, almost dies giving birth, and becomes a vampire. After surviving these ordeals, Bella and Edward receive a stone cottage with a key as a wedding gift (*Breaking Dawn*).

The hero has a loyal band of companions:

Bella's ever-loyal and highly reliable companions include the Cullen vampires and Quileute werewolves.

The hero makes a stirring speech to his/her companions:

Bella makes a significant and stirring speech in each *Twilight* book:

- Bella confesses to herself that she is "irrevocably in love with a vampire" (*Twilight*, p 171) and she is willing to die in order to become one (*Twilight*, p 432). Edward is shocked and surprised that Bella is willing to end her life just to be with him.
- Bella calls a Cullen family meeting and asks everyone to vote about her future as a vampire (*New Moon*).
- Bella is willing to cut herself and bleed to death, if this will distract Victoria and stop her from killing Edward (*Eclipse*, p 487).
- Bella has a moving chat with Renesmee. She tells her only daughter that they will always be together forever in each other's hearts (*Breaking Dawn*, p 628).

The hero engages in tests or contests of strength (physical and/or mental) and shows pride in his/her excellence:

Bella confronts James alone in the ballet studio (*Twilight*).

Bella travels to Italy to save Edward from being executed by the Volturi vampires (*New Moon*).

Bella helps to implement warfare strategies to fight an oncoming army of newborn vampires. She also copies the third wife sacrifice (*Eclipse*).

Bella uses her psychic shield to protect dear ones from the Volturi's attack. On a lighter note, Bella arm wrestles with Emmett and pulverizes a boulder (*Breaking Dawn*).

Bella dominates Edward in the bedroom, chooses to stay in Forks after the brutal attack at the ballet studio, calls a Cullen family vote regarding her wishes to become a vampire, and rises as a star in the final battle with the Volturi, whom she defeats with her shield. The hero suffers an unhealable wound, sometimes an emotional or spiritual wound from which the hero never completely recovers:

Bella develops great heartache and a deep emotional scar (a hole inside her chest) when Edward breaks up with her.

At the end of *Breaking Dawn*, Bella fulfills her quest. She is the 'superhero' of the day.

Of course, the criteria of the 'hero' can apply to various characters in *Twilight* – Bella, Edward, Jacob, Carlisle, and others. Every individual is on a heroic quest, striving for personal fulfillment.

Bella's Likeness to Other Heroes

Jane Eyre – In literature, Bella Swan resembles a famous heroine called "Jane Eyre". This character from Charlotte Bronte's *Jane Eyre* is an 18 year old orphan girl who is plain, scrawny and not particularly attractive. When employed as a governess by the mysterious and wealthy Edward Rochester, Jane becomes obsessed with him (like Bella is with the mysterious Edward Cullen). Nevertheless, Jane shows heroic qualities like independence, strong-mindedness, defiance, and non-conformity. She doesn't hook up with Edward Rochester, after all (Schmoop, 2008).

Artemis – Bella resembles the moon goddess Artemis from Greek myth. This helps to boost Bella's heroic status. In particular, Artemis is depicted wearing a crescent moon. Bella also bears the mark of the crescent moon (a silver vampire bite scar on her hand). Just like Artemis, Bella is an independent feminist who makes her own life choices and resists the idea of marriage. The only reason why Bella marries Edward is so he can turn her into a supernatural being himself. Just as Artemis does in Greek myth, Bella nurtures the needy and helps others, especially her parents. The goddess Artemis defends the powerless from unjust treatment at the hands of the Olympian Gods, just as Bella is the up and coming *Twilight*-style goddess who protects her baby daughter from the Volturi. While Artemis goes hunting with a pack of hounds by her side, Bella becomes acquainted with the Quileute werewolves, a pack of fierce hunting dogs. Such similarities between Bella and Artemis are uncanny.

The Byronic Hero: Edward
Beautiful but Damned

Another type of hero from the point of view of literary analysis is the Byronic hero. Although various characters from the *Twilight Saga* show some features of this type of hero, Edward is the prime example. Just as the Byronic hero type suggests, Edward is, above all, heroic. In *Twilight*, for example, Edward saves Bella's life several times. This includes saving Bella from 1) a car skidding on ice; 2) Port Angeles thugs; 3) a killer called James; and 4) from becoming a vampire. Above all, Edward loves Bella, wants to protect her, and does not want to hurt her. Overall, many examples from the *Twilight* books suggest that Edward fully satisfies the criteria of a Byronic hero.

Features of a Byronic Hero

Highly intelligent and perceptive:

Edward is intelligent, well educated, has nearly a century of life experience, and is perceptive due to his sensitivity and mind reading. He has learned over many years how to read people both literally and figuratively.

Cunning and adaptive: Edward seems to be arrogant and stuck-up at first. However, unlike other Cullen vampires, Edward is open-minded enough to trust Bella who is a human. Edward adapts to her and learns to control his thirst for blood when he is around her to such an effective extent that it astounds the Volturi vampires. Hard-wired to feast on human blood, Edward and the Cullen family adapt to drinking animal blood so that they don't have to hunt people. As Edward explains "we call ourselves vegetarians" (*Twilight*, p 164).

Often sophisticated and highly educated:

Edward has multiple university degrees, an appreciation for the arts, and is musically talented.

Self-critical and introspective: Edward has an introverted personality and the kind of mind that wonders, worries, and analyzes things. He also tends to be hard on himself and puts himself down repeatedly. On one occasion, when Edward asked Bella to sit at his table at the school café, he tells her: "I decided as long as I was going to hell, I might as well do it thoroughly" (*Twilight*, p 75).

Mysterious, magnetic and appealing: Edward is certainly a closed, cold, and complex character. However, this seems to make him all the more appealing to Bella. As Bella explains herself:

- "I was consumed by the mystery Edward presented. And more than a little obsessed by Edward himself… I dreamed of Edward Cullen" (*Twilight*, p 57).
- "When I thought of him, of his voice, his hypnotic eyes, the

magnetic force of his personality, I wanted nothing more than to be with him" (*Twilight*, p 121).

- Bella clearly acknowledges "the magnetic force of his personality" (*Twilight*, p 121).

Seductive and sexually attractive:

Edward is certainly seductive and attracts sexual interest. For example:

- Bella's very first dream in the *Twilight Saga* is about "Edward Cullen" (*Twilight*, 57). This clearly suggests that deep down in her unconscious mind, it is Edward who she truly, madly loves.
- "I was consumed by the mystery Edward presented. And more than a little obsessed" (*Twilight*, p 67).
- "I'm the world's best predator, aren't I? Everything about me invites you in – my voice, my face, even my *smell*" (*Twilight*, p 231). In other words, Edward is a supernatural creature who is designed to be seductive and lure his prey.

Dominant in sexual relationships and interaction with people: Edward has shown dominant behavior in a variety of situations. For example, Edward clearly says "no" to Bella's sexual advances in his bedroom at the Cullen house, despite her pleading. His dominance matures in the *Twilight Saga*. For example, Edward is the one who leads the talks and converses with Aro during the *Breaking Dawn* war. Edward establishes his dominant personality tendencies early on in the *Twilight* series. For example:

- Edward tells Bella he will be "overbearingly protective" (*Twilight*, p 287).
- Bella tells Edward he is "pushy!" (*Twilight*, p 89).
- Bella describes Edward as "intimidating" (*Twilight*, p 179).

Conflicting emotions, bipolar tendencies, or moodiness:

Edward experiences considerable inner conflict. This may explain some of his mood swings. Basically, Edward wants to be with Bella because he loves her. At the same time, Edward thinks it is a bad idea because his natural diet is human blood. This makes the vampire-human dating game a little dangerous. Some examples of Edward's inner conflict and moody behavior:

- "What if I'm not the superhero? What if I'm the bad guy?" (*Twilight*, p 79).
- Bella notices Edward's moodiness in that "his sudden mood changes left me always a step behind, dazed" (*Twilight*, p 233).
- Edward confesses to Bella that: "Sometimes I have a problem with my temper" (*Twilight*, p 152).
- "Do you have multiple personality disorder?" (*Twilight*, p 70), Bella asks Edward, when he keeps chopping and changing his mind about being with her.
- A good example of Edward's mood swings is when he tells Bella: "'I wasn't mad at *you*'... He was suddenly intense, all trace of teasing gone." This reminded Bella of his "black moods" (*Twilight*, p 319).

A distaste for social institutions and social norms:

While Edward and the Cullens do try to live peacefully alongside humans, Edward certainly has a wild social side to him. In particular, Edward once rebelled against Carlisle's vegetarian vision to the point where he drank the blood of would-be murderers and other human offenders for a while. Edward also dislikes high school, quarrels with the Quileutes, and avoided humans altogether until he met Bella.

Being an exile, an outcast, or an outlaw:

Edward is certainly one-of-a-kind. For example:

- Bella describes him as a "bizarre, beautiful boy" (*Twilight*, p 43).
- Edward does not mix with students outside his family at school.
- Edward and the Cullens drink animal blood to survive, not human blood. This makes them outsiders according to the social vampire norms.

Has 'dark' attributes not normally associated with heroes:

- Although Edward is good-hearted and heroic, he has a dark and destructive side. For example, Edward has killed humans in the past. Edward also has an overwhelming urge to kill and drink the blood of his true love. As Edward warns Bella: "It's not only your company I crave! Never forget that I am more dangerous to you than I am to anyone else" (*Twilight*, p 233).
- In another scene, Edward's "expression was pained" (*Twilight*, p 165). This is because he wants to be with Bella, but he knows it is "wrong". This is because of his darkest attribute – he is a vampire.
- Edward confesses to Bella that when they first met: "The scent was maddening. I so very nearly took you then… But I resisted… I went straight to Carlisle, at the hospital, to tell him I was leaving" (*Twilight*, p 237). In fact, Edward went all the way to Alaska that time.
- Another dark attribute not typical of vampires is Edward's destructive death wish. As Edward's sister Alice explains: "You don't get a lot of suicidal vampires" (*New Moon*, p 431).

A lack of respect for rank and privilege:

Edward definitely doesn't like the Volturi, the Italian vampires who enforce laws. Furthermore, Edward feels so bad for being a vampire that he denies the personal privileges associated with being a vampire and his eternal life. At first, Edward does not show much respect for the Quileute werewolves either, not until Bella makes friends with Jacob and eventually brings the two sides together.

A troubled past, guilt over some past crime, struggles with integrity:

Edward has had a troubled past and feels guilty for a number of reasons. For example, Edward has killed humans in the past, he had a rebellious period where he left Carlisle and the Cullens, he has felt lonely for almost a century, and he believes that he has no soul and is a "monster". Looking at Edward's face, Bella once noticed that: "His eyes were ancient with their sadness" (*Eclipse*, p 474). In other scenes, Bella notices that Edward worries a lot and picks up on his emotional struggles:

- "He closed his eyes, lost in his agonized confession… I was filled with compassion for his suffering" (*Twilight*, p 238).
- Edward's "expression was torn, almost pained, and so fiercely beautiful that the ache to touch him flared" (*Twilight*, p 193).
- "His stunning face was unexpectedly vulnerable" (*Twilight*, p 56).
- Edward finds it excruciatingly painful and difficult to abstain from drinking Bella's blood, but "I couldn't live with myself if I ever hurt you. You don't know how it's tortured me" (*Twilight*, p 239).

Since Edward is a vampire who strives to do the right thing, this makes him vulnerable to worry and guilt.

Cynical, demanding, and/or arrogant:

- Edward admits to Bella "I was arrogant" (*Twilight*, p 238).
- The way Edward treats and talks about the Quileutes

werewolves is extremely cynical, distrustful and scathing.

Self-destructive, self-critical and introspective:
Edward seems to really hate himself at times. For example, Edward tells Bella, "I'll never forgive myself for leaving you" (*Eclipse*, p 28). In another adventure, Edward tells Bella: "I'm just going to do what I want now, and let the chips fall where they may" (*Twilight*, p 75). Edward says this even though his behavior is potentially unhealthy and destructive.

Loner, often rejected from society:

- When Edward's parents died from the Spanish influenza, he was truly "alone" (*Twilight*, p 251).
- Edward cannot fully fit in with human society as he is a vampire.
- The other Cullens are paired off, but Edward is alone.
- Charlie and the wolves initially reject Edward from their lives.
- When Bella jumps off a cliff in *New Moon*, Edward cuts himself off from others and his family, as he tries to deal with this highly stressful situation alone, far away from others.

(Source: *Teaching Twilight: Edward as Byronic Hero*. http://teachingtwilight.wordpress.com/about/)

How Does the Byronic Hero Involve Lord Byron?

The idea of the Byronic hero was not invented by Lord Byron, but he did help to make it famous. The Byronic Hero was a core figure of the Romantic movement, a hero with a dark side, an era in which Lord Byron was a prominent writer. In the *Twilight* world, Edward has a dark side in that he has killed some humans and he also craves Bella's blood.

According to academics, many Romantic vampire novels feature a Byronic hero and Lord Byron is often linked to the vampire genre. This is due to the strange company Byron kept as well as his eccentric lifestyle – like drinking blood and using human skulls as mugs. There are also tales of Byron requesting skulls and hearts from funeral pyres. Apparently, Byron believed that drinking blood made him sexually attractive to others, as other authors of the vampire genre did. An 1831 description of Byron's work helps to explain what makes Edward a convincing Byronic hero: *"strange union of opposite extremes, proud, moody, cynical – with defiance on his brow, and misery in his heart; a scorner of his kind, implacable in revenge, yet capable of deep and strong affection"* (Thomas Babington Macaulay). Despite Edward's vampiric nature, the very thing that makes him a 'monster', Edward is capable of loving a human girl.

Honey

Honey is a rich and rare liquid food most famous for its golden color and sweet taste. It is the effort, labor, and alchemy of bees. The product of honey can only be achieved by honest effort and a great deal of collective hard work by bees, which transform pollen dust and nectar from flowers into honey. Someone is *busy as a bee* when she or he works diligently and tirelessly. Honey therefore symbolizes the idea that precious gold can only be achieved by sincere productivity. These honey meanings help to explain why the Cullens may have links with honey.

The honey-eyed Cullens, Edward's honey-like fragrance, and their past emotional hardships fit well with honey alchemy and symbolism. Each Cullen family member has experienced hardship or a near death experience. For example, Edward lost his parents to a flu outbreak, Esme leaped off a cliff to commit suicide, and Rosalie would have died from murder had Carlisle not saved her. A wild bear nearly mauled Emmett to death and Jasper's war experiences fighting newborn vampires were terrifying. The three-day experience of becoming a vampire is also grueling. The Cullens felt intolerable pain as a raging fire spread through their bodies. After becoming vampires, starting with Carlisle, it has taken much thought, effort, diligence and action for the Cullens to abstain from drinking human blood and establish themselves as vegetarian vampires who only drink animal blood. Indeed, it is so hard that Jasper is still working on it. When you consider the symbolic meanings of honey, the Cullens deserve to have amazing gold eyes and other honeyed qualities.

Since honey is such a sweet and luscious liquid it also has romantic meanings. This has lead to ideas such as affectionately calling someone you love 'honey' and describing the blissful state of newlyweds as the 'honeymoon' phase. The oldest known poem that used honey as a synonym for love comes from ancient Sumaria (Southern Iraq). More than 4000 years ago, the overjoyed bride of a king wrote these honey-sweet lines in a song:

Your allure is a sweet thing, as sweet as honey.
My precious sweet, let me bring you honey.
In the bedchamber dripping with honey
let us enjoy over and over your allure, the sweet thing
(Songs of Songs. In Sumerian Songs)

Sounds like someone describing Edward from the *Twilight Saga*!.

The sweet experience of falling in love forever is something that many people strongly desire. Immortality is certainly a honeybee quality because honey is a non-perishable food; it is a sweet delight that never decomposes. As such, the bee is an authentic symbol of alchemy because it turns pollen dust into a sweet life-giving liquid gold that lasts forever and forever. No wonder honeybees, signifying immortality and resurrection, were royal emblems of ancient societies. Not only is honey long-lasting, which links it to immortality, but it has healing and antiseptic properties. A drop of honey smeared onto a wound will sterilize it and promote the healing process.

With its healing properties and supernatural links with immortality, wisdom, poetry, and love, the busy bee is a magnificent and magical insect. In line with bee symbolism, it is worth noting that Edward has positive supernatural powers too. In the *Twilight Saga*, Edward's honey-colored eyes dazzle, and so does his scent once Bella becomes a vampire. Edward's love and romantic words for Bella are as sweet, pure, and healing as honey. This makes Edward a real honey!

By all means, taste the sweetness and behold the beauty of honey. But beware the bee's danger. A painful sting can kill certain people who have allergies. What could be more analogous to the toxic sting of the bee than the venomous bite of a vampire?!

House

A house is a special dwelling place. It is a home, residence, or private abode where people and families have sheltered since the earliest times. When people hunted and gathered food, their survival depended on making protective cover with their hands if no natural shelter was available. Shelters protected people from wild weather, fierce creatures, and evil spirits at night. To survive, people preferred to settle around places rich in natural resources. They built shelters near fresh water, food, trees and other supplies. Considering themselves lucky to find such natural wealth, they would thank and celebrate nature. This is how the dwellings acquired symbolic meanings and were considered to be spiritual havens. Naming houses was once an important and ancient practice. "If a house had a name, it was believed that it had a spirit, a soul, an existence in its own right" (Colin, 2000, p 269). To this day, some places are believed to be charged with positive or negative energies, giving them either a welcome or hostile feel. In Ukraine, for example, (traditional vampire homeland), every house in the village would have a house-spirit called a *domovik* that protects the house or else, if disturbed, plays pranks.

Houses also came to be associated with mothers, as being places where people can gather, enjoy intimacy and seek refuge, shelter, protection, or love. It is no wonder Esme makes everyone feel welcome at the Cullen house. She is the heart of the house.

Every house, depending on where it is, what it looks like, and how it is managed reveals telltale symbolic clues about the occupants. A visit to a house or dreaming about a house can be interpreted in countless ways. Is the visitor/dreamer inside or outside the house? What is the house's shape, structure and location? Which room of the house is the visitor/dreamer in? In the *Twilight Saga*, each house sure has its own unique flair.

Charlie Swan's House

In *Twilight*, we learn that Charlie the police chief lives in a "small, two-bedroom house" which he bought when he was married to Bella's mother (p 7). Bella's bedroom has "light blue walls" and "yellow curtains" (*Twilight*, p 8). The white-yellow kitchen is "small". The family room was about as big as a "handkerchief" and filled with family photos, including Charlie's old wedding photo. This house is homely, cozy and practical (after all, there's less housework to do in a small house). Charlie is clearly a humble and sentimental individual because he keeps the house his wife once lived in and continues to display early family photos. The house also suggests security and safety – Charlie is not a financially irrational guy who has upgraded his abode to a flashy castle he can't afford. And although the house seems a bit dusty and neglected (a symbol of a busy work life and a strong devotion to career), it is definitely not in disrepair – it lacks crumbling walls, leaking taps, and creaky floorboards.

The Cullen Manor

The Cullen Mansion is arguably the most interesting house in the *Twilight Saga*. Occupied by a family of vampires and described in detail, this is no surprise. It is depicted as a "huge white mansion buried deep in the forest beside the river" (*New Moon*, p 19). As Bella describes it, the grand house was three storeys tall and looked: "timeless, graceful, and probably a hundred years old" (*Twilight*, p 281). She describes it as a large, uncluttered, and neutral-colored home. It is situated in a large clearing, next to six huge cedar trees and the riverbank. The house inside was "very bright, very open, and very large" and the first floor was designed to be "one wide space" (*Twilight*, p 281). The wall facing south was made of clear "glass", and the lawn, shaded by the cedars, reached the Calawah riverbank (*Twilight*, p 281). A "massive curving staircase dominated the west side of the room" and to the left of the front door was a "spectacular grand piano" (*Twilight*, p 281).

The Cullen house is unfenced, surrounded by wilderness, nature, light, space, and filled with a few stylish and artistic objects. This surely reflects the Cullens' open-minded natures, their unwillingness to be untamed by the Volturi, and their desire for freedom of expression. Adding to the Cullens' strong sense of family, the Cullens also value creativity and personal growth. The pale white colors of the house may be a symbolic tribute to the pallid white vampire skin of the Cullens. A neutral color scheme is also much like a blank canvas – an open or empty background waiting for someone to make their mark and express themselves creatively. The open spaces, shared living area, and the clear glass view strongly suggest that open and transparent communication is a Cullen clan strength. The house is very modern, open and protective.

On the second floor at the top of the staircase, Carlisle's huge wooden cross from the 1630s hung (*Twilight*, p 288). This is not necessarily a morbid reminder of a dark past though. The

Cullens value historical knowledge and they like to learn lessons from the past so that they can move forward in the future. Rosalie and Emmett's room is situated on this floor. So is Jasper's study, and Alice and Jasper's room (with a clothes closet larger than the room itself). Carlisle's office is next, with an area inside for Esme's study and Carlisle's personal library.

On the third floor, Carlisle and Esme's room is at the top of the staircase, there is Edward's room, and also a library.

Carlisle's office had a "high ceiling", a "west-facing window", and the room was filled with "towering bookshelves" (*Twilight*, p 292). These house features may be a symbolic salute to Carlisle's high moral aspirations (high ceiling), his intense contemplation of death and the afterlife (his office faces west where the sun dies), and his pursuit of knowledge (numerous books). The wall of Carlisle's office was "crowded with framed pictures of all sizes, some in vibrant colors" (*Twilight*, p 293). This includes the "large", "colorful" and "ornately framed" painting of the three Volturi rulers (Aro, Marcus, and Caius) standing next to Carlisle (*Twilight*, p 297). This symbolizes Carlisle's appreciation for history, culture, and the arts. The whole Cullen house certainly reflects an appreciation for the arts. It has color (the paintings), music (the piano), architectural style (the spiral staircase), and culture (the cross).

Edward's bedroom has a "wall-sized window" facing south out with a great view (*Twilight*, p 300). Edward's bedroom and bed have a black and gold color theme, the same color as his eyes. In one undefined corner, there's a state of the art sound system which Bella feels unable to use. There's a thick golden carpet and thick fabric curtains "in a slightly darker shade" for the walls. In *Eclipse,* Edward buys a big, beautiful bed for Bella to sleep in. "The coverlet was dull gold, just lighter than the walls; the frame was black, made of intricately patterned wrought iron. Sculpted metal roses wound in vines up to the tall posts and formed a bowery lattice overhead" (*Eclipse,* p 134). The bed is also reminiscent of Edward's golden eyes, fringed by long black lashes. As one *Twilight* fan has noticed, Edward's room has "the best view" and his gaze is turned outwards onto the Sol Duc River valley and the Olympic Mountain range because it is most probably the Cullen family lookout. "Edward's room is the crow's nest of the Cullen fortress" (TwilightMOMS, posted by scoundrel, 2011).

Edward's bedroom features a massive CD collection and wide black leather sofa, but no bed. Edward's cool, bleak, detached, music-filled room probably helps to fill Edward's emotional emptiness inside. No bed may also be a symbolic clue that Edward has had no romantic life either, not until he meets Bella.

In *Eclipse*, Edward gets a big bed for his room for Bella to sleep in. This clearly reveals Edward's romantic and nurturing side. He enjoys watching and doting over Bella as she sleeps and looks on with adoration as she talks in her sleep and dreams.

In *Breaking Dawn* Bella spends most of her time inside the Cullen House. The Cullen house is a truthful physical expression and extension of the Cullens themselves, a "unique blend of Gothic mystery and engaging humanity" (TwilightMOMS, posted by scoundrel, 2011).

The Black House

In *New Moon*, Bella visits the Black house – the residence of Jacob and his father Billy Black. It is "a small wooden place with narrow windows, the dull red paint making it resemble a tiny barn" (*New Moon*, p 130). Jacob's garage is located at the side of the house, hidden from view by trees and shrubs. On Bella's first visit there, she noticed that Billy was in "a tiny square living room" (*New Moon*, p 132). In a subsequent visit, she noticed that Jacob's room was also very small, like a "tiny closet" (*New Moon*, p 302). The physical structure of the small Black house accurately reflects the small close-knit two-person family that lives there. The *red* house also symbolizes the red/bronze Quileute skin, the blood-related family ties, and the magic that flows in Quileute blood.

Emily Young's House

Emily's house appears in *New Moon*. Bella describes it as "a tiny house that had once been gray. There was only one narrow window beside the weathered blue door, but the window box under it was filled with bright orange and yellow marigolds" (*New Moon*, p 331). The bright flowers give the house a cheerful atmosphere. The appearance of Emily's kitchen was bright and friendly too, with its "white cupboards and pale wooden floorboards" (*New Moon*, p 333). This house is not only Emily's home; it serves as a hangout for the whole La Push wolf pack.

Isle Esme Home

Isle Esme near Rio is a tropical island that Carlisle gave to Esme as a gift. This is where Edward and Bella spend their honeymoon. This island has a large and airy house furnished by Esme. A dominant feature of this island home is its large glass windows, and it has very pale color tones like the Cullen house in Forks (*Breaking Dawn*, p 73). The house has two bedrooms, one large bathroom, a modern kitchen, and a window overlooking the beach. The main bedroom was "big and white" with a glass wall, a "*huge* white bed" draped with white mosquito netting" (*Breaking Dawn*, p 73). A light, bright, relaxing room, no doubt, colored white to suggest a new and fresh start in life. Another feature of the Isle Esme house was a "blue room" with a bed, dark teak wall panels, and blue silk features (*Breaking Dawn*, p 91). A room to promote bonds perhaps, since blue suggests honesty and sincerity.

Bella's Stone Cottage

The Cullen family gave Bella a stone cottage as a gift for her nineteenth birthday in *Breaking Dawn*. Esme thought that Bella and Edward might like a place of their own as newlyweds, so she renovated an old building in the forest for them. Bella describes it as "a tiny stone cottage" with flowers, dark windows, and a stone path leading up to a cute "arched wooden door" (*Breaking Dawn*, p 440).

Once inside, "stone mosaics", "warm wood" and a "fire" give the cottage a magical feeling (*Breaking Dawn*, p 443). The assorted interior furnishings include a medieval chair, a modern ottoman, and a well-stocked bookshelf (*Breaking Dawn*, p 443). The miscellaneous materials used to build the cottage and the eclectic furniture inside seem to symbolize Bella's new family really well. It is also a unique and cozy ensemble of three very different individuals. There's Bella (a newborn vampire), Edward (a vampire), and Renesmee (a half-vampire). And they are all part of a larger family network that comprises several adopted children. The cottage's symbolic message? If you don't have any biological family, if you feel all alone in the world, there is still hope – you have the power to create a happy family setting of your own. You can use unrelated family members (eclectic furniture pieces) in the form of friends, flowers, or maybe even animal companions to build yourself a harmonious home. After all, as the Cullen vampire family shows, the best family homes are forged with the power of love, not with hard materials such as bricks or genetics.

Hunting/Gathering

The *Twilight Saga* suggests important food themes. In particular, Bella smells sweet and irresistible to Edward, while Edward's delicious scent intoxicates Bella. No wonder they feel like eating and biting each other all the time. Beyond the pleasure principle, however, some deeper dietary signs and symbols seem to emerge.

Hunting Behavior

What is the one thing that vampires love to eat? No, not vampire cereal. It's human blood – their natural food source. This throws up some interesting symbolic dilemmas in the *Twilight* world:

Do vampires symbolize evil?

Vampires devouring humans is considered brutal and evil. Can't vampires get sustenance some other way that does not involve killing humans? After all, some vampires have acquired a new taste, a moral diet – they only drink animal blood. What's more, animal blood-drinkers are environment aware. They only hunt those animals that are plentiful, not rare. This suggests that not all vampires are evil.

Do *Twilight* vampires symbolize human evil?

If vampires can refrain from consuming human products (and drink animal blood instead), can't humans refrain from killing and consuming animals (and eat plant material instead)? Maybe the greedy human blood-drinking vampires in the *Twilight* world are a symbol for greedy flesh-eating humans.

What does vegetarianism symbolize?

Vegetarianism is a main *Twilight Saga* theme. Some vampires are vegetarian – they hunt animals, not humans, for food. Edward and the Cullens are 'vegetarian'. They are all committed to protecting human life – preferring the flavor of large predators to satisfy their dietary needs (*Eclipse*, p 23). What's more, vegetarian vampires and human vegetarians symbolize much more than just the food they eat. Vegetarians also symbolize empathy, compassion, a higher way of life.

What does hunting *really* symbolize?

In the *Twilight* world, all vampires hunt. Some hunt people and some hunt animals. Werewolves hunt animals to eat too. Then there are the humans who hunt in the *Twilight* world. Charlie goes fishing almost every weekend. Other people hunt native wildlife. For example, Bella comes across "SAVE THE OLYMPIC WOLF" flyers in *Eclipse* (p 88). Given that hunting is a main theme in the *Twilight* world, what does hunting symbolize? What is this theme trying to tell us?

As a symbol, hunting means different things:

Survival – hunting is one of the most ancient and vital life-sustaining human activities. Humans originally hunted and gathered wild animals, birds, fish, vegetables, fruits and nuts for food.

Strength – hunting is also a test of physical strength, mental confidence, and skill.

Quest – hunting is also a quest. It is a glorified form of combat, a challenge between humans and animals to determine superiority of a species.

Power – Hunting is also a power motif. Ultimately, hunting involves one party completely dominating another party, predator and prey, an executioner and a victim (Colin, 2000).

As the hunting adventures in the *Twilight* books suggest, hunting is not just tied to survival issues and food themes, it involves power issues too. *Twilight* hunting scenes show that regardless of who is the hunter (vampire, werewolf, human), the motive and the method of the hunt is what makes a hunter evil or not. Hunting habits say a lot about the mind and morals of the hunter.

In the *Twilight* world, some forms of hunting are not for the purposes of finding food. For example, James hunts Bella for the thrill of it. This is considered brutal. But some hunting by humans is not for the purposes of finding food either. Some humans hunt animals, like wolves or deer or fish, for fun or sport – just for the thrill of it. How is this less brutal than vampires hunting humans for the same reasons? Some symbolic food for thought.

Vegetarianism Gathers Force

Vampires hunting humans is presented as brutal and abhorrent. Vampires devouring animals for food is presented as bloody and macabre, e.g. Bella's first hunt. Yet, eating a deer in the woods is no different to humans devouring the flesh of slaughtered farm animals such as chickens, cows, pigs, and sheep. In fact, the Cullens appear to be especially aware of the animal life force which they extinguish during their hunts. Just like many ancient and native cultures, the Cullens show respect for these animals which have lost their lives in a hunt. The Cullens consider what they hunt. They conduct magical and ritualistic 'farewells' to animals they kill. Quileute fishing is related to culture and survival, need not greed, food not power.

Bella gives up fishing after "killing three fish in a row" (*Twilight*, p 226). What might Bella's natural vegetarian tendency symbolize? Empathy towards animals. It foreshadows Bella's natural vegetarian potential, her success as a vegetarian vampire, and an ability to live a life with higher meaning.

Who eats who, who hunts who, and why, is a symbolic exploration of the motives that drive human behavior. These include survival and power, need and greed, cruelty and kindness, and good and evil.

I

Ice

Freezing cold ice in drinks is great on a hot summer's day. But ice can sure be a cold and bitter metaphor. In the *Twilight Saga,* ice describes different things. This includes the cold outdoors. For example, once Bella noticed the frosty Forks weather. "A fine layer of snow" in the yard had frozen the rain, "coating the needles on the trees in fantastic, gorgeous patterns, and making the driveway a deadly ice slick" (*Twilight,* p 45). On another occasion, Bella touched Edward's super-cool vampire skin. She noticed that Edward's "fingers were ice cold like he's been holding them in a snowdrift" (*Twilight,* p 38). As the *Twilight* world shows, icy things like winter weather and vampires can be beautiful, but also dangerous. What's more, ice is a popular symbol for cold and detached emotions.

Icy Isolation

The cold and icy Forks weather reinforces a sense of isolation (ice-olation, get it?) that important characters such as Bella and Edward feel. When Bella moves to Forks, she isolates herself in a number of ways. At a geographical level, there's the physical isolation. Forks is a secluded, rainy, rural town with a small population. There's also the social isolation. Bella is the new girl in school, an outsider who looks plain and acts clumsy. There's also a strong sense of emotional isolation. Bella is an only child who has chosen to leave her mother and move in with an emotionally distant father. Furthermore, Bella has an introverted personality style that tends to isolate her from others even more. She is a thinker, dreamer, loner. As Bella explains: "I found myself reveling in the aloneness" (*Twilight,* p 46). Symbolically speaking, it feels as if Bella's inner emotional world has hit freezing point.

Then there's Edward – arguably the loneliest character in the *Twilight Saga*. Edward was an only child who lost both his parents when he was still a teen. Although Edward is an important member of the Cullen clan, all the other members in his family are paired off, except for him. Edward has not had a romantic partner for over a century, until he finds Bella. Being a vampire makes Edward's social and emotional world colder and lonelier too. Since *Twilight* vampires sparkle in the sun, they must hide themselves away in the coldest, gloomiest, and darkest corners of the earth to minimize their exposure to the sun. The natural food source they crave, human blood, isolates the Cullen family further. As vampires, the Cullens need to keep their distance from humans. Losing control over one's inner vampire urge could prove disastrous and fatal. By moving to a small town where the rain always falls and the place is not so crowded helps to reduce the Cullens' contact with humans. To keep their supernatural identity a secret, the Cullens must never lose control of their desire to drink human blood.

As if Edward and the Cullens weren't isolated enough, their choice to be vegetarian vampires (drink animal blood) separates them further from all the other vampires. Edward and his family banish themselves to the highest and rockiest mountaintops, and the thickest and wildest parts of the forest, to feed on big cats and grizzly bears. Without a doubt, the geographic, social, and emotional worlds of Bella, Edward and the Cullens are ice-cold.

Frozen Feelings

Edward is a vampire with ice-cold skin who is 'frozen' in a state of immortality. Turned into a vampire at the young age of seventeen, Edward will always look like a teenager forever. Charlie, however, is perhaps *Twilight's* best example of a human who is frozen in his mortal life. This is because Charlie hangs on to his past, his marriage, his memories. Charlie hides himself in his work, watches TV, and goes fishing often, which thwarts his personal progress to bond intimately with others, including his only child. Even after his daughter Bella comes to live with him, Charlie sticks to the same routine – work, TV, fishing. Symbolically speaking, Charlie's emotional world is frozen and lifeless like ice. He still has old photos of his ex-wife and former life, dusty and untouched, in his house. Charlie continues to focus on his job, has not learned how to cook, and he has not formed any new romantic relationships for nearly twenty years. After separating from his wife, Charlie's emotional world becomes cold and barren; his life is frozen solid. Unable to move forward, Charlie's life stands still in time and space. You can either freeze personal progress, like Charlie does. Or, you can set your world on fire with exciting choices. By contrast, Carlisle seeks to make warm emotional connections – he engages others. This approach leads him to bond with the lovely Esme, his wife. And to find several foster children too.

Some other scenes in the *Twilight* books also suggest the idea that ice means negative emotions and getting stuck:

- Edward's feelings were once frozen for a while. As Bella tells it, Edward was "dead set against any future that changed me… made me immortal, too. An impasse, he called it" (*New Moon*, p 10). In this example, Edward freezes the possibility for change.
- When Edward tells Bella he wants to break up with her, "her whole body went numb. I couldn't feel anything below the neck" (*New Moon*, p 71). She is frozen in a state of shock – an ice statue.
- From October to January in *New Moon*, Bella's life freezes up emotionally. She experiences a deep depression and becomes socially inactive and "lifeless" (p 95).
- When Jacob tells Bella not to see him anymore, she feels

> "so cold". She was "still freezing" after having a long, hot shower (*New Moon*, p 274). Symbolically, when Jacob withdraws the warmth of his friendship, Bella's emotional world becomes barren, empty and ice-cold.

The ice in "*Twilight* symbolizes the icy cold of Bella's and Edward's life. Neither one of them have really experienced any warmth in their years. They are both sort of frozen when it comes to emotion" (TwilightMOMS post by Joanna Maria, February 27, 2010).

Melting the Ice

Edward's icy skin is only vampire-skin deep. As Bella describes him, Edward's chest was "hard and cold-and perfect – as an ice sculpture" (*New Moon*, p 17). Underneath the icy skin, however, is a very different Edward. This young male vampire has "warm eyes" (*New Moon*, p 65) and a burning love for Bella in his heart. As Bella notices, "the gold became liquid again, molten, burning down into mine with an intensity that was overwhelming" (*New Moon*, p 71). Edward may be a cold-skinned vampire. On the inside, however, Edward is warm-hearted, he is fire and ice in one. It's how you love and live your life makes you warm, not your skin type.

The *Twilight* world's references to ice also help to illustrate Bella's increasing love for Edward. In *Eclipse*, Bella gets used to the cold weather and grows less fond of the heat. For example, when Bella visited her mother in Phoenix, she found the heat "smothering" and the "air was so heavy with moisture" that it was hard to breathe (*Eclipse*, p 59). Bella's new affinity for cold weather may be a symbolic tip to her growing love for Edward, a cold-skinned creature. Bella's increasing preference for cold and ice may also symbolize the fact that Bella is choosing "ice" (Edward) over "fire" (Jacob).

Fire and Ice

In the *Twilight* books, fire and ice metaphors help to symbolize personality differences between Edward and Jacob as they compete for Bella's love. In a noteworthy scene, just after a snowstorm, Bella climbs out of her tent into "the bright, icy morning". She notices that "the sun" was "glancing off the snow that lingered and stabbing at my unadjusted eyes. The air still had a bite to it, but it was dead calm and slowly becoming more seasonable as the sun rose higher" (*Eclipse*, p 457). The sunlight on the snow (Jacob is Bella's sun) "stabs" Bella in the eye. Meanwhile, the icy snow "bites" Bella with its bitter coldness (Edward is Bella's ice-cold vampire). What ideal symbolism, to describe Jacob and Edward competing for Bella's love using – fire and ice, hot and cold, Jacob and Edward using their fiery and icy influences, fighting it out on a mountaintop for Bella's love. By referring to symbolic opposites such as sun and snow, fire and ice, and hot and cold, the *Twilight* text helps to capture and contrast the different supernatural personalities of Edward and Jacob perfectly.

In a much later scene in the *Twilight* epic, fire and ice is used to suggest that two different forces, two people from very different backgrounds, can get along and love each other, if they really want to. During her honeymoon with Edward, Bella refers to herself as fire and Edward as ice to highlight the idea that harmony, despite diversity, is possible. Bella's observes that "Fire and ice, somehow existing together without destroying each other" makes Bella feel happy (*Breaking Dawn*, p 80).

Island

As a symbol, an island is a source and center of life. The island is a center of the world. Imagine our ancestors, from long ago, sailing the wild, open, unchartered and dangerous waters of an open sea. And then finding an island – a source of food, shade, tools, protection, and great beauty. The experience must have been truly amazing. An island can give you a strange feeling that you are on another plane of existence, and that something unexpected could happen at any moment, perhaps somewhere on the horizon or else something encircling the island. In fact, an island experience usually entails an atmosphere of adventure and excitement as well as calm, pleasure and relaxation. All over the world, the island represents a place of refuge and protection.

Another important symbolic meaning of islands is birth and death. An island is a place of life – animals, food, water, luxurious vegetation. But island life is also linked to destruction and death – reefs, sharks, storms, waves, cyclones, tsunamis. An island can also mean shipwrecks.

In the *Twilight Saga,* tropical Isle Esme certainly fits with the beautiful, exotic and pleasurable meanings of islands. An island is "the enchanted and wonderful place that we long for, dream about and discover. It is therefore the symbolic representation of the place within each and every one of us where we can find peace and harmony" (Colin, 2000, p 285). On their island near Rio, both Bella and Edward can free their feelings fully and be themselves. Since islands are surrounded by open waters and hidden reefs, they are wild places where anything can happen. The visit to Isle Esme certainly fits this island meaning also. In particular, Bella falls pregnant with Edward's child. Impossible? Not after absorbing some island magic, it seems. An emotional tsunami follows – Edward reacts badly to the news. He loses the plot with regards to Bella's unplanned pregnancy and his control undergoes a total wipeout. As you can see, Isle Esme embraces both positive and negative island meanings. The emotional island we create inside ourselves can be a paradise or a storm, depending on whether our feelings are steady or choppy, it seems.

J

Jacksonville

In the *Twilight* series, Jacksonville is where Bella's mother Renée moves to live with her new husband Phil. After Bella has a violent encounter with an evil vampire, and ends up in the Forks Hospital, Renée entices Bella to live there. "Jacksonville! It's always sunny" (*Twilight*, p 406). By this time, however, Bella has fallen madly in love with Edward, so she wants to stay in Forks.

In real life, Jacksonville is the largest city in land area in the American state of Florida. It is located near the oldest continuously occupied American settlement, St. Augustine. In 2008, its population was 807,815 people. Jacksonville is the most crowded city in Florida, making it the twelfth most populous city in the United States.

So how did this city get its name? The name "Jackson" is defined as being a patronymic name meaning 'son of Jack'. Jack may also be a version of *John* or *James*, or a derivation of the Old French given name *Jacque*, the French form of *Jacob*. The suffix *ville* means protector. Always sunny in Jacksonville, this place provides plenty of protection from *Twilight*-style vampires who tend to shy away from the sun so as not to reveal their secret identity.

Jester

> Great, now I was the court jester.
> (*Breaking Dawn*, p 231)

Since Jacob calls himself a "jester" in the *Twilight* series, and is a happy character who likes to joke around, it might prove useful to explore the jester metaphor.

In sixteenth century Europe, jesters of the royal court entertained kings and queens, much like Jacob thinks he is doing at the Cullen house. The jester was a 13th century character of Italian theatre known as the *Arlecchino* or 'Harlequin' of the *Commedia dell'arte*. The word harlequin is derived from the Old French hellquin and similar words, which mean demon, imp or will-o-the-wisp. This means that a jester not only has funny features, but supernatural features too. A harlequin has some qualities in common with the Fool (the last card in the tarot deck) and also the joker (in a modern deck of cards). But the difference between a jester and a clown is that a jester makes fun of other people like the king, while other people laugh at the clown.

In the *Twilight Saga,* Jacob is definitely the best-ever jester. Jacob also possesses supernatural powers, which a jester or harlequin is said to have. Though Jacob may make some bad vampire jokes and sick blonde jokes, especially in acts of self-defense against Rosalie's mean remarks, his humor is never intended to be truly evil or malicious. Clearly, Jacob has an important role in the *Twilight Saga* looking on the bright side, dissolving anxiety in tense scenes, and injecting humor into many mysterious, scary, and chilling adventures.

Jewelry

Jewels are sparkling objects traditionally associated with play, joy, and pleasure. The English word 'jewel' derives from the Old French words *juel* or *joel,* which mean 'game' or 'plaything'. In eleventh century France, the word jewel became associated with *joy* (joi, joie) and *pleasure* (jouissance). It may therefore be symbolically meaningful, and not random, when Bella throws Aro's diamond necklace onto the floor for Renesmee to play with. According to Bella, "she liked sparkly things" (*Breaking Dawn,* p 697).

In the deepest collective parts of the human mind, jewels have magical and sacred meanings. The term jewelry arose at a time when tools of divination (stones and bones) were worn as necklaces by mystics and fortune-tellers. Amulets and talismans are prime examples of protective jewelry. Of course, jewelry can mean different things in different situations. In a dream, for example, receiving a ring is an omen of present or future joy, profits or bonuses. But such a ring can also foreshadow a test, trial, task or dangerous mission to accomplish soon (Colin, 2000). When Bella receives a diamond engagement ring from Edward in *Eclipse*, this certainly seems to be the case. Bella achieves great rewards (a happy family, everlasting life, love), but only after she puts in great effort to overcome the dark and difficult challenges that involve the Volturi vampires.

The way people wear jewelry or dream about wearing jewelry can mean certain things also. For example, tight bracelets are said to be a sign of dependence. A loose, dangling bracelet, however, does not suggest an attempt to constrain an individual's personality or behavior. In the *Twilight* world, the bracelet that Jacob gives Bella is not tight fitting. Rather, it is silver, delicate and easy to fasten, and features a little wolf charm that "swung lightly" from Bella's wrist (*Eclipse*, pp 332–333, 365). The looseness of this bracelet suggests that although Jacob wants Bella to love him, he is not trying to limit or restrict Bella's freedom or choices in any way.

Another important piece of jewelry in the Twilight world is Aro's necklace. A necklace is a sign of an emotional bond. The looser the necklace and the lower down it is on your chest, the stronger the symbol of loyalty. However, if a necklace fits close around the neck, the emotional attachment is considered constraining. In *Breaking Dawn*, it is interesting to note that Aro's diamond necklace sits in the hollow of Bella's throat (*Breaking Dawn*, p 628). As such, Aro's necklace symbolizes constraint. Volturi jewelry, just like Volturi law, is clearly designed to limit autonomy and limit free will.

Journey

A journey is not just an act of travelling across an area of land. A true journey is also a philosophical and spiritual quest for new horizons. Hence the joke:

Question: "Where are you going?"

Answer: "Geographically or philosophically? Geographically – over there. Philosophically – I don't know."

As a symbol, a journey might suggest an urge for escape, a desire to be free, a need for independence, inner growth, personal development or an attempt at avoiding stagnation (Colin, 2000).

In fact, fiction, folklore and fairy tales have always featured some kind of journey. Not just an outside one but an inner one. A trip that involves a hero and which produces great change. The traditional symbolic significance of journeys, and their effects on important characters certainly applies to the *Twilight Saga*.

Archetypal JourneysIn fiction stories and myths, there are several different types of journeys that individual characters can experience. These are:

- The quest for identity.
- The epic journey to find a promised land (a good city, inner peace).
- The quest for vengeance.
- The warrior's journey to save the people.
- The search for love (to rescue a princess/damsel in distress).
- The journey in search of knowledge.
- The tragic quest (self-punishment or self-denial).
- The fool's errand (a quest that cannot be accomplished because of fate or because it is a joke, e.g. receiving an impossible or imaginary task, trying to find something that

does not exist).

- The quest to rid the land of danger.
- The Holy Grail quest (quest for perfection).

The Hero's Journey

One of the most well-known journeys in fiction is the hero's journey. Everyone knows what Superman, Batman, Wonder Woman, Hercules and other famous characters went through to become the great heroes they are – they suffered hard, trained hard, fought hard, jumped through hoops and went through heaps. In the *Twilight Saga*, Bella would be the main hero, since the books are written mainly from her perspective. Also, events in the *Twilight* world change Bella more than any other character.

Typically (or archetypically) a hero's journey involves dealing with a number of challenges and overcoming important obstacles. In particular, a true hero must "go on a journey, learn a lesson, change in some way, and return home."

More specifically, a Hero's Journey can be divided into stages. Using Bella to illustrate, these stages are:

- **Departure** – in Bella's case, she begins her journey by leaving sunny Phoenix and moving to rainy Forks.
- **Initiation** – Bella gets to know Edward. Meeting Edward's vampire family is like an early initiation. Sacrificing her life to save others is perhaps the ultimate initiation rite.
- **The Road of Trials** – In order to be with Edward, Bella endures many trials and tribulations throughout the *Twilight Saga*. She almost dies several times, she gets depressed, takes risks, and makes sacrifices.
- **The Innermost Cave** – Bella's best example is when she withdraws into a depressed state and then dives off a cliff. In the deepest parts of her mind, Bella realizes that she truly loves Edward.

What makes the *Twilight Saga* extra intriguing is that the story describes three heroic journeys. Although Bella, Edward, and Jacob are different characters who come from totally different backgrounds (human, vampire, werewolf). Each character must make important choices to achieve resolution and make the best of fate. In other words, the *Twilight* world has three main characters, three journeys, and three heroes of equal importance. Since all three teenage characters are on an individual hero's journey, it's no wonder the *Twilight* books are so gripping. All three characters have strong desires, important goals, a sense of purpose, and the courage to put themselves in danger. This *triples* the story's excitement and suspense. Will Bella be happy as a vampire? Will Edward cope well with Bella's change? Will Jacob ever find true love and happiness, without Bella? Archetypally speaking, we need each hero to succeed to achieve a happy ending in the *Twilight Saga*. If only one hero 'returns' fulfilled from a journey (experiences growth, achieves spiritual rebirth, and reintegrates adequately into the world), the story will be *incomplete* because just *one* individual has succeeded. Ideally, Bella, Edward, and Jacob all need to experience a resolution, if *Breaking Dawn* is to achieve a truly peaceful ending.

In the *Twilight Saga,* we do (but nearly don't) achieve a successful return of each hero's journey:

- Bella got what she wanted. She hooked up with Edward, became a vampire, gets to love Edward forever, and didn't go to war with the Volturi. She even got a bonus – a daughter.
- Edward got what he wanted. He got Bella, married her, did not have sex before marriage, and can have safe sex with Bella now that she is a vampire. Edward even made a few unexpected friends along the way – werewolf allies like Jacob and Seth.
- Jacob got what he wanted (but he nearly didn't). Jacob

> accepted Quileute spirituality, became boss wolf, and although he didn't get the girl of his dreams (Bella), he got something much better – Nessie, his true blue soul mate.

The most important goal of any journey is to find your own true place in the world, to triumph over whatever obstacles are in your way, and achieve authentic happiness.

Of course, all characters in the *Twilight Saga* are on their own heroic journeys, just as we are all on journeys in real life. For example, Carlisle underwent heroic effort to overcome his brutal vampire nature. His quest was to embrace the passion and compassion of humanity. Carlisle found peace as a vegetarian vampire and has found a level of acceptance by both the Volturi and humankind. He is a father figure and inspiration to others. Carlisle's ongoing quest is how to deal with the potential reappearance of the Volturi.

A true hero is always on a journey, is always seeking to evolve, improve himself or herself, and reach a higher place somewhere. Carol Pearson, author of a classic book called *The Hero Within*, says that:

> "Heroes take journeys, confront dragons, and discover the treasure of their true selves."

Everyone in the fiction world and in the real world is on his or her own heroic journey.

K

Key

Keys might seem like an insignificant symbolic object in the *Twilight Saga,* especially when a vampire or werewolf can easily bust down a door. Nevertheless, since keys are used to lock or unlock doors, they have other special meanings. You see, keys are linked to the idea of mystery, secrets, obstruction, closure and death. Keys also promise an opening, opportunity, clarification, and liberation. To be happy and successful in life, it is not enough just to have a key. You also need to know how to use that key, and what it opens or closes. As such, the key is a powerful symbol of choice and free will, which happens to be an important theme in the *Twilight* world.

The most straightforward key in the *Twilight* world is the key Bella uses to get in and out of her house. Much later, in *Breaking Dawn,* Bella and Edward get a key for their new stone cottage. Alice gives Bella a "brass key with an oversized pink satin bow tied around it" on Bella's nineteenth birthday (*Breaking Dawn,* p 434). Why? Because keys symbolize the road to freedom. They point to a rite of passage. "The key is a symbol of power, a visible sign of this initiation" (Nozedar, 2008, p 111). In this light, Bella's key, tied with a pink ribbon, and placed in her left hand by Alice, is a mark of power, maturity, and finishing a rite of passage (Bella's marriage to Edward). The key, a rite, is repeated again when Edward gives Bella a "long and silver" key with a "blue bow" – the key to her new car, her wedding gift (*Breaking Dawn,* p 436).

However, keys do not need to be physical objects. Secret language, sacred words, or special actions are also powerful keys. The key symbolizes access to something that otherwise remains hidden or secret. Keys unlock the door to wisdom. "Initiation, too provides a key that unlocks secret knowledge or information" (Nozedar, 2008, p 111). When Jacob takes his clothes off and phases into a wolf on the spot right in front of Charlie's eyes (and nearly gives him a heart attack), he also gives him a symbolic key to secret knowledge. Just before Jacob changes into an animal he tells Charlie: "You don't live in the world you thought you lived in. The good news is, nothing has changed – except that now you know" (*Breaking Dawn*, p 459). Jacob has opened a door to a supernatural world. Morphing in front of Charlie is a key-like metaphor. With this newfound knowledge, Charlie will never be the same again.

Kiss

What does a kiss mean? Other than being one of the most romantic gestures of love, the kiss is a powerful symbol. "Symbolically, a kiss is a merging of breath, a fusion of spirits" (Colin, 2000, p 300). When you kiss, not only are you kissing someone you love, it also means "embracing something, someone's interests or a cause" (Colin, 2000, p 302). So the kiss symbolizes a bond. Sometimes people kiss the ground they walk on. This enables an individual to unite his or her spirit with the great forces of nature and the source of life.

The main meaning of a kiss is that it symbolizes union. When you kiss someone on the lips, this symbolizes an exchange of the spirit. The reason why the bride and groom kiss, just after the marriage vows are taken, has great symbolical significance. "The mingling of their breath symbolizes the fact that the couple breathe the same air, a sign of the union of their marriage in a physical and spiritual sense" (Nozedar, 2008, p 593).

The *Twilight Saga* has several momentous kisses that mark romantic progress in Bella and Edward's relationship. Three special kisses are these:

First Kiss

Edward hesitated to test himself, to see if this was safe, to make sure he was still in control of his need.

And then his cold, marble lips pressed very softly against mine.

What neither one of us was prepared for was my response.

Blood boiled under my skin, burned my lips. My breath came in a wild gasp. My fingers knotted in his hair, clutching him to me. My lips parted as I breathed in his heady scent.

(*Twilight*, p 247)

Wedding Kiss

He kissed me tenderly, adoringly; I forgot the crowd, the place, the time, the reason… only remembering that he loved me, that he wanted me, that I was his.

(*Breaking Dawn*, p 46).

First Kiss as Vampires

He kissed me, soft as a whisper at first, and then suddenly stronger, fiercer... Though I didn't need oxygen, my breathing sped… How different this kissing was!

(*Breaking Dawn*, p 364)

As Bella and Edward's three kisses show – the passionate kiss, the tender kiss, and the exciting kiss – a kiss sparks and sustains true love and an invincible spiritual union.

L

La Push

In the *Twilight* series, La Push in Washington is a remote area where the Native American Quileute people live. It is the home of Bella's best friend Jacob Black. Bella spends a lot of time with Jacob and other Quileute shape-shifters there, especially in the second book of the *Twilight Saga, New Moon*.

In real life, La Push is a small community in Washington state. It is located near Forks and houses the Quileute community. This place is well-known for surfing and whale-watching, which attract many tourists there.

The Quileute's first contact with white people occurred in 1855, when a treaty was signed with delegates of Territorial Governor Isaac Stevens. In February 1889, President Grover Cleveland established a one-mile square reservation at La Push, where at which time 252 residents lived. While villagers were picking hops, cruel arsonists destroyed their town that year.

Modern-day La Push sits above First Beach and comprises the La Push Ocean Park and Shoreline Resort. This area features motels, townhouses, cabins, a store called Lonesome Creek, and a post office. The Quileute people celebrate their cultural heritage and modern lifestyle during July 17–19 at La Push. This important festival features fireworks, a traditional salmon bake, dancing and songs, field sports, a horse show, an arts and craft exhibition, and local foods.

Light

Once upon a time, light was regarded as "the purest, most precious and most wonderful expression of life" (Colin, 2000, p

316). In every culture around the world, light has always been linked to happiness, joy, the soul, and spiritual awakening. As such, light is an ultimate symbol of life and everlasting life to which all mortals aspire. Light can also symbolize a good force that has the power to destroy darkness and evil. As a result, light symbolizes hope and happiness for humanity. While there is a physical form of light that is made of waves and particles, light also symbolizes spiritual light. This light is associated with profound personal enlightenment, inner vision, and great spiritual insight.

An important way that light symbolism appears in the *Twilight Saga* is in scenes that involve dawn. As a symbol, dawn suggests the birth of a new day and the triumph of light over darkness and the night. Go to *Dawn* for more information.

The *Twilight Saga* also links the soul and spiritual power to light, in line with the spiritual meaning of light. An excellent example is Bella's supernatural shield. When Bella extends her shield to protect good vampires and other good characters in the Volturi war, they appear as "sparks", "lights", and "glimmering shapes" underneath her cover (*Breaking Dawn*, p 653). Bella's shield itself is a positive light force, a beautiful dome of glowing crimson light. Go to *Shield* for more information.

Lightning

Since lightning is sudden, spectacular, unpredictable and dangerous, lightning symbolizes sudden, unexpected, and threatening events. Anything can happen in a lightning storm. The force and violence of lightning is so powerful that it can strike down huge trees, burn down forests, and split the earth open. In ancient times, people viewed lightning as an angry display by gods. Many myths, from ancient Greece to the Australian Dreamtime, describe angry spirits making lightning or hurling huge lightning bolts from the sky. Lightning is such a powerful natural force that in ancient Greece only the mightiest gods, such as Zeus who ruled over everything on Mount Olympus, possessed the power of thunder, storms and lightning.

In the *Twilight Saga*, the Cullens play super-fast, super-strong, extra-loud baseball during a thunderstorm (*Twilight*, p 323). Due to the symbolic meaning of lightning, this unusual baseball game may have several meanings. While baseball is a popular game that traditionally symbolizes teamwork and family bonding, playing baseball during lightning suggests the involvement of divine forces and vampires are supernatural creatures. As mentioned, lightning also symbolizes sudden, unpredictable and dangerous events. What could be more sudden, unpredictable and dangerous than the appearance of James, Victoria and Laurent on the baseball field during that storm?

M

Marriage

Marriage may well be one of the most important rites of passage in life. Every country and belief system in the world has its own marriage ceremony that seeks to unite two individuals, namely male and female, together. The practice of marriage helps to encourage order and harmony, promote settled life, increase feelings of security, and calm extreme emotions and reckless behaviors. "The struggle for survival, which may be desperate and suicidal if waged alone, becomes a happy, salutary experience if undertaken together" (Colin, 2000, p 324).

Weddings are packed with symbols that point to romantic union. For example:

Wedding flowers – these symbolize love between two people.
Wedding ring – the ring's circle shape symbolizes eternal love.
Wedding kiss – this symbolizes the merging of two breaths, two spirits, two souls.

Ancient alchemists loved using symbols to depict the union of two opposites or complements, especially male and female. In alchemy, birds and lions, for example, symbolize important unions. So do birds and snakes. Does this mean that the marriage between Bella (linked to birds) and Edward (linked to lions) is an alchemical union? Probably!

Meadow

Love, Magic, Power

I reached the pool of light and stepped through the last fringe

> of ferns into the loveliest place I had ever seen. The meadow was small, perfectly round, and filled with wildflowers – violet, yellow, and soft white. Somewhere nearby, I could hear the bubbling music of a stream. The sun was directly overhead, filling the circle with a haze of buttery sunshine. (*Twilight*, pp 226–227)

The meadow that Bella and Edward spend time in is one of the most magical and symbolic places in the whole *Twilight* world. It is a circle, a place of light and love, that is situated somewhere in the middle of a lush green forest maze. The meadow, a sunlit clearing in the heart of a dark forest, traditionally symbolizes the revelation of insight, illumination, or some kind of inner light. In *Twilight*, Edward reveals his dark secret in this sunlit meadow. He shows Bella that as a vampire – his skin sparkles in the sun. Just before Edward steps into the sun to reveal himself to Bella, she saw "a lightening of the trees ahead, a glow that was yellow instead of green" (*Twilight*, p 226). This fits with symbolic meanings that a meadow is a place of insight and inner light, especially in relation to positive thoughts, secret desires, and spiritual power. After all, Edward reveals his love for Bella and the truth about himself inside a sunlit meadow.

Bright Thoughts

A sunlit clearing in a forest, like Edward's meadow, symbolizes thoughts and mental processes. Forest darkness, shadows, towering trees, and thick canopies are supposed to symbolize the deepest and wildest parts of the human mind. Finding a forest clearing, however, symbolizes the discovery of a bright idea, happy thought, or powerful solution. Since Bella spends special time with Edward in the sunlit clearing, this suggests that both Bella and Edward are connecting to her best thoughts and brightest ideas. In a *Twilight* chapter called "Confessions", Edward makes some of his most positive and tender statements to Bella. It is here, in the bright and safe *Twilight* meadow that Edward, for example, reassures Bella not to "be afraid" (p 230), that he "*can* control" his urges (p 232), that he constantly "craves" her company (p 233), and that Bella "is the most important thing" to him ever (p 240).

A meadow is secret, lush, green, warm, fertile, full of wildflowers, and associated with the power and magic of the sun. While Edward presents as a dark, cold and mysterious character on the outside (just like a dark forest), his innermost personal space is warm, kind, and lovely (just like a sunlit meadow). Once again, despite Edward's dark and brooding mystery (symbolized by the dark and gloomy forest), Edward has a good heart, a bright mind, and positive thoughts.

Deep Desires

As well as positive thoughts, meadows also symbolize inner desire. In myths, folklore and fiction, some crucial emotional scenes take place in secret little clearings. This includes Bella and Edward's meadow in the *Twilight* world. The meadow is a wild place where Bella and Edward reveal their deepest love for each other, as well as their darkest desires. For example, it's in a meadow that Edward shows his true self in the light and sparkles in the sun, revealing that he is really a vampire. Edward also confesses something terrible – his urge to kill Bella. Bella and Edward's initial meeting in the meadow is not completely romantic; it's dangerous too. Bella's sweet scent brings out the worst predatory feelings in Edward. In many ways, their first meadow adventure is a symbolic way to affirm their romantic but dangerous relationship, as well as their deepest desires for each other.

Even though Edward admits he lusts for Bella's blood in *Twilight*, that he is "more dangerous" to her than anyone else (p 233), and calls himself a "deplorable creature" (p 243), she accepts him. Bella doesn't turn away in disgust or run away from

Edward either. She stays with him, gets to know him, and notices all the goodness beyond Edward's thirst for human blood. As Bella explains, "I couldn't make myself be afraid. I couldn't think of anything else except that he was touching me" (*Twilight*, p 242). In the sacred meadow, love overpowers danger. In fact, Bella continues to expresses her deep desires by stroking Edward's cheek, his eyelid, and lightly tracing his lips (*Twilight*, p 242). Bella and Edward consecrate their romantic relationship with a powerful symbolic gesture, a soft, cool and truly passionate kiss (*Twilight*, p 247). The meadow symbolizes a hallowed place, a perfect garden blooming with passion. A place that features true love, forbidden fruit, mortal danger and supernatural power. Just like the meadow, Bella blossoms and grows emotionally herself whenever she is with Edward, fading and withering when he goes. And, just as the meadow is a circle, so is Bella and Edward's deepest love for each other – perfect, complete, and eternal.

A Magical Place

The meadow is where Edward reveals his supernatural powers to Bella. Not only does Edward sparkle in the sun, he is super-strong, super-fast and ice-cold (*Twilight*, p 227). Bella tries to recapture Edward's magic in an attempt to convince herself that vampires are real by returning to the meadow. To Bella, the meadow has always been "a magic place, full of light" (*New Moon*, p 195). So, when Edward moves away from Forks for a while, Bella goes searching for the meadow in the forest by herself. Although Bella finds meadow magic again, this time it's different:

- "I stepped through a low arch made by two vine maples – pushing past the chest- high ferns – into the meadow (*New Moon*, p 233).
- "It was as perfectly round as if someone had intentionally

created the flawless circle… beautiful and serene" (*New Moon*, p 234).

- "The meadow was a magic place again. A darker magic… but magic all the same" (*New Moon*, p 236).
- At this moment in the meadow, a vampire named Laurent reappears and tries to kill Bella.
- While standing in the meadow, Bella sees Jacob in wolf form for the first time. The other Quileutes also appear in wolf form to save Bella from Laurent's imminent kill.
- After five werewolves chase Laurent away and Bella has just heard Edward's voice in her mind: "A cold breeze whipped through the meadow, swaying the grass like something was moving through it" (*New Moon*, p 245). The meadow, it seems, has some spiritual power and presence, as if Edward's cool and soothing soul is passing through.

Traditionally, the center of a circle is a very magical place. In the *Twilight* world, the meadow is in the heart of the forest, in the middle of a labyrinth, in the center of a great green maze. In fact, Bella had "never seen anything so symmetrical. It was perfectly round… a flawless circle" (*New Moon*, p 234). This round clearing with its colorful wildflowers, soft grass, warm sunlight, and gilded air – is a fairy tale haven in a lovely living forest.

"Our Meadow"

A critical feature of the meadow is that it belongs to Bella and Edward. As Edward says to Bella: "Let's go to our meadow" (*Eclipse*, p 545). Filled with white and yellow flowers in green grass under a cloudy sky, Bella describes their meadow as "a peaceful, happy place" (*Eclipse*, p 545).

When Bella plans to revisit the meadow in *Twilight*, she also recalls that this was the "one place that would always belong to *him* and no one else" (*New Moon*, p 195). In fact, when other people try to find Bella and Edward's meadow, they fail. When

Bella asks Jacob to help her look for the meadow he cannot locate it, despite his excellent knowledge of the forest and the help of a map and compass.

It is probably no coincidence that Bella cannot find the meadow with Jacob, even after hiking more than six miles in different directions. Bella's attempt to find the meadow is a bit of a 'fool's errand', really. Asking Jacob to find a magic place that belongs only to her and Edward is bound to go wrong. In fact, Bella herself describes it as a "silly quest" that was "pretty much doomed" (*New Moon*, p 199).

Meadow vs. Driftwood Tree

Just as Edward and Jacob compete for Bella's love, the meadow and the driftwood tree scenes in the *Twilight* books – Team Edward and Team Jacob symbols – contrast and compete with each other. The meadow is a place of beauty for Bella. The colors, sounds, feel, and sunlight all indicate a special and magical place with Edward. By contrast, La Push Beach, although beautiful and breathtaking, is somewhat remote and desolate for Bella. Still, it is a special and magical place that she shares with Jacob.

When Edward breaks up with Bella, she becomes an uprooted driftwood tree, like the one washed up on Jacob's beach. Jacob nurtures Bella but she does not want to establish a romantic relationship with him because Edward is her true love. Bella's deep feelings for Edward (the perfectly round meadow in the forest) and Jacob (the driftwood tree that can't take root in the shifting sand) are symbolized using scenery from nature. The circle-shaped meadow and crescent-shaped driftwood beach are juggled and juxtaposed, to illuminate the conflict between Edward and Jacob in the *Twilight Saga* as well as their personal character differences (TwilightMOMS post, Immortal Diamond, 2009).

The Deathly Meadows

Edward and Bella experience some of their most ecstatic and romantic moments in their forest meadow . It is also noted that Edward is a blood-drinking vampire from the world of the undead who takes Bella, a living human girl with blood flowing in her veins, to that meadow. According to an insightful report by one *Twilight* fan, this links the *Twilight* meadow to a macabre place from Greek myth known as the Asphodel Meadows. The Asphodel Meadows are ghostly plains said to exist somewhere in between heaven and hell. Souls that were neither good nor evil were condemned to reside there. Only tastes of blood offered to them in the world of the living could reawaken their sensations of humanity for a while. Asphodel flowers, a type of lily, were sacred to Persephone from Greek myth, queen of the underworld. The ancient Greeks believed that this flower of death fed fallen heroes in the fields of heaven. In Harry Potter's magic world, asphodel flowers were used to brew a powerful potion called the "Draught of Living Death" (Rowling, 1997). Since the *Twilight* meadow is visited by a deadly blood-drinking creature who takes a human there, this could be a subtle foreshadow to the Asphodel Meadows. Both the Asphodel Meadows and the *Twilight Saga* meadow are deathly meadows that have links to blood-drinkers, blood sacrifice, the undead, and death (TwilightMOMS post, whome March 2, 2010; Wikipedia, 2011).

The Cullen Meadow

Adding to the meadow that Bella and Edward share, there is another less obvious meadow in the *Twilight* world. It is a much darker and shadier one, found at the foot of the Cullen mansion:

> We were suddenly in a small meadow, or was it actually a lawn? The gloom of the forest didn't relent though, for there were six primordial cedars that shaded an entire acre.
> (*Twilight*, 280)

Unlike Bella and Edward's private meadow, the Cullen family meadow seems to be for everyone. This meadow suggests unity and completeness. It is there, for example, that everyone (family circles and circles of friends from everywhere) meets to celebrate Edward and Bella's union of marriage. As such, this meadow symbolizes the Cullen family's approach to life. The Cullens want to integrate with society, live together with humans, live in harmony with nature (with supernatural creatures, plants and animals), and promote a healthy circle of life.

As vampires, however, the peaceful Cullens are vulnerable to persecution by humans. So they must keep their identity a secret. The six towering trees that shade the Cullen house may be nature's sentinels, playing a magical and protective role guarding the Cullens' meadow.

Midday

Midday is a brief moment of time that marks the midpoint of the day. It is when the sun is at its highest point in the sky, in a 24-hour day. At this time, a remarkable celestial event takes place – the sun reaches its zenith and there are no shadows on earth. Ancient mystics linked midday to illusions. What they mean is that when the world is fully flooded with sunlight, at midday, people are blinded by illusion – the sunlight is so intense and shocking that it brightens and distorts the things we are supposed to see. When we are plunged into darkness, at night, that's when we are supposed to see things clearly and grasp the truth about reality (Colin, 2000). Noon is also a magical time and a chime hour (every third hour is a chime hour, e.g. 3 am, 6 am, 12 pm). Midday is also a time of endurance and perseverance (Eason, 2002).

At midday in *New Moon*, a near-disaster occurs. Edward almost dies when he tries to step out into the noon sun at the Volterra city plaza. When Bella and Edward were at their most disconnected, had spent a terrible time apart, this sunny midday scene was their darkest moment in the whole four book series. This *Twilight* adventure aligns with the beliefs of mystics that sunlight can blind you from seeing the truth. Edward was blinded and misguided by a shocking and erroneous belief that Bella had committed suicide, and this illusion drove him to die. As such, the plot in *New Moon* clearly embraces negative midday meanings.

Midnight

Midnight is a brief moment of time that marks the midpoint of the night. Midnight is when the sun is at its lowest point in the sky, in a 24-hour day. At midnight, there are no remarkable celestial or physical phenomena taking place. But this has not stopped people from regarding midnight as being the darkest, deadliest and most disturbing time of a 24-hour day.

A memorable midnight scene in the *Twilight Saga* is when Edward and Bella take a "midnight swim" in *Breaking Dawn* on the beach at Isle Esme. In complete contrast to the dreadful midday scene at Volterra in *New Moon*, Bella and Edward are at their most connected at midnight, this being their wedding night. This midnight experience marks the most intimate physical moment between Bella and Edward in the whole four book series. They finally consummate their marriage by engaging in their first sexual encounter. The midnight swim under the light of the bright full moon was a dazzling and illuminating event for both Edward and Bella. This aligns with the beliefs of mystics that there is light in the darkness and that dark times can be very illuminating.

Midnight is supposed to be a powerful time to heal illness, repair quarrels, and deal with spiritual forces. According to ancient folklore, midnight is used "for healing and restoration of mind, body and spirit. The chime hour is midnight" (Eason, 2002, p 442).

In the dictionary, 'mid-night' means:

1 The middle of the night, specifically 12 o'clock at night.
2 Intense darkness or gloom.
3 A period of darkness and gloom.

The Witching Hour

Bella and Edward's first sexual encounter happens to occur at the most magical moment of the 24 hour day. Midnight is most famous for the witching hour, which occurs from midnight for an hour until 1 am. According to Wikipedia, one of the earliest, if not the first, appearance of the term 'witching hour' occurred in Washington Irving's short story *The Legend of Sleepy Hollow*. Here, the famous writer uses the phrases "witching hour" and "witching time". Both terms relate to midnight and are used to conjure up an atmosphere of supernatural anxiety.

A modern meaning of the term witching hour describes a time when supernatural creatures such as witches, demons and ghosts are thought to appear and be at their most powerful. The midnight hour is a "time in the middle of the night when magic things are said to happen" and when magic and spells are at their most effective (Wikipedia, 2011).

In several of William Shakespeare's plays, ghosts and other supernatural forces become most active at midnight. In the play *Hamlet*, for example, a depressed young prince remarks:

'Tis now the very witching time of night,
When churchyards yawn and hell itself breathes out
Contagion to this world.
(*Hamlet*, 3.2.277–279)

While Bella and Edward's midnight skinny dip may not be spooky, it is nonetheless an intense magical and supernatural moment.

Mirror

Mirrors are traditional symbols of spiritual power. They play a big symbolic role in the *Twilight Saga* in several ways.

Invisible Bella

Mirror, mirror on the wall
I can't see my vampire self at all!

A main myth is that vampires cannot see their own reflections in a mirror. In many tales, vampires are not reflected in mirrors and do not appear in photos, but Edward does. The *Twilight Saga* is an inverse of myth, because Edward appears in mirrors and photos and is the beautiful one whereas Bella is invisible, unseen, and unattractive. In the *Twilight Saga*, Bella is "invisible". She does not think she is interesting, beautiful, or special. Nor does Bella like to pay much attention to mirrors – especially in terms of grooming and visual appearance. For example, Bella "was careful never to look in the long mirror" (*Eclipse*, p 514).

The first time Bella looks at herself in a mirror in the *Twilight Saga*, she looks "pallid" (*Twilight*, p 9). While this may be a clue that foreshadows the vampire that Bella will become, it also has a deeper meaning. Bella does not think she looks so great in a mirror (she looks sickly and pale). This is because she does not *feel* so great about herself. Just like the Forks weather, Bella's view of herself is somewhat gloomy. When Bella gets together with Edward and her mood brightens, the world (including her own reflection in a mirror) looks brighter and better too. When Bella looks at herself in a later mirror scene and she is happy, she notices that "the face in the mirror was practically a stranger – eyes too bright" (*Twilight*, p 274). Our emotions alter our perceptions. Mood manipulates our self-images.

In *New Moon*, Bella denies her own beauty (p 65) and folds a part of herself in a photo away (p 66). This only leaves Edward visible in her album. Symbolically speaking, this could be an omen that Bella is not meant to exist in the human world anyway – she is destined to be a vampire. Psychologically speaking, Bella's tendency to see herself as invisible, unimportant or unattractive in a mirror or photo is most probably a sign of depression or maybe low self-esteem. Despite having access to mirrors, Bella does not see herself accurately or as positively as she could.

Introspective Bella

Mirrors are supreme symbols of deep self-reflection and the soul. When people look at themselves in a mirror, they discover themselves and may reflect on themselves. This increases self-awareness. In a dream at the start of book two, Bella looks at an image of her grandmother, only to find that she is gazing at her own reflection "in a mirror. Me – ancient, creased, and withered" (*New Moon*, p 6). Upon waking up, Bella immediately checks herself in the bathroom mirror only to find that she hasn't "changed" at all (*New Moon*, p 7). This scene is doubly introspective because it involves a mirror (a symbol of looking inwards) in a dream (a path to the deepest part of the mind). This extra introspective scene suggests that Bella is thinking deeply about issues. When Bella sees an image of an old woman reflected in the mirror, what she is really seeing is her hidden fears – she fears getting old because she thinks Edward will not love her anymore. What Bella desperately wants is to be with Edward forever.

The ballet studio adventure at the end of *Twilight* is perhaps the most significant and symbolic mirror scene in the whole series. Mirrors symbolize the deepest level of introspection, a person's reflection of the innermost self. In a multiple mirror moment, Alice foresees James entering a room with "mirrors everywhere" (*Twilight*, p 362). Just as Bella has chosen to confront James in the ballet studio, this symbolizes a choice to confront her true self by reflecting inwardly. So now Bella knows what she really, really wants. Bella decides that she truly loves Edward so much that she is willing to die for him (*Twilight*, p 376). As such, Bella confronts an evil vampire (James) in the ballet studio filled with wall to wall mirrors (*Twilight*, p 392). Symbolically, Bella confronts her inner self. She deeply desires Edward and is willing to face her darkest fears to save someone she truly loves. Shortly after Bella's battle with James in front of a maze of mirrors, when Bella is in hospital, she makes her decision to become a vampire. This choice shocks Edward (*Twilight*, p 413). Nevertheless, that particular choice in *Twilight* determines the turning point in Bella's journey for ever more.

Spiritual Bella

> *Mirrors were believed to reflect the soul. This is why, according to myth, you cannot see the reflection of a bad witch in a mirror. It was considered unlucky to smash a mirror as you were damaging your immortal soul.*
> (Eason, 2002, p 102)

In other words, this myth explains why so-called evil creatures, including vampires, could not see their reflections in mirrors. This would have fuelled Edward's belief that he is an evil and soulless monster. Mirrors appear in myths and legends all over the world. The mirror is a mystical gateway to another world. The mirror always reflects the impartial truth, and therefore it symbolizes honesty and purity. A broken mirror is a symbol of doom. A black bowl filled with water makes a reflective surface and acts as magic mirror that serves as tool for divination. The ancient Greek mathematician Pythagoras had a magical mirror, which he placed in the moonlight in order to "charge" it with lunar, occult powers. He then used the mirror to foretell the future. The eye, itself a reflective surface, is called the Mirror of the Soul and is said to convey what is really hidden inside the mind of its owner. In the

Twilight Saga, Edward can see his own reflection in a mirror. And Bella can see all the way into his soul when she looks into his eyes. This suggests that Edward has a soul.

Money/Wealth

Money and material wealth is an important theme in the *Twilight Saga*. Edward is wealthy and has plenty of money. The Cullens live in a magnificent three-storey mansion, they drive expensive cars, and they wear designer clothes. Carlisle is medical director who has been earning a living for about 300 years. Meanwhile, Alice can predict the stock market, which keeps their profits up. In contrast, Bella lives in a small house, drives an old truck, and works part-time at a local sports store. Above all, Bella does not like Edward spending money on her. She prefers old and sentimental gifts.

Edward's financial wealth also differs greatly to Jacob Black's circumstances. Jacob lives in a small house with his father Billy Black, who is physically disabled and wheelchair bound. Jacob's mother is no longer alive. The Black house does not contain any new furniture, but it is cozy and comfortable.

Does this mean money matters in the *Twilight* world? Not necessarily. According to Bella, she loves Edward for his personal qualities, not his bank account details. As Bella explains to Jacob in this important scene:

> "I love *him*. Not because he's beautiful or because he's *rich*!" I spat the word at Jacob. "He'd still be the most loving and unselfish and brilliant and *decent* person I've ever met." (*Eclipse*, p 98)

What is true wealth anyway? Bella, for example, is truly rich in that she has found a kind and caring young man who loves her and adores her.

As for Jacob, he does not have enough money to buy a new car so he builds one. Jacob does not have enough money to buy new motorbike parts either, so he scrounges around for some at the dump. But Jacob is filthy rich spiritually and culturally. He has the spirit of a warrior, magic in his blood, lives on sacred land, and is part of a strong Quileute community.

Is Edward really wealthy? Edward may have money. But he has experienced great emotional poverty and spiritual deprivation. Edward's life has been sad, lonely and empty for more than 100 years. He also believes he has no soul until he meets Bella. Psychologically speaking, Edward does not seem well-off at all. In real life, some of the most materially wealthy people on the planet are utterly miserable. And some of the poorest people on earth are really happy. As the *Twilight Saga* helps to show, there are some things that money just can't buy. Personal, spiritual, and cultural riches. Things like a positive attitude, a good heart, and true love – these are the greatest treasures of all.

Moon

When the moon rises in the *Twilight Saga,* some of the most magical scenes and situations arise also. Sometimes the moon makes the dark landscape more beautiful. Sometimes the moon promotes strong romantic feelings. What's more, the *Twilight* world strongly suggests that the moon is a symbol that belongs to Bella and Edward.

Bella the Moon

The best clue that the moon is a metaphor for Bella is when Edward breaks up with Bella in *New Moon*. She describes herself as "a lost moon" left "to circle in a tight little orbit around the empty space left behind" (*New Moon*, p 201). In a later scene, Edward describes his life without Bella as "a moonless night. Very dark" until the moment he meets her in *New Moon* (p 514).

Clearly, Bella is Edward's moon.

When Edward breaks off with Bella and she calls herself "a lost moon" (*New Moon*, p 201), not only does Bella (the moon) circle a cosmic black hole (the empty space left behind when a planet goes missing), Bella also experiences a depressing symbolic hole (an empty chest). Bella's empty chest symbolizes her cheer-less, hope-less, and life-less life without Edward, just as Edward's life without her is like a moon-less night.

Bella the Moon Goddess

In the *Twilight* books, Bella is always running around the forest – from secret fern groves to sunlit forest clearings to spruce-fringed beaches, to snowy mountaintops. This is not unlike a significant moon goddess from Greek myth. Artemis was a beautiful and independent goddess of nature, hunting, and the moon. Artemis often travelled to wild places with faithful dogs by her side. As the *New Larousse Encyclopedia of Mythology* explains:

> *Artemis, accompanied by… her pack of swift hounds gave herself to the pleasures of the chase. On the shady mountainside, on the wind-lashed mountaintops, she bends her bow of sparkling gold and lets fly her deadly arrows.*

If anyone were to try and harm Artemis, her protective hounds would attack them at her command.

Just like Artemis, once Bella changes into a vampire, she becomes a beautiful supernatural being and a hunter too. Bella is also often accompanied by a pack of powerful dogs. As Bella explains, when "Jacob, Renesmee, and I were hunting together" the hunting experience was more exciting (*Twilight*, p 494). Whenever Bella has been in danger, the Quileute werewolves have repeatedly protected her – in the meadow when Laurent appeared (*New Moon*), when the newborn vampire army attacked (*Eclipse*), and when the Volturi vampires came to Forks (*Breaking Dawn*). It seems that Bella has Artemis down to an art!

Both Bella and Artemis have striking similarities as moon metaphors. The moon, in fact, is a very old sign of the Triple Goddess. The moon's appearance lunar cycle reveals three distinctive shapes – a crescent (new moon), a circle (full moon) and nothing (no moon). This suggests three life phases (maiden, mother, and elder). The progress of Bella's life in the *Twilight* world certainly reflects these three lunar phases.

At first, Bella is a maiden – a naïve young girl who knows nothing about vampires. Then Bella becomes a mother – she mothers Edward by showing him the good side of wolves and she nurtures Jacob by promoting the Cullens' goodness. Just as the silver moon in the sky grows full, Bella grows emotionally mature. She sacrifices her own life to save others and gives birth to a baby daughter. Eventually, Bella becomes a wise and experienced woman – a vampire. She has lived, she has died, she has reached a supernatural state, and she proves wise regarding earthly and non-earthly matters. Indeed, think of what Bella has witnessed and lived through to achieve happiness and to become what she has always wanted to be. Even Bella's negative experiences in life would have empowered her with knowledge, skills, confidence and more. It's easy to why the Volturi fear her. Bella not only has a powerful psychic gift, she is blessed with extraordinary determination and willpower. With her attitude, courage, and achievements, Bella is both venerated and feared. Bella (maiden, mother, elder) – *Twilight's* Triple Goddess!

Bright Moon

In the *Twilight Saga,* the bright silver moon is linked to Edward because both are cold and silver. The silver of the moon is Edward's color. This is probably because Edward has a silver Volvo, silver venom, and his vampire skin is silver-like – pale, white, shimmers in the light. For example, Bella once dreamed she was standing on the rocky crescent of First Beach one dark, cold night. Suddenly, "as if the moon had suddenly broken from the clouds, I could see everything" (*Eclipse*, p 234). Symbolically, this scene suggests that Edward's influence (the cold and silver moonlight) dominates Jacob's influence because the bright moon (linked to Edward) lights up the beach, and not the sun (linked to Jacob).

A bright silver moon tends to appear during the most romantic interactions between Bella and Edward. For example, just after twilight in *Twilight* at the school prom, Edward took Bella outside the back door (back door – subconscious mind, get it?). Bella noticed that "the moon was already up, visible through the gauzy clouds, and his face glowed pale in the white light" (*Twilight*, p 430). Meanwhile, Edward sat next to Bella under a tree, just "staring at the moon" (*Twilight*, p 430). Edward gazing at the moon (a symbolic nod that he is thinking about Bella, no doubt) and the moonlight (Bella's influence) somehow highlights Edward's presence on that special night.

The bright moon appears in another important romantic adventure involving Bella and Edward. The first time Bella sleeps at the Cullen house she notices that "the light of the moon brightened the clouds outside the window… highlighting the tops of the trees, and glinting off a small slice of the river. I watched the silver light, waiting for my eyes to get heavy" (*Eclipse*, p 135). This scene illustrates that whenever Bella is around Edward, the moon is bright, Bella feels bright, and the atmosphere is serene.

As a symbol, the moon stands for the unconscious mind, inner feelings and a person's mysterious side. The moon relates to dreams, the soul and renewal. This is because the moon disappears and then reappears in the sky during the lunar cycle. Moonlight suggests inner enlightenment and the glow of spiritual power because the light of the moon can guide a lost soul on a dark night – through darkness and difficulty in life, that is. Bella's mind is very moon-like. For example, Bella dwells a lot in the unconscious realm of dreams, private thoughts, inner feelings, and she loves Edward. Her psychological journey ahead is dark and difficult – she is a depressed human who desperately wants to be with Edward forever. And just like moonlight on a dark night, her eventual choice – to become a vampire – lights her path ahead. As this insightful *Twilight* fan puts it:

> *Where the sun will boldly bear down its blaze upon an object – the moon softy gains our attention, gently illuminating our deep feelings and lighting the path ahead in a soft and silvery glow.* (TwilightMOMS Post, Joanna Maria 2010)

In another lovely link between the moon and Bella and Edward's romance, Bella feels "ready to join [Edward's] family and his world" at the same time that she is gazing "at the moon" (*Eclipse*, p 386).

It wouldn't be surprising if Debussy's romantic melody *Clair de lune* (*Twilight*, p 90) was another symbolic gesture to Bella – the *Twilight* world's moon. After all, the word *lune* does mean 'moon' in French.

Half-Moon

The shape of the moon alludes to Bella's romantic relationship with others. In *New Moon*, the cliffs on First Beach were at the "the southern edge of the beach, where the flat, rocky half-moon dead-ended against the sheer sea cliffs" (pp 351–352). Symbolically, this half-moon comment suggests that romantically, Bella and Jacob's relationship will always be half-formed and at a dead end. While a full moon appears whenever Bella and Edward are romancing each other, a full moon never appears in Jacob's presence – only half-moons and crescents appear. Just after Bella's cliff-dive at the half-moon bay, Bella realizes that she has strong romantic feelings for Jacob. She kind of half-loves

Jacob, which is symbolized by the half-moon beach.

Of course, Bella's cliff jump also triggers a visit from Alice. This makes Bella recall that she has strong feelings for Edward too. This accentuates the idea that her heart is half-full of love for Edward and half-full for Jacob. However, as the reality of Edward's existence grows stronger, Bella realizes that she really does love Edward more than she loves Jacob, symbolic of a half-moon that grows fuller in the sky. Bella's feelings have now moved beyond the halfway point. As Bella confirms to herself: "After all, I'd picked the *bloodsucker* over him" (*New Moon*, p 406). Steadily, Bella's heart swells up again and fills up with love for Edward. This is surely a symbolic sign of a bright full moon to come.

Maybe Bella, the moon, is waxing, growing fuller – growing emotionally stronger. After all, when Edward broke up with her at the start of a new moon in *New Moon*, Bella was just a very thin crescent, a fragment of herself emotionally. Now she is at a half-moon point in an emotional way and is semi-confident. Eventually, when Edward and Bella reunite again at the end of *New Moon*, Bella feels full and complete inside, the big gaping hole is gone. "My heart inflated like it was going to crack right through my ribs. It filled my chest and blocked my throat so that I could not speak" (*New Moon*, p 527). Bella is a full moon once more and no longer at a half-moon stage of life.

Full Moon

The full moon is a potent time for love magic and achieving your deepest desire. According to one source, the full moon is "a time of fruition and assessment, the time to let go old, outmoded habits and whatever is holding you back" (Bowes, 1999, p 109). As the moon reaches fullness, the growth in positive energy that follows can move people forward to reach their goals more fully also. In the *Twilight Saga,* the most striking romantic scene between Bella and Edward occurs underneath a full moon on their wedding night. In Bella and Edward's case, once their love reaches fruition and they arrive to Isle Esme as newlyweds, the full moon seems to unleash its power. As Bella observes, "I saw only blackness at first, and the moon's white trail across the water" with "the sheen of moonlight on the waves" (*Breaking Dawn*, p 71). When Bella reaches the island's wooden dock, she noticed it was "bleached into whiteness by the moon" (*Breaking Dawn*, p 71). This gives the scene a magical feel. Many magical purification rituals involve leaving objects outside at night to expose them to the light of the full moon. That night on the island, "the moon was bright on white sand" and "almost full, and the sand was bright white under its shine" (*Breaking Dawn*, pp 73–75). It is as if the full moon is cleansing and purifying everything, including the romantic fullness and richness of Bella and Edward's love. The bright silver moonlight starkly contrasts the darkness of the night, silhouettes in the island landscape, the midnight water, and Edward's wet black hair. As a result, "everything was black-and-white, leached colorless by the moon" (*Breaking Dawn*, p 77). The romantic and magical mood of this romantic scene is wholly due to the visual effects of the moonlight and the power of the full silver moon.

Motorbikes

As well as suggesting traditional symbols, the *Twilight Saga* introduces its own symbols. An interesting and informative symbol used is motorbikes. The two broken motorcycles that Bella brings to Jacob's house to fix symbolize their lives in several important ways. In the *Twilight* world, the bikes symbolize Bella's broken heart (after Edward left her), Jacob's broken home, and the impaired romantic relationship between Bella and Jacob.

You see, in *New Moon*, Edward dumps Bella. She subsequently experiences depression and heartbreak over her loss and becomes "broken beyond repair" (*New Moon*, p 219). At around the same time, Bella finds two 'broken' motorcycles 'dumped' on a trash heap. They were two "dilapidated motorcycles rusting in the Markses' front yard" with a "FOR SALE, AS IS sign" attached to them. This message "seemed to serve some higher purpose" (*New Moon*, p 126). Feeling a bit adventurous, Bella purchases the bikes lying on the dead branches, to ease her depression and bring some excitement back into her life (*New Moon*, p 127). She recalls Jacob being mechanically inclined, and thinks of taking the pair of bikes to him to fix up.

The *Twilight Saga* strongly suggests that Bella's old red motorbike symbolizes her depressed broken emotional state, badly in need of repair. In *New Moon*, the red bike ends up belonging to Bella (p 137). The black motorbike, meanwhile, is owned by Jacob *Black* (p 169). The old black bike appears to reflect Jacob's impoverished background. Or maybe it reflects the romantic relationship between Bella and Jacob that will always be broken, especially since Jacob never actually gets the black bike going properly. One day, after Bella visits the empty Cullen house, and is feeling less broken and empty inside, she sees "the red bike standing up, looking like a motorcycle rather than a pile of jagged metal" (*New Moon*, p 163). Even though Bella suffers depression and becomes an emotional wreck, Jacob helps her to stand up by herself, makes her drivable again, makes her feel alive again. Symbolically, Bella is on the emotional mend, and looks a bit more shiny and new, just like the restored red motorbike.

Mountain

Adding to the beach and forest scenes in the *Twilight Saga*, mountain scenes have important meanings too. As a symbol, a mountain is:

An inaccessible place, a link with heaven and the gods, the

> *mountain, whose mysterious summit is often wreathed in clouds, symbolizes the legendary axis of the world. The mountain is a bridge between earth and heaven.*
> (Colin, 2000)

One of the most famous mountain myths is the one about Moses. God presented the Ten Commandments to Moses on top of Mount Sinai. Long before Christian times, the peak of Mount Olympus was believed to be the dwelling place of ancient Greek gods and goddesses. "Long thought to be a hostile, inaccessible place, at whose summit the elements were unleashed (the volcano's fire, the burning cold of ice and snow, storms and tempests), the mountain was primarily regarded as the earthly seat of the gods" (Colin, 2000, p 348). It may therefore be no coincidence that in the *Twilight Saga* supernatural creatures take action and make important exchanges on mountaintops. Edward and Jacob, for example, had an important interaction on top of a mountain in *Eclipse*.

The highest adventure in the *Twilight Saga* is when Bella treks with Edward and Jacob to the top of a mountain and camps there for the night (*Eclipse*). That is where Edward and Jacob have their first deep and meaningful chat to each other about Bella. There, on the peak of this mountain, a critical turning point occurs in the relationship between these two supernatural guys – Edward and Jacob understand each and other and subsequently relate to each other much better. In fact, the moment Edward and Jacob stop fighting about Bella and reach a truce, even the wild wind on the mountaintop has rest (*Eclipse*, p 447). As such, this scene accurately captures "the symbolic meaning of the mountain, a place that links high and low, the pinnacle of reconciliation, of perfect, absolute union" (Colin, 2000, p 349). The *Twilight* mountain scene is consistent with the mighty meanings of mountains – as a place to unite, and not fight.

Music

Musical scenes in the *Twilight Saga* are emotional experiences, with meaning and messages to boot. While music may not be mentioned in significant quantity or quality in the *Twilight* text, the musical moments that do occur tend to be rather moving and memorable.

When Edward plays the piano for Bella at the Cullen house for the first time, he merges with the music as one. Absorbed in the music – Edward's fingers flow across the keyboard fluidly and with ease. In fact, Bella, who is mesmerized by the lovely music, inspired the piece Edward plays because he composed it himself. Edward even acknowledges the power of the Muses indirectly when he tells Bella that "you inspired this one" (*Twilight*, p 285). The Muses in myth inspire individuals to create music and other forms of art, just as they seem to have inspired Edward.

The Muses are goddesses from Greek myth who personify the arts and sciences. Originally, there were three Muses associated with the goddess of memory Mnemosyne. Memory is an essential ability since without memory no one can learn or remember the finest poems or songs. During the time of Homer, it became popular practice to call on the spirit of the appropriate muse before performing. Altogether, there were nine divine Muses with different names:

Clio – history
Euterpe – flute playing
Thalia – comedy
Melpomene – tragedy
Terpsichore – lyrics, poetry, dance
Erato – love poetry
Polyhymnia – mimicry
Urania – astronomy
Calliope – eloquence, epic poetry

Other *Twilight* characters have also been inspired artistically. Bella's mother Renée is also a musically talented pianist. When Renée played her second-hand piano "she was happy, absorbed – she seemed like a new, mysterious being" (*Twilight*, p 284). These days, artists still speak of finding their muse, which symbolizes a source of inspiration that drives the creative force.

The word 'music' happens to share the same origins as 'amuse'. To 'muse' upon something means to consider something. Edward, who chuckles a lot in *Twilight*, finds Bella extremely amusing.

N

New Moon

> Tonight the sky was utterly black. Perhaps there was no moon tonight – a lunar eclipse, a new moon. A new moon. I shivered, though I was not cold.
> (*New Moon*, p 74)

This is the most direct remark about a new moon in the *Twilight Saga* books. It is also the most symbolic one. As a symbol, a new moon means the start (or the end) of a phase or process. In Bella's case, when Edward ended his relationship with Bella, he also left her to begin a new life without him. Just as the night in this scene is very dark when the moon is new, so is Bella's future without Edward – uncertain and unknowable. Yet, a new moon eventually grows bigger and brighter in the dark sky. And Bella's dark depression phase dissolves after she does some serious soul-searching. Steadily, Bella discovers new insights about the world and she develops a deeper understanding her innermost self. Just as a new moon grows thicker and brighter over time, Bella grows psychologically wiser and stronger over time. A new moon (a bright crescent rising in a dark night sky) symbolizes Bella's growing friendship with Jacob, her deepening romantic love for Edward, and her rise from dark uncertainty to increased psychological confidence in life. Bella's future brightens and her purpose becomes more clear – she loves Edward and must go to Italy to save him.

Night

There seem to be about as many night adventures in the *Twilight* world as there are daytime scenes. This nocturnal tendency makes sense because night is an old and traditional symbol. According to ancient Greek legends of long ago, night was the daughter of chaos. In other words, darkness originated from the world of cosmic forces and undifferentiated life forms. And it is only at night time, in the darkness, that you can see the moon, the stars, and other subtle forms of light. Similarly, dark and difficult times can help you to see and appreciate your bright inner light. When Bella becomes depressed in *New Moon*, this is a symbolic or psychological night for her, a time of intense darkness, sadness, loneliness and uncertainty. It is certainly helpful and inspiring to remember that the night reveals light and always passes, no matter how dark or cold or long the night is.

Nudity

Even though everyone is born naked, many people, many cultures, and many social situations regard nudity as something shocking or offensive. In addition, people in the modern world are so used to wearing clothes that being nude seems strange and unnatural. Nevertheless, nudity symbolizes a state of innocence, because people are born naked, with a clean slate. That is, evil acts have not yet been committed. The soul has not yet been corrupted. This means that "nudity symbolizes not only truth, purity and authenticity, but also completeness, perfection and achievement" (Colin, 2000, p 362).

In the *Twilight* series, when Bella and Edward swim nude in the warm tropical waters at Isle Esme, this is not just a pre-sex skinny dip. It means that the *Twilight* newlyweds are shedding away their insecurities, worries, inhibitions, and tainted beliefs. During that late night swim, Bella and Edward are acknowledging their deepest feelings for each other (darkness), retreating to the source of emotional life (ocean/water), and are innocent beings cleansing themselves in the water (nudity). Bella and

Edward's naked get-together – with no barriers, walls, or disguises 'covering' them or obstructing their behavior – is a pure and perfect union.

Numbers

Most people think of numbers as good math. Numbers are useful for counting objects, quantifying things, and managing money. But numbers also explain patterns, laws and powers hidden in nature and the universe. Certain numbers have very unique properties and some numbers help to form special structures and configurations. In the *Twilight Saga*, certain numbers keep recurring for some reason, such as the number *three*, for example. Although a number of interesting number theories abound, numerologists agree that certain numbers do have certain meanings. Without a doubt, the *Twilight* world is a mystifying mathematical puzzle.

One: Best and Only

The main meaning of the number 'one' is the oneness of all. Everyone and everything exists together in one big universe. The number one also acknowledges individuality and achieving first place in something. It is certainly a suitable number for an only child and a social outcast such as Bella in the *Twilight* universe. The main meaning of the number one is that it "stands alone, at ease with its individuality, symbolizing the ego and the self" (Nozedar, 2008, p 485). This symbolic meaning is embraced in modern phrases such as 'one of a kind' or the 'odd one out'. The Greek philosopher Plato described one as "the summit of many" – which means to be the best at something (such as a skill) or coming first at something (such as a race).

In tarot cards, one is the Magician's number. This unique and secretive loner is a figure with the powers to amaze and confound us all. This sounds much like Bella, Edward, and even other unique characters like Renesmee perhaps. The *Twilight Saga* certainly uses the symbolic meanings of number one to describe important characters:

- Bella thinks to herself that: "As a human, I'd never been best at anything" (*Breaking Dawn*, p 484). As a vampire, however, Bella is the strongest – she is number one.
- Since Bella is immune to the psychic intrusions of other vampires, including Volturi guards such as Jane and Alec, this makes her "the only one who *could* fight" (*Breaking Dawn*, p 534).
- "Renesmee was beautiful and gifted and unique – she was one of a kind" (*Breaking Dawn*, p 493). This makes Renesmee an important symbolic character, whose power and behavior would be very difficult to predict.
- "I was the only one whose thoughts he could not hear" (*Breaking Dawn*, p 493). Bella's strong mental glitch make her unique, a one and only.
- Bella chooses a 'one of a kind' name for her baby: *Renesmee* (*Breaking Dawn*, p 299).
- Renesmee's unique gift is that she communicates in images. This enhances her oneness.
- Because Renesmee is a hybrid (half-human, half-vampire) she does not fit in with vampires, werewolves or humans. "You're special" Bella reassures her (*Breaking Dawn*, p 539).
- Aro says Renesmee is "utterly, impossibly unique" and therefore "there *is* danger" (*Breaking Dawn*, p 664). As such, Aro argues that Renesmee is an unknown risk, a vulnerability (p 665). This becomes Aro's rationale for killing Renesmee. Unfortunately, some people are threatened by those who are unique or special in some way. And in the *Twilight Saga*, some characters definitely stand out from the crowd.

Two: Fit or Split

In a numerical sequence, the number two is the first even number and it is the only even prime number that exists (a prime number is a number that can *only* be divided by itself, e.g. 2, 3, 5, 7, 11, 13). Two means connection, duality, balance and separation. The number two can unite and complements things. Or else, the number two splits and separates things. For example, it takes two people to fall in love and join together in marriage. On the other hand, the number two suggests two sides to a story. It also has the power to differentiate and separate everything into positive and negative categories. Consider, for example, these binary opposites – day and night, light and dark, good and bad, love and hate, life and death. This 'splitting' role of two links it to conflict because two different sides often compete with each other for resources or just to prove a point. In tarot cards, two is the number of the High Priestess – she rules both sides of a situation and tunes in to flip sides of an issue.

In the *Twilight Saga,* when Billy Black warns Bella to "Take care" (*Twilight,* p 309) with Edward, for example, he is opening up a can of dichotomous worms. He introduces another side to the Edward issue. Bella can either avoid Edward and stay safe or date him and increase the risk of danger. As you can see, it is: Billy versus Bella, elders versus youth, tradition versus innovation, obedience versus rule-breaking, and werewolves versus vampires.

Twilight Dichotomy

When you think about it, the *Twilight* world is very much a twofold world. Many of its topics and themes have two clear sides. Consider the dual nature of these *Twilight* themes, some of which are very obvious and that may have already picked up on:

Vampires/Werewolves
Mortal/Supernatural

Humans/Monsters
Humans/Animals
Good/Evil
Darkness/light
Sun/Rain
Fire/Ice
Warm/Cold
Ugly/Beautiful
Pleasure/Punishment
Freedom/Rules
Responsibility/Recklessness
Past/Future
Choice/Chance
Compassion/Cruelty
Love/Hate
Life/Death

For example, let's examine a dichotomy in detail:

Past/Future – The Cullens are *future*-oriented. They drive new and expensive cars, they wear designer clothes, they are innovative vampires (e.g. drink animal blood), and Alice can foresee the future. In contrast, Billy Black and the Quileute people are *past*-oriented. They cherish ancient legends. They value tradition, modesty, and resourcefulness. Rather than buying a new car, Jacob fixes up an old classic model which he uses to take Bella to the movies (*New Moon*).

Twilight Harmony

Of course, two forces can merge together to balance, complement, or support each other. Examples of good two-factor fits in the *Twilight* books include:

Bella/Edward (love)
Bella/Jacob (friendship)

Male/Female
Sun/Moon
Sea/Land
Beach/Forest
Vampires/Werewolves

The field of alchemy is based on dualism, especially the male/female dynamic. The Great Work in alchemy involves an important union or conjunction, as every 'characteristic' of an element has a counterpart:

Sulfur/Mercury Male/Female Fire/Water Hot/Cold
Dry/Humid Gold/Silver Sun/Moon
King/Queen
(Spindler, 2011)

In an alchemical light, Edward and Jacob may represent a Mercury/Sulfur union. Edward is mercury (because he resembles the mythical Greek messenger Hermes, whose Roman name is Mercury). In *Breaking Dawn*, Edward is the main messenger and key negotiator in the Volturi war. Edward is also the sensitive, emotional, lunar type. Jacob seems to be a sulfur symbol because solar qualities describe him. Plus he is athletic and masculine. Only when Edward and Jacob unite (Mercury and Sulfur), act as one divine duo, and become a fighting pair, do they defeat the Volturi's dark magic at the end of *Breaking Dawn*.

Another example of perfect harmony and alchemical union in the *Twilight Saga* is Renesmee. She is the daughter of a human and a vampire. As such, she is proof that two opposite sides can coexist peacefully together, just like the two magnets that Bella has tried to stick together on her fridge. This makes Renesmee a true 'magnet for harmony'.

It is interesting to note that in the *Twilight* world, vampires and werewolves are initially introduced as opposites, as traditional enemies. By the end of *Breaking Dawn*, however, the two sides merge closely together. For example, Edward and Seth's strong friendship was "mind-boggling" to Bella and shows that "vampires and werewolves could get along just fine" (*Breaking Dawn*, p 10). Alice inspired the idea of vampires and wolves uniting against newborns. "Separately we could all get killed. Together" they could win (*Eclipse*, p 338). Then Jasper invited the wolves to a strategic meeting and considered the possibility of everyone working together. Vampires and werewolves have teamed up ever since.

Three: Magic and Complete

Of all the numbers that occur in the *Twilight* world, the number *three* is the most frequent. It is also a significant symbolic number. In the *Twilight Saga*, three appears in a wide variety of ways.

Consider these scenes from the *Twilight* books, for example:

- The very first number to be mentioned in the *Twilight* world is the number three. A "large black 3 was painted on a white square on the east corner" (*Twilight*, p 13).
- Bella, Edward, and Jacob are three individuals involved in a love triangle.
- There is a main group of three Forks High school boys (Eric, Mike, Tyler).
- There is a main group of three Forks High school girls (Jessica, Angela, Lauren).
- Three nomadic vampires (James, Victoria, Laurent) turn up at Forks (*Twilight*, p 325).
- The Cullen mansion has three floors (*Twilight*, p 281).
- Edward's bedroom is on the *third* floor of the Cullen house (*Twilight*, p 300).
- Edward saves Bella three times in *Twilight* (he stops the van, he stops James from killing Bella, he sucks vampire venom out of Bella's blood).

- Three Quileute boys hang out together (Jacob, Quil, Embry) (*New Moon*, p 138).
- Sam, Jared, and Paul form a strong werewolf trio (*New Moon*, p 174).
- The love triangle between Romeo, Juliet, and Paris is mentioned (*New Moon*, p 371).
- There are three male leaders (Carlisle – Cullen Leader, Charlie – Police chief, Billy – Quileute chief).
- There are three Volturi rulers (Aro, Marcus, Caius).
- Three storms take place (the storm during the *Twilight* baseball game, Bella's cliff- jumping in *New Moon*, and the snowstorm just before the newborn vampires attack in *Eclipse*).
- The *Third Wife's Sacrifice* is an Indian legend about the wife of the last great Spirit Warrior. She sacrificed her own life to save a Quileute tribe from being devoured by a vampire (*Eclipse*, p 229).
- The driveway to the Cullen house is "three miles" long (*Eclipse*, p 323).
- Bella receives three diamond gifts (Edward's heart charm, Edward's engagement ring, Aro's necklace).
- Bella's pregnancy appears after she has had sex with Edward three times in *Breaking Dawn* (in the sea, p 78; in the white room, pp 80–81; and in the blue room, p 98).
- Bella's first three pregnancy symptoms are dizziness, sleeping for 12 hours, and an increase in appetite (*Breaking Dawn*, pp 99–100).
- It takes three days to change into a vampire. It's a "painful three-day conversion" (*Eclipse*, p 66).

As you can see, the *Twilight Saga* loves the number three. But why? What makes this number so special and significant?

Powerful Three

In the *Twilight Saga*, one reason why number three may be so popular is because according to legend and folklore, powerful and magical things happen when three things meet or repeat. For example, an eclipse is a cosmic junction between three planets (the moon, the sun, the earth). The literature on symbolism says that the number three is the most magical and complete number. It relates to spiritual power, supernatural power, and great wisdom. The number three is the first true magical number because its points, when spaced equally apart, can form either a triangle (three lines) or a circle (three arcs). Some of the most famous groups of three that appear in nature, magic and history, for example, include these:

Existence – birth, life, death
Humans – mind, body, soul
Family – mother, father, child
Time – past, present, future
World – earth, heaven, hell
Moon – crescent, full moon, no moon
Sun – sunrise, day, sunset
Magic – cauldrons have three legs, candelabras have three prongs, spells are recited three times
Triple Jewel – Buddha, Dharma (truth), Sangha (virtue)
Triple Goddess – Maid, Mother, Elder
Holy Trinity – Father, Son, Holy Ghost
Fairy tales – often feature three things, e.g. *Goldilocks and the Three Bears*

These famous trios above may help to explain why the *Twilight Saga* has so many trios of its own. A group of three is mystical and divine, it suggests hidden power, and is the simplest pattern of the universe.

Circle or Triangle?

Of course, three points joined together make two important shapes: a *circle* (three points joined by arcs), or a *triangle* (three points joined by lines).

In the *Twilight Saga*, an example of a symbolic circle is Bella, Edward and Renesmee. These three individuals make up a small and complete family circle. In fact, the influence of this family circle is so powerful that it helped the African half-vampire Nahuel to stop hating himself. When Nahuel first met Bella, Edward and Renesmee and "saw the three of us – and realized for the first time that just because he is half immortal, it doesn't mean he is inherently evil" (*Breaking Dawn*, p 696), it gave Nahuel great comfort. For the first time ever, Nahuel saw a natural family unit, a family that he could have and should have had. As Edward explains, this family circle of three will protect Nahuel from further emotional pain.

The *Twilight Saga* also presents a few powerful triangles (three points joined up by lines). If a triangle points upwards, it looks like an arrowhead – a sharp, pointed weapon that attacks others. For example, the Volturi leaders (Aro, Caius and Marcus and James) are described in sharp, menacing and triangular ways in *Breaking Dawn*. If you want to read about dark Volturi triangles now, go to *Triangle*.

Four: Safe

The number four is a symbol for the earth, order, solidity and understanding. Four lines make up a square, a safe and stable shape that contains things securely. It also relates to the square and the cross (four points or lines form these shapes). In a cosmic cross (+), the vertical line symbolizes action and the horizontal line symbolizes the stable earth. We struggle to survive across the life span on earth (horizontal line) and yet we also aspire to higher spiritual enlightenment (vertical line) (Bowes, 1999). Crossroads indicate four possible directions – people can move backwards or forwards, left or right. The crossroad symbol gave rise to the idea that land or territory could be divided or quartered. A crossroad also symbolizes free will – a choice of travelling in four possible directions. "When you are at crossroads and you decide to take one direction rather than another, you are in fact deciding your fate" (Colin, 2000, p 374). In the *Twilight Saga,* there are lots of references to the four axes – north, east, west and south (see *Axis* to discover what each direction means). Since four lines help to organize and categorize nature, four suggests a perfect world. For example, there are:

Four spatial directions – up, down, left, right
Four compass directions – north, south, east, west
Four natural elements – earth, air, water, fire
Four seasons – winter, summer, spring, autumn

As you can see, the number four 'boxes' people, nature, and the world into a safe and stable physical pattern and reality. According to the Greek philosopher Pythagoras in the 6th century BC, four is the closed, perfect and essential structure of the cosmos (Colin, 2000).

According to alchemy, Renesmee may be the *Axiom of Maria Prophetissa,* a process based on the number four. This principle suggests that: "One becomes Two, Two becomes Three, and out of the Third comes the One as the Fourth." This strange statement emphasizes the antagonism between numbers three and four, and has been used in Alchemy for almost two thousand years (*Alchemy Dictionary,* 2009). What this rule suggests is that the number four helps to balance the number three. In the *Twilight Saga,* Renesmee is a much-needed fourth addition that resolves deep emotional conflict, once and for all, in the Bella-Edward-Jacob love triangle. This makes Nessie alchemy's *Axiom.*

As the meaning of the number four suggests, by creating a world bounded by four lines, a square, people felt safe and secure. Anything outside the four points or lines or the square, implied an "unknown world, the forbidden" (Colin, 2000, p 373). The biggest downside of four boundaries, however, is that it can make people feel limited, enclosed, 'boxed in'.

Five: Human

The number five symbolizes humanity. This is because people have five fingers on each hand, five toes on each foot, and five senses to perceive the world (sight, hearing, taste, touch, smell). Five also symbolizes a grown human standing upright (one head, 2 arms, 2 legs). According to ancient Greek philosophy, the universe has five elements – fire, water, earth, air and quintessence (spirit). Five dots, spaced apart equally, form a five-pointed star or pentagram, a shape also known as the wizard's foot. While five does not seem to play a huge role in the *Twilight Saga*, it does crop up here and there. For example:

- The Cullen family comprises five foster children.
- Five wolves protect Bella from Laurent in the meadow.
- Maybe there are other symbolic fives to discover and decode in the *Twilight Saga*.

Six: Creative

The number six does not appear to be especially significant in the *Twilight Saga*, but its meaning could be very relevant to some adventures. For example, the number six traditionally symbolizes marriage, male and female union, and the balance of opposites. This is exactly what happens in the *Twilight* world. Bella and Edward marry, girl and guy hook up, and vampires and werewolves end up complementing each other. As for shape, six points or lines can form a hexagon or a six-pointed star (two triangles overlapping each other). In the *Breaking Dawn* battle, the positions of the Volturi (Aro, Marcus, and Caius) and the *Twilight* world's three heroes (Bella, Edward and Jacob) may be suggesting a six-pointed star at the very center of the battlefield (two triangles meeting up).

Since five symbolizes a *human* adult, six becomes the number of *creation*. It symbolizes an unborn child developing inside the mother's body. Thus, a human's first stage of creation is the number six while a fully-grown human is a five. This would make Renesmee the only character linked to the number six as we learn a lot about Renesmee well before she is born. In Genesis, it took six days for God to create the world. In Avesta, the earliest writings of the bible written by the Hebrews say that the world was created in six stages.

Seven: Perfect

Seven is used to group supernatural characters in the *Twilight Saga*. In particular:

- There are seven Cullen family members (Edward, Carlisle, Esme, Alice, Jasper, Rosalie, and Emmett.
- There are seven male werewolves in the Quileute pack (Sam, Jacob, Quil, Embry, Jared, Paul, Seth). Leah (the first female wolf) and others join the pack later on.
- When Bella's father raises an embarrassing topic, it makes Bella feels as if she has travelled "beyond the seventh circle of Hades (*Eclipse*, p 52).

The number seven may have been strategically chosen to group the supernatural Cullens and the spiritual Quileutes. As a symbol, the number seven is a magical number that denotes intelligence, spirituality, and the occult. The most remarkable and significant events, both natural and divine, tend to be grouped in sevens. For example, there are:

- Seven days in the week
- Seven rainbow colors

- Seven notes in a musical scale
- Seven ruling planets in the zodiac
- Seven deadly sins
- Seven cardinal virtues

Seven is therefore the number of perfection.

In ancient Egypt, a spiritual teacher called Hermes Trismegistus said the universe is made up of seven elements in a certain order. Earth, air, water, fire, quintessence, soul, spirit. The number seven appears often in the Bible. The character Noah built an ark seven days before the Lord unleashed a terrible flood on earth. Noah also took seven pairs of flying birds with him on the ark. Did you know that the Old Testament mentions the number seven 77 times? The New Testament mentions seven items that it groups in sevens: 1) seven churches; 2) seven seals; 3) seven angels with 4) seven trumpets; 5) seven signs; 6) seven plagues; and 7) seven vials (Colin, 2000; Nozedar, 2008; Spindler, 2011).

In alchemy, seven metals are said to grow on the Philosophical Tree. These metals are gold, silver, copper, iron, mercury, lead, and tin. The fruit of this Tree is the eternal and incorruptible Mercurial manifestation known as the *Philosopher's Stone* (*Alchemy Dictionary*, 2009).

The number seven also appears in many traditional fairy tales, which are filled with special symbols. In *Snow White*, for example, Snow White finds shelter with seven dwarfs, whose house she cleans. The dwarves (creatures who dwell deep in the earth) are supposed to symbolize seven psychological processes. These are instinct, emotion, intelligence, intuition, reason, will and awareness (Colin, 2000).

The *Twilight Saga* seems to group certain adventures, experiences, and truths in multiples of seven too. For example, Bella makes seven trips away from Forks:

1 Port Angeles (to the bookshop)
2 Phoenix (to the ballet studio)
3 Port Angeles (to the movies)
4 Italy (to save Edward)
5 Jacksonville (to visit mother)
6 South America (for honeymoon)
7 Seattle (to meet Jenks)

Who knows? This could be a symbolic tip by author Ms. Meyer in that Bella must overcome challenges in seven different places before the Volturi emerge from their underworld and Bella can activate her invincible psychic shield to defeat them in the great *Breaking Dawn* war.

Seven Cullens

It may be worth noting that the seven Cullens may be linked to the seven ruling planets. The planets were named after mythical Gods and possess certain character traits.

1. Carlisle is the family leader – so he is linked to Jupiter, the ruling planet that is linked to expansion and spiritual growth through knowledge and understanding.
2. Esme is down to earth and motherly – she is *Twilight's* earth, the planet that sustains life. The Goddess of Life is a "nurturing mother" and "nature is her embodiment on earth" (Bowes, 1999, p 6).
3. Edward is a fast and intelligent vampire, a messenger who translates the silent thoughts of humans, vampires, and werewolves to others – so he resembles Mercury, the winged and speedy messenger of the Greek gods. Just like Edward, Mercury (Hermes in Greek myth) was athletically fast and strong, was fostered as a child, and musically talented. The classic writer Homer described Mercury as "a bringer of dreams… a watcher by night and one who was

soon to show forth wonderful deeds among the deathless gods." Like Mercury, Edward makes Bella dream about him, watches over her at night, and does good deeds. The planet Mercury symbolizes mentality and a great consciousness beyond physical life

4 Alice has visions, makes prophecies, and has a bright/sunny personality – and the sun symbolizes vision, clairvoyance, and happiness. The sun is a symbol of self-expression, a meaning that captures Alice's happy, creative and expressive pattern of behavior well.

5 Jasper is a war expert and war survivor – and Mars is the planet of war. As a symbol, Mars symbolizes the power, energy, and spirit needed to take successful physical action, which fits with Jasper's military personality well.

6 Rosalie is tall, statuesque, golden-haired, "gloriously beautiful", and *Twilight's* Aphrodite (*Twilight*, p 16, p 26) – so she would be linked to Venus, the planet of love and beauty. Love also encompasses divine love. Once Rosalie apologizes to Bella for being a "monster" and tells Bella that Edward loves her more than anything, she commits an act of divine love (*Eclipse*, p 150).

7 Emmett is physically strong, "muscled like a serious weight lifter" (*Twilight*, p 16) – and Saturn represents physical life, time, karmic tests, and strength. This suggests an apt link between Emmett and the planet Saturn.

(Source: Cullens and Planets: TwilightMOMS Post, whome Feb 2, 2010. Planet meanings: Bowes, 1999)

Eight: Justice

The number eight symbolizes infinity, eternity, and justice. In alchemy, an *ouroboros* is a dragon, or a snake, biting its own tail – a number eight on its side. A horizontal eight is also a symbol of eternity and infinity. The eight's continuous circuit shape suggests that matter and spirit can continually and eternally dissolve into each other (Bowes, 1999). An eight represents the end of a great work, perfection, and eternity. It also suggests that a beginning and an end can occur at the same time. One specific meaning of the ouroboros is that some individuals may 'bite their own tail' and cancel themselves out in the end. This seems to happen in the *Twilight* world. In *Breaking Dawn*, Edward duels with Aro in a word game regarding whether Renesmee is "unique" or "rare". But when Alice introduces a half-vampire to prove that Renesmee is *not* a "unique risk", Aro must swallow his own words – and so he defeats himself with his own trap.

The number eight also symbolizes justice because it looks like an hourglass (time) and balancing scales (used to compare, evaluate, weigh up). In tarot cards (a mystical and magical card system) it is interesting to note that the eighth card of the Major Arcana signifies justice. The image on this card is a bold female figure sitting on a throne. She holds an inverted sword in her right hand and balancing scales in her left hand. Together, the sword and scales are universal symbols of divine justice. In the *Twilight* world, note that Bella calls a Cullen family vote in the middle of the night at the end of *New Moon*. In this sense, Bella represents a female justice figure who raises the issue of immortality and asks others to assess it – these are number eight meanings. In addition, eight people were seated at a round Cullen family table when Bella asked everyone to weight up her plans to become a vampire.

Some other *Twilight* eights that may or may not be symbolically significant:

- Renesmee catches a perfect "eight-pointed" snowflake in her hand (*Breaking Dawn*, p 495).
- In the *Breaking Dawn* battle, a pack of "sixteen enormous regiment wolves" (two branches of eight) bordered the Cullens and surprised the unsuspecting Volturi (p 691).

Since eight symbolizes justice, the presence of wolves may be a tip to their quest for natural and uncorrupted justice.

- A big theme in the *Twilight* world is choice, symbolized by chess, which is pictured on the original cover of *Breaking Dawn*. A chessboard happens to be organized in multiples of eight. There are 8 x 8 squares (64 units of playing space altogether) and each player has sixteen (8 x 2) playing pieces.
- The first three consecutive numbers Bella thinks of in her vampire mind just happen to be multiples of eight: "Ten thousand" (8 x 1250) "Twenty thousand" (8 x 2500), and "Eighty-six thousand, four hundred" (8 x 10800) (*Breaking Dawn*, p 353). The first event Bella analyzes mathematically is the time it took for her to leap off a bed. Her estimate was "a sixteenth of a second" (*Breaking Dawn*, p 359). This number, incidentally, is a multiple of eight. Mathematically beguiling, or what?

Nine: Experience

While the number nine does not feature significantly in the *Twilight Saga*, it may be worth noting that the Cullen family grows from seven members to nine, once Bella marries Edward and has a child. As for the evil side, the Volturi have nine permanent guards. But the details of this sinister symbolism are revealed in a mythical discussion in *Volturi*.

While the number nine has some interesting symbolic meanings such as limit, the unlimited, experience, completion, and virtue, the extent of nine's influence in the *Twilight Saga* is not yet fully clear.

Ten: Cycle

In the *Twilight* world, ten relates to several important character groupings:

- Ten wolves attended Jasper's first battle strategy session in the baseball clearing at night (*Eclipse*, p 348). Colin and Brady (aged thirteen) are the pack's youngest and latest additions (*Eclipse*, p 385).
- A group of ten stand together in the *Breaking Dawn* battle. Seven in the front line (Carlisle, Edward, Emmett, Rosalie, Tanya, Kate, Eleazar) and three at the back (Bella, Benjamin, Zafrina) (*Breaking Dawn*, p 629).
- When Jacob imprints on his soul mate and future wife Renesmee in *Breaking Dawn* (p 415), this will round off the Cullen clan to ten supernatural family members. The importance of ten for the Cullen clan has been previously foreshadowed. One late afternoon at the Cullen house, the seven Cullens, Jacob and Nessie were all together outside in the meadow when:

  > The sun suddenly burst through the clouds, shooting long beams of ruby and gold across the ten of us, and I was lost in the beauty of my skin in the light of the sunset.
  >
  > (*Breaking Dawn*, p 484)

In alchemy, ruby and gold are the colors of perfection. They symbolize the idea that one has successfully attained inner riches. The lovely late sunset casts a hallowed glow over the group of ten, as if to suggest that ten is the number this family is meant to be.

The patterns of ten in the *Twilight Saga* seem to be meaningful and consistent with regards to the traditional meanings of the number ten. The number ten is supposed to symbolize a completed cycle, perfection, death and rebirth. When counting, once you reach ten, you start counting in tens all over again. As such, the number ten symbolizes a total revolution, the return to unity, and the achievement of a goal (Bowes, 1999). The *Twilight Saga* ends with a Cullen clan of ten members, which includes their latest additions, Jacob and Renesmee. How's that for symbolic closure?

Specific Numbers

In case these are symbolically important, it is worth noting that several specific numbers get a special mention in the *Twilight Saga*.

Eleven

The number eleven does not seem to be of any obvious significance in the *Twilight Saga*. Although, it may prove handy to know that the Forks High School Graduation Ceremony and Alice's graduation party at the Cullen house, for example, occurred on the 11th of June (*Eclipse*, p 238).

According to a symbolism of numbers, the number eleven means new beginnings. This number, written as two vertical rods ('11') suggests a fresh and advanced cycle or process, which builds upon the knowledge of the previous '1 to 10' cycle. The number eleven and its magical meaning suggests "a higher level of understanding" (Bowes, 1999, p 79).

Thirteen

In the *Twilight Saga*, Bella's 18th birthday is September the 13th. She also marries Edward the following year on August the 13th. According to the literature, the number 13 is considered to be a very unlucky number in some countries. It even has a specifically recognized phobia: *Triskaidekaphobia*. The superstitious sufferers of triskaidekaphobia fear the number thirteen and try to avoid bad luck by keeping away from anything numbered or labeled thirteen. As a result, many companies and manufacturers use special numbering or labeling systems to avoid the number. Some hotels and tall buildings, for example, do not have a thirteenth floor. It is certainly considered unlucky to have thirteen guests at a table. And Friday the 13th is said to be the unluckiest day of all. Why is the number thirteen so unlucky? Here are some interesting theories: Last Supper – At Jesus Christ's last supper, thirteen people sat around the table, counting Christ and the twelve apostles.Knights Templar – On Friday the 13th of October in 1307, King Philip IV of France ordered the arrest of the Knights Templar.Full Moons – a year which contained 13 full moons instead of 12 moons posed problems for monks who designed calendars. A thirteen-month year would upset the schedule for church festivals. A repressed lunar cult – In ancient cultures, the number 13 represented femininity, because it corresponded to the number of lunar (menstrual) cycles in a year (13 x 28 = 364 days). When the solar calendar came to dominate the lunar, the number thirteen was considered to be cursed (Wake, 2011).

Poor thirteen.

In the *Twilight Saga*,, the number thirteen does not appear to have a clear-cut positive or negative meaning.

Fifteen

For some reason, the number fifteen is specifically mentioned in the *Twilight* books.

- The distance from Forks to La Push is "fifteen miles" (*Twilight*, p 98).
- Bella's house is fifteen miles from La Push (*Eclipse*, p 65).
- Renesmee jumps fifteen feet in the air to catch a falling snowflake (*Breaking Dawn*, p 495).

The number fifteen is probably a random number choice more than a number deliberately chosen for its symbolic value, especially as this number does not appear to have significant meanings according to the literature. Of course, fifteen is a multiple of five, in case that's useful to any symbol detectives out there.

Eighteen

Six formal important rites of passage or things happen when Bella turns *eighteen* years of age:

1 Bella has an 18th birthday party.
2 Bella graduates from Forks High.
3 Bella gets married.
4 Bella falls pregnant.
5 Bella dies and becomes a vampire.
6 Bella gives birth to Renesmee.

Whether it is a deliberate plot plan, an unconscious mental idea, or simply a freak random fact, it is not clear what the number eighteen means in the *Twilight* books.

Nineteen

The number nineteen does not seem to be an important symbolic number. However, it does appear several times in the world of *Twilight*:

- Bella's first day at Forks high school was on the 19th of January (*New Moon*, p 158).
- The anti-vampire festival, Saint Marcus Day, is celebrated on the "nineteenth" (*New Moon*, p 440).
- Edward, whom Bella falls in love with, was born in the nineteenth century.

Any special significance with regards to the number nineteen, if it exists, is yet to be uncovered.

Battle Numbers

For whatever reason, the *Breaking Dawn* battle mentions a few specific numbers. For example, 32 vampires make up the Volturi army and more than 40 angry vampires serve as witnesses. The

Cullen side has 19 fighting vampires, 10 wolves, 7 witnesses, plus Renesmee.

Maybe the *configuration* of these numbers is more important than the actual numbers themselves. For example, Bella explains that the line of Cullens was "uneven" (*Breaking Dawn,* p 634). Maybe the "uneven" Cullen line suggests a tendency to think more flexibly because it contrasts the "rigid" formation of the Volturi army.

O

Olympic Peninsula

In the *Twilight Saga,* the Olympic Peninsula is the main geographical setting (*Twilight,* p 3). Of course, the Olympic Peninsula is a large stretch of land in the western Washington state of the USA, near Seattle. The Pacific Ocean borders the western side, with the Strait of Juan de Fuca to the north, and Puget Sound to the east. Cape Alava, the westernmost tip in the United States, appears on this peninsula. For a long time, the Olympic Peninsula remained unexplored and unmapped until its topography and timber resources were identified in 1898. The many green forest scenes in the *Twilight* books, with their big, tall and old trees, accurately reflect the Olympic Peninsula as a place covered in temperate rain forest, especially in the mountain ranges.

The Olympic Mountains, where Bella nearly froze her fingers and toes off in *Eclipse,* are located in the center of the Peninsula. This mountain range happens to be the second largest one in Washington state. Its highest peak is Mount Olympus. In Greek myth, the gods ruled from the top of Mount Olympus, the seat from which the king of gods, Zeus, ruled over all. Since the Cullens have links to the seven planets and seven mythical gods (see *Seven*), it is interesting that the *Twilight* story is set in a name that relates to the mythical Olympus.

Major salmon-bearing rivers on the Olympic Peninsula such as the Quillayute, the Sol Duc, and the Lyre, wind their way through the green forest-covered land. Charlie Swan would have many favorite fishing spots here, no doubt. Large natural lakes feature in the peninsula as do many state and national parks. At present, much effort is being made to protect wilderness areas and salmon streams in the Olympic National Peninsula. These conservation efforts will help to keep the forests, rivers, mountains and beaches to stay wild, beautiful and magical forever.

One-Eyed Pete's

It may be hard to imagine what a bar that serves alcohol could possibly mean in the *Twilight* books. After all, it is a place where humans get drunk and the local *Twilight* world riff-raff hang out in Port Angeles. However, the name of the bar in the *Twilight Saga* may be a quirky reference to an important Greek myth. You see, the Cyclopes are one-eyed monsters in Greek myth. And the bar "One-Eyed Pete's" may be a subtle nod to these mythical monsters (*New Moon*, p 108). You see, the Cyclopes were huge giants that had a single eye in the middle of their forehead. The Greek poet Hesiod wrote about three Cyclopes brothers: Brontes (which means thunder), Steropes (lightning), and Arges (brightness). These Cyclopes were best known for their magnificent metalwork, and together they fashioned the thunder bolts for Zeus, a trident for the sea god Poseidon, the helmet of invisibility for Hades, and other powerful tools. There was another group of Cyclopes giants of which the most famous one is called Polyphemus. According to Homer's epic poem, the Greek hero Odysseus blinded this giant while trying to escape from his cave. When some people get really, really drunk, they can get blind, act like terrible monsters and not see things too clearly. What's more, the bar "One-Eyed Pete's" does happen to have a big 'green' sign (*New Moon*, p 108). A pointer to a big, green one-eyed monster, perhaps?

Onyx

Onyx is a precious stone that comes in various colors – dark red, striated, patterned and black. The word *onyx* means 'claw' in

Greek. In Arabic, the word for onyx is *el jaza*, which means 'sadness'. The stone is believed to drain energy and cause melancholy. When vegetarian vampires are hungry and their bodies desperately require nutrition, their eyes turn onyx black. Once they feed on animal blood, however, vegetarian vampire eyes lighten up once more with glowing golden energy. The *Twilight Saga* refers to the onyx eyes of Edward Cullen a number of times, and his brooding manner fits with the melancholy meanings of this stone. When Edward declared his love for Bella when they reunited in *New Moon*, "his eyes were liquid onyx and utterly sincere" (p 519).

P

Paradise

Many people desire to reach a place of paradise in the future – a perfect, peaceful and beautiful place. The famous tale of Adam, Eve and the apple is not just a story of past sin and the loss of paradise; it also suggests how people can find paradise again. In the same way, the apple in the *Twilight* tale symbolizes the growing fruit of Bella and Edward's forbidden, foolish, insane, and even deadly love for each other. However, the power of love is also good, gallant, clear, and pure – and therefore a fine and valid way to regain a lost paradise. In ancient times, people often viewed paradise as "the finest representation of the afterworld, frequently symbolized as a beautiful garden" (Colin, 2000, p 410). As such, the apple's hidden message about paradise is this: *If you do your best, follow your heart, and try to be good and pure, you can reclaim your inner paradise.* That is why Carlisle Cullen always strives to do his best – he still has hopes for his soul. Carlisle strongly believes that good thoughts and behaviors can help individuals to find their lost paradise.

The garden of paradise metaphor provides important symbolic closure for the end of *Breaking Dawn*.

Bella and Edward's stone cottage is a gift from Esme after Bella attains immortality and "reaches the afterlife" so to speak. Her cottage has a beautiful garden, full of fragrant flowers and a tranquil pond. Symbolically, Bella's garden may well be a symbol for paradise found. Just like Christian scripture, the *Twilight* tale suggests that those who strive to be good, brave and loving can reach a beautiful and peaceful place. Of course, Carlisle and his gold-eyed vampire followers are striving to such a paradise by living respectfully and harmoniously with humans, animals, nature, werewolves, and even other vampires. In the *Twilight* world, good and virtuous behavior is the garden path to paradise. So, while the apple at the start of *Twilight* may stir up feelings of desire and temptation, the paradise at the end of *Breaking Dawn,* after the Volturi battle, provides perfect and peaceful symbolic closure. As Bella explains: "We continued blissfully into this small but perfect piece of our forever" (*Breaking Dawn,* p 699).

Phoenix

Phoenix, Arizona is where Bella Swan was raised in the *Twilight Saga,* as was author Stephenie Meyer. Bella's mother, Renée, moved to Phoenix after she separated from Charlie in Forks. Renée's last words were, "Let me go, Charlie" (*Twilight,* p 344). It is also where Bella took ballet classes and lived for almost seventeen years of her life. In the *Twilight Saga,* Bella moves from Phoenix to Forks, Washington state. She moves from a sunny city to a rainy town to live with her father, after her mother remarries. But Bella must return to Phoenix, to her old ballet studio because an evil vampire wants to kills her there. What's more, this Phoenix scene has some interesting symbolic meanings.

To escape James, a lethal vampire gifted in tracking his prey, Bella returns home to "the Valley of the Sun" (*Twilight,* p 355). Despite this city's sunny reputation Bella, upon arriving there, notices that the sun causes the palm trees to cast "shadows across the freeway" (*Twilight,* p 355). These shadows in the valley are like an omen of evil to come. In a symbolic sense, this makes the Phoenix adventure a psychological thriller. The hidden meaning of Bella's menacing challenge in Phoenix is to walk through one of the most sinister, shadowy and terrifying valleys of all:

Yea, though I walk through the valley of the shadow of death, I will fear no evil: for thou art with me.
(*Psalms 23:4*)

Get it? In *Twilight* terms, Bella's return to Paradise Valley is like walking through a valley of shadows to face death (from James). In nature, deserts often symbolize barren and lifeless places – where Paradise Valley is. However, Bella does not fear James because Edward's loving memory is with her. Evil cannot touch love. It suggests that anyone can overcome a dark and difficult time with love in their heart and support from a positive spirit. Just as a mythical phoenix rises from its ashes of death, anyone can rise from tragedy and misery to happiness. This makes the Phoenix adventure pretty inspiring.

As swell as Bella's symbolic connections with Phoenix, this city is also a real city in Arizona, in the United States. A hot, cactus-dotted desert with blistering heat, Phoenix is a complete contrast to cold and rainy Forks.

Pink

The color pink makes a grand debut in the *Twilight Saga* on the night of Bella's 18th birthday party. Alice decorates the Cullen house with plenty of "pink roses", lots of "pink candles", and a "pink birthday cake" (*New Moon*, p 25). The pink decorations really stand out against the Cullens' large white living room, crystal dishes, and presents wrapped in silver.

Why pink? Alice's pink party probably means well. Pink is a color that traditionally symbolizes femininity, good health, love, and patience. It is a feminine color – flirty, girlish, and innocent. In particular, pale pink is the symbol for a baby girl.

The pink party theme could also echo a pretty pre-twilight time of day. The sky at Forks, with its overcast weather, has been known to be covered in silver-gray clouds shot with streaks of bright pink sunshine in the late afternoon.

Port Angeles

In the *Twilight Saga,* teenagers visit Port Angeles for entertainment. The town has a cinema, restaurants, a bar, and a bookstore. In *Twilight,* Bella travels to Port Angeles with Jessica and Angela to buy dresses for the school prom. When Bella checks out a bookstore, she encounters four drunken men who plan to sexually attack her. Edward, who followed Bella to Port Angeles to make sure she was safe, hears the violent thoughts of these men, and arrives just in time to rescue Bella. When Bella and Edward visit the La Bella Italia restaurant afterwards, Bella and Edward's romantic relationship really begins.

In the real world, Port Angeles is a large town in the Clallam County, Washington state. According to a 2000 Census, it is the biggest city on the Olympic Peninsula. The harbor was dubbed *Puerto de Nuestra Señora de los Ángeles* (Port of Our Lady of the Angels) by the Spanish explorer Francisco de Eliza in 1791. By the mid-1800s, this name was shortened to Port Angeles. Since Port Angeles means 'port of angels' or 'angel's entry', it is an apt place for Edward, whom Bella considers to be an angel, to makes his first angel's entry to rescue Bella from four thugs who try to attach her there.

Purple

The traditional meanings of purple are power, majesty, wealth, and royalty. Except for the beauty of "purple" wildflowers blossoming in Bella and Edward's meadow, purple takes on a mean and menacing streak in the *Twilight Saga*. The color purple tends to be associated with suffering, injury, anger, evil, and death:

- Edward has a "purple shadow in the hollow under his eyes" (*Twilight*, p 242)
- The gray storm clouds looked "a gruesome purple color" (*New Moon*, p 355).
- When Bella nearly drowns after cliff diving, and Jacob pulls her out of the sea, she opens her eyes to see "dark purple clouds" (*New Moon*, p 365).
- When Edward felt really suicidal, he had "deep purple" rings under his eyes (*New Moon*, p 451).
- Charlie gets so angry at Bella going to Seattle that he makes his face "flush purple" (*Eclipse*, p 18).
- A menacing sky heralded a terrible storm in *Eclipse*: "a solid wall of purple-black cloud was racing in from the west, blackening the forest beneath it" (p 427).
- "There was a dark purple cloud hanging low over the tree… smoke" (*Eclipse*, p 500).
- A fire of "thick, purple-black smoke, hovering like a disease against the bright grass" appeared where a group of newborn vampires burned (*Eclipse*, p 503). Gruesome.
- Bella had "large purplish bruises" across her arm" (*Breaking Dawn*, p 81).

Despite using purple in ghastly ways, the true magic and meaning of purple does shine through occasionally. The meadow is scattered with wild "purple" wildflowers (Twilight, p 226). In *Breaking Dawn*, the first time Bella visits her small stone cottage it looked "lavender gray in the light of the stars" (p 440), underneath "a deep purply night outside" (p 434). The color purple certainly fits well in a setting that has magical and supernatural themes.

Q

Queen

Bella is the main character, narrator, and hero of the *Twilight* epic. It is therefore fitting that Bella symbolizes qualities fit for a Queen. The strongest example of Bella as queen is the original image of the *Breaking Dawn* cover. Two chess pieces are depicted – red pawn in the background (the weak, human Bella) and a white Queen in the foreground (the strong, vampire Bella). By virtue of her strong determination, strategic choices, brave behaviors and other Queen-like qualities, Bella rises from being a naïve and fragile human girl to a powerful vampire Queen – whose empathy for others involves super self-control. Meanwhile, Bella's supernatural gift to shield others with the crimson light of her protective love reigns supreme.

What's more, Bella is a Queen who rules with smart choices and tries to enforce fair and honest justice. For example, it is Bella who arranges a democratic vote regarding her idea to become a vampire. Bella is also the catalyst who promotes a positive alliance between vampires and werewolves. She starts off as a neutral Switzerland force to settle the dynamic between Edward and Jacob. This culminates in a powerful defense force in the *Breaking Dawn* war and an unbreakable bond once Jacob (a werewolf) imprints on Bella's daughter Renesmee (his vampirish soul mate).

In alchemy, the White Queen is a moon symbol (Bella's symbol) and her metal is silver or quicksilver (Edward's color). Since Bella is the "moon" in the *Twilight Saga*, is in love with Edward (his color is silver), and is pictured as a White Queen on the original *Breaking Dawn* cover, the alchemical meaning of the White Queen is an incredible fluke (*Alchemy Dictionary*, 2009).

An amusing symbolic idea, plotted or unplanned, which

suggests that Bella is a queen is when Bella and Emmett arm wrestle each other on a big rock. This funny scene occurs at the "granite boulder" among a pile of rocks at the riverbank in the Cullens' backyard (*Breaking Dawn*, p 482). Symbolically speaking, it happens to be a challenge rather reminiscent of traditional magical challenges that are designed to test the strength of kings and queens. In particular, the legend of King Arthur involved a young Arthur pulling out "Excalibur" – a jewel-encrusted sword that was stuck inside a rock. Arthur, the true king, was the only one who could do it. This royal test is echoed in Bella's adventure. She is so strong supernaturally that she splits the boulder into two pieces with just one karate-chop and pulverizes the rock into pebbles and powder with her bare hands. Bella, the vampire queen, rules!

Quileutes

Twilight Quileute

In the *Twilight* saga, fictional Quileute characters live around Forks and La Push, in Washington state. The main Quileute character in the *Twilight* world is Bella's best friend Jacob Black. Other important Quileutes include Jacob's father Billy Black, who is the chief of the tribe. There is also Sam Uley, the wolf pack's leader, and a few more figures. According to Quileute folklore in the *Twilight* series, the ancestors were once great spirit warriors who developed the power to transform themselves into wolves. Since then, the magic has never disappeared from their bloodlines.

Quileute People

Stephenie Meyer has certainly based her story on important facts. The Quileute people are a real Native American community with a rich culture. Their native land is the Olympic Peninsula. About 750 Quileutes live in the southwest corner of the state at the mouth of the Quileute River on the Pacific coast. The reservation's main population center is the community of La Push, just as the

Twilight books describe. The language of the Quileute tribe belongs to the Chimakuan language family from the Northwest Coast indigenous peoples. The Quileute language is unique and resilient, and only one of five languages in the world that does not use nasal sounds (m, n). Traditional Quileute people were once great whalers who fished in local rivers and the Pacific Ocean for seafood.

A few interesting facts about Quileute Indians are that:

- The word 'Quileute' is pronounced 'quill-ee-yoot'. The name of their tribal place is *Kwo'liyot*, which is derived from the Quileute word *kwoli* (wolves).
- The Quileute Indians are the original people of the Pacific Northwest Coast.
- Today, the Quileutes live on a reservation in Washington state and they own and control this land.
- In the past, the Quileute tribe made large dugout canoes by hollowing out cedar logs. They used these canoes to trade, fish, hunt, and engage in warfare.
- The Quileute Indians have fished for salmon, trout, seals, sea lions, and they have even hunted whales from their canoes. They also gathered plants, berries, roots, shellfish and clams.
- Quileute people are famed for their fine basket weaving and woodcarving arts.
- In the *Twilight* series, the story about the "Cold Ones" is not real. There are no vampires in traditional Quileute folklore. However, the legend that Quileute people descended from wolves is a true Quileute legend. Wolves are sacred animals to the Quileute people.
  (Source: Redish and Lewis, 2011).

Although the *Twilight* books are fictional, they have played a positive role in increasing awareness about Quileute culture.

R

Rain

Bella's Inner Rain

At first, Bella really hates the rain in Forks. She dislikes rainy weather and shows a strong aversion to water. When Bella arrives at Port Angeles airport it is "raining", which she interprets as a sign of "goodbye" to the sun and the end of a happy life (*Twilight*, p 5). Bella's disdain for the rain not only symbolizes her feelings of resentment coming to Forks (even though it was her own choice). At a deeper level, Bella's rejection of water may be suggesting that she is not yet in touch with her true feelings that flow within her. Maybe Bella's move to a wet place like Forks is a purification process. Rain is supposed to wash away pain, sorrow and negative energy. As such, the Forks rain may be trying to purify Bella in a symbolic way.

As a symbol, rain has both positive and negative meanings. In ancient times, people saw rain to be a blessing or gift from the heavens. The best example of rain in nature is when it manifests as a cool, refreshing life-giving force following a long tough drought. Rain helps plants to grow, animals to thrive, and makes the earth healthy and fertile once again. However, rain can also be a destructive force. Heavy downpours can cause floods, submerge land, and drown everything in their reach.

When Edward breaks up with Bella in *New Moon*, she has a heavy rain day in the forest. The rain starts to fall as Bella lies on the ground, struggling to hold onto the numbness in her body. The rain keeps falling, pooling around her cheek. Not only is Bella being swamped by rain, she is drowning in the pain of her loss. As the *Twilight* world shows, rain can be a comfort or a threat; it can mean either life or death, tears of joy or great sorrow.

It's Raining Love

The rain in the *Twilight* world adds atmosphere to Edward's character. It enhances his gloomy, mysterious, and romantic presence. For example, the *Twilight* novel reveals a number of links between Edward and the rain:

- The first day Bella met Edward at school, it was "sheeting rain" (p 8) and Bella could hear the "whooshing of the rain and wind" (p 10).
- The rain "continued heavily" as "the weeks passed" (p 60), at the same time as Bella contemplates the mysterious Edward in her first weeks at school.
- When Edward drives Bella home after she faints from blood-typing class, it was, of course, "raining harder" than ever (p 89). Then Edward "stared out through the rain, lost in thought" as the rain "blurred everything outside the window" (p 90). Just as the hard rain makes it hard to see clearly, Bella is struggling to figure Edward out at this time.
- In the early stages of Bella and Edward's relationship, it seems to rain quite heavily (p 93). Surprised?
- Whenever Edward is around, so is the rain, e.g. "pounding rain" (p 95), the "rain picked up" (p 308), "pouring hard outside" (p 313) and "heavy" rain (p 314). The rain is surely a meaningful metaphor that enhances Edward's mystery and signifies his presence. Or maybe the rain is trying to suggest that deep feelings are starting to "flow" and "pour out", as Bella and Edward's romantic feelings for each other intensify.
- When the communication channels open between Bella and Edward in his car, the rain pours also: "The sky darkened and rain plummeted around us in a sudden deluge." At the same time, Bella becomes more emotionally expressive and was "talking freely" (p 203).

Does this suggest that the emotional floodgates have just been opened, or what?

- The "rain was louder" and it then became hard to see through "the rain" (p 204). Symbolically speaking, lots of rain means lots of emotion to sift through – Bella and Edward are falling in love.

In the *Twilight* world, the rain continues to symbolize Edward's presence, even after Jacob enters Bella's life. The day that Bella visits Jacob so they can start fixing the bikes "the rain came down like water slopped from a bucket" (*New Moon*, p 144). Yet, "a strange feeling of warmth bubbled up in my throat, despite the icy rain splattering on my cheeks" (*New Moon*, p 144). It is as if the rain (Edward's presence) is trying to interfere with the motorbike repairs, but Jacob's sunny presence (feeling of warmth) is competing with Edward's cold, icy presence. Later that night, after spending a nice sunny day together, Bella and Jacob attend a dinner party with the Clearwater family (Harry, Sue, Leah and Seth) at the Black house. But the "rain eventually broke up the party" (*New Moon*, p 150). A jealous or overprotective rainy Edward presence? Maybe!

It's worth noting that when Jacob picks Bella up in his Rabbit to take her to the movies, it is not raining (*New Moon*, p 218). It was a cloudy, dry, and nice day, even for Forks (*New Moon*, p 232). Maybe there is less rain because Jacob's sunny, happy, and romantic influence is stronger somehow. However, as soon as Jacob joins Sam's pack, and tells Bella that he is "not good" for her and not to visit him anymore, he leaves Bella standing alone, hurt and lonely. At that exact moment the rain returns. "The rain started to drizzle, stinging here and there against my skin… The rain picked up, and so did the wind… My hair whipped in my face, sticking to the wet places and tangling in my lashes" (*New Moon*, p 272). In fact, since Bella left the truck windows open, the seats had become really wet. Does the return of the rain suggest the return of Edward? Edward's romantic rain trying to comfort Bella? Makes sound symbolic sense, don't you think? It is also worth noting that Jacob 'turns into' Edward in Bella's very next dream. This suggests that it is symbolically raining in Bella's heart, meaning that Edward is her true love, and not Jacob – a sun symbol.

Rainbow

The *Twilight Saga* is famous for its beautiful vampires who sparkle like diamonds in the sun. But what about rainbows? They too appear in the story. While shimmering white diamonds are linked to Edward (see *Diamonds*), rainbows tend to be more strongly connected with Jacob and the area around La Push. While vampire skin can appear rainbow-like (e.g. *New Moon*, pp 4, 466; *Eclipse*, p 458), these descriptions seem less significant compared to the meaningful, magical and spiritual rainbows that appear alongside Jacob and his beach.

Jacob's Rainbows

Sea Life

The rainbow is strongly linked to Jacob, especially in scenes that involve La Push Beach. The first time Bella visits First Beach (Jacob's beach), she notices colorful sea life in a tidal pool. At the edge of the forest at La Push Beach, Bella finds "shallow pools that never completely drained" and that were "teeming with life" (*Twilight*, p 101). Sitting on a rock above these "ocean ponds", Bella describes herself as being:

> Spellbound by the natural aquarium below me. The bouquets of brilliant anemones undulated ceaselessly in the invisible current, twisted shells… crabs… starfish… one small black eel with white racing stripes wove through the bright green weeds.
> (*Twilight*, p 101)

Bella's observation of colorful sea life on Jacob's beach and sacred Quileute territory is a positive experience. This fits with the positive meanings of rainbows as symbols of good news and good luck. As a symbol from nature, the appearance of a rainbow signifies good news and 'beneficial renewal', as it never predicts disaster or a bad situation.

Colored Stone

In another outdoors adventure, Bella notices colorful stones during her first visit to La Push Beach. A thin, sandy strip of beach "grew into millions of large, smooth stones that looked uniformly gray from a distance, but close up every shade a stone could be: terra-cotta, sea green, lavender, blue gray, dull gold" (*Twilight*, p 99).

In a much later adventure, Bella again notices the multi-hued stones at the driftwood wall when she is with Jacob at the beach. Although the sea and clouds are gray, Bella notices rainbows, especially when she saw Jacob walking "back to the driftwood bench, staring at the rainbow-colored pebbles" from "our tree" (*Eclipse*, p 101). As soon as Bella and Jacob become absorbed in an intimate conversation at the beach, "the sun broke through the clouds" and the stony rainbow beach became even more beautiful. "Everything changed color – the waves turned from gray to blue, the trees from dull olive to brilliant jade, and the rainbow-hued pebbles glittered like jewels" (*Eclipse*, p 113). That's a beautiful image, full of color, that surely links Jacob with rainbows.

Giftwrap

The rainbow motif is clearly linked to Jacob when he produces a colorful gift bag to Bella. At Alice's post-graduation party, Jacob gives Bella a "small bag of a loose-woven, multi-colored fabric" which contained "a hand-made silver bracelet" (*Eclipse*, p 332). Jacob's colorful bag is yet another subtle reference to rainbows.

Just like a colorful rainbow is supposed to bring good news, Jacob's colorful bag brings good news too – a handcrafted gift that Jacob made himself, a wooden charm for the bracelet.

Inner Life

As a symbol, rainbows reflect inner life – the colorful world of ideas, images, and dreams. This meaning is acknowledged in the *Twilight Saga*. For example, after the Volterra ordeal and a safe reunion with Edward, Bella has "strange, colorful dreams" (*New Moon*, p 500). When Renesmee communicates her thoughts, her stream of consciousness is presented as a burst of rainbow colors. As Bella notices: "A flickering of colors like a handful of butterflies was scattering from her thoughts" (*Breaking Dawn*, p 433). Dreaming about a rainbow is supposed to put you in touch with your inner self and plunge you into the heart of your finest spiritual energy. This makes the rainbow "a symbol of revelation, regeneration and personal accomplishment" (Colin, 2000, p 428). In other words, a person's mind can be full of colorful ideas, just as the *Twilight* books suggest.

Divine Color

> Everything was so CLEAR. Sharp. Defined.
> The brilliant light overhead was still blinding-bright, and yet I could see the glowing strands of the filaments inside the bulb. I could see each color of the rainbow in the white light, and, at the very edge of the spectrum, an eighth color.
> (*Breaking Dawn*, p 357)

Rainbows become even more important once Bella becomes a vampire. The rainbow reference above from *Breaking Dawn* captures the moment when Bella awakens from her change. Now she can see, not seven, but eight colors in the rainbow spectrum. This fits with the divine power that rainbows are said to have. In myth, the rainbow was considered to be a divine force, a path between heaven and earth. "The rainbow is often seen as a bridge between heaven and earth... and used by the gods to visit the world of mortals" (Colin, 2000, p 427). In myths and legends around the world, the rainbow is a universal symbol that suggests a link between heaven and earth. It is therefore a symbol of divine power.

When Alice smiled "the light sparkled off her teeth, another eight-color rainbow" (*Breaking Dawn*, p 359). Once again, once Bella is a supernatural being, she detects the supernatural power of the rainbow in the form of its eighth color.

Some ancient societies believed that the rainbow carried mortals to heaven. Another old idea was that rainbows could suck people up into the clouds. The ancient Incas did not dare look at a rainbow and they covered their mouths with their hands should one appear. In India, the seven rainbow colors belong to each of the seven heavens. Buddha used the rainbow as a seven-colored stairway to travel from heaven to earth. "The seven colors of the rainbow were also associated with the seven 'heavens' or rungs of the cosmic ladder that initiates had to climb, one by one, to reach the eighth heaven of the revelation and liberation of the soul" (Colin, 2000, p 428). So the eighth color of the rainbow Bella sees after her transformation may symbolize her journey to a higher level. Symbolically speaking, Bella has finally reached a spiritual, supernatural, divine, and celestial plane.

Twilight's Iris

A beautiful rainbow myth concerns a Greek goddess called Iris, a divine messenger for god Zeus and the goddess Hera. As "the harbinger of good news", Iris would "come down to earth from heaven along the path of the rainbow. She was depicted wearing a dress of dewdrops in the sparkling colors of the rainbow, which is why her name was given to the iris of the eye" (Colin, 2000, p 428). A subtle hint to this rainbow myth may well be when Bella notices Jacob's "jewel-like eyes" (*Eclipse*, p 205).

In the *Twilight* world, note that Irina (whose name is somewhat similar to 'Iris') is inversely related to the rainbow goddess in some ways. While Iris refers to the "colorful sparkle" in one's eye, Irina is a lone dark spot in the Volturi army, in the eye of the brooding storm (*Breaking Dawn*, p 633). Just like Iris, Irina has the role of messenger too. But the *Twilight* world symbolically inverts the Greek myth. Instead of bringing good news, *Twilight's* Iris (Irina) is the harbinger of bad news. She heralds the threat of death and destruction for the Cullens, and anyone who supports their cause. In point of fact, Irina triggers a supernatural war. Of course, this is just a theory. It is also possible Irina's work is not a planned perversion of the Greek rainbow myth. Nevertheless, the link between Iris and Irina are worth noting. After all, classic villains are notorious for having a "wicked gleam" in the irises of their eyes.

Red

Red is a powerful and passionate color. It is expressed in various ways in the *Twilight Saga*. For example:

- Bella's face "flushed tomato red" (*Twilight*, p 13).
- Bella's hair shines "red" in the sun (*Twilight*, p 124).
- Bella's favorite gemstone was "red" (*Twilight*, p 201).
- Edward's skin glittered in "ruby-tinged sparkles" (*Twilight*, p 124).
- Jacob's skin is "red-brown" (*New Moon*, p 270).
- Bella dreams about an evil vampire whose "red hair was brilliant as fire" (*New Moon*, p 251).
- The wolves were on "red alert" for danger (*New Moon*, p 342; *Breaking Dawn*, p 197).

These scenes from the *Twilight* books illustrate different symbolic meanings of red. These include emotion, energy, beauty, and danger.

As a symbol, the color red is a very positive color that relates to ideas like action, vitality, creativity, desire, passion, excitement, energy, and emotion. Red is a symbol of life because fire (a dynamic element) can be red. Similarly, blood is a powerful life force that flows through the body. The *rubedo* or red phase of alchemy means that someone is no longer attached to earthly life and the chains that hold one back. When people are 'in the red', they are ready to reach their best possible selves.

In alchemy, Bella's journey suggests red activity because red, the color of passion, symbolizes Bella's true love for Edward. Bella's 'red-iness', her strength and courage to change destiny, enables two ill-fated lovers to be together forever in the end. Bella's love, strength, and selfless behavior are red-hot.

According to symbol experts, red has been a color of power and protection for more than 2000 years. Amulets made from rubies and garnets were most valuable and were believed to make the wearer invincible. Bella's preference for garnets is interesting because red is a protective color. It is also symbolically curious that Bella's protective shield is a "crimson" color too (*Breaking Dawn*, p 576).

The Reddest Scene

Perhaps the reddest adventure of all in the *Twilight Saga* happens in Italy. The city of Volterra was "very windy" and "the color red was everywhere. Red shirts, red hats, red flags dripping like long ribbons beside the gate, whipping in the wind" (*New Moon*, p 444). This is because the locals were having a festival. It may sound strange but it is as if Jacob (who loves Bella and is red-skinned) is desperately trying to hang on to Bella, trying to breathe air into her lungs, trying to make his color stand out.

A symbolic red climax of the Volterra Plaza scene involves a single red ribbon. Bella saw that a "brilliant crimson scarf one woman had tied around her hair was caught in a sudden gust. It twisted up into the air above her, writhing like it was alive. She reached for it, jumping in the air, but it continued to flutter higher, a patch of bloody color" (*New Moon*, p 444). This red scarf is a very significant symbol. The red scarf escaping into the air most probably symbolizes the breaking of Jacob's ties with Bella. The woman's red scarf becomes lost in the wind, as if to suggest that, in the end, Jacob's breath is leaving Bella and that Bella is no longer Team Jacob (red). In the crowded Volterra scene, humans everywhere wear red to symbolize they are anti-vampire, just as Jacob is red-skinned and competes with pale-skinned Edward for Bella's love. In a symbolic way at least, the Volterra residents are sort of Jacob's army. At a symbolic level, these local Italians are on Jacob's vampire-hating side in a city where Volturi vampires rule. It is an anti-bloodsucker festival, after all.

The flood of bloody red, the fiery sun blazing high in the sky, Edward about to kill himself – all this points to the whole scene being on Jacob's side. Jacob is desperately and symbolically fighting for Bella's love. "The wind *whooshed* into me, flinging my hair into my eyes and blinding me further" (*New Moon*, p 448). This suggests that Jacob's breath (symbolically speaking, of course) is trying to stop Bella from saving Edward (who doesn't breathe) one last time. The red scarf blows away soon after Bella has rejected Jacob and at the moment that Bella reunites with Edward in Italy. Pretty symbolic.

Of course, a bright red ribbon, tearing apart, is pictured on the original *Eclipse* book cover. Bella was once strongly attracted to Jacob, and felt torn between choosing Edward or Jacob. However, the romantic gains that Jacob made during Edward's absence disappear forever when Edward and Bella come back together as lovers.

Ribbon

In *Eclipse*, the ribbon on the original book cover symbolizes

Bella's feelings of being torn between Jacob and Edward. The ribbon is also a type of thread, which therefore links it to fate, destiny or a certain path in life. Had Bella not met Edward and made the choice to be with him, the natural course of fate would have pushed Bella and Jacob together. So, the tearing ribbon symbolizes the idea that Bella's choice is a difficult one. It also symbolizes triumph over fate because Bella chose Edward over Jacob. What's more, the ribbon on the *Eclipse* book cover is not completely torn. This suggests that Bella will always have strong ties to both Edward and Jacob, no matter what happens.

When Bella is finally ready to leave Jacob (and choose Edward) during a visit to First Beach, she was "trying to pull her hand free" but Jacob "refused to let go" (*Eclipse,* p 116). This handholding also resembles the idea of a tearing ribbon, breaking a bond. It is interesting that on the way home from that visit, when Bella reunites with Edward but still feels close to Jacob, she notices "the road that shimmered wetly in the sun" (*Eclipse,* p 117). This road looks like a wet ribbon glistening in the sun. Symbolically speaking, this may suggest that Bella's choice is a difficult one. The path home is affected by both the sun (Jacob) and the rain (Edward) because the ribbon of road is both sunny *and* wet. Both Jacob's sunny influence and Edward's rainy influence is affecting Bella's path in life. Bella is emotionally and symbolically attached to both Edward *and* Jacob.

The ribbon, which symbolizes ties to others, has been used in marriage rituals since ancient times. The hand-fasting ceremony is an old pagan marriage rite. Usually, pagan hand-fasting rituals include tying a couple's hands together with a ribbon during the formal marriage rite. These are usually conducted outside to allow people to be at one with the power of nature. "A pagan hand-fasting is a simple, natural and joyful celebration of love without the involvement of any established religion. A bonfire, dancing, engraved chalices and garlands of flowers are traditional features of the festivities." According to traditional folklore, hand-fasting couples should also wear "garlands of flowers, made from a combination of roses, gardenias, daisies, jasmine and orchids on their heads or around their necks" (Bowes, 1999, p 152). These traditions, which involve nature, flowers, ribbons and festivity, are rather reminiscent of Bella and Edward's wedding day:

- The wedding featured blossoms, lilacs, freesia and roses (*Breaking Dawn*, p 38).
- The wedding took place outside on the Cullen meadow under two huge cedar trees.
- Garlands of "white blossoms" were hung everywhere, as were "long lines of white gossamer ribbons" (*Breaking Dawn*, p 44).
- Edward the groom waited for Bella at "an arch overflowing with more flowers, more gossamer" (*Breaking Dawn*, p 44).

Since this wedding scene is similar to a hand-fasting ceremony, the ribbon symbolism winds its way even more deeply into the *Twilight Saga* story.

Ring

In a romantic climax in *Eclipse*, Bella receives a beautiful engagement ring from Edward when he asks her to marry him at his house:

> Elizabeth Masen's ring sparkled in the dim light. The face was a long oval, set with slanting rows of glittering round stones. The band was gold – delicate and narrow. The gold made a fragile web around the diamonds. I'd never seen anything like it.
> (*Eclipse*, p 406)

When Edward presents his mother's ring to Bella, this may be the most significant ring scene in the *Twilight Saga*. Not only does this event occur somewhere in the middle of *Eclipse,* but it also happens in the middle of an *eclipse* that overshadows Jacob's sunny love for Bella, no doubt. The start of *Breaking Dawn* opens with Bella wearing this "delicate ring" (*Breaking Dawn,* p 3).

What is so special about a ring? Since a ring is round, it has similar symbolic meanings to the circle and the wheel. In particular, rings mean unity, infinity, and eternity. Above all, a ring's most distinctive feature is that it symbolizes "an alliance, bond, union, association or attachment" (Colin, 2000, p 430). Edward's ring belonged to his mother, and by giving it to Bella, it stays in the family circle. More importantly, the wearing of a ring indicates an existing bond. The most famous example in society is the wedding ring. This is exchanged by a couple on their wedding day at the same time that they exchange their vows of eternal love and loyalty to each other. A ring reinforces the eternal, infinite, continuous, and cyclic nature of life:

- the spiral shape of DNA
- the recurring rhythm of day and night
- the cycle of the seasons
- the circular orbits of the sun, moon, planets and stars
- the ever-spinning circles, cycles, and spirals of the cosmos

The famous tale of King Solomon, whom Jacob mentions in *Eclipse* (p 530), featured a magical ring. According to legend, the Seal of Solomon was a ring which was the source of all his wisdom and power. The king used it to conjure up demons and enslave them. One day, when King Solomon lost his ring, all his power and wisdom disappeared also, until his ring was eventually returned to him. The ancient Greek philosopher Plato also described a powerful ring that belonged to a shepherd named Gyges. Apparently, when a special part of this ring was turned inwards, the wearer became invisible. In medieval times, physicians once gave their patients stone or metal rings to wear to cure certain ailments. Sometimes rings were used to cast spells or bewitch others. A person wearing an enchanted ring could therefore become irresistible to the one whose love they craved.

In the *Twilight Saga,* Bella's antique engagement ring accurately reflects important ring meanings. Since Bella's romantic union with Edward is accompanied by the giving of rings and formally established in a marriage ceremony, this suggests that her love and desire for Edward is truly fulfilled symbolically.

S

Sacrifice

Bella's Sacrifices

> I would rather die than stay away from you.
> (*Twilight*, p 240)

When Bella is willing die for her vampire boyfriend, is she just an idiot teenager? Or, is Bella on a serious psychological mission? Is it possible that Bella has found higher spiritual meaning in her world?

The *Twilight Saga* star, Bella, is pretty much a selfless character anyway. She risks her life to protect her family and friends. She keeps her worries to herself for the sake of other people's happiness. She is willing to give up her own human life just to be with Edward forever.

Bella makes many noble sacrifices like these:

- Bella volunteers to move to Forks to make her mother happy. As Bella explains: "She didn't send me here. I sent myself" (*Twilight*, p 41).
- When Jacob tells Bella that the Cullens are "cold ones" (vampires), she does some Internet research and starts to figure things out for herself. Bella decides that she loves Edward too much to resist him, even if he is a vampire. In this sense, Bella sacrifices her own safety just to be with him.
- Bella knows that Edward thirsts for her blood. Although he repeatedly warns her that she should be afraid of him and stay away if she's smart, she continues to love him dearly.
- Jacob's father Billy is a Quileute elder who warns Bella to

stay away from the Cullens, a message which she ignores.

As Bella shows, her readiness to sacrifice her life is not a random act or irresponsible teen madness. There is a meaningful motive underlying those acts. To Bella, love is more important than life. To save the life of someone you love is more important than saving your own life. Love is the greatest power.

Edward's Sacrifices

Bella's love-interest Edward is another important character who makes significant personal sacrifices in the *Twilight* world to be with a girl he loves. In particular, Edward risks his life (execution by the Volturi) by telling Bella he is a vampire and dating a human. Some revealing sacrifices that Edward makes in the *Twilight* world are these:

- A boy's truck almost squashes Bella at school after skidding on black ice. But Edward uses his body as a shield to save her. Edward has just used his superhuman vampire strength which exposes him as a vampire, and which could get him and his family killed by the Volturi.
- When Bella visits Port Angeles and becomes lost, some thugs try to attack her in a dark alley. All of a sudden, Edward appears in his shiny Volvo and rescues her. At dinner together, Edward tells Bella that he is a vampire. By disclosing his secret, Edward puts himself and his whole vampire family in grave danger.
- The Cullens rescue Bella from an evil vampire called James, but he has already bitten her. Edward must suck the venom out of her blood before Bella turns into a vampire. Though it is difficult for Edward to control his urge, Edward manages to cure Bella without draining all her blood and killing her.
- When Bella asks Edward to bite her at the end of *Twilight*,

Edward declines. Edward sacrifices his own happiness to preserve Bella's human life and soul.

- Edward continues to romance Bella, even though the smell of her blood makes his throat burn, causes great pain, and drives him mad with desire. Love can be tough, sometimes.
- Regardless of their physical differences, and the danger, Edward and Bella are devoted to one another completely.
- Edward tells Bella "if leaving is the right thing to do, then I'll hurt myself to keep from hurting you, to keep you safe" (*Twilight*, p 185). Edward will forsake his own happiness for Bella.
- Edward mistakenly thinks that Bella has committed suicide (*New Moon*, p 18). He is willing to die to be with her, rather than continue existing without her, just like Shakespeare's famous tale about *Romeo and Juliet*.
- Edward leads Bella into the forest, tells her that he is "leaving", and says he is "no good" for her (*New Moon*, p 69). What a painful sacrifice Edward makes, pretending he doesn't want Bella, just to keep her safe. Deep down, however, Edward loves Bella more than anything else in his world.

As you can see, the sacrifices Edward makes symbolize an individual's truest love, deepest truth, and most devoted pledge. It reveals a person's highest values, greatest aspirations, and purest spirit. Above all, a brave and noble sacrifice is an ultimate expression of love. Both Bella and Edward are willing to give up absolutely everything just to ensure each other's safety. Why? Because they love each other so much.

Bella, Edward, the Cullens, the Quileutes and other characters in the *Twilight Saga* make many important sacrifices in the name of courage and compassion, love and spiritual power.

Scar

Scars are important marks and metaphors in the *Twilight Saga* that appear in a wide range of forms. Not only are there physical scars, there are emotional wounds too. A scar, whether a visible one or an invisible one, has an important story to tell.

What might scars in the *Twilight* world mean? A scare can convey:

- Life experience
- Proof of survival
- Overcoming difficult challenges
- Past pain
- A unique marker of personal progress
- A visual map of one's life
- A shape from the past, but it's your choices that shape your present and future
- A life lesson to guide personal growth
- A reminder that life can be unpredictable and dangerous
- Fate can be cruel – violent, evil, deadly
- Scars express personalities, how someone chooses to move past the pain
- Scars map journeys – where people have been and where they may be headed
- How people choose to react to their tragedies determines their progress and power in life
- Scars influence the future
- Scars can change the course of destiny
- Physical scars point to an emotional time that made us fight, suffer, nearly die
- Some scars are secret, hidden, emotional, invisible to others
- A sign of healing that has just started or is just finishing
- Scars test others – they find people who are willing to look

beyond imperfect physical appearances
- Scars don't disfigure you, scars define you
- Marks of maturity – life experiences
- Evidence of courage and heroism
- Inner beauty counts
- A visible scar is a sign of great inward impact
- Scars can invite people to get the know us
- Scars can compel people to reach out to others
- Scars attract true friends – people willing to listen to our stories, people who want to know us for who we truly inwardly are

To move forward in life, people must demonstrate an ability to integrate a scar and make it a positive part of who they are. As such, a scar is often considered to be the mark of a hero.

Physical Scars

What scars do the important *Twilight* characters show? More importantly, what do those scars show about the characters? Physical scarring is a prominent theme in the *Twilight Saga*. A physical scar is also a sign of some psychological payment – energy, effort, action, suffering, coping. A number of *Twilight Saga* characters have physical scars that mark them. Bella herself receives quite a few. Some notable scar scenes in the *Twilight* world are these:

- Bella receives a vampire bite. This forms a "crescent-shaped scar" on her hand that is "cool" and "sparkles faintly in the sun" (*New Moon*, p 19).
- Bella receives seven stitches to her forehead after crashing her motorbike (*New Moon*, p 192).
- Emily has a scar on her face, from the hairline to the chin marked by "three thick, red lines" (*New Moon*, p 331). Once Emily was standing too close to Sam, who lost his temper,

changed into a werewolf, and attacker her. Emily's arm is also scarred "all the way down her arm to the back of her right hand" (*New Moon*, p 333).

- Billy Black has a significant loss of mobility and is wheelchair bound.
- Jacob cuts his palm with a sharp knife in Bella's kitchen. This causes "a long, deep gash" to his hand (*Eclipse*, p 194). Later on, only an "angry pink, puckered line was all that was left of his scar" (*Eclipse*, p 196). This is because werewolves heal so fast.
- Another teen werewolf, Paul, has a visible physical scar (*Eclipse*, p 196). Jacob's fight with Paul caused "a fading pink line on Paul's forearm" that will be "perfect by sundown." This suggests that Paul is strong psychological character, who is not pensive nor dwells on negative ideas, and who therefore heals quickly.
- Jasper Cullen is extensively scarred from warring so often with newborns. To human eyes, Jasper's scars look like "curved half-moons crisscrossed in a feathery pattern" (*Eclipse*, p 254). Newborn vampires have bitten Jasper "thousands" of times on his arms (*Eclipse*, pp 254, 255).
- Some scars remain, and some disappear.

What do these physical scars suggest?

In *New Moon*, Jacob notices the "long silvery crescent" on Bella's hand (p 214). Why is this scar so special? This scar is symbolically significant because it foreshadows Bella's future as a vampire.

It is also interesting to note that the small round table at Emily's house has "a cracked blue-and-white china pitcher" on it "overflowing with wildflowers" (*New Moon*, p 333). The cracked pitcher itself symbolizes Emily's scar, while the flowers symbolizes Emily's happy home life with Sam. Despite Emily's physical scars, she is emotionally happy.

Jasper's body is extensively scarred from fighting so many newborn vampires. Despite Jasper's numerous battle scars, Alice doesn't see the physical scars, just the beautiful person on the inside. As such, Jasper's scars also reveal Alice's inner beauty – she is a non-judgmental person who appreciates others and sincerely cares about other people's happiness and feelings.

All these scars leave visible physical damage or injury to the body, but they are also indelible and undeniable marks of survival and strength.

Emotional Scars

> Edward admits: "I left you bleeding. Jacob was the one to stitch you back up again. That was bound to leave its mark – on both of you. I'm not sure those kind of stitches dissolve on their own."
> (*Eclipse*, p 473)

As with physical scars, many *Twilight* characters are emotionally scarred too. Different characters have experienced different emotional hurt. Some suffering is self-inflicted. For example, Edward *chose* to break up with Bella and leave Forks in *New Moon*. Some emotional challenges are driven by fate. For example, Jacob was *destined* to become a werewolf in *New Moon* whether he liked it or not. Whatever produces emotional scars, one thing is certain. They are there – despite their physical invisibility. In the *Twilight Saga,* emotional scars range from subtle to significant, as these adventures show:

- Bella moves to Forks to make her mother happy. Deep down, however, she is sad to leave her sunny home.
- When Bella's parents separated, this would have resulted in some stressful times.
- After the vampires trigger Jacob's ability to change into a werewolf, he feels that "the damage is done" (*New Moon*, p

269).

- Jacob and Bella describe themselves as "a pretty messed-up pair" (*New Moon*, p 349).
- When Edward broke up with Bella, she felt like she had "died" (*New Moon*, p 398).
- Jacob's face was "crumpled in pain" (*Eclipse*, p 34).
- The way Bella looked on the night Sam found her lying on the forest floor has "always haunted Sam" (*Eclipse*, p 114).
- Jacob explains that ever since Edward broke up with Bella he has painful memories of her being broken, sad and wrapping her arms around herself (*Eclipse*, p 115).
- Edward worried so much about Bella's pregnancy, that he looked "half-crazed" and "on fire" (*Breaking Dawn*, p 157).
- Leah tells Jacob telepathically that she knows how it feels *"being unwanted"* (*Breaking Dawn*, p 209). Leah is a lonely she-wolf.

In the *Twilight* books, references to emotions scarred and relationships marred are everywhere:

- Edward's parents died from a flu, leaving Edward alone and emotionally wounded (*New Moon*).
- Jacob's mother died when he was a young boy. Billy Black lost his wife and physical mobility.
- Edward denies his own soul and thinks he is a soulless monster.
- Carlisle's father was an incredibly cruel and hurtful man.
- Esme lost a child and attempted suicide.
- Alice was abandoned at a mental institution by her parents.
- Jasper has accumulated years of traumatic war memories.
- Rosalie was raped and murdered by her own fiancée, and his drunken friends. Her life was brutally stolen from her.
- Leah lost her partner Sam after he fell in love (imprinted) on Emily (*Eclipse*, p 111). This experience has hurt all three

of them.

- The Denali sisters were "left with unhealing hearts" after their mother was executed by the Volturi (*Breaking Dawn*, p 32).

As you can see, each *Twilight* character has very different emotional scars for very different reasons. So, why are they there? What is their message? Ultimately, what's in it for people like us? A good story poses challenges and problems, and then shows how those problems can be overcome. That's how a good story sells a hero. A great story strives to free the inner hero in you. This is what the *Twilight Saga* surely sets out to do.

Emotional Power

The role of emotional scars in the *Twilight* world is educational and instructive. Everyone has the power to turn their emotional scars into emotional growth. Consider how these three *Twilight* characters deal and cope with their negative life experiences, and how they achieve emotional triumph in life:

Bella Finds Strength – At first, Bella perceives Edward as a beautiful and perfect individual who can do no wrong. In *New Moon,* however, Edward breaks Bella's heart, ripping a "huge hole" inside her chest. Bella develops a huge emotional scar as a result. What this painful information tells Bella, however, is that Edward is *not* perfect. As a result, Bella grows stronger and smarter from this experience. This allows her relationship with Edward to make positive progress later on. The pain of losing Edward and the subsequent scarring process has afforded Bella the confidence and courage to pursue her true desires and to seek a Cullen family vote. Despite what Edward wants, Bella chooses to become a vampire. When Bella achieves her deepest desire and unites with Edward forever as a vampire, she finally feels truly happy and complete.

Rosalie Finds Peace – Rosalie lost her human life and everything that mattered to her, after her boyfriend and his gang attacked her. Then Carlisle changed her into a vampire, an existence that Rosalie would never have chosen for herself. Rosalie's dark pain, hidden deep inside her, has been allowed to brew and bubble and make her bitter. Poor Rosalie. Will that deep wound ever serve a higher purpose? Will it offer Rosalie a way to find emotional fulfillment? Well, as the message in Madonna's song *Deeper and Deeper* suggests: "if it's bitter at the start, then it's sweeter in the end." At first, when Rosalie chose to deal with her scars in a bitter way (by being hostile to Bella), she made herself miserable. Later on, Rosalie gets a chance to help Bella and her unborn child. When Rosalie apologizes to Bella, accepts her, and helps her, she can move forward emotionally and spiritually. Rosalie even gets a chance to be a doting and loving aunt to Renesmee.

Esme Finds Family – When Esme was a human, she lost a young child and then attempted suicide by jumping off a cliff. It is not hard to imagine such a caring and compassionate person becoming so hurt. How does Esme learn to deal with her pain in a constructive way? Due to her deep emotional scars, Esme has made efforts to foster several children. She resolves her deep emotional void by helping to care for an 'adoptive' family. Esme triumphs emotionally by actively creating a happy family life, full of love.

As these three *Twilight* characters show, it is certainly not profitable to view scars as signs of impairment, imperfection or weakness. On the contrary, scars can be inspiring. They can trigger powerful inner change.

Bella's Empty Chest

Of all the emotional scars in the *Twilight* series, the most crucial one psychologically and symbolically is Bella's empty chest. In fact, this book's analysis found that Bella's "hole/empty chest" experiences were mentioned '36' times *in New Moon*. Bella, for example, describes:

- "A huge hole had been punched through my chest" (p 118).
- "Aching around the edges of the hole in my chest (p 123).
- Edward's words *"It will be as if I never existed"* (p 123) "ripped the hole wide open" (p 124).
- "What if this hole never got better?" (p 124).
- "I felt hideously empty" (p 162).

(Appendix 2 – presents the full list of 36 "empty chest" references)

A hole is a powerful symbol that mainly suggests birth, fertility, and a door to life. Holes can also signify a trap into which someone might fall. In particular, the hole is a transit point through which you must pass if you are to develop or transform in some way. So dreaming about a hole predicts a big change that will eventually prove beneficial. Caves, being deep holes inside the earth, are mystical and hallowed places – doorways to unknown otherworlds, offering a way into the underworld and the afterlife. Since the earliest times, people used caves as dwellings and refuges. The experience of depression can often feel like you have fallen into a deep black hole, a place marked by dread and uncertainty about the future (Colin, 2000).

Inner Abyss

According to religious literature, a hole or an abyss symbolizes the terrible feeling of emptiness and despair someone feels after they have committed a sin. As such, an abyss is a bottomless pit, an underworld, the lowest possible level, or hell. The English word 'abyss' derives from the Latin word *abyssimus*, which borrowed from the Greek *abyssos* based on the Greek elements 'deep' and 'bottomless'. In the *Twilight Saga,* Bella has certainly taken action that has plunged her into a divine abyss. She has bitten the apple, the forbidden fruit, by falling in love with a vampire – a dark and dangerous desire. Literature-wise, maybe Bella's empty chest is mentioned 36 times because it alludes to the idea that Bella has sinned, fallen from paradise into a dark and miserable abyss that follows sin. Indeed, Bella describes this abyss experience perfectly when she visits the meadow in *New Moon*:

> The meadow was empty of atmosphere, empty of everything, just like everywhere else… There was no way I could have disguised the abyss I was plunging into now… I had to curl into a ball to keep the empty space from tearing me apart.

Bella's newfound and dangerous knowledge that Edward and his family are vampires, despite the fact that Edward thirsts for her blood and his warnings to stay away, caused Bella to lose her beautiful Edward and her perfect paradise. So she experiences a "gaping hole" inside her chest and tumbles down, down, down into a deep emotional abyss.

In the *Twilight Saga,* Carlisle adamantly believes that it is worth doing good, even if you're a vampire. If you perform good deeds, then you stand a chance to climb out of the eternal abyss, avoid the flames of hell, reach heaven, and regain paradise. In agreement with Carlisle, the great fable of Lazarus featured a great abyss or chasm between the righteous dead and the wicked dead (Wiki, 2011).

Seattle

Seattle is a city that features in the *Twilight* series. At the start of *Twilight,* Bella's plane lands at Seattle's airport before she catches another plane to Port Angeles. Seattle reappears in *Eclipse,* where many unexplained murders are taking place. Apparently, the reason for this killing spree is to create an army of newborn vampires to attack Bella and the Cullens. With so much killing going on, it would be no surprise if people were getting sleepless in Seattle. At the end of *Breaking Dawn,* Bella travels to Seattle by herself to meet the mastermind of fraud – J. Jenks. At Bella's request, Jenks produces false passports and other fake identification for Bella.

In the real world, Seattle is the northernmost city in the state of Washington, in the United States. It is a major seaport and the largest city in its state. The city is respectfully named after Chief Sealth 'Seattle', of the Duwamish and Suquamish Native American people. The nickname for Seattle is the 'Emerald City' due to the plentiful evergreen forests around the area. The Port of Seattle, which has an international airport, is the major gateway for trade with Asia and cruises to Alaska. Seattle has a famous music history. The Jackson Street jazz scene emerged in 1918 (around the time that Edward was born). This city also launched famous musicians such as rock legend Jimi Hendrix, Ray Charles and 'grunge' and 'indie' music styles. With its lush green forest surroundings, overcast weather, and musical history, Seattle would be a safe and interesting place for *Twilight*-style vampires to visit, especially musicians like Edward and Rosalie, as long as they could control their urges to drink human blood.

Shield

I have forged me in sevenfold heats
A shield from foes and lovers,
And no one knows the heart that beats
Beneath the shield that covers.
– Mary Coleridge, *The Shield* (1986)

This shield, from a 19th century verse written by an English poet, sure has an uncanny resemblance to Bella's mental shield that protects and covers all that she loves in the *Twilight* world.

Bella's Shield

In the *Twilight Saga*, Bella has a unique "glitch" inside her brain that shields her from the negative and intrusive energy of others.

As Bella describes it, Edward "couldn't see into my mind... some strange glitch in my brain that made it immune to all the extraordinary and frightening things some immortals could do" (*Breaking Dawn*, p 22). In particular, it first comes to light when Edward confesses that he cannot read Bella's mind at Port Angeles: "It's harder than it should be – keeping track of you" (*Twilight*, p 152). Once Bella becomes a vampire, that glitch becomes a powerful supernatural shield that is immune to the psychic powers of other vampires.

A shield is a supreme symbol of defense. In the *Twilight* world, Bella's supernatural shield is the ultimate defense force field against evil vampires. In ancient times, shields helped ancient warriors to defy death and achieve victory in battle. They used their shields to deflect deadly strikes from enemies. No wonder people once thought that shields had magical powers. This is why ancient shields were embellished with magical symbols, such as fire, teeth, or snakes – to spook, terrify, and beat the enemy.

The symbolic meaning of shields, such as Bella's, can vary widely. A shield suggests:

- A need for help or protection
- A tendency to be defensive or self-protective
- A mistrust of the outside world and subsequent efforts to block it out
- Feelings of vulnerability or uncertainty that must be guarded
- A method of fighting or protecting yourself

Whatever meanings Bella's shield upholds, there's no doubt that she has forged superlative armor that keeps both foes and lovers amazed.

Shield Alchemy

Bella's supernatural shield resembles a result that alchemists call *Corpus Glorificatum* – the final immutable Philosopher's Stone and its red transparent tincture. In other words, Bella's crimson shield is a red Philosopher's Stone in the *Twilight Saga*. As Bella describes it, "My shield took on a strange reddish tint… a layer, a thin film that covered me from head to toe" (*Breaking Dawn*, p 575). According to legend, this astonishing stone could turn raw metals into gold. As an alchemy symbol, however, what this stone really stands for is spiritual gold. This robust red rock depicts the final, perfect, and immutable stage in a conversion process, which supposedly grants magical powers to its owner (*Alchemy Dictionary*, 2009). In exactly the same way, Bella's shield reflects this powerful meaning. After many trials and tests throughout the *Twilight* series, Bella's red shield is an invincible, perfect, and magical force field that no vampire can overcome.

Shield Magic

Of course, Bella becomes a "superhero" in the *Twilight* world for the very reason that she has a tough red shield (*Breaking Dawn*, p 693). As Edward declares: "Their gifts were rendered useless by Bella" (*Breaking Dawn*, p 690). That is, Bella's "glitch" was a protective mechanism that evolved into a super-psychic defense, which served to repel any outside forces. What's more, Bella's powerful shield has a fascinating resemblance to the most powerful shield from Greek myth. Bella, the hero, has a shield that is similar to the shield of the great mythical hero Hercules. His shield was made famous in a work written in the 6th century BCE (Janko, 1986; Shapiro, 1984; Wikisource, 2011).

An epic Greek epic poem called *The Shield of Heracles* describes a battle mighty between Hercules and the son of Ares – a god of war whose name sounds like Aro, whom Bella challenges. The shield of Hercules (Heracles) was so powerful and extravagant that its image was recorded in great detail: "His armor adorned with bronze clashed about him." Just like this supernatural shield of Hercules, made for him by a god called Hephaestus, Bella's shield has a metallic flavor about it as her "tongue tasted like burning metal" (*Breaking Dawn*, p 575) and she "blew out... a mushroom cloud of liquid steel" (*Breaking Dawn*, p 642). Other lines about this round shield explain that the "whole orb shimmered with enamel and white ivory and electrum, and it glowed with shining gold." Hey, this sounds pretty similar to Bella's shield – a round "dome" of "glowing light" that feels "electric": "I flexed it now into a low, wide dome that arced over our company" (*Breaking Dawn*, p 652). Another striking similarity between the two shields is that the center of the Hercules shield had "a mask of Fear (*Phobos*) with the staring eyes and teeth of a gorgon." The snake heads engraved on the shield would "clash their teeth" when fighting Ares' son. Well, these ancient lines do point to Bella's sharp new vampire teeth "grinning" at the Volturi vampires. Bella wanted nothing more than to "sink [her] teeth into them, to rip their limbs from their bodies and pile them for burning" (*Breaking Dawn*, p 635). Bella's shield magic rules, just like the all-powerful shield of famous mythical heroes.

Shield Strategy

After arguing with Jacob at her wedding party, Bella feels guilty for causing a "disaster". To stop emotional pain, Bella thinks to herself: "My idiocy would not ruin anything else tonight. I would put this away, shove it in a drawer and lock it up to deal with later" (*Breaking Dawn*, p 63). By postponing worries and putting negative thoughts at the back of her mind, Bella shields herself from worry and anxiety, a highly effective CBT (Cognitive-Behaviour Therapy) strategy.

As the *Twilight* world shows, many different kinds of shields keep people safe from pain and harm. Some of the most effective shields are forged deep inside us. The message? Anyone can create a powerful shield, fit for the hero in everyone.

Silver

Silver is a special color in the *Twilight Saga* and it is a special symbol too. In the *Twilight* books, Edward is the character who seems to have the strongest links to silver. As a shimmering white hue, the color silver and the metal silver are linked to the moon. In contrast, the color yellow and gold metal are linked to the sun. In particular, Edward is a vampire whose pale-white skin sparkles silver in the sun. Edward's vampire venom also looks "all silver, like it was made from steel" (*Breaking Dawn*, p 325). Edward's car is silver too – a silver bullet as he speeds down the highway to rescue Bella from danger. Edward's silver theme is most beautiful and magical in *Breaking Dawn*. The ocean at Isle Esme looked silvery at night when Bella and Edward arrived there. And Edward's "eyes looked silver" in the bright moonlight (*Breaking Dawn*, p 78). Silver's white, lustrous and luminous appearance and the ability of silver to reflect light clearly also makes it a symbol of thought, purity and wisdom. The metal silver is associated with lunar myths and symbols related to the moon, femininity, fertility, receptiveness, purity. Silver is especially sacred to the moon and moon goddesses in many cultures. Soft and luminous, silver is "a source of psychic and intuitive abilities, especially when its ruling moon is full" (Eason, 2002, p 333). These meanings reflect the characters of Edward (silver) and Bella (the moon) well. Edward is a pensive and brooding vampire who can read people's thoughts. Meanwhile, Bella is a thinker, dreamer, academic achiever with superior intuition.

At the very end of *Breaking Dawn*, as Bella and Edward walk to their cottage, the night is silver and blue. These two colors unite to create a peaceful and perfect "silver-blue night" (*Breaking Dawn*, p 697). Since Bella is associated with the color blue (see *Blue*) and Edward is silver, these two colors finally merge together in the calm night sky. This color scheme surely symbolizes Bella and Edward's beautiful life together for evermore.

Skin

The skin is a symbol of protection. It is the outside layer of the human body and is the largest single organ as well. A 'thick-skinned' person is supposed to be emotionally insensitive while a 'thin-skinned' person is too sensitive. In ancient times, shamans wore skins and pelts of certain animals to absorb the power of those animals. Skin has also been used to symbolize power and difference between people. In particular, skin color has resulted in racial prejudice and even genocide. In humans, fair skin is considered a symbol of wealth because pale-skinned people did not need to subject themselves to manual labor and work all day in the sun. Dark skin, however, carries the opposite meaning – poor, uneducated, the working class.

In the *Twilight Saga*, the white paleness of vampire skin suggests a materially wealthy status. The reason why pale-skinned aristocrats called themselves 'blue bloods' was because their blue veins were more visible under their skin. In contrast, Jacob and the native Quileutes in the *Twilight* world are red/bronze-skinned characters. People with colored skin have been historically and stereotypically associated with a primitive mentality, an outdoors lifestyle, and material poverty. And yet, it is so interesting to note that while Edward and the Cullens long for spiritual peace, the Quileute people are emotionally wise, spiritually rich and thrive in legend, community and culture. As the *Twilight* books show, you can't judge true wealth by skin color.

Sky

The vast and impressive sky has inspired the human imagination in many different ways. A popular view around the world is that the sky is a dwelling place of spirits, souls, and divine forces. Angels are winged creatures who live in the sky, coming down to earth with reports or messages from the heavens. These days, some people believe that terrestrial beings live in the sky, far away in a distant galaxy. Across the ages, the sky has always been a special place reserved for dreams, hopes, fantasies, and visions, which the *Twilight* world strongly suggests. A cloudy, rainy, or sunny sky in the *Twilight* books produces certain moods, situations and adventures. For example, a sky brewing with storm clouds suggests an imminent threat. In *New Moon,* a sudden storm emerged just before Bella leaped off a cliff. In *Eclipse,* the newborn vampire battle was preceded by a fierce and freezing blizzard. The last sky scene in the *Twilight Saga* ends underneath a peaceful silver-blue sky in *Breaking Dawn*. Such sky scenes surely stir up the imagination, directing our attention to a distant and dreamy horizon, to another time and place somewhere far away, well beyond the worries and woes of the present. Since sky scenes free the imagination, the interpretation of a sky is a very individual experience.

See also: *Blue, Clouds, Rain, Storm,* and *Sun*.

Snow

Snow is cold, white, pure, pretty and potentially deadly stuff that falls from the sky in the coldest weather conditions. In the *Twilight Saga,* good vampires are sometimes described using snowy terms. For example, the first time Bella hugs Edward in *Eclipse* it is a "cool stone embrace" as Bella presses her lips against Edward's "snow-cold neck" (p 29). In such a scene, snow is cool and soothing. It is presented as a pleasant thing to feel and touch.

The White Christmas snowscape that many people often dream about appears in *Breaking Dawn*. In a magic moment outdoors, Renesmee "was staring at the snowflakes fluttering high above her head" and caught a "perfectly formed eight-pointed ice star in her palm" (*Breaking Dawn*, pp 494–495). In this adventure, the snow symbolizes innocence, to reflect Renesmee's childhood innocence. Everyone is born with a clean, white spiritual slate that has not yet been corrupted or damaged. Snow tends to acquire pure, innocent and spiritual meanings because it is so white.

Sometimes, however, snow foreshadows danger and appears whenever wicked characters are around. In the *Twilight Saga*, for example, Victoria and her army of newborn vampires visit the Forks forest. As they did, a furious snowstorm blew in. In fact, it became especially cold at that time:

> The wind shook more fiercely through the trees around us, and it felt like it was blowing straight off a glacier. The sharp sound of wood cracking echoed off the mountain. Though the light was vanishing as the grisly cloud covered the sky, I could still see the little white specks that fluttered past us. (*Eclipse*, p 430)

This storm from *Eclipse* turns "black" and becomes "sprinkled with the swirling bits of snow" (p 431). A little further on "the storm howled like an animal attacking the tent" (*Eclipse*, p 437) while "the wind shrieked insanely through the trees" (*Eclipse*, p 438). As Victoria's newborn army gets closer, the snowstorm intensifies.

In particular, a climactic duel between cold-hearted Victoria and warm-hearted/blooded Bella occurs on top of a cold, snowy mountain. Victoria is the coldest and cruelest vampire vixen in *Eclipse*, so this cold hilltop scene reflects her extreme emotional coldness. As Bella, Edward and Jacob awaited Victoria's chilling visit, Bella's night on the mountain was freezing and painfully cold. Although snow can appear as white and pure on the surface, it also alludes to bitter and chilling forces, corruption and even death. Bella uses her warm blood (a symbol of emotional warmth, passion, and life) to save Edward and defeat Victoria's cold, brutal attack in the snow.

The battle with the Volturi at the end of *Breaking Dawn* also occurs in a cold, winter snowscape. This cold snow scene helps to symbolize the cold, bleak and bitter emotional world of these human blood-drinkers and the below-zero empathy of the Volturi.Get the (snowflake) drift?

Soul

Though as people we may change physically, our most precious inner essence, the immortal soul, never seems to change. This is something Bella finds out for herself in her first moments as a vampire. "'How do you feel, Bella?' Carlisle asked… 'I feel like me. Sort of. I didn't expect that'" (*Breaking Dawn*, p 365). This *Twilight* scene illustrates what spiritual teachers explain – the soul is an invisible and timeless power above and beyond earthly life. The consciousness of a soul is believed to be far greater than the five senses we use to understand the outside world (Colin, 2000). According to folklore around the world, the soul has been symbolized in various ways. For example, air, wind, birds and butterflies are popular images for the soul. In fact, the word for soul derives from the Latin word *anima* ('breath', 'air' or 'wind') and the Greek word *anemos* ('air' or 'wind'). When individuals, like Carlisle in the *Twilight* world, search for spiritual meaning, this soul-seeking process helps people to master death and connect to eternity.

Spiritual themes and symbols that appear in the *Twilight* series may have occurred for a purpose or maybe they appear by divine accident. When Stephenie Meyer was interviewed about the religious themes in her books, she explained that: "because I'm a very religious person, it does tend to come out somewhat in the books, although always unconsciously (*Time Magazine*, 2008).

Consider the three main *Twilight* characters – Bella, Edward, and Jacob – and how their spiritual journey is symbolized and suggested.

Bella Glows

Bella starts life off in a gloomy town with no deep beliefs in anything much, until she encounters a spiritual and supernatural world of vampires, werewolves, love and sacrifice. When Bella finally achieves immortality as a vampire, she does not feel spiritual bliss because she gets to live forever. She becomes a true mistress of death only because she acknowledges to the truest and purest feelings deep inside – her love for Edward. As seventeenth century scientist Emanuel Swedenborg puts it: "Love in its essence is spiritual fire."

Bella's most stunning symbol of spiritual strength in *Breaking Dawn* is her shield. This human mental glitch develops into a supernatural force field created by Bella's love for others. It also seems to reveal the spiritual best in other people too. When Bella hurls her shield over her loves ones, she "could feel the life force of everything it covered like points of bright heat, dazzling sparks of light surrounding me" (*Breaking Dawn*, p 642). In other words, whoever Bella protects with her shield, they appear as "glimmering shapes" and "brilliant sparks" of light (*Breaking Dawn*, p 653). When Bella projects her love, she draws out the lights within, she sees the spiritual power. Compared to the Volturi vampires, who are dark sports across the cold white field of ice, devoid of light (soulless), Bella's family and friends were "sharp plumes of light" and Edward was "the very brightest" light of all (*Breaking Dawn*, p 652). Even the good undead have soul. That's strong spiritual symbolism.

Edward Shines

Edward believes he has lost his soul because he is a vampire. Worse, Edward believes he is a doomed and soulless creature forever (*New Moon*, p 37). As he explains to Bella: "I know that you believe I have a soul, but I'm not entirely convinced on that point" (*Eclipse*, p 242). Despite Edward's negative beliefs about himself, others can easily see and sense his spiritual energy. Carlisle, for example, can see the "strength, his goodness, the brightness that shines out of him – and it only fuels that hope, that faith, more than ever" (*New Moon*, p 37). In fact, Edward must have spiritual strength because he moved away from Forks and sacrificed his own happiness to protect Bella. As Bella explains, "he had only been trying to save me when he'd left, trying to save my soul" (*Eclipse*, p 28). According to health experts, when you help and support others, in the kind of way as Edward has helped Bella, you transform yourself into a shooting soul star. "Giving and integrating. It transcends the physical and psychological dimensions" (Granstrom, 1985).

Jacob Shifts

At first, Jacob "scoffs" at the Quileute legends and calls Billy Black a "superstitious old man" for his views that the Cullens are the cold ones (*Twilight*, p 206). When Jacob finally experiences the werewolf magic himself, he becomes a devoted follower of spirit wolf legends and law (*New Moon*, p 268). The first great spirit warriors of the Quileute people could soul-travel. That is, their spirits could leave their bodies, to observe the world around them and blow fierce winds to scare off enemies (*Eclipse*, p 217). The last great Spirit Warrior Taha Aki shared his bodiless spirit with the body of a large wolf (*Eclipse*, p 222). Ever since then, the descendants of Taha Aki could transform themselves into strong and glorious wolves. The spiritual magic continues to play a role in the lives of the Quileute shape-shifters. For example, imprinting is how werewolves find their mates, their life partners, their true "soul mates" (*Eclipse*, p 109). The magic experience of imprinting helps to symbolize the great and invisible power of the spirit.

Stone

Stone is a hard, strong, and long-lasting. It's a material that suggests immortality. Although not everlasting, stone is one of the toughest substances in nature. It suggests continuity, durability, and permanence. In the natural landscape, stone structures last for ages and resist change. Stone is tough enough to withstand the worst weather conditions and the passage of time. Ever since people could sculpt and shape stone, buildings and monuments made from stone have assumed a magical and sacred aura. In ancient times, stones were used to form the earliest temples, a home for gods.

Stony Qualities

Stone is an important symbol in the *Twilight Saga* because vampires have a physical body that is as hard and cold and strong as stone. Bella described Edward's body as "a perfect statue, carved in some unknown stone, smooth like marble, glittering like crystal" (*Twilight*, p 228). Bella and Edward's cottage at the end of *Breaking Dawn* is the only building that is described as being built from stone. This stone cottage is a fit temple for supernatural beings such as Bella and Edward. Or else, the stone home is a symbolic gesture to the durable and permanent nature of their romantic union perhaps.

Romancing the Stone

The vampires in the *Twilight* series feel like statues with skin like stone. For example, when Bella touches Edward "his skin was cold and hard, like a stone" (*Twilight*, p 151). Again, Edward's hand was a "perfect texture, satin smooth, cool as stone" (*Twilight*, p 277). According to an insightful fan, the idea that Edward the statue-like vampire falls in love with a human girl resembles an ancient Greek tale. A sculptor called Pygmalion was uncomfortable with the culture of his times. People were rejecting the idea of divine and romantic love in favor of lust, promiscuity and sex, sex, sex. Nevertheless, Pygmalion (an old-fashioned romantic at heart) kept making offerings to the goddess of love at her abandoned altar, always wishing that a beautiful stone statue of a woman he created was real. So Venus rewarded him for his faithfulness. When Pygmalion went home, he found his statue warm with flesh and alive with a beating heart. She became his wife and lover, and together they had a child. His impossible dream came true (TwilightMOMS post, Shimmerskin, June 17, 2011).

In the *Twilight Saga*, the reverse occurs. Instead of statues coming to life, Edward and his family were once living and breathing human beings with beating hearts who were later turned into stone-like beings – vampires. Just like Pygmalion, Edward rejects promiscuous sexual relationships in favor of a traditional relationship. Love, courtship, marriage, and *then* sex. Edward's moral views are rewarded when he encounters a girl made of blood and flesh and who later becomes his wife and lover. Together they have a child, and their impossible dream comes true. The *Twilight* tale is therefore a fractured fairy tale, the Pygmalion myth reversed in that a warm human girl has been turned into a stone cold vampire (TwilightMOMS, post by Shimmerskin, June 17, 2011).

Storm

Storms can have both good and bad meanings, and the *Twilight* world is no exception. Three key storms take place in the *Twilight* world and each have their own stormy meanings.

Baseball Thrill

> Alice says there's going to be a real storm tonight, and Emmett wants to play ball.
> (*Twilight*, p 302)

The first storm to appear in the *Twilight Saga* is a positive one – fun, energetic, exciting, a social scream.

The positive meanings of storm relate to ideas like excitement, energy, a forecast that rain will come to refresh nature and make the land green, healthy, and fertile. Just as lightning and heavy thunderclouds are charged with electricity, a storm can make us feel charged with energy.

Brooding Storm

As a symbol, storms have another important meaning. They suggest unsettled, restless, negative, volatile emotions. This certainly holds true in the *Twilight Saga*. The stormiest scenes symbolize emotional turmoil. A great example is when Bella is so upset that she leaps off a cliff in *New Moon* – in the face of an oncoming storm. Here's how the symbolism brews in this *New Moon* cliff-hanger:

> The heavy warm pressure of the atmosphere… hinted at something major in the storm department. A glance at the sky backed this up; the clouds were churning sluggishly despite the lack of breeze on the ground. The closest clouds were a smoky gray, but between the cracks I could see another layer that was a gruesome purple color. The skies had a ferocious plan in store for today.
> (*New Moon*, p 355)

But this storm is much more than just a weather forecast. It is a symbolic forecast of Bella's intensifying emotional pressure. It may also be a gesture to Edward's brooding supernatural presence and the imminent reunion that will happen between Bella and Edward shortly in Italy. After all, Byronic heroes do tend to sulk a lot, are moody, bossy, and explosive. They're stormy characters.

What's more, this dramatic weather change in *New Moon*, a

sudden clash of warm and cold air pressures, may also be trying to symbolize a clash between warm Jacob-like and cold Edward-like forces. Symbolically speaking, Edward and Jacob are kind of fighting it out for Bella at a 'half-moon' point – at the halfway point. Will Bella choose Edward or Jacob? It's a worrying and troubling choice because Bella really likes both guys. So the developing storm helps to highlight Bella's troubled feelings really well:

> The waves picked up as I paced, beginning to crash against the rocks, but there was still no wind. I felt pinned down by the pressure of the storm. Everything swirled around me, but it was perfectly still where I stood. The air had a faint electric charge.
> (*New Moon*, p 353)

As the wind picks up, as the waves crash harder against the rocks, and the pressure of the storm whirls and wheels, Bella feels electricity building up in the air. Clouds against sky. Chemistry/electricity against air/wind. Edward against Jacob. Symbolically speaking, Edward's emotional charge and Jacob's breath is competing for Bella. As Bella's emotional pressure grows to choose between the guys, so does the storm pressure. That's pretty good storm symbolism.

On the shore, the waves get "angrier" and they "batter" the cliffs at the beach, "spraying big white clouds of sea foam into the sky… It was eerie" (*New Moon*, p 356). When Bella jumps of the cliff at the peak of the storm, this symbolizes the peak of her own emotional turmoil. So she jumps. When Bella finally chooses to jump, she symbolically chooses Edward over Jacob – Bella finally sees Edward's perfect image in her mind as she sinks beneath the cold, black water.

Stormy Courage

Another important meaning of storms is that they are a chance to show courage. The *Twilight* world storms not only symbolize Bella's unsettled emotions, they also seem to draw out Bella's courage. Once, for example, Bella had a dream about a storm. "I dreamt I was outside in the storm, the wind whipping my hair in my face and blinding my eyes. I stood on the rocky crescent of First Beach" (*Eclipse*, p 234). Just before Bella had this dream, she listened to a Quileute tale about human sacrifice. A chief's wife stabbed herself with a knife to save her tribe from an evil vampire. In Bella's dream, she does not seek to shelter from the storm. Rather, Bella confronts it as the wind "whips" at her hair. This may be a symbolic pointer to Bella's inner courage. In her dream, Bella prefers to *face* the storm. Symbolically, this suggests that Bella is the kind of girl who would prefer to face her fears and problems rather than hide and shelter from them. Bella is brave and this storm reveals her courage.

Sun

As a symbol, the sun signifies an individual's "instinctive will" as well as "courage, determination, dominant strength, authority, kindness and generosity" (Colin, 2000, p 480). In ancient Egypt, people worshipped the sun and the sun god Re to the extreme. In Greek myth, Helios was a sun god and a demon who crossed the sky each day in a fiery chariot. The warm, bright power of the sun almost always symbolizes a happy attitude, clear thinking, social success and positive directions in life. In the *Twilight Saga,* the sun is an obvious symbol. The original titles of all the books describe cosmic events that relate to the positions of the sun in the sky – twilight, new moon, eclipse and dawn. In particular, the power of the sun in the *Twilight* world is explored in three important ways using three main characters – Bella, Jacob and Edward.

Sun-Loving Bella

The first sunny passages in the *Twilight* series acknowledge Bella's love for sunny weather. At first, Bella loves the sun, misses the sun, and recalls positive memories about the sun. For example:

- "I loved Phoenix. I loved the sun and the blistering heat" (*Twilight*, p 4).
- When Bella first meets Jacob, she enjoys "the sun" that appears in the sky (*Twilight*, p 97).
- "The sun shone bravely" at La Push (*Twilight*, p 99).

These sunny examples help to illustrate Bella's character – she loves the sun. At a deeper symbolic level, these sunny scenes may also be trying to suggest that Bella is drawn towards sun-like values and virtues. In particular, Bella deals with her world by searching for light (goodness), clarity (truth), gold (courage), and love (warmth) – sun qualities.

At the start of the *Twilight* series, Bella grieves over leaving sunny Phoenix. In *Twilight*, Bella feels like she is saying goodbye to the sun when she arrives at Port Angeles airport where it is raining. Slowly and steadily, however, Bella's relationship with the sun changes. She begins to like the cloudy weather and increasingly rejects the sun. Symbolically speaking, this may mean that Bella is starting to withdraw from her personal sun – Jacob. It may even be foreshadowing Bella's rejection of life, which the sun symbolizes, and her own human mortality.

Sun-Like Jacob

There is no doubt that Jacob with his happy, friendly and sunny nature is *Twilight Saga's* 'sun'. Jacob's cheerful and beaming personality makes him confident, outgoing, cheerful and emotionally expressive in public. He shines in the social spotlight, like a sun that shines on a clear day. Many examples support the idea that Jacob is sun-like and is linked to sunny symbolism. For example:

- Bella calls Jacob her "personal sun" (*New Moon*, p 198). Jacob is a source of light and warmth who dispels dark shadows in the woods and dark feelings inside Bella's heart.
- Jacob says to Bella: "I see that you can't live without him now… But I would have been healthier for you. Not a drug; I would have been the air, the sun" (*Eclipse*, p 531).
- Bella notices "the bright yellow light of a sunny day" (*Twilight*, p 122) in Forks, surprised when her bedroom window "opened silently, without sticking" (p 122). It is as if Jacob is trying to reach into Bella's private world with his sunshine.
- "I was daydreaming watching the sunlight play on the red-barked trees" (*Twilight*, p 123). Bella *day*dreams about *sunny* weather and *red*-barked trees (Jacob symbols).
- The day after Edward breaks up with Bella, the sun appears. "The sky was no longer black outside the window. Somewhere behind the rain, the sun was beginning to rise" (*New Moon*, p 82). When Edward leaves, the rain stops, the clouds disappear and the sun comes out. Symbolically speaking, this foreshadows Jacob's active presence in Bella's life soon.
- One of the most well-known sun quotes in the *Twilight* series is: "Jacob was simply a perpetually happy person… an earthbound sun, whenever someone was within his gravitational pull, Jacob warmed them" (*New Moon*, p 145).
- When Jacob shows up at the beach, the sun rises (*New Moon*, p 304).
- The first time Bella visits Jacob, his smile looked like a "sun breaking free of clouds" (*Eclipse*, p 89).
- When Jacob grins a "most, sunny and warm" smile, the

rain disappears (*Eclipse*, p 158). This may be a symbolic clue that Jacob's sunny influence is dissolving Edward's dreary rain.

- When Bella wakes up one morning after sleeping next to Jacob on a freezing cold night on the mountaintop: "it was very bright – even inside the tent, the sunlight hurt my eyes" (*Eclipse*, p 449). The strong sun may be reflecting Jacob's increased desire to stake a claim on Bella, as he recently said he loved her.

A gorgeous *Twilight* adventure that symbolizes Jacob's link to the sun is also one of the most romantic. When Jacob overwhelms Bella with a passionate kiss on top of a mountain, the sun's power becomes dazzling:

> He was everywhere. The piercing sunlight turned my eyelids red, and the color fit, matched the heat. The heat was everywhere. I couldn't see or hear or feel anything that wasn't Jacob. (*Eclipse*, p 468).

As the sunlight pierces Bella's eyes, Jacob's sunny love surely pierces her heart. In fact, Jacob's influence is so strong that Bella thinks she really might love Jacob after all: "He was more than just my friend… I was in love with him, too" (*Eclipse*, p 468). When Jacob wins that sweet, joyful kiss, the sun is high in the sky.

Sun-Spooked Edward

The sun is a deadly and dangerous force against Edward. Edward is a cold-skinned creature who is not safe in the sun. As Edward explains to Bella: "You asked if the sun hurt me, and it doesn't. But I can't go out in the sunlight – at least, not where anyone can see" (*Twilight*, p 165). Since the glaring sunlight causes Edward's skin to sparkle, it is dangerous. The sun exposes his deep "secret", that he is a vampire.

The worst time for Edward in the *Twilight* world was when the sun was blazing down over Volterra at noon. At Volterra, Edward planned to kill himself when the sun was at its brightest, highest, and strongest power. Approaching Volterra, "the sun was terrifyingly high in the pale blue sky… The sun continued to climb in the sky while Alice raced against it. It was too bright" (*New Moon*, pp 441–442). In this edgy adventure, Bella felt "trapped by the brilliant sunlight" as it "beat down from the highest point in the sky" (*New Moon*, p 2). Trapped – meaning suicidal. She planned to die herself if she failed to save Edward. As the time of Edward's suicide attempt was near, the sun (Jacob's influence) was strong. If Edward were to die, Jacob – the sun – would have full romantic access to Bella. In this climactic life-death scene, the moment that Bella hugs Edward she stops him from stepping out into the harsh daylight, blocking the sun. "My lungs filled deep with the sweet scent that came off his skin" (*New Moon*, p 452). Cool shadows replace burning sunlight. Edward's gloom replaces Jacob's glow. Edward's scent replaces Jacob's air. Bella chooses Edward over Jacob.

T

Table

A table symbolizes a meeting, union, and a desire for togetherness. Sitting down at a table to share a meal or to talk about something shows a willingness to join forces with others, hear someone else's point of view or reach an agreement. The table is therefore a symbol of union and sharing. The expression 'round table conference' alludes to the legendary round table made by Merlin for King Arthur and his knights. To 'lay all your cards out on the table' means to be honest and to share all the information you have available. This helps everyone to make the best choice possible.

The word 'table' is based on the Latin word *tabula*, derived from the word for stone tablets upon which the first scribes etched their works.

One of the most important table scenes in the *Twilight Saga* is when Bella calls the Cullens to a meeting in *New Moon*. This family meeting happens to occur around an oval-shaped table. Another important table scene is when the Cullens and their friends discuss heroic feats at the Cullen table in *Breaking Dawn*. These table top scenes fit with the symbolic meanings of a table as a place to meet, unite, share information, and be together. As a symbol of togetherness, the table is one of the most salient objects to suggest family, family life, social life, and community. A dream that you are sitting at a table may indicate a strong need to confide in someone, offload worries, express secrets or feelings to reduce anxiety, or a desire to engage with others.

Tears

What do tears mean? As a symbol, tears suggest pain, joy,

survival, and cleansing. Above all, tears are an emotional release and acknowledge the fact that a person still has feelings. They are a physical manifestation of an invisible force that humans too often hide away – feelings.

Bella's Tears

Bella clearly cries tears in the books, which flow fast and furious in some scenes:

- Bella cries a "tears" in her bedroom just after she arrives in Forks (*Twilight*, p 8).
- Bella had "tears" in her eyes when Edward played music for her (*Twilight*, p 287).
- "Tears" spilled when Bella packed for Phoenix to protect her father from an evil vampire (*Twilight*, p 342).
- Bella's "tears streaked noiselessly" down her face on the way to Phoenix (*Twilight*, p 352).
- Bella cried "tears" when the evil James blackmailed her to meet him at a ballet studio (*Twilight*, p 375).
- Bella cried watching a *Romeo and Juliet* movie at school (*New Moon*, p 18).
- Bella cried listening to Edward's lullaby on a homemade CD (*New Moon*, p 49).
- When Jacob tells Bella not to visit him anymore (*New Moon*, p 270).
- When Jacob visits her in her bedroom, just after he rejected her (*New Moon*, p 282).
- When Bella thought of Esme and her "kind, lovely face" (*New Moon*, p 298).
- When Alice returned to Forks (*New Moon*, p 371).
- When human tourists are fed to the Volturi (*New Moon*, p 483).
- After reuniting with Edward after spending months apart (*New Moon*, pp 518–519).

- When she sees Jacob laying injured on his bed, just after the newborn battle (*Eclipse*, p 528).

This scenes show that Bella cries plenty of tears for others. This makes sound symbolic sense because Bella's feelings for others help her to achieve success in her life and is the very foundation of her powerful shield.

Jacob's Baseball Tear

Perhaps the most talked about tear in the *Twilight Saga* is Jacob's tear in *Breaking Dawn*. In a sweet farewell scene, when everyone thinks they are doomed to die, Bella says to Jacob: "I love you, too, Jake. You'll always be my best man." A tear the size of a baseball rolled into the russet fur underneath his eye" (*Breaking Dawn*, p 671). On the brink of war, Jacob shed a tear the size of a baseball. A variety of theories try to explain what this special tear may mean.

Cullens – This baseball-sized tear occurred on the same field where the Cullens once played baseball in *Twilight*. So maybe this tear symbolizes a secret wish, Jacob's sad internal longing to have been part of that baseball game too, rather than be an outsider, an enemy, a "dog", especially now that he has got to know and like the Cullens.

Care – The tear could also symbolize Jacob's strong positive feelings for the Cullens. The tear is a sign of endearment – a show of love – for the Cullens. Jacob projects his positive feelings for the Cullens as a "baseball" shaped tear because the Cullens are such a close-knit family that they play baseball together. To Jacob, the Cullens may seem very loyal, cohesive, and an ideal pack of individuals, just as Quileute wolves are meant to be.

Chief – Jacob's baseball tear may be a tribute to the Cullens on behalf of the whole pack, for all the wolves as a team. As the Alpha wolf (team leader), Jacob's tear may reflect everyone's sad feelings. It is a somber farewell gesture to new friends and allies, who are risking their lives to fight a terrible war.

Combination – Maybe Jacob's baseball-shaped tear is a combination of all these factors. It wouldn't be surprising, as Jacob does have an awfully sociable nature and a wide emotional reach.

Teeth

Teeth symbolize energy, aggression, power, and death. In the animal world, when a creature shows or bares its teeth, this is a sign of aggression to attack or to kill, to ward off a threat. When Bella bares her teeth in *Breaking Dawn*, maybe the Volturi should heed her determined and aggressive signal. At the height of her anger and fury, Bella describes her reaction: "My lips curved back automatically, and a low, fierce snarl tore up my throat from the pit of my stomach. I realized the corners of my mouth were turned up in a smile" (*Breaking Dawn*, p 635). People from ancient societies once wore necklaces made from teeth of wild animals they hunted. They believed that these animal teeth would make them more aggressive and powerful. In Greek myth, the god of sleep – Hypnos – is pictured as a winged figure holding a tooth. The tooth of Hypnos means 'assimilation' and 'adjustment' because human teeth grow, fall out, regrow and adjust themselves during the human life span.

As strong skeletal tools designed to tear flesh and chew food, teeth relate to physical, emotional, or spiritual nourishment. The phrase to 'take a bite of life' means to live life deeply and fully. And 'to grit your teeth' is a sign of willpower, determination, or endurance. So when Bella dreams of sharp fangs and wide vampire grins in the *Twilight Saga*, the teeth she sees in her mind may be a symbolic reminder that she should take a bite out of life, go for her goals, and become the vampire she has always wanted to be. If you are reading this right now, then you too have plunged your fangs into the dark world of vampires, werewolves, and Gothic fiction – the *Twilight Saga*.

Thread/Fate

Fate

The *Twilight* world explores important themes like choice and chance and the influence of personal control in life. Bella teams up with choice. She believes that choices largely determine the quality of life. For example, Bella chooses Edward regardless of his race or background. She tells him: "It doesn't matter to me what you are" (*Twilight*, p 161). On the other hand, characters like Edward and Jacob support destiny. For example, no matter how good he is or how hard he tries, Edward believes he has no soul and is eternally damned (*New Moon*, p 37). Jacob's view that fate rules is even stronger. For example, Jacob tells Bella "You see it everywhere… Nature taking its course" (*Eclipse*, p 97).

The thread images in the *Twilight* books are apt because thread symbolizes fate or destiny. Compared to chess (a symbol for choice), fate is symbolized by threads, ropes, ribbons, or strings. These suggest that our paths in life unwind before us in ways we cannot control. As the tearing ribbon on the cover of *Eclipse* shows, the way events unfold is not always smooth or easy. Even Bella acknowledges the power of fate and thread symbolism on one occasion. For example, she thinks about Jacob's wolf legend that "had begun so many different, tangled threads of my life" (*New Moon*, p 303).

Fates' Loom

> I imagined how the thread of my life might look in the Fates' Loom – who knew but that it actually existed? I was sure my thread must have changed color… It felt like it must be bright crimson, or maybe glistening gold.
> (*Breaking Dawn*, p 486)

As the *Twilight* scene above suggests, threads symbolize fate. In fact, the *Twilight* books use threads, ropes, ribbons and woven objects in a number of important scenes. The thread image is based on a Greek myth about threads and human destiny. Zeus, who ruled over all the Greek gods and goddesses, had a romantic relationship with Themis – the Goddess of Law. This affair produced several daughters – the Fates. Somewhere high in the heavens, the Fates sat spinning human fate. A thread depicted the course of a person's life that was spun, which was measured and cut up by the Fates. A short string meant that death will come early. A person who received a long string would live a long and happy life. As such, the thread scenes woven into the *Twilight Saga* would have been inspired by the Fates from Greek myth.

Three of the most important fate scenes in the *Twilight Saga*, symbolized by thread, involve a red ribbon, Bella's vampire change, and werewolf love.

Torn – The original cover of *Eclipse* shows an image of a red ribbon that is a bit torn in the center. The ribbon symbolizes fate, especially with respect to relationships. What it suggests is that Bella's romantic fate can transpire in two directions – she can either choose Edward, or choose Jacob. However, Bella loves both. She only feels complete when both Edward *and* Jacob are in her life. The choice proves difficult, impossible. Hence, the torn ribbon. The dilemma is tearing Bella's world apart. Which path should Bella follow? When Bella chooses Edward and rejects Jacob, she clearly confirms that the choice has torn her world apart. "I knew that the new tear in my heart would always ache" (*Eclipse*, p 540).

Tied – Thanks to an experience told from Jacob's direct perspective, the most powerful thread/fate scene in the *Twilight Saga* involves werewolf love. When Jacob imprints on Renesmee, it is an experience like no other:

> Everything inside me came undone as I stared at the tiny porcelain face of the half-vampire, half-human baby. All the

> lines that held me to my life were sliced apart in swift cuts, like clipping the strings to a bunch of balloons. Everything that made me who I was… disconnected from me in that second – snip, snip, snip – and floated up into space.
>
> I was not left drifting. A new string held me where I was. Not one string, but a million. Not strings, but steel cables. A million steel cables all tying me to one thing – to the very center of the universe.
>
> (*Breaking Dawn*, p 331)

Jacob has imprinted, surrendered to destiny, fallen suddenly and madly in love, an experience way out of his control and way out of this world.

Turned – Once Bella has been turned into a vampire, she imagines that the thread of her life has turned too. Specifically, Bella imagines her human life as having been a beige thread, which has now turned crimson. A rich and strong color, crimsoon symbolizes Bella's happy new life with Edward. Bella even mentions the Fates from Greek myth herself:

> When I looked back over my first three months as an immortal, I imagined how the thread of my life might look in the Fates' loom… bright crimson, or maybe glistening gold. The tapestry of family and friends that wove together was a beautiful, glowing thing, full of their bright, complementary colors.
>
> (*Breaking Dawn*, p 486)

The thread of Bella's life is a beautiful rich color, to reflect the richer quality of her new life. No longer is Bella a single, loose, lonely thread. She has woven herself into a colorful family tapestry.

Topaz

Although the topaz, a precious gemstone, can be blue, red, or pink, it is best known for its golden-yellow hue. The *Twilight Saga* just loves linking Edward's eyes to this sunny and tawny shade. In *Twilight*, when Bella falls in love with Edward, she declares that her favorite gemstone used to be garnet, but now it is "topaz", to match the color of Edward's eyes (*Twilight*, p 201). In *New Moon*, Edward's eyes are "liquid topaz" (p 9), "liquid gold" (p 70) and "topaz, clear and deep" (p 70). The topaz is said to symbolize something that is hard to find or figure out, since the word *topazein* means 'conjecture' in Greek. This makes the topaz a fitting gemstone to describe the eyes of a mysterious and brooding vampire like Edward.

According to a famous Greek legend, the most beautiful topaz gems could be found on a place called Serpent Island. Since *Twilight* vampires do show some snake-like features (e.g. fanged, venomous, cold-blooded, hiss a lot), the idea that topaz is found in a famous snake-site is an interesting link, don't you think?

What's more, the topaz has some peculiar physical qualities. It cools down very quickly after being soaked in hot water. It is also believed to have the power to cool tempers and calm passions. The Indian sages, in particular, acknowledged the coolness and cooling effects of this stone. It is symbolically spot-on to connect a cool stone like topaz with a cool-skinned and morally cool creature such as a golden-eyed vegetarian vampire. Given the mystery and secrecy of *Twilight*-style vampires, especially Edward, and the idea that vampires are cold-skinned and snake-like, the author's choice of topaz vampire eyes is symbolically apt and artful.

Tree

The main feature of the natural *Twilight* world landscape is trees,

trees, trees. They provide shade, scenery, safety, symbolic ambience, and more. The area of Forks is really special because of magnificent trees. As Bella notes: "The forest spread out around us in a boundless labyrinth of ancient trees" (*Twilight*, p 226). Deep in a wild forest, huge trees may be hundreds of years old. Some plant species may even be prehistoric. Tall, thick, wild and overgrown, the forest around Forks twists, turns, wraps and arches over everything like a living green maze.

All around the world, the tree has been "universally revered as a sacred, living being" (Nozedar, 2008, p 385). Trees are a main element of life on earth, associated with the magical, mysterious, and life-giving forces of nature. Not only do trees absorb carbon dioxide, they produce oxygen in the air we breathe. With their towering heights, thick trunks, long lives and food bearing features, it's no wonder people have always regarded trees as magical, powerful, and the center of life. "We are still filled with awe when contemplating a centuries-old tree or the depths of a forest that is both an inviting haven of peace and quiet, and a mysterious and disturbing unknown world" (Colin, 2000, p 498). The fact that an inverted tree (with its roots up) looks like a human nervous system or respiratory or circulatory system makes the tree extra sacred. A tree can also produce sap, which resembles blood. The three main parts of a tree (trunk, branches, roots) suggests it has links with three different worlds – earth, heaven, and the underworld). As you can see, the tree has many powerful meanings.

Tree Species

The *Twilight Saga* makes sure to mention specific trees. And each species of tree has its own symbolic meanings. Tree species mentioned in the *Twilight Saga* are:

- Cedar Tree
- Fir Tree

- Hemlock Tree
- Madrone Tree
- Maple Tree
- Palm Tree
- Sitka Spruce
- Yew Tree

In ancient cultures, shamans, druids and witches considered every tree to have a spirit. In one of the earliest writings about trees ever recorded, the Egyptian *Book of the Dead* says that: "twin sycamores of turquoise stood on the gate of heaven from which the sun-god Re emerged each morning" (Colin, 2000, p 499). Different trees have different powers and offer different gifts. For example, trees can provide food (fruits, nuts), medicine (aspirin comes from willow trees), heat (fire, cooking), shade (leafy branches in summer), wood (for building houses), and tools (weapons, spears, dishes). In the thick, wild forests of the *Twilight* world, just what might the different trees mean?

Cedar Tree

At the Cullen house, six huge cedar trees cast a protective shadow across their meadow (*Twilight*, p 280). It seems apt for a supernatural vampire family to have cedar trees in their garden. The ancient Egyptians thought the spooky sound of wind blowing through cedar leaves was the moaning of powerful spirits. Since cedar trees are big, dark, old and strong, cedar forests were said to be dwelling places of divine spirits. The *Twilight Saga* wedding party is set up underneath two "ancient cedars" (*Breaking Dawn*, p 47). The wood of the cedar is so tough and durable that the cedar tree is linked to incorruptibility and purity. Evergreen and ever-present in nature, this highlights the cedar's immortality. Ancient Egyptians discovered that cedar oil was antiseptic and an excellent embalming ingredient, which linked the cedar to rebirth. A cedar grove in a vampire meadow and a vampire wedding under cedar trees are certainly fitting symbolic gestures. Just like the cedar, vampires are immortal, are reborn as vampires from human form, and their venom embalms a mortal to live forever.

Fir Tree

The tall fir frees in the *Twilight* books create a spiky green fringe along the coastline. First Beach was "crowned with austere, soaring firs" (*Twilight*, p 99). In nature, firs have needle-like leaves and cylinder-shaped pinecones that disintegrate to release seeds (Wiki, 2011). A fir tree is a symbol of honesty, truth and forthrightness because the trunk grows 'straight', like a pillar of truth. Since fir trees grow in groups, they symbolize friendship. The evergreen nature of firs (they never loose their green vitality and hue) encourages awareness about life-long links with others. The fir's long life, its ability to survive tough winter conditions and grow in poor soil enhanced its reputation for resilience and determination. If fir trees can survive long, cold, dark, and difficult times, maybe we can too. Endurance and determination is what Bella must show in order to overcome her many challenges and fulfill her true destiny.

Hemlock Tree

In the *Twilight Saga*, the hemlock tree is mentioned more times than any other tree species. Bella notices hemlocks during her first hike in the forest (*Twilight*, p 118), in a dark forest dream (*New Moon*, p 168), in a forest meadow (*New Moon*, p 246), and near the Cullen house (*Breaking Dawn*, p 433). The worst meaning of the hemlock is death. The philosopher Socrates is famous for killing himself by drinking hemlock when he was given a death sentence. During great battles, hemlock was once rubbed onto the blades of knives and swords to make them extra deadly. Although the hemlock is deadly for humans, it does not harm domestic animals.

Madrone Tree

In the *Twilight* books, the madrone tree features in the most romantic settings. In *Twilight,* on the night of the school dance, Edward and Bella sit next to madrone trees when the moon comes out just after twilight. "As soon as we were alone, he swung me up into his arms, and carried me across the dark grounds till he reached the bench beneath the shadow of the madrone trees" (*Twilight,* p 430). The madrone is an evergreen tree that is native to Western Europe, North America and the Mediterranean. In fact, its nickname is 'Strawberry tree' because the fruit resembles strawberries. With its edible red fruit and its immortal (evergreen) qualities, it seems fitting for a vampire to romance a human in the company of a madrone tree.

Maple Tree

The maple tree is mentioned several times in the *Twilight* books. Bella notices maples during her first hike in the forest (*Twilight,* p 118), she notices maple leaves shudder when Edward leaves her in the forest (*New Moon,* p 73), and she pushes past maples on the edge of the forest meadow (*New Moon,* p 233). As a tree, the vine maple looks spectacular – a brilliant red during autumn. A maple is also a social tree because it grows happily among great firs and cedars. The maple leaf is Canada's national emblem and maple syrup, made from the tree's sweet sap, is Canada's national product. In North America, the maple has long been a symbol of life, longevity and vigor, with the power to ward off demons and nocturnal spirits. The maple's sweet honey-like syrup and its positive supernatural power points to Edward's sweet allure and good nature.

Palm Tree

In the *Twilight Saga,* Bella and Edward visit a tropical island in South America:

> A small island rose out of the water ahead of us, waving with palm fronds, a beach glowing pale in the light of the moon. (*Breaking Dawn*, p 71)

The palm tree, which is often associated with islands, suggests a fun, happy and carefree lifestyle, the perfect place for a honeymoon. The palm tree has a number of important symbolic meanings. The palm leaf has been a symbol of triumph and victory since the earliest times. The Romans rewarded champions of the games and celebrated military successes with palm branches. In Christian art, martyrs were often depicted holding a palm frond. This is supposed to suggest the victory of spirit over flesh. In *Breaking Dawn*, Bella falls pregnant falls pregnant on an island full of palms. Then Bella becomes a vampire – spirit triumphs over flesh. These days, palms remain a symbol of a tropical island paradise. In the Western world, palms suggest the idea sunny skies and good times. "The palm is a sun symbol, a tree whose fronds spread and splay outwards and upwards from the center, like sunbeams radiating from the sun. Beautiful symbolism, isn't it?" (www.whats-your-sign.com, 2011). Some consider the palm a tree of alchemy because it unites male parts (tall, erect trunk) and female parts (lush leaves, rich fruits, and flowering fronds). This is why palms are such strong symbols of unity, fertility, and balance. In support of this symbolic meaning, the sexual union between Bella and Edward leads to the birth of Renesmee.

Sitka Spruce

In the *Twilight Saga*, during Bella's first big hike alone in the forest "the trail wound deeper and deeper into the forest" and "snaked around Sitka spruces" (*Twilight*, p 118). This tree grows in the northwest of North America on the Pacific coast of America and Canada. It is in the top five of tallest tree species. Sitka spruce is the largest of all spruces, and often grows to 180 feet tall.

Cultures have held the spruce as a protective tree. The spruce tree was once a symbol of the protective female, a tree of life, and mother tree; the maypole often was made of spruce. Some towns in Bavaria still practice this tradition.

Yew Tree

Bella notices "yews" during her first hike in the forest (*Twilight*, p 118). Yew trees may be the oldest-lived tree in the world and are associated with the goddess, the grave, the afterlife and immortality. The yew is the traditional cemetery tree, because Celtic priests and priestesses regarded it as a symbol of immortality planting it in their sacred groves. Revered by ancient wise ones, yews can be found in many ancient sites and churchyards. It is linked to dead lovers and is said to spring to life from their graves, as if to mark forever what has been. Often used to enhance magical and psychic abilities, and to induce visions, the yew's evergreen leaves were said to be symbolic of everlasting life. The Greeks considered yew trees sacred and associated them with Hecate, queen of the underworld. Although the yew tree was revered in nearly every culture of the northern temperate zones, yew trees were almost wiped out completely for their utility. Because of its great longevity, the yew is a symbol of everlasting life. It grows in an unusual way, too, its new stems growing down the outside of the tree, giving the yew an association with rebirth and regeneration, as the new is born from the old. In the *Twilight Saga*, Bella's new vampire body is born from her old human body and she becomes immortal like a yew.

Triangle

The triangle possesses all the symbolic power of the number *three*. In ancient times, the triangle was a sign for light. If a triangle points upwards and sits on its base, it is an arrow, a male sign and symbolizes fire, light and divine powers. If a triangle points downwards, it is a cup, a female sign and symbolizes water, darkness and deep instincts (Bowes, 1999; Colin, 2000).

Wolvish V

In the *Twilight Saga,* triangles tend to have aggressive male meanings. When Laurent is about to kill Bella, five werewolves step out of the forest to protect her. The first wolf, a "gigantic black monster" appears with a pair of wolves on each side "lined up in a V, like geese flying south" – the shape of a deadly black arrow (*New Moon,* p 242). The pattern of the five wolves forms an aggressive arrowhead shape, ready to deal with danger. However, this wolvish V has positive and protective meanings too, because the wolves are trying to save Bella's life and geese form V shapes to support each other when flying over long distances as a flock.

Dark Fan

The strongest triangle shape in the *Twilight Saga* is the dark display of the Volturi vampire army. *Breaking Dawn* describes these vampires approaching in: "a rigid, formal formation… a dark, unbroken shape that seemed to hover a few inches above the white snow" (*Breaking Dawn,* p 631). The advancing army folded outwards, like "the opening of a fan, graceful but very angular" (*Breaking Dawn,* p 632). The black Volturi triangle spreads out much like a proud peacock might spread out its tail. But it is a black triangle of doom, death and destruction. Compared to the positive meaning of the Holy Trinity (love, light and peace), the tip of the "black-shrouded triangle" made up by Aro, Marcus and Caius suggests death, evil and sorrow (*Breaking Dawn,* p 670). As such, the Volturi trio corrupt and pervert positive spiritual meanings.

Battle Shapes

In the *Breaking Dawn* war, striking geometrical designs and color schemes appear upon the field of white ice. In particular, a black Volturi triangle offsets Bella's rosy glowing circle of protection. While the black Volturi triangle is geared to attack, Bella's shield is a red dome of light that covers everyone she wants to protect. Note also that the Volturi (black triangle) seek "power", "domination" and the army moves "rigidly", "formally" and in "synchronicity" (*Breaking Dawn*, pp 631, 666–667). In contrast, Bella's defense (round shield of light) "flexes", "wraps" and "stretches" just like "elastic armor" as if it "wants to cooperate" (*Breaking Dawn*, pp 652–653). The stiff black triangle represents the evil side and Bella's round dome of light is the good side. After all, the Volturi want to destroy free will. Their true purpose is the "quest for dominion" (*Breaking Dawn*, p 667). In contrast to Volturi authority, the Cullen family bonds are "based on love" (*Breaking Dawn*, p 656). This presents striking visual and symbolic differences between the Volturi vampires and the Cullen vampires:

Triangle/Circle
Black Fan/Glowing Dome
Darkness/Light
Evil/Good
Oppression/Freedom
Power/Love

Clearly, the dark Volturi triangle, devoid of light and love, looks like a toxic black arrow about to shoot down the light and destroy all that is good in the world.

In the *Breaking Dawn* war, some geometric shapes mirror each other. As one attentive *Twilight* fan has noticed: "You see the pack, then the Volturi army. You have Bella, Edward, and Jake (good triangle); Aro, Caius, and Marcus (bad triangle)" (TwilightMOMS, post by Blushingmommy, 2008).

What's more, if you think about it, the *Breaking Dawn* war may have been deliberately designed to look like a game of life-sized chess. The black cloaks and white snow do suggest a black and white checkered chessboard. Even the playing pieces on the field resemble chess pieces. This include figures such as kings (Aro), queens (Bella), knights (Jacob), towers of truth (Garrett), pawns (witnesses, bystanders) and more. After all, the *Breaking Dawn* war is meant to be a test of mental strength and strategy. As Ms. Meyer explains "the battle with the Volturi is one of wits and strategy, not physical violence" (2011)).

Twilight

When the unquiet hours depart
And far away their tumults cease,
Within the twilight of the heart
We bathe in peace, are stilled with peace.
– *The Hour of Twilight,* George William Russell

The world may never view the word 'twilight' in the same way again now that it has starred in the *Twilight Saga* phenomenon. Stephenie Meyer explains that she initially picked the word "twilight" from a list of "words with atmosphere" when she and her publisher were trying to find a title for her first book. Meyer recalls that this title: "isn't absolutely perfect; to be honest, I don't think there is a perfect title for this book… The word twilight was on a list of 'words with atmosphere'" (www.stephenie meyer.com).

Twilight is a very special time of day, well-known for its peaceful and entrancing atmosphere. Due to the strange and ambient quality of light at this time, writers and artists call it the 'blue hour', after a French expression. The blue haze of twilight is a boundary point between day and night, darkness and light, and black and white. As such, twilight is a dividing line that both *separates* and *joins* two opposite forces. The dim 'half-light' of twilight suggests the idea of being 'split' and 'suspended' in space (suspended like the Hanged Man card in tarot cards). Of course, twilight can be a busy time when crepuscular creatures – such as crickets, dragonflies, owls and bats – hunt for food and become active. To the human mind, twilight is romantic and tantalizing. It signals the onset of night, dark delights, sweet surprises and secret fantasies yet to be experienced.Twilight Turning Points

The first time 'twilight' is mentioned is in *Twilight*, chapter seven, when Bella wanders through the forest for the first time. It is here, in the intimate forest gloom, where Bella figures out her true feelings. She decides to pursue her heart's desire – Edward:

> I had my answer… When I thought of him, of his voice, his hypnotic eyes, the magnetic force of his personality, I wanted nothing more than to be with him right now… in the darkening forest… dim as twilight under the canopy… with the rain."
> (*Twilight*, p 59)

Even though it isn't twilight time yet, the darkness and rain gives the forest a twilight-like atmosphere. Just as twilight marks the turning point from day to night, this twilight scene is the first major turning point in the plot. From this twilight forest moment on, Bella pursues her love interest in Edward.Twilight Safety

The next twilight scene that appears is in *Twilight*, chapter eleven. Edward drops Bella off at the end of the day, and declares that: "twilight is the safest time for vampires." Why might twilight be so safe? Well, for one thing, the fierce sun no longer subjects its blind scrutiny onto the world. The darkness of night can be a good time to reveal delicate matters. Twilight is neither night nor day, not dark nor light, not black nor white. Twilight time is 'just right', a hazy gray half-light that teeters in on the edge of both day and night.

Another reason why Edward might like twilight time is that it is traditionally supposed to be a magically powerful time. Spirits and supernatural creatures can roam around more freely and easily at twilight time and Edward is a supernatural vampire. Fairies and pixies, elves and sprites, and spirits both good and bad belong to the twilight and can be glimpsed more easily at this time.

Twilight Suspense

The third obvious twilight scene that appears in the *Twilight Saga* is at the end of *Twilight*, on the night of the school prom. Bella and Edward arrive at the prom just on twilight because Bella notices "a few streaks of sunlight escaping through far away in the west" (*Twilight*, p 423). Just after Bella and Edward leave the dance hall to be alone outside, Edward notes that it is: "Twilight again… No matter how perfect the day is, it always has to end" (*Twilight*, p 430). Edward's comment could be symbolic. No matter how perfect Bella and Edward's relationship is, it must eventually, and sadly, come to an end. This is because Bella is a human girl, a mortal, she will get older, she will die. End of romance. End of perfect story. Edward could be grieving ahead for his loss. Unless, of course, Bella becomes immortal.

That same night, when Edward kisses Bella's neck, he asks her if she is truly willing to die and make this "the twilight" of her life (*Twilight*, p 452). Of course, this would mean the symbolic twilight of Bella's life, as to become a "dark creature" must entail her human death. Of course, Edward refuses to bite her… for now. Just as twilight hangs suspended between night and day, Edward suspends his decision to turn Bella into a vampire and they reach an "impasse" at the hospital (*Twilight*, p 415).

Secretive Twilights

Adding to these twilight scenes described in the *Twilight Saga*, a few secret twilight scenes hide in the books. Yet, strange and significant things happen at twilight time...

Twilight Rescue

After visiting the bookstore at Port Angeles, it "was getting dark" and the sky grew dark and gray, streaked with "pink and orange" (*Twilight*, p 137). Of course, not only is this twilight time, it happens to be the time that Edward and his silver Volvo skid out onto the tarmac to rescue Bella from four horrible thugs.

Twilight Games

The baseball game, which the Cullens play during a storm, is scheduled "around dusk" (*Twilight*, p 305), which is another way to refer to twilight. This twilight time is also a turning point for destiny. This is because three travelling vampires hear the Cullens playing, so they join in. Unlike baseball, however, these nomad vampires decide to play a much deadlier game – hunting Bella for dinner.

Twilight Split

Edward's act of breaking up with Bella after school would have occurred at twilight time. This is because Bella notices Edward's car in the driveway after school just before her father is due to come home from work (*New Moon*, p 67). Soon after Edward leaves, Bella looks for him in the forest that is growing "darker and darker" (*New Moon*, p 73). Not just another twilight, but another symbolic twilight – a critical turning point in Bella's life. After dating a vampire for a year, Bella has just embarked on a long, cold boyfriend-less time without him.

Twilight Risk

When Bella goes out for the first time with Jessica to see a zombie movie, the girls happen to attend the "twilight showing" of the movie (*New Moon*, p 105). Well, strange things happen at twilight. This time Bella engages in risky behavior by striking up a chat with some drunk men at One-Eyed Pete's bar. This is a significant scene in the *Twilight Saga* because it is the first time Bella hears Edward's voice in her mind warning her to take care.

Twilight Nightmare

Bella's first nightmare after Edward leaves shows her wandering around an empty "nothing" world. This dream clearly has a twilight atmosphere because: "It was dark, like dusk on a cloudy day" and Bella "hurried through the gloom without a path, always searching, searching, searching" (*New Moon*, p 123). Not only did Bella's dream occur at a twilight-like time, her dream accurately reflects the time of day that Edward broke up with her (twilight).

Twilight Tours

In the *Twilight Saga*, Bella treks to the forest during twilight time. For example, Bella desperately wants to find the meadow that she and Edward shared together the previous year. She gives up on her search for Edward's meadow at twilight when "it started to get darker, the sunless day fading toward a starless night" (*New Moon*, p 200). The second time Bella looks for the meadow, she finds it. But she also finds a vampire who wants to kill her. Luckily for her, a pack of huge wolves saves her from the evil bloodsucker. As soon as Bella arrives home after visiting to the magic meadow, "the sky was already dusky" (*New Moon*, p 246). Twilight again, of course.

Twilight Wedding

It is worth noting that the wedding reception party started just on "twilight over the river… allowing the sun to set behind the trees. The lights in the trees glimmered" (*Breaking Dawn*, p 47). The most important things just keep on happening at twilight.

Twilight Tactic

The werewolves are shocked to hear about Bella's pregnancy, which they discover during a meeting at (you guessed it) twilight time. "It was almost dark – the clouds covered the sunset completely… We met up about 10 miles from La Push in a clearing" (*Breaking Dawn*, p 182). At this meeting, the Alpha wolf Sam Uley orders the pack to kill Bella and her unborn baby.

Twilight Mission

Bella heads out to meet Jenks in Seattle at twilight time. Bella wants to finalize some plans to keep Jacob and Renesmee safe. She launches into her mission at twilight time. "It was a dreary afternoon, already dark as dusk" (*Breaking Dawn*, p 619).

As these significant, secretive and symbolic scenes show, interesting changes and events take place at twilight time. It is truly a powerful, magical and beguiling time, especially in Stephenie Meyer's *Twilight Saga*.

U

Underworld

The Volturi vampires rule the vampire race. Their address? A spooky underground chamber. A secret place far beneath the city of Volterra in Italy. Somewhere in the sewers, shadows and gloom. But one of the most striking features of the Volturi underworld is its striking symbolic similarity to another chilling world of the dead from Greek myth.

A Death Pit

In the *Twilight* world, the undead Volturi clearly live in an underground kingdom. When Bella first visits their lair, Jane (a Volturi guard) takes her on an "alley angled slightly downward", which kept "slanting downward" (*New Moon*, p 457). Bella and her companions then "slid down an open hole in the street" that was "small, and black" and took visitors "lower into the blackness" (*New Moon*, p 458). Clearly, Bella has entered a "subterranean tunnel" (*New Moon*, p 459). The path slanted down to another "low, arched tunnel" (*New Moon*, p 460). At this point of the journey, a "grate" and a "small door" made of bars appear at the end of the "ghoulish stone sewers" (*New Moon*, pp 461–62). A hallway took Bella to an ornate hall, which opened up into a cavernous stone chamber (*New Moon*, p 465). This underground Volturi world has an uncanny resemblance to another terrifying underworld called 'Hades' – the kingdom of the dead.

According to Greek myth, Hades was a god of death who ruled the underworld. The place where dead people went and the souls of dead people dwelled. Similarly, the Volturi chamber in the *Twilight* series is underground, is ruled by powerful supernatural beings, and is a place where the undead hide and reside.

It is also a place of death in that unsuspecting people are lured there so that the local vampires do not have to leave their lair to hunt for human blood. Rather than eating out, the Volturi vampires delight in feasting on home-delivered 'tourist take-away' meals. Both Hades and the Volturi hideout are death pits.

Secret Laws

In the *Twilight Saga*, the Volturi lair is a vampire command center underneath the Volterra city plaza. Not only is it a place where undead vampires dwell, but the oldest known vampires – Aro, Marcus, and Caius – rule the vampire race from there. Though rulers in both Hades and the Volturi lair can be evil and abuse their power if they want to, each undead world fills an unpleasant but necessary duty in enforcing supernatural laws and justice. Exposing vampire secrets results in death. As Bella once observed: "Caius pointed a skeletal finger at me. 'She knows too much. You have exposed our secrets… *her* life is forfeit'" (*New Moon*, p 478).

Going into the Volturi domain in the *Twilight* world surely symbolizes a descent into Hades, especially when the only way to exit this deadly world is if the ruler grants access. The only reason why Bella, Edward and Alice can leave the Volturi underground is because the leader Aro allows them to go, so enthralled by their visit that he invites them to "please visit again" (*New Moon*, p 480). Similarly, no one can enter or exit the Greek world of the dead without the ruler's permission.

When you consider the physical structure of the Volturi chambers, the layout offers strong symbolic supports for the Volturi's secretive lifestyle. The Volturi vampires, for example, live in a closed fortress setting, a cold stone structure deep under the ground. The dark, cold and closed nature of their supernatural abode suggests secrecy, emotional coldness, supremacy, and closed-mindedness. The way the Volturi vampires greet and treat Bella supports the cold and secret nature of the Volturi empire also. As one perceptive *Twilight* fan has noted:

> Bella was wet through from her charge through the fountain and the Volturi offered her no warmth, no change of clothes. Most of them are indifferent to Bella's quiet suffering as she is trawled through the sewers into their barren and comfortless, lifeless building. They think she's about to become lunch anyway.
> (TwilightMOMS Post by scoundrel, 2011)

The cold, closed and macabre Volturi fortress enhances the cold and menacing reputation of the Volturi, for sure.

Water Crossing

The path to an underworld can be difficult to find and follow. The only way to reach Hades in Greek myth, for example, is to travel across a river. In order to cross that river, one has to pay a ferryman called Charon with money. This gruesome skeletal figure, cloaked in black, will then row you across the river Styx, a powerful and poisonous waterway. 'The nine circles of Hades' refers to the river Styx, a swirling river that looks like a spiral and coils nine times around Hades. It flows between Earth and the Hades, and circles this dead underworld nine times. When Charlie tries to have a "safe sex" talk with Bella in the kitchen, she felt is this experience was worse than "the seventh circle of Hades" (*Eclipse*, p 52). What this means is that having a sex talk with Charlie was really horrible. Since the Styx circles Hades nine times, making a visit to Hades is a tricky and treacherous trip. When Bella charges through the fountain in the Volterra city plaza to reach Edward in *New Moon*, just before he tries to die, this was pretty anxiety-provoking and may well be a symbolic gesture about crossing water to reach Hades.

A fascinating property of the river Styx is that a single drop of its water is fatally poisonous. In a similar sense, a single drop of vampire venom can kill a mortal, change a human into a vampire. Since the Styx is a body of water at a transitional point between two worlds (life and death), it is accessible to water birds. A water bird, such as a pelican or swan, can move effectively in three different elements: air (flying), earth (walking), and water (swimming). For this very reason, alchemists saw such birds as messengers between gods and mortals, the living and the dead. Maybe this is where Bella's symbolic links with bird symbolism comes in so handy. You see, Bella has links with eleven different birds, especially water birds such as the swan (see *Birds*). This makes Bella's visit to the Volturi underworld extra intriguing symbolically; Bella is the only mortal in the *Twilight Saga* who visits the Volturi underworld and survives the trip. Furthermore, Bella acts as a messenger, a spokesperson for the living and the undead, and unites supernatural vampires and wolves. For example, it is Bella who speaks up in *New Moon* to save Edward from Jane's grueling torture (*New Moon*, p 475). Bella is a *Twilight Saga* swan bird who safely travels across the fountain water to the Volturi's world and back.

Triple Guard

Another striking similarity between the Volturi underworld and the Hades underworld is that the entrance to each world is extremely well guarded. In the *Twilight* series, the Volturi's three most important guards seem to be Jane, Alec and Demetri. All three vampires have powerful psychic gifts. Jane has the supernatural power to cause excruciating pain, Alec deadens the senses, and Demetri tracks down any target he wants to without fail. Altogether, these three torments suggest pain, loss of sensation, and being chosen for death, which do foreshadow the experience of dying. The symbolic conclusion? These three powerful vampires are a fitting guard for a world of death.

In *New Moon*, the triple Volturi guard meet Bella and Edward above ground at the clock tower just outside the Volturi lair, as if guiding their visitors underground. When Bella and Edward are guided into the Volturi lair by three black-cloaked members of the guard, this seems to symbolize the terrifying Hades guardian in Greek myth – Cerberus. According to this myth, Cerberus is a giant, black three-headed dog who guards the entrance to Hades. The three-headed dog is often depicted with razor-sharp teeth, a mane of live serpents and a snake's tail – which sounds a bit like the venomous vampire threesome. Not only did this terrifying dog not let the living enter the kingdom of the dead, but made sure that no ghosts, souls or others escaped from this dark and macabre realm. The only way out of the underworld is if Hades lets you go. Similarly, the only way out of the Volturi underworld is if Aro, Marcus and Caius let you pass the triple vampire guard and leave.

It is symbolically interesting that Demetri (one of the three Volturi guards) has a name that is a version of the name *Demeter*. In Greek myth, Demeter was an earth goddess whose daughter Persephone was kidnapped by Hades and taken into his gruesome underworld. In a similar way, Demetri is gifted "tracker" who hunts down and captures individuals that the Volturi underworld rulers wish to claim. Demetri takes his victims deep undergrounnd, or else he ruthlessly kills them.

Stone Altar

In a way, the Volturi lair is like a stone altar, a place of slaughter and sacrifice, deep within their underworld. The Volturi's stone chamber was a "brighter, cavernous room, perfectly round like a huge castle turret" (*New Moon*, p 465). This round chamber, from which the deadly and venomous Volturi rule, would have to be the most evil circle in the *Twilight* series. Of course, the dark tunnel that leads you there and swallows you up in its darkness is a fitting idea for hungry Volturi. In the center of this circular room was a "depression" or drain in the floor (*New Moon*, p 466). Bella wonders whether the Volturi travel through this cavity.

When Bella, Edward and Alice are allowed to leave the gloomy stone room, a group of human tourists – Volturi food – arrive and start "screaming" (*New Moon*, p 484). This reveals the real purpose of the ditch in the stone room – it is surely meant to drain the blood of the brutally slaughtered humans.

Unicorn

The *Twilight Saga* mentions the unicorn just once. In *Breaking Dawn*, Bella describes her new stone cottage in the forest as "a place where anyone could believe magic existed. A place where you just expected… a unicorn to stop and nibble at the rosebushes" (*Breaking Dawn*, p 444). Bella may well represent the innocent young girl who lures the unicorn, a sweet symbol of temptation that lures powerful magic to her, especially as Bella means harm to no one, not even after she becomes a vampire. The unicorn even seems to have deeper links with Bella, once you see what unicorns mean.

The unicorn is a beautiful mythical creature, pure, chaste and innocent. This fabled animal has the body of a white horse and a long single horn protruding from the center of its forehead. Since the horn grows in the middle of its head, the unicorn symbolizes knowledge and wisdom. It was a popular image in medieval tapestries, a white shimmer against a dark green forest background. According to legend, only a young girl pure of mind and body can touch a unicorn. Even after becoming a vampire, it is easy to imagine a good-hearted person like Bella attracting such a shy and gentle creature.

The Greek historian and physician Ctesias (423–401 BC) provided the earliest writings about unicorns. He described the medicinal properties of the unicorn horn, most probably inspired by the white Indian rhinoceros – a shy, reclusive herbivore that lived in the marshes. The unicorn is one of the symbols alchemists used to describe mysterious processes. In alchemy, the union of a unicorn (a symbol for the mind, male and sulfur) and a stag (a symbol of the soul, female, and mercury) produced a divine being. In the *Twilight* world, Edward is a shy vampire with venom that burns just like sulfur (Edward, the unicorn), who attracts an innocent girl, pure of heart, close to him (Bella, the deer). Their sexual union on Isle Esme produces a divine being – Renesmee. Potent alchemy? Maybe.

An old poem called *New Year Letter* (1940) describes the unicorn's lovely magic as if was happening in the deep green cedar forest where Bella lives:

O, Unicorn, among the cedars,
To whom no magic charm can lead us,
White childhood moving like a sigh
Through the green woods unharmed in thy
Sophisticated innocence,
To call thy true love to the dance.

Since the image of a unicorn emerges in Bella's mind and the *Twilight* world is a supernatural setting, it would be no surprise if such a fantastic creature were to visit Bella's garden and nibble on roses, after all.

V

Vampire

A Dark Figure

There is no figure so terrible, no figure so dreaded and abhorred, yet delights with such fearful fascination, as the vampire.
(*Twilight*, p 116)

The vampire is arguably the most salient symbol in the *Twilight Saga*. This dark and chilling figure is explored and developed in the most intriguing ways in the *Twilight* books. A fanged and venomous creature that feeds on human blood in order to live forever, the vampire is linked to a range of different themes and modern issues. Even some discussions about the original cover of *Twilight* argue that the two arms extended down to hold an apple may well be a deliberate design because the arms form a 'V' shape – that's 'V' for vampire, of course. *Webster's International Dictionary* defines a vampire as:

A blood-sucking ghost or reanimated body of a dead person; a soul or re-animated body of a dead person believed to come from the grave and wander about by night sucking the blood of persons asleep, causing their death.
(encyclopedia.com)

So, just where does this mysterious, alluring and yet terrifying creature come from in the first place? And as a symbol, what does the vampire really, truly mean?

The Word 'Vampire'

According to language and culture experts, the English word

vampire is most probably based on the German *vampir*, which borrowed the word from early 18th century Slavic language. The Slavic terms for vampire include *upir* (Ukrainian), *upyr* (Russian), *vampir* (Serbian) and *wąpierz* (Polish). The original source of this term is uncertain. But it most probably derived from the Slavic word *pi*, which means to 'drink' or 'drain' – a good way to describe thirsty vampires who drain humans of their blood. The first written use of the word vampire in old Slavic (Upir) dates back to 6555 (1047 AD). A priest transcribed a book for the Novgorodian Prince Vladimir Yaroslavovich, and wrote *Upir Likhyi* (*Evil Vampire*). According to the *Oxford English Dictionary*, the first published appearance of the word 'vampire in English appeared in a 1745 travelogue story, *Travels of Three English Gentlemen*. Vampires were already a popular topic in German literature. After Austria gained control of Serbia and Oltenia in 1718, officials noted the local Slavic practice of exhuming bodies and "killing vampires". These reports, prepared between 1725 and 1732, received widespread publicity.

Slavic Origins

> *Of all the peoples who fought for supremacy on the vast eastern European plains, the Slavs have proved the most enduring. Despite manifold cultural and religious changes, traces of their spirit have survived in the magical stories which fill the forbidding landscape with fantastical characters. These include the vampire whose wretched specter still stalks our world today.*
> (Time-Life Books, 2003)

Where do vampires originally come from? Myths about blood-drinking vampires have Slavic origins. Even though vampires seem to be everywhere these days, vampire legends are based on the rich folklore of Eastern Europe. Vampires feature in the culture of Ukraine, Croatia, Poland, Russia, and, of course, Transylvania. These creatures of the night have frightened and terrorized their audiences for centuries ever since.

These days, vampires might roam forests around Forks in the Pacific Northwest, but they originally emerged from the deep, dark forests and the wild Carpathian Mountains of Eastern Europe. According to *Forests of the Vampir: Slavic Myth* (2003), it was somewhere beyond the Oder River.

A widely held belief in Slavic culture was that vampires were the souls of individuals who had departed the earthly realm, yet could not enter the next world. A vampire was often a tragic figure, a lost soul, just like the lonely, brooding, and melancholy Edward seems to be. Individuals of poor moral character, such as drunks, thieves, and other criminals were also prime candidates. The most common causes of vampirism in Slavic folklore included being a magician, an immoral person, suffering an unnatural or untimely death, improper burial rituals, an animal jumping or a bird flying over the corpse or an empty grave, or even being born on certain days. In South Russia, people who talked to themselves were believed to be at risk of becoming vampires. In Ukraine, human blood drinking was once very prevalent. Some Slavic vampires appeared as butterflies. This echoes a much earlier belief that the butterfly symbolizes a departed soul.

Blood Drinkers

Tales of the undead craving blood are found in nearly every culture in the world. Vampire-like spirits called the Lilu appear in Babylonian demonology and Sumerian myths have blood-sucking Akhkharu. These female demons would roam at night, hunting and killing newborn babies and pregnant women. A demon named Lilitu was adapted into Jewish demonology as Lilith. She is sometimes called the mother of all vampires. In India, tales of ghoul-like beings that inhabit corpses are found in old Sanskrit folklore. Meanwhile, the ancient Egyptian goddess Sekhmet became full of bloodlust after slaughtering humans. In Homer's Odyssey, Odysseus summons underworld creatures called *shades* by using the blood of freshly sacrificed rams. Roman tales feature the *strix*, a nocturnal bird that feeds on human flesh and blood.

An old vampire poem written by Lord Byron, called *The Giaour* (1813), celebrates the vampire as a heartless corpse that rises from "its tomb" to kill its own family. The ghastly creature returns home to "haunt thy native place, and suck the blood of all thy race" and then:

Wet with thine own best blood shall drip
Thy gnashing tooth and haggard lip;
Then stalking to thy sullen grave,
Go – and with Gouls and Afrits rave;
Till these in horror shrink away
From Spectre more accursed than they!

What this verse means is that the vampire's mouth drips with "blood", and that this graveyard stalker is more terrifying than 'specters', 'ghouls' and other frightening spirits there.

Vampire-Spotting

How do you spot a vampire? A traditional way is to note the absence of a vampire's reflection in a mirror. This is because mirrors are believed to reflect the soul – something that a vampire does not possess. The *Twilight* series, however, throws out some symbolic and behavioral clues that foreshadow Bella's future as a vampire before she becomes one. Maybe you have already spotted some signs in the books. Here are a few of the Bella vampire omens that appear in the *Twilight* world:

- Bella "hisses" for the first time in *Twilight* (p 54). She demands to the truth from Edward about the van – a cute and early vampire clue.
- Blood "smells like rust... and salt" Bella explains (*Twilight*,

p 86).

- Jacob tells Bella: "I've never seen anyone paler than you" (*New Moon*, p 179). Pale-skinned – Bella already looks a bit like a vampire.
- Jacob warms Bella's "cold fingers" (*New Moon*, p 253). Cold-skinned, like a vampire.
- Jacob looks at Bella's hand and says "This is your scar, the cold one" (*New Moon*, p 347). This points to Bella's future as a cold one.
- When Bella feels that Charlie is interfering with her social life too much Bella "stabbed her fork viciously" into her spaghetti "and "growled fiercely" through her teeth (*Eclipse*, p 12). This is cute fang-like behavior.
- There was "acid" in Bella's voice, when Jacob tells her something she didn't like (*Eclipse*, p 97).
- Bella "spits words" at Jacob in an argument (*Eclipse*, p 98).
- Bella "hissed through her teeth" (*Eclipse*, p 130) and her "voice turned acidic" (*Eclipse*, p 131).
- Alice paints Bella's toenails "bloody red" (*Eclipse*, p 131).
- Bella "*seduced*" Edward into having sex with her (*Breaking Dawn*, p 100). Vampires lure their prey sexually.
- Bella drinks blood, to save her unborn child, which is her "first vampire act" (*Breaking Dawn*, p 224). The blood not only "smells good", it "*tastes* good" too (*Breaking Dawn*, p 229).

Psychological Vampires

These days, the vampire metaphor is used to describe a certain personality style. Psychologically speaking, the vampire symbol describes a "dominant individual who refuses to adapt to the world, to change or transform himself, who wants the world and other people to submit to him, and who has enough power or strength of will to succeed" (Colin, 2000, p 515). The Swiss psychoanalyst Dr. Carl Jung identified a dark vampire-like side of human nature which he called the *shadow*. This is the weak, uncivilized, and destructive part of our inner selves. The shadow might appear in a myth or a dream as a menacing presence, a negative, evil, or frightening figure – such as a vampire figure. If we do not keep check on the shadow part of our personality, manage it poorly, let it feed greedily on positive energy, and allow it to drain others inappropriately, then our inner vampire will rise, dominating the rest of our personality.

As you can see, the vampire symbol helps to explain positive and negative psychological qualities. In the *Twilight Saga*, for example, many vampires are violent, ruthless and give in to their desire for human blood. But the Cullens don't. The Cullens don't exploit others or suck resources dry. Carlisle's mission is to avoid evil and selfish acts altogether. Carlisle's vision and will is to encourage other vampires to survive and thrive without feasting on human blood. For a young vampire like Edward, it isn't easy overriding strong urges to drink human blood, especially with the luscious lip-smacking Bella around. What the *Twilight* world is trying to show is that your race or background doesn't make you a monster. It's your choices and behavior. The Cullens may be physical vampires, but they are certainly not psychological vampires. As Bella's Internet research reveals "good vampires" from Italy do exist (*Twilight*, p 117).

The worst thing about psychological vampires is that this type of individual "cannot live simply by being himself: he needs other people to survive" (Colin, 2000, p 515). These vampirish traits certainly feature in well-known personality disorders For example, a person with antisocial personality disorder has a strong urge to exploit and violate other people, property and social norms. People with this personality disorder may:

- Repeatedly violate others.
- Deceive and manipulate others to gain personal profit or pleasure.

- Show impulsive behavior and failure to plan ahead.
- Display irritability and aggressiveness, as indicated by repeated physical fights or assaults.
- Have reckless disregard for the safety of self or others.
- Demonstrate consistent irresponsibility, such as failure to sustain work behavior or honor financial obligations.
- Have lack of remorse – being indifferent or rationalizing having hurt, mistreated, or stolen from another. (American Psychiatric Association, 2000)

In other words, people who use you, abuse you, hurt you and bleed you dry are psychological vampires.

In the *Twilight* world, the vampire James, for example, is a psychological vampire. He is cruel, selfish, and used others like Victoria and Laurent to help him track down the victims he wanted to hunt. A vampire named Maria was another psychological vampire. She used Jasper to train and manage newborn vampire armies so she could seize and control as much land as she could. Not just blood-sucking vampires, they are soul-sucking vampires.

Even though the royal Volturi *are* blood-drinking vampires, they are also psychological vampires. Why? They are ruthless. They are hungry for power. They crave dominion. They are greedy for material riches and other "treasures". This includes turning talented individuals into slaves for their guard. The Volturi clearly have overwhelming and destructive psychological urges to overpower others completely.

In the modern world, the psychological vampire figure may be on the rise. Self-centeredness, narcissism, addictive behaviors, a lack of empathy for others, a fixation to achieve material wealth, capitalism, racism, terrorism, and driving individuals to consume and devour everything in their way in order to be super powerful. If you suspect or relate to any of these ideas, then you are already in tune to the psychological vampire. As you can see, the dark and ancient vampire symbol haunts the modern world. As Simon Bacon (2011) explains:

> *Myths of vampires and the undead are as old as civilization itself, wherever humans gather these 'dark reflections' are sure to follow. Whether as hungry spirits, avenging furies or as the disgruntled dearly departed, they have been used to signify the monstrous other and the consequences of social transgression.*

As long as humans exist, the vampire metaphor will live on. However, as the environmental, moral, humane and spiritual Cullens from the *Twilight* world suggest, it doesn't necessarily have to be so dark.

Virginity

Virginity, virtue and abstaining from sex before marriage is a big prominent theme in the *Twilight Saga*. Despite their strong adolescent desires, Bella and Edward do not engage in premarital sex. Rather, they remain virgins until their wedding night. While such behavior may reflect moral standards, some kind of interpersonal respect, or the ability to control sexual and peer pressures, the virginal states of two romantically entwined characters can also symbolize other things. For example, both Bella and Edward have good hearts, positive intentions, and pure spirits. The virginity of Bella and Edward symbolizes the idea that their minds, hearts and souls have not yet been corrupted by evil forces, even though the Volturi vampires want to.

Volterra

Volterra is a real town in Tuscany, Italy. It is a walled city – an ancient protective fortress inside and out. This city has a history going back to the Neolithic age. It became a municipality in the

Roman Age. The city was a bishop's residence in the fifth century and popes established power there in the twelfth century. When this religious empire declined, the Florentines seized Volterra. In 1530, the Florentine Republic collapsed and Volterra fell under the control of the Medici family and then followed the history of the Grand Duchy of Tuscany. The Medici family were a very rich and powerful clan. Their patronage financed the Renaissance era and some family members were popes. It is believed that the Volturi vampires were fashioned off the Medici family who ruled Volterra.

Stephenie Meyer has always planned for the Volturi to live in a fictional city with a clock tower in Tuscany. After scanning a map of Italy, she discovered Volterra and learned that the city had a clock tower like the one she had described in her book. So Ms. Meyer based the *Twilight* series on this city. The Volterra scenes in the film *New Moon* were filmed in a place called Montepulciano, Italy.

In the *Twilight* series, the Volturi vampires live in Volterra and they rarely leave their city. The beautiful buildings are made of light brown stone and Volterra is considered the safest place in the world from vampire attacks because the Volturi do not permit any vampires to hunt humans in their home town. When Bella visits Volterra in *New Moon*, the city is celebrating Saint Marcus Day, when Saint Marcus is believed to have driven away all vampires from the area. As a city that features ancient tradition, authoritative rule, hard stone buildings, strength and power, the symbolism of Volterra certainly embraces the Volturi's ancient, hard, and imperial approach to life.

Volturi

Hades

In the *Twilight Saga*, the Volturi vampires live underneath a city in Italy. As Alice explains, the Volturi have been around for centuries. These vampires are over three thousand years old. As rulers of the vampire race, the Volturi enforce laws, rules, and justice, and they punish any transgressors. In particular, they zealously guard the secret that vampires exist at all. The word "Volturi" is unique to the *Twilight* world. It could be just a phonetic variation of the "Volterra", but it also sounds a bit like 'vulture'. After all, the Volturi are a bit like vultures, with their swooping black cloaks, flesh-eating lifestyle, and constant hunger for carrion. In line with classic myth, the Volturi underworld has an uncanny resemblance to other deathly underworlds in myth.

Cerberus

The three Volturi rulers resemble a terrifying supernatural monster from Greek myth that dwells in Hades – a three-headed beast called Cerberus. In the *Twilight* world, it's already apparent that "there were three of them originally, Aro, Caius, and Marcus" (*New Moon*, p 428). Just like their triple guard (Jane, Alec, Demetri), the ruling trio can also symbolize the three-headed Cerberus, the monstrous mythical hound that guards the gateway to the world of the dead. Storyteller Tony Allan describes what happened when the hero Heracles (Hercules) approached this frightening howler from hell:

> *The sight of the monstrous creature, its three heads maned with serpents, would have deterred a lesser man, but Heracles gripped it… relying on his impenetrable lionskin to protect him from its gnashing jaws… The foam that slavered from its mouth congealed to form the plant known as deadly nightshade.*

The way that Volturi vampires operate corresponds with the role of Cerberus too. Just as the three Volturi rulers determine who enters and exits their underworld, Cerberus makes sure that no one escapes the kingdom of the dead ruled by Hades, except those who are granted passage. Just as Heracles grabbed and tamed the three-headed hound, without killing it, Bella tamed and amused the three Volturi leaders in *New Moon*. They did not hurt her with the deadly venom that would have slavered from their glistening fangs. Instead, they set Bella and her friends free.

Furies

With regards to Greek myth, the Volturi's top three guards (Jane, Alex, Demetri) may have been inspired by the three Furies. The Furies are divine entities from Greek myth who personify vengeance. They relate to the aspect of the triple goddess as a lawmaker and one who punishes. The names of these Furies are:

- Alecto (unceasing)
- Megaera (grudging)
- Tisiphone (the avenger)

The heads of the Furies are crowned with serpents and their eyes are said to drip blood. Since the Volturi vampires have snake-like features and relish in blood-thirsty activities, both the Volturi and the Furies share the same horrific image. The name Alecto (the unceasing Fury) has a name that sounds similar to Alex, the Volturi guard whose cruel ability is to numb the senses unceasingly. Also, the role of the Volturi guards is to track down perpetrators of vampire law to administer justice and vengeance, just as the Furies are said to do.

It is possible that other threesomes in the *Twilight Saga* are linked to the three Furies and their quest for vengeance. This includes the tracker's gang (James, Victoria, Laurent). When James hunts down Bella as his prey, and is killed by the Cullens, the begrudged Laurent and especially Victoria hunt Bella down relentlessly in an act of blood-boiling vengeance. The three Denali sisters (Kate, Tanya, and Irina) seem reminiscent of the Furies too. Their mother was killed by the Volturi, executed for creating an immortal vampire child. One of the sisters, Irina, thinks that Bella has created an immortal vampire child too. She informs the Volturi immediately. Unfortunately, Irina's action was fuelled by vengeance and blinded by bitterness because the werewolves killed her partner Laurent earlier to save Bella. Irina pays the ultimate price for her thoughtless, resentful, and furious mistake – her life.

Hydra

Another feature of the Volturi empire is that the three rulers (Aro, Marcus, and Caius) are protected by *nine* guards altogether. This feature is symbolically intriguing because it points to yet another terrible monster from Greek myth. As explained in *New Moon*, the Volturi have a powerful guard, "nine members" that are permanent (p 429). This nine-pronged weapon is somewhat reminiscent of a snake-like monster in Greek myth called a *hydra*, a nine-headed mythical creature. Whenever someone fighting a hydra cut one of the serpent's heads off, two heads would grow in that place.

As a symbol, the hydra is supposed to symbolize personal challenges in life, some of which can be very difficult to overcome and which require patience, learning, strategy and courage. The hydra also has a powerful psychological message. Negative thoughts can increase, intensify, multiply and grow if we don't deal with them effectively or if we only try to eliminate them superficially. If you want to overthrow a bunch of evil vampires, for example, such a task is not easy. It may require much thought, research, discussion, skill building, practice, and suitable alliances or acquiring the right resources.

W

Water

Water Means Life

Water is a powerful natural element and the original source of life on earth. It can express itself in many different forms. It can appear in liquid, solid or gas states – as pools, streams, mist, spray, the ocean, rain, ice, snow and dew. Since water is the source of life, by drinking or immersing ourselves in it, we "wash and purify ourselves. Natural spring waters and thermal waters are renowned for their therapeutic effects and some are even believed to have magical properties" (Colin, 2000, p 530). Since ancient times, the sudden appearance of a spring has always been considered a divine gift. A dried up river or stream, however, is considered to be a curse. Rain makes the earth lush and fertile. If rain does not fall and rivers do not flow, the earth becomes dry and barren. As such, water gives life. According to the *Dictionary of Symbols, Myths and Legends* water mainly symbolizes:

- Wisdom
- Purification
- Fertilization
- Regeneration
- Everlasting love
- Eternity
- Spiritual life
- The source of all life

As the *Twilight Saga* shows – from pool to sea to river to rain – the ways of water flow on wisely, wildly and in many wonderful ways.

Water Means Emotion

Water is also a symbol for emotion. Feelings can trickle as gently as a calm stream or be released in a sudden flood of tears. The *Dictionary of Symbols, Myths and Legends* says that "water" is an "emotional and intuitive" force into which one "plunges to be born or reborn" in some personal way. In the *Twilight* books, water symbolizes Bella's feelings in a number of important scenes. The link between water and emotion is a recurring theme in the *Twilight* world. In a depressing adventure, for example, Bella literally drowns in despair after jumping off the cliffs as she sinks deeper and deeper in the cold water in *New Moon* (pp 83–84). When Bella thinks deeply about Edward leaving her, "the waves of pain that had only lapped at me before now reared high and washed my head, pulling me under. I did not resurface" (*New Moon*, p 84). Bella stayed under water so to speak, drowning in despair during October, November, December, and January (*New Moon*, pp 85–92).

Another *Twilight* scene that used water to symbolize life and emotion is the moment before Edward tries to kill himself at midday in *New Moon*. Just when the clock tower in the Volterra city plaza is about to chime noon, and Bella thinks she has no hope reaching Edward to save him from suicide, she encounters water. Bella notices a "wide, square fountain set into the center of the plaza… I flung my leg over the edge and ran through the knee-deep water. It sprayed in the sun, the wind was glacial" (*New Moon*, p 449). Water fountains symbolize life. And becoming immersed knee-keep in this fountain enabled Bella to save Edward, to save the love of her life. This, in turn, revived her dead emotional life.

Sea

The sea is an all-powerful life force. All life originated from the sea. The sea not only creates life (like a womb) but it also absorbs and recycles life. The sea teems with life as a "constantly moving, endlessly changing world in a continued process of formation" (Colin, 2000, p 447). A wide, open sea suggests that a sea of endless possibilities, opportunities open to all, and a wide range of destinies to experience. The ocean is a place of chaos too, cyclones and whirlpools, where the wild things are. Imagine a deep idea taking shape in the watery depths of your mind, waiting to surface and float away, carried off by your stream of consciousness and waves of emotion, that can chop and change any time just like waves on the windy sea. As a symbol, the sea suggests that "infinite richness... resides within us. We can bathe in it to revive ourselves, but we may also find ourselves out of our depth or in danger of drowning" (Colin, 2000). In the *Twilight Saga,* the sea is used to reflect feelings and emotions from calm contemplation to stormy turmoil to waves of joy.

Drowning in Despair

In an early scene in *New Moon,* Bella is in deep thought as she watches the deep, fathomless sea. The sea was "dark gray under the clouds. We were above the shore, on top of the cliffs that bordered the beach here, and the view seemed to stretch on forever" (*New Moon,* p 170). Just as the sea view stretches forever, so do Bella's feelings for her missing Edward, it seems. The moment Bella plunged into the sea, her deepest feelings were refreshed, and she realized that she really does love Edward after all. As Bella explains: "I plunged deeper into the freezing black water" (*New Moon,* p 359). This sea scene symbolizes Bella immersing herself in her emotions, her deep love for Edward. She embraces her vampire true love, and he embraces her back in the form of an image floating in the black icy sea. Thus the dark sea dive has dislodged a beautiful and "flawless" vision of Edward's "face" from the dark depths of Bella's mind and heart (*New Moon,* p 361).

When Bella dives off a cliff at La Push Beach, she happens to be at one of her lowest emotional ebbs ever. Just before Bella makes her cliff jump into the big black ocean, the rain drenches her before she hits the surface. This reinforces the idea that Bella is drowning in despair. Drowning in the storm-tossed waves symbolizes Bella drowning in a deep depression. Bella sinks deeper and deeper into the dark cold water, deeper and deeper into her own cold emotional world. Her final thought is, "Goodbye, I love you." The words she didn't speak to Edward in the forest, the words she truly means deep down in her heart. Sinking down further and "drowning" surely symbolizes Bella "drowning" in her sadness without Edward. As Bella sinks "deeper into the dark" sea, she also gets in touch with her deepest feelings. When Bella starts to drown, she decides that she loves Edward so much that she would rather die without him. In other words, he is what she really, really wants. "I saw him, and I had no will to fight. It was so clear... In the icy cold, I was content. I'd forgotten what real happiness felt like" (*New Moon*, p 361). Edward is Bella's deepest desire.

Waves of Joy

Another significant sea scene suggests a totally different mood. This time the ocean is warm and soothing, a relaxing spa glittering in the moonlight. The visit to Isle Esme reflects the warm love between Bella and Edward on their wedding night, sparkling with excitement. The first time Bella and Edward have a sexual experience occurs in the water, at midnight, under a full white moon. "It was very warm, like bath water. I stepped in... I waded through the weightless current till I was at his side, and then I placed my hand lightly over his cool hand lying in the water" (*Breaking Dawn*, p 77). The sea is a creative and fertile force. In another important scene at the end of the *Twilight Saga*, Bella felt a "tidal wave of happiness" at the very end of the *Twilight* series (*Breaking Dawn*, p 697).

Beaches

The symbolism and power of the water is also suggested in three *Twilight Saga* beaches. The first beach to appear is "First Beach" – the wildest and darkest one. The second beach occurs on Isle Esme, a warm tropical paradise. The third beach is the smallest and calmest of all. Each beach symbolizes Bella's emotional highs and lows, shifts and flows.

First Beach

First Beach at La Push is an awesome slim crescent that stretches out for a mile. The dark steel-gray water, capped with white, swells to and fro along a rocky gray shore. Cliffs topped with tall spiky firs tower over the water. The shore is fringed with piles of large driftwood trees, bleached white. A brisk sea wind ensures that "clouds still circled the sky, threatening to invade at any moment" (*Twilight*, p 99). As a wild, windy and breathtaking place, this beach is a fitting setting for Bella to hear Jacob's scary story about the cold ones. She stares at the "rough surf", a symbolic gesture to the mighty sea and her own unsettled emotions (*Twilight*, p 109).

Just as the meadow is Bella and Edward's sacred place, this beach belongs to Bella and Jacob. It is a source of dark secrets and scary stories. It is at this beach that Bella's discovers the existence of the "cold ones" and Jacob's descent from "wolves". It is where other myths and legends are revealed, such as imprinting. It is where Bella almost drowns in the sea, and where Jacob resuscitates her with his breath – the kiss of life. A mystical place where secrets are unveiled – all the legends become reality at First Beach. It is here that Bella reveals her true love for Edward, just before she leaps off the cliff. First Beach is not only desolate, but turbulent – with its eerie grey mood, sweeping tides, volatile storms, remote location, gigantic trees and white driftwood piles. A lonely place, First Beach surely reflects the grand and sweeping emotions of every individual lost, confused or beached up somewhere in life.

The *Twilight* world tends to suggest that First Beach loses its magic without Jacob. Once, when Jacob was sleeping, Bella visited the beach, had a panic attack and he found her curled up and crying on the ground. Another time when Jacob was out hunting Victoria, Bella jumped off the cliff at the beach. When Jacob returns to the beach, he saves Bella by resuscitates her. First Beach seems to serve multiple purposes – as a place of magic, danger and refuge. Help from a supernatural escort like Jacob brings out the beach magic.

Island Beach

The sea at Bella and Edward's honeymoon beach looks healing. The waves glistened in the moonlight, and the "gentle swells" were "warm, like bath water" (*Breaking Dawn*, p 77). On the shore of Isle Esme, Edward pulls Bella "gently into deeper water" (*Breaking Dawn*, p 78). At this point, they both immerse themselves in their soothing love and their deep feelings for each other too, coming emotionally alive in each other's arms in the sea. Bella tells Edward: "We belong together" and its "forever" he replies (*Breaking Dawn*, p 78). The water in that scene is bright under a full moon – warm, calm and comfortable. In this scene, the sea surely symbolizes a womb and a source of life. It is likely Nessie was conceived in the ocean on the night of Bella and Edward's honeymoon, which gives her sea serpent nickname "Nessie" extra symbolic significance.

Cottage Beach

In *Breaking Dawn,* when Bella finally achieves what her heart desires (Edward and becoming a vampire) she also achieves deep emotional peace. An important symbolic indication of her newly found emotional contentment is the pool in the cottage garden. It was a "small round pond, smooth as a mirror and edged with shiny stones. A tiny, calm ocean for us" (*Breaking Dawn,* p 445).

Just as the little pool is still and unruffled, so is Bella's emotional state. Finally, she is happy and relaxed. The pond is a body of water (symbolizes emotions), a mirror (symbolizes inner self-reflection), *and* a circle (symbolizes harmony/eternity) that is surrounded by shiny stones (symbolizes security). Peaceful emotional symbolism, for sure.

Tidal Pool

An important scene in *Twilight* which shows how water symbolizes Bella's feelings and how her emotions steadily grow is the first time she visits the beach. At the edge of the forest at La Push Beach, Bella finds "shallow pools that never completely drained" and were "teeming with life" (*Twilight*, p 101). Bella was "spellbound by the natural aquarium" in the ponds below, as she noticed sea anemones, crabs, starfish, eels, and more (*Twilight*, p 101). Exploring the tidal pools, the call of the sea surely symbolizes Bella listening to her own underlying emotional forces, a secret world full of flowing feelings that teems with psychological life. As a maturing adolescent, Bella's romantic feelings are truly awakening.

For the first time, Bella examines these ocean pools (her emotions, that is) closely and carefully. That is why she can see sea-creatures stirring there. Not only does Bella discover that she has always had powerful feelings inside (just like an eternal spring, the pools here "never drain"), she also observes that these pools (her emotions) are "full of life". It is here, in this scene, that Bella "wonders" about Edward and admits she is "absorbed" by him (*Twilight*, p 101). This beach visit symbolizes the fact that Bella is exploring deep unconscious forces, a secret emotional world teeming with life, and that her feelings for Edward are coming to life and growing stronger. What do you think?River

The river is yet another water way that is both an important symbol of life and an important feature of the *Twilight* world. The first river to appear in the *Twilight Saga* is when Bella travels through the forest on her way to La Push. Driving along the road, Bella notices "the wide Quillayute River snaking beneath it twice" (*Twilight*, p 99). On another occasion, when Bella first visits the Cullen house, she could "hear the river close by" (*Twilight*, p 281). So, a river leads Bella to the spiritual world of the Quileutes, and then to the supernatural Cullen family. This idea is consistent with traditional meanings of rivers.

Since rivers are central to the survival of plants, animals and people, rivers have always been regarded as divine and sacred forces. Many civilizations were founded and flourished on riverbanks like the Nile in Egypt, the Yellow River in China, and the Ganges in India. With their power to fertilize or flood the land, rivers were once seen as powerful gods in whose vicinity all sorts of water divinities, spirits and sprites lived. According to symbol experts, "following the course of the river as it flows to the sea symbolizes the path of life that leads from birth to death" (Colin, 2000, p 432). The water that flows in a river also evokes the idea that certain processes follow a natural, normal or obvious course that flows in the right direction. Ancient and logical wisdom, for example, tells us not to swim against the current, and to go with the flow of things. As a character, Bella demonstrates an ability to flow with the current, she is intuitive and in tune with her world. On the other hand, Bella has also resisted the river of life. She chose to get romantically involved with a vampire, which is deemed an unnatural course of action.

Rain

See *Rain*.

Werewolf

Even a man who is pure in heart
And says his prayers by night
May become a wolf when the wolfbane blooms
And the autumn moon is bright.

This rhyme, which villagers recite whenever the topic of werewolves comes up, comes from a movie called The *Wolf Man* (1941). This American horror classic, created by Curt Siodmak and George Waggner, was remade in 2010.

As a symbol, the werewolf is the most sinister and terrifying beast that has ever existed. The idea that humans can shape-shift into wolves, known as lycanthropy, is ancient. A well-known belief is that people turn into werewolves at the appearance of a full moon. What's more, this change is not voluntary. True werewolves have no reflection in a mirror, just like vampires, nor do they cast shadows on the ground.

In the *Twilight Saga*, the Quileute guys (and one girl) who can change into wolves are called werewolves at first. What they really are, everyone learns much later in the story, are spiritual shape-shifters. They can change their form at will and this magic power is triggered whenever people need protection from the cold ones – vampires. Nevertheless, *Twilight*-style wolves are supernatural creatures. This makes them fierce and powerful beings. No wonder the *Twilight Saga* revels in describing their wolvish features. In *New Moon*, where Jacob and other Quileute Indians rise to wolf-like power:

- Jacob "barked out a bitter laugh" (p 270).
- Jacob "growled, still pacing" (305).
- Bella noticed Jacob's "mouth twisting into a snarl" (p 306).
- "Something like a growl… rumbled in Jacob's chest" (p 315).

- The wolves protect people from vampires (p 309).
- Quileute werewolves can read each other's mind and communicate telepathically (p 317).
- "Paul punched Jacob on the shoulder and Jacob went for a kidney jab in return" (p 334). Wolf play!

A unique feature of *Twilight Saga* werewolves is that vampires like Alice, who can foresee the future, cannot see the future of the Quileute werewolves in her mind. Maybe the wolves have a natural or magical defense. Another theory is that the future of werewolves is too unpredictable because they shape-shift rapidly in response to sudden changes in the environment (*Eclipse*, p 56). The Quileute werewolves do not age when vampires are around. They patrol the land as wolves, phasing back and forth, and listening to each other's thoughts (*Eclipse*, p 112).

Today, the biggest symbolic significance of the werewolf is that it alludes to the darkest and wildest parts of ourselves, as well as the most emotionally disturbed individuals among us. Beware of howls and growls when stress is at its peak and emotions are overloaded (the moon is full). Maybe a dreadful feeling is about to descend on you, such as an anxiety attack, or your darkest fear is about to flare up. Or maybe, you sense the threatening behavior of another person about to ambush you. The werewolf is a headstrong and hungry predator, literally or figuratively, and it may be lurking out there for a chance to commit a string of bestial attacks. Imagine how it would feel to be alone and hunted by a pack of thugs in a small town at night, just as Bella was in *New Moon* before Edward saved her. While the werewolf metaphor is most popular in fiction books and horror films, one cannot help but wonder what wolf-like lurk in the shadows of the real world.

White

> His eyes looked silver in his ice-colored face... I raised my free hand... and placed it over his heart. White on white, we matched, for once.
> (*Breaking Dawn*, p 78)

This honeymoon scene is the whitest adventure in the entire *Twilight Saga*. Standing in the water in the bright moonlight next to Edward, everything looks white on Isle Esme – the moon, the sand, eyes, skin, and the moonlight glitter on the sea. Everything is cleansed, washed, bleached, and purified by the light of the full bright moon.

The color white is an important one throughout the entire *Twilight* series. At first *Twilight* highlights Edward's white appearance – his "chalky pale" complexion (p 16) and that "smooth white skin" (p 224), making him look like a white marble figure. *Eclipse* features a snowscape that was very "bright" with white snowflakes (*Eclipse*, pp 449, 458). But *Breaking Dawn* has the whitest world of all. There's Bella's white wedding dress, the white wedding, white flowers and white "wedding decorations" everywhere (pp 23, 44). There's Bella and Edward's honeymoon scene bathed in "white light" on "the snowy sand", which the bright moonlight whitens even more (p 78). There's also the Volturi war that takes place on a clean and fresh white snowscape. "Edward and I held hands as we stared across the glittering white field" (*Breaking Dawn*, p 627). Not even the evil Volturi vampires, an army that looks like a dark fan, can corrupt Bella and Edward's pure and powerful white love for each other. It is as if nature is preparing Bella for these adventures – lightening and brightening, purifying and cleansing, and bathing and washing Bella's spirit, but blinding and bleaching her energy when times are really tough.

The white *Twilight* scenes match the symbolic meanings of

white: peace, purity, perfection, innocence, insight, illumination, incorruptibility, death and rebirth, a start or an ending. White is colorless (the absence of pigment) and yet is it all the colors of light summed together. So it can mean nothing or everything, a blank canvas with complete potential to be creative or a whole and fulfilled spiritual state. The *albedo* or white phase in alchemy is a purifying stage. An alchemist becomes pure by relinquishing earthly desires or selfish behaviors in favor of following a light and bright spiritual path. In the *Twilight* books, Bella's true love for Edward and her aspirations to become immortal intensify and purify over time, which reflects her whitening just as alchemy suggests. Bella gives up her desire to be human as her choice to become immortal becomes whiter and brighter, dearer and clearer, as pure and pristine as a blanket of fresh fallen snow.

Wind

The wind blows through the *Twilight* world in all kinds of adventures. It can appear from a cool breeze to a wild tempest to a bitter blizzard on a mountaintop. But the wind is also an important symbol that expresses various moods and meanings.

Winds of Fate

A traditional meaning of wind is that it stands for fate. When a really strong wind blows, you are at its mercy. "The raging wind scours the land in a storm, sweeping aside everything in its path, carrying water, fire and earth along with it, because no element can withstand the fury of the wind" (Colin, 2000, p 538). In ancient times, people observed just how sudden, strong, and unpredictable the wind could be. To survive, they had to rely on certain warning signs in the weather, to anticipate, predict and deal with the wind. Wind patterns and directions regarding imminent cyclones, hurricanes or tornadoes were especially significant. If you know 'which way the wind blows', then you know which is the best direction to travel in – to maximize speed, survival and success. You can function to optimum capacity in life, much like the sails of a boat that catch the wind to achieve maximum effect. A popular expression 'the winds of change' means new and good influences on the way. The power of the wind is supposed to release magical energy. Windy weather can "clear stagnation in your life, blow you in a new direction or carry you forward to success" (Eason, 2002, p 16).

Have you noticed that the wind picks up whenever something wicked approaches Forks? The windiest weather in the *Twilight* saga occurs as a snowstorm in *Eclipse* (check out *Storms*, too). A strong and freezing blizzard of ice and snow wreaked havoc on a mountaintop, just before a newborn army of vampires arrived in Forks. This windy adventure is an excellent example of how wind helps to symbolize the wild, brutal and blood-thirsty vampire characters who plan to destroy and kill everyone in the forest. This enhances the volatile mood of the adventure.

Spirit Forces

The wind is also a symbol for spiritual and supernatural forces. Moaning through trees, whistling through rocks, or maybe just whispering in the leaves, the wind is said to carry the voices of spirits and the dead. "When the wind blows in mountains or valleys, deep in the desert or in the midst of the ocean, its voices can be enchanting or frightening, depending on the circumstances" (Colin, 2000, pp 538–539). In Greek myth, the famous sailor Odysseus heard the sweet and haunting song of the sirens carried on the sea winds. Similarly, Edward caught Bella's sweet and seductive fragrance carried on a breeze in biology class. This made Edward very tense and stiff as he made a big effort to resist her blood (*Twilight*, pp 20–21).

In the *Twilight* world meadow, the wind is mellow. The spiritual forces of nature, symbolized by a light breeze, dresses

Bella and Edward up in her love. Bella notices that "the wind was gentle, it tangled my hair and ruffled the grass that swayed around his motionless form" (*Twilight*, p 229). In a later adventure, after some werewolves chase Laurent away, Bella feels a "cold breeze" blowing through the meadow, "swaying the grass like something was moving through it" (*New Moon*, p 245). Edward's cool spiritual presence, or maybe Quileute magic. This *Twilight* scene helps to show that the wind can be cooling and calming.

Window

A window symbolizes an entrance, opening, outlet and a mode of passage. Windows are sacred portals – a way into another world. Throughout time, windows have been focal architectural features of shrines and temples and cathedrals. It's no wonder enigmatic and uplifting expressions such as "window of opportunity" have evolved. Some of the most critical scenes in fairy tales and famous stories have involved windows. Consider the cursed prisoner and princess *Rapunzel* who throws down her long, golden hair through a tower window to a young man below. In *Harry Potter and the Chamber of Secrets*, Harry and his owl, locked in an upstairs bedroom, escape through a window – in a flying blue car! Perhaps the most romantic window scene ever is Shakespeare's *Romeo and Juliet*, which the *Twilight Saga* story follows. Standing on a balcony outside her window, Juliet calls out the famous lines: "*Romeo, Romeo, Where for art thou, Romeo*?" It makes symbolic and literary sense that Edward and Jacob (romantic suitors) visit Bella through her window at night.

It is symbolically spot on that Edward (a supernatural creature) enters Bella's private human world through her open bedroom window. In a Shakespeare-like window scene, Bella sprints over "to the window" on tiptoes in a Juliet-like way: "I threw it open and leaned into the night. My eyes scanned the darkness" (*Twilight*, p 259). This suggests that Bella's mind and heart is wide open to her love interest Edward. In a much later adventure, Bella confirms her strong feelings for Edward with window-talk. In *Eclipse,* Edward tells Bella to: "Shut your window if you want me to stay away tonight," but she leaves it wide open for him (p 56).

In contrast, the window symbolism supports the theory that Bella's feelings are not the same for Jacob. When Jacob visits Bella, her bedroom window is closed. He must ask her to "open the window" (*New Moon,* p 279). It is symbolically significant that the window is left wide open for Edward to enter, but not Jacob. Edward is Bella's true love. A perceptive *Twilight* fan describes windows in the *Twilight* world like this: "Not only does it stand for her open mindedness, the Open Window is also a wonderful barometer to read Bella's emotions, it is an extension of her body language (TwilightMOMS post, JQ48, August 11, 2011).

Perhaps the most symbolically significant window scene in the *Twilight* world appears in *Breaking Dawn*. It is fitting that Bella launches into supernatural life through an upper story window of a vampire house. Bella makes her first inaugural leap as a vampire from the upstairs window of the Cullen mansion: "Clenching my teeth as I concentrated, I tried to copy his casual step into empty air. Ha! The ground seemed to move toward me so slowly that it was nothing at all to place my feet" (*Breaking Dawn,* p 377). Bella's deep desire is fulfilled. She is finally the vampire she has always wanted to be. How appropriate, theatrical and symbolic!

Bella's window is also a good metaphor for Bella's open personality and receptive approach to life. While some readers may view Bella as a closed or reserved character, the "open window" in Bella's bedroom symbolizes Bella's open-mindedness and open-heartedness.It is Bella's underlying openness (symbolized by the open window) that:

- Enables Bella to love a vampire that many others would shun.
- Helps Bella to see Edward's goodness.
- Instills faith that good vampires have souls.
- Gets two traditional enemies collaborating together (werewolves and vampires).
- Gives her an open outlook on life.

The open window of Bella's bedroom explains Bella's ability to uncover knowledge and the truth (she is open-minded) and her ability to love vampires and werewolves despite the negative prejudices and walls/barriers against them (she is open-hearted).

Once the Cullens leave Forks, the windows of their house suggest a terrible emptiness. "Though nothing had changed on the outside, the emptiness screamed from the blank windows. It was creepy" (*New Moon*, p 161). The glass windows (eyes/soul of the house) have lost their luster and their life.

The best way to interpret windows in the *Twilight Saga* is to have an open view about it, much like an open window. As one bright fan puts it: "The role of the window portal is huge in *Twilight*" (TwilightMOMS post, Lauralee, Aug 9, 2011).

Wood

> The miniature wolf was utterly realistic. It was even carved out of some red-brown wood.
> (*Eclipse*, p 332)

Wood is a valuable and useful material. It is also the flesh of a tree, which many cultures believe has a spirit (see *Tree*). Powerful magicians, sorcerers and witches made their wands and divining rods from wood. Branches and bark were used to make amulets too. Meanwhile, oak, yew, mountain ash, hazel, birch, apple and pine were often used in magic rituals, spell casting, and divinity by ancient Celts (Colin, 2000).

The fact that Jacob makes a hand-crafted ornament from wood for Bella is surely a sign that he is in tune with the supernatural power of nature and his magical heritage, even if he does not yet fully realize it.

Y

Year

A year suggests a circle. It takes one year for the earth to complete its circular orbit around the sun. As such, annual days and seasons such as spring, winter, midsummer night, and Halloween celebrated the power of nature, hidden in the cycle of seasons and the cosmic circles of the planets.

Since it takes a year for the earth to make a complete revolution around the sun, ancient astrologers measured and established time based on this cycle. While days, nights and months were calculated by observing the phases of the moon, the yearly cycle is linked to the movements of the sun. In the old days, the measurement of time was guided by nature. For example, the new year was celebrated at the time of the spring equinox, on March 21. This day of triumph for the sun marked the moment when the days started to grow longer and brighter. In fact, the word 'year' is derived from the Polish *jar,* which means 'springtime'. Later, when Christian culture became more established, the New Year, anniversaries, and yearly calendars became associated with people, Jesus Christ, the triumph of human life on earth, and spiritual light over darkness. The New Year became person-centered, losing its contact with nature.

It is worth noting the year as a symbol in the *Twilight Saga.* After all, the *Twilight* world celebrates birthdays, Christmas, marriage anniversaries, school calendar events, annual holidays, and the number of years (or centuries) one has been a vampire. An anniversary is a time of celebration or reflection and marks the circle of the year. The birthday is the most well-known example of an anniversary. Bella's human birthday is especially important and acknowledged in the *Twilight Saga.*

Yellow

Yellow is the brightest and most dazzling of all three primary colors. As a symbol, yellow means many good things: the sun, power, authority, intellect, intuition, goodness, light, life, truth, and immortality. Yellow is a positive color that is closely linked to the sun. Just as the sun shines clearly and brightly, yellow is a solar color that symbolizes truth, honesty, and the good forces of light. It can also suggest betrayal in that sometimes people use their sunny strengths or a sunny cover to perform dark or evil deeds. As such, yellow has positive and negative meanings. It can be a sign of triumph and happiness or deceit and treachery. Yellow is often linked to gold, a precious and valuable metal. To decode the meaning of yellow in a dream or some other important scene, it is essential to consider how and where yellow appears. Is yellow the color of an object, background, a beautiful flower, a strong animal or some dry, barren landscape?

In the *Twilight Saga*, yellow has positive and negative meanings. For example, Bella once noticed "the bright yellow light of a sunny day" in Forks (*Twilight*, p 122). In this scene, yellow suggests happy feelings and the good power of the sun. The meadow that Bella and Edward share is also a positive and powerful yellow. As Bella describes it, the edge of the meadow was a "pool of light" that glowed "yellow" (*Twilight*, p 226), and it included "yellow" wildflowers bathed in "buttery sunshine" (*Twilight*, p 227). On the Quileute reservation, Emily's house had "bright yellow and orange marigolds" in a window box and the crockery in her bright white kitchen was "yellow" (*New Moon*, p 331). Here, the yellow color helps to promote a cheerful atmosphere. At the end of *Eclipse*, Alice finally receives the gift she always wanted – a "shiny canary yellow Porsche" *Eclipse*, p 130). Bella's graduation outfit is also "yellow" and "yellow hats rained down" at the end of the school ceremony (*Eclipse*, p 315). Yellow boosts happy and festive feelings at the end of the school year.

The most spectacular yellow adventure in the *Twilight Saga* is when Alice steals a "bright yellow Porsche" in *New Moon* (p 439). Not only does this adventure reflect Alice's sense of optimism and cheerful nature, it also embraces yellow's betrayal meanings. Alice's new hot wheels is an act of grand theft auto, after all. Using yellow to symbolize Alice's happy personality also works in a later betrayal adventure in *Breaking Dawn*. At first, the Cullen family thinks that Alice has betrayed them in a Judas-like way. Judas, who betrayed Jesus Christ, wore yellow robes that subsequently charge this color with treachery to this day. Just before the Volturi war, the Cullen family believes Alice has betrayed them when she disappears with Jasper and leaves her family a note: "We're so sorry that we have to leave you this way, with no goodbyes or explanations. It's the only way for us" (*Breaking Dawn*, p 517). Nevertheless, Alice's golden sincerity shines through like a yellow sun. She returns from her quest with a bright surprise that prevents an all-out supernatural war.

You

The *Twilight Saga* books and films are a hit because of *you*.

Whether you are a serious book detective, a carefree movie buff, or maybe a bit of both, you, the fan, have launched Stephenie Meyer's books to the stars. Not only has your interest and faithful fandom made the *Twilight* series hot, hot, hot, some of you are clever and attentive literature detectives already. Your observations regarding *Twilight, New Moon, Eclipse* and *Breaking Dawn* have helped to uncover the story's true artistic depths, breadth and heights. Informative and insightful comments and reviews lurk on *Twilight Saga* websites such as *Bella and Edward*, the *Twilight Lexicon* and of course, the family-friendly adult network *TwilightMOMS*.

Not only have *you* revealed interesting motifs, meanings and messages hidden in the *Twilight* books, your love of these books says a lot about you as a person. If you have fallen in love with the *Twilight Saga* books and movies, then here are just some of the incredible things that you suggest about yourself. You show:

- A bright and imaginative mind because you like books and show an interest in fantasy fiction.
- A sensitive nature and feelings for others. Bella's life has not been so easy. Edward has had a lonely life too.
- Courage in the face of many critics who slam the *Twilight* books as teen trash, condemning fans who love *Twilight*.
- A creative streak. Some of you write your own stories, share your own fan fiction on the net, paint beautiful art and fan art, design awesome websites, network with others, and you even raise money for charity.
- A desire to link with people all over the world. Some of you send cards and gifts to your fellow fans. Or else, your gift has been a joke or warm message posted on the net, Facebook or in an email.
- Somewhere in your world, you make shiny choices, you dazzle others, and your spirit sparkles.

You are not just a fan of *Twilight* culture, you are an amazing part of it.

Z

Zombie

In the *Twilight Saga,* Bella and her school friend Jessica go to Port Angeles to see a movie called *Dead End*. This scary movie is about zombies and shows "gruesome zombie attacks and endless screaming" (*New Moon,* p 106). A zombie is a kind of monster. According to one definition, a zombie is an animated corpse brought back to life by mystical means such as witchcraft. It is also a term used to describe a person who looks hypnotized and lacks self-awareness, yet that person still walks around and gets around in their environment. Creepy! Zombie folklore became popular in the late 19th century, especially in North America and Europe. In modern times, the term 'zombie' described an undead race of walking corpses in horror fiction. Famous zombie adventures include the 1929 novel *The Magic Island* by William Seabrook, a 1932 horror film called *White Zombie* starring Béla Lugosi, and the 1968 film *Night of the Living Dead*. Zombies have appeared in books, films and on television ever since.

Zombie Action
Lifeless Bella

Bella expressed a zombie-like state in *New Moon,* when she became depressed, withdrawn and lifeless. At this time, Bella describes herself as "not beautiful, and I probably looked closer to a zombie" (*New Moon,* p 124). This terrible state of doing nothing lasted for months, as Bella becomes an unresponsive being with no friends and no life. After months of seeing Bella in a zombie-like state, Charlie gets so frustrated that he threatens to send Bella back to her mother. This prompts Bella to change her behavior and go out with school friends. In fact, when Bella watches the zombie movie with Jessica, she makes a frightening discovery:

> I felt uneasy, and I wasn't sure why at first…
>
> It wasn't until almost at the very end, as I watched a haggard zombie shambling after the last shrieking survivor, that I realized what the problem was. The scene kept cutting between the horrified face of the heroine, and the dead, emotionless face of her pursuer… And I realized which one resembled me the most.
>
> (*New Moon*, p 106)

In other words, when Bella sees the lifeless zombie character on the big screen, it reminds her of her own lackluster self. Despite Bella's zombie stage, this *Twilight Saga* scene has an empowering message. People can get depressed and the depression can become worse if people get less active and withdraw from the world. The good news is that, just like Bella did, even if it didn't feel fully perfect without Edward, it helps to take positive action and reach out to others.

Alec's Anesthetic

Another less obvious zombie reference in the *Twilight Saga* concerns a Volturi vampire who has the power to deaden all the senses. Alec's gift enables him to completely numb people's senses so that they cannot see, hear, smell, taste or feel anything. In effect, Alec turns people into zombies, rendering his victims passive and powerless. In a way, Alec's anesthetic resembles the poison of certain insects and arachnids that paralyze their prey. Just like Alec, the venomous bite of a spider or snake, or maybe the sting of a scorpion or wasp, is meant to anesthetize and incapacitate victims, to make the killing easy. *Ew!*

Which Monster is the Worst?

The *Twilight Saga* does mention a number of different monsters. These include vampires, werewolves, zombies and even mythical monsters like the snake-haired Gorgon "Medusa" (*Eclipse*, p 460) and the "Loch Ness Monster" (*Breaking Dawn*, p 417). So, using *Breaking Dawn*-talk, which one is the most creep-tacular? (p 586). Which monsters are the worst? If you had a choice, which ones should you dodge on a dark night in a dimly lit back alley? Symbolically speaking, when you really think about it, the worst monster in the *Twilight Saga* is not a particular species. It is the worst in a species. The true monster is the worst side of ourselves.

A monster is a metaphor for the monstrous behavior of humans. Some people may insist that only all vampires, werewolves and other supernatural creatures are evil because they are icy, hairy or smelly. But humans are capable of monstrous acts too. People murder, rape, attack and abuse other people. Just as vampires are accused of being filthy bloodsuckers, people incarcerate, torture, distress and kill animals in a vampire-like way on a massive scale just to eat their flesh and blood – steak, chicken, bacon, black sausage, rare meat, liver pâté. Unlike the Cullen vampires who limit and select what they eat, modern humans have taken their hunger for flesh to excess. Millions of animals around the world are tortured and killed ever day for greed and pleasure, not survival anymore.

Any individual is capable of being a monster and human beings are no exception. As the *Twilight Saga* shows, it's the choices we make and the actions we take that make us cruel and brutal monsters or not:

> I was being herded…
> The raucous laughter started again behind me.
> I braced myself…
> I probably would have a chance against one of them, and there were four.

(*Twilight*, pp 139–140)

As this gang of men who plan to assault Bella show, monsters don't dwell somewhere 'out there'. The worst kind of monsters can represent our own species, festering somewhere deep down inside the worst individuals among us.

We Are Our Own Worst Enemy

A monster, such as a zombie or a vampire, symbolizes the worst parts of ourselves. In the *Twilight* series, it's not the zombie, vampire, werewolf or some other monster that is bad. We can act like monsters by showing unhealthy anger, aggression and destruction. Sometimes we direct negative energy at ourselves. In other words, we can be our own worst enemy. The *Twilight Saga* provides plenty of examples of self-hate and self-criticism. The most common form of hate in *Twilight* is self-hate. Edward hates himself for the danger he brings into Bella's life, and he is horrified at his bloodlust. Do you recall the degrading words Edward used to describe himself? He uses the emotionally damaging words like "monster", "deplorable", and "bad guy". Once, when Edward was talking to Bella: "A hard, mocking edge entered his voice. 'You don't care if I'm a monster? If I'm not *human*?'" (*Twilight*, p 161). The best example of Edward's self-hate is when Bella falls pregnant and fatally ill. In his blackest moment in the *Twilight* series, Edward tells Jacob: "Even you, Jacob Black, cannot hate me as much as I hate myself" (*Breaking Dawn*, p 165). As you can see, self-hate and negative self-talk are pretty monstrous behavior.

Everyone has a dark side, an ugly personality part we prefer not to acknowledge – our hidden, repressed, unfavorable, wicked and monstrous characteristics. Beating the dark side is never easy. There are always challenges to face, evils to overcome, demons to fight, and monsters to battle. This theme is explored in the *Twilight Saga*. As the main *Twilight* characters help to show, we can be our own worst enemy. How many times has Bella denied her own beauty, even though Edward and others finds her attractive? How many times has Bella suggested that she is a misfit, freak or klutz? In his book *Man and His Symbols,* Dr. Carl Jung believes that a person only becomes "whole, integrated, calm, fertile and happy when the conscious and unconscious have learned to live at peace and to complement one another" (Jung, cited in McLellyn, 2011). In other words, accepting the dark and bright side of ourselves, expanding our self-views, and continuing to develop our strengths can help Bella, Edward and Jacob and characters like us to reach our full individual potential. Symbolically and psychologically, the monster symbol – whether it be zombie, vampire, werewolf, human or some other terrible creature – is just a dark theatrical reminder that we have the power to control our behavior and to better ourselves. Let's use the dramatic power of the dark symbols to add more depth, value, knowledge, skills, and meaning to our lives.

The Saga Continues

To outsiders, critics, and unsuspecting readers, Stephenie Meyer's Gothic fiction series the *Twilight Saga* is nothing more than a freak success. At deeper levels, however, the books *Twilight, New Moon, Eclipse* and *Breaking Dawn* shine, shimmer and sparkle with symbolic significance. The *Twilight Saga* is a psychological and philosophical thriller that is filled with haunting, seductive and alluring symbols everywhere. The *Twilight* symbols have the power to guide you, inspire you, and motivate you in real life.

Does the *Twilight Saga* drive people to drink human blood? Of course not. The symbols and scenes in the *Twilight Saga*, whether they are dark or delightful, have a much higher purpose. Sure, Bella is a teenage girl who runs around with vampires and werewolves in a spooky forest. But dark, dramatic, and dangerous symbols also make a story more educational. Survival skills cannot be learned without struggle, suffering, and a chance to show strength. Bloodsuckers, shape-shifters, and other anxiety-provoking motifs are simply a colorful cover for the true story underneath.

What is the *Twilight* tale really about? It is a story about love, freedom, happiness, humanity, spirituality, the triumph of good over evil, and the fulfillment of personal destiny. What makes Bella so compelling is not her new fangs or vampire clothes, it is her unwavering determination to follow her dreams. What makes Edward really sparkle is not the idea that he is a vampire, it is his capacity to love. What makes Jacob so amazing is not his thick werewolf fur, but his incredible optimism and sunny nature, no matter what happens. What *Twilight* fans really crave is to embrace their favorite character's core qualities so that they can be more like the heroes they admire so much. Hope, happiness, and love are the overriding themes here, conveyed by visually and emotionally evocative symbols. The *Twilight Saga's* symbols, from A to Z, are riveting and they resonate with people everywhere.

Just like Bella, Edward, and Jacob – the *Twilight* world's main heroes – everyone is on a heroic quest in life. But many people never realize that because they lack confidence, procrastinate, stay stuck in their comfort zone, watch too much TV, or else they miss the critical symbols and the signs. As Bella Swan shows, fulfilling your true destiny is your only responsibility in life. Every bad thing that you experience can make you stronger and is a step that you can use to lead you to reach your greater goal. Every single setback you have had can show you who you really are and prepare you to become what you were truly meant to be. Even tough times can get you there. If *The Twilight Symbols* has helped you to appreciate the *Twilight Saga* a little more, if it has helped you to understand symbols a little more, or if it has shown you a symbol or two that you can use to set your world on fire, then you are already on a personal saga that can launch you into your own glorious new dawn.

Appendix 1

Score Regarding Edward Cullen's Communication Style in *Twilight* Eye–Voice–Smile Scores

So what makes Edward Cullen so alluring? His eyes? His voice? Or his smile? When you quantify his communication style in *Twilight* by counting the number of times he uses his eyes, voice, and smiles when interacting with Bella, the results are:

Eye expressions used – 335 times
Voice used – 330 times
Smiling behavior – 174 times

What does this mean? It means that in numerical terms in a novel, Edward's eyes and voice are equally alluring. Edward uses the power of his eyes as well as his voice to the same extent, when communicating to others, almost always Bella. 'Eye' communication occurs nearly twice as much as 'smiles'. The number of times Edward uses his 'voice' is also nearly double that of 'smiles'. It is interesting to note that while many fans adore Edward's "golden" eyes, the color of his eyes was mentioned 16 times in *Twilight*, just under 5% of all 'eye' communications, which is a very small proportion. Perhaps visual information is more important and compelling to the perceiver than other aspects.

Eye References (with page numbers)

dark eyes 17, met my gaze 17, black eyes/revulsion 21, eyes flashed over 35, our eyes met 35, Edward Cullen is staring at you 36, still staring 36, staring 39, frustrated eyes 39, different eyes

39, strange/ocher eyes 39, dark gold eyes 41, penetrating eyes 41, eyes intense 42, staring at me 42, gaze appraising 42, staring intently 44, staring frozen/shocked 47, innocent expression 49, force of his gold-colored eyes 49, full/devastating eyes 49, gold eyes 49, he glared 54, eyes were cold 54, glared back 55, staring 55, golden eyes grew darker 60, staring curiously 62, frustrated/black eyes 62, gaze with probing intensity 62, his eyes released me 63, eyes were on me 66, tawny eyes 70, his eyes were wickedly amused 71, his eyes were gloriously intense 72, staring at you again 74, staring at me 74, wicked glint in his eyes 75, ocher eyes were serious 75, deep gold eyes 76, stared 77, eyes turned brooding 78, intensity of stare 78, ocher eyes scorching 79, eyes still smoldered 79, eyes were impenetrable 79, eyes full of emotion 80, eyes troubled 80, bright/exited eyes 84, staring with unfathomable expression 86, eyes mocking 88, staring forward 88, eyes narrowed 88, glanced down 88, eyes danced 89, stared at rain 90, curious eyes 90, eyes searching mine 91, raised one eyebrow 92, burning gold eyes 93, expression murderously angry 141, closing his eyes 141, squeezing his eyes 142, opened his eyes 142, staring at ceiling 142, eyes hard 143, eyes were curious 146, looked at me 146, watching me 146, watching me 148, stared into my eyes 148, light/golden butterscotch eyes 148, brow furrowed 148, stared stunned 148, eyes narrowed 148, eyes tight 148, raised one eyebrow 149, eyes flickered 149, rolling his eyes 150, eyes warm 150, eyes locked 151, stared 152, raised one eyebrow 152, eyes flashed 152, looked anxiously 152, staring past me 153, stare over 153, covering his eyes 153, his eyes seeking mine 153, looked down 154, looked at me 157, eyes enigmatic 157, rolled eyes rolled 158, looked down 159, honey eyes gentle 159, staring 160, eyes fierce 160, staring 161, stared 161, watchful eyes 161, look at me 162, golden eyes 162, eyes cold 162, looked at me quickly 163, eyes gentle but intense 164, anguished eyes 166, gaze on 166, eyes tight 168, looked like he was joking 174, eyes were capable 175, brightened his eyes 175, glared at me 181, glanced up 182, troubled eyes 182, dark golden eyes piercing 183, eyes surprised 183, he frowned 183, eyes were gentle 183, "his liquid topaz eyes were penetrating" 183, eyes narrowed 184, eyes knowing 184, "the look" in his eyes 184, looked wary 186, he frowned 186, rolled his eyes 186, serious eyes 186, eyes smoldering 187, eyes suddenly fierce 187, stared at me 188, eyes were scrutinizing 188, followed my gaze 189, eyes suddenly furious 189, glared at me 190, eyes peering 192, eyes smolder 192, eyes cautious 192, conflict raging in eyes 193, eyes shifted slightly 194, eyes slid back 195, rolled his eyes 195, eyes shrewd 196, eyes burned sincerely 196, staring at me 196, measuring me with eyes 196, humor in eyes 196, humor there 196, gazing morosely 197, eyes held 197, closed his eyes 197, eyes on clouds 197, eyes roamed 199, gaze lingered 199, staring 200, peculiar eyes 200, raised an eyebrow 200, looking at me 202, eyes ambivalent 202, looking at horizon 204, gazed unseeingly 204, eyes shifted to mine 204, raised one eyebrow 204, eyes darkened 213, golden eyes troubled 214, eyes innocent 214, rolling his eyes 214, eyes on face 215, he looked down 215, without looking away 216, looked me over 221, gaze 222, eyes annoyed 224, stared at me 224, holding my glance 225, eyes wary/reluctant 227, eyes satin smooth 229, eyes were open watching me 229, eyes butterscotch/warmer/lighter 229, golden eyes 229, eyes watching me 230, eyes mesmerized me 230, stared 231, eyes dark 231, eyes never left mine 231, eyes of a snake 232, lovely eyes glowed 232, eyes dimmed 232, he winked 232, eyes soft 232, looked into his eyes 233, gazing 233, looked back 234, looking into eyes 234, looked across 235, stared 235, glanced swiftly 235, gazed at sky 235, looked away 235, lifted his eyes 235, eyes burned 236, watched intently 236, glanced grimly 236, looked up 236, golden eyes scorched hypnotic/deadly 236, force of stare 237, eyes flashed 239, eyes tender 239, he looked down 239, glorious/agonized eyes 239–240, golden eyes were on me 240, eyes met 240, stared 240, looked at me 240, looking to see 241, never moving eyes from mine 241, eyes peaceful 242, closed his eyes 242, hungry eyes 243, excited/flaring eyes 244, "hear his eyes rolling" 245, guarded expression 247, eyes wild 247, dazzled my eyes 247, eyes excited/faded 247, raised eyebrows 249, gazed 250, glanced 250, gazed 251, looked into my eyes 251, looked into sun 251, glanced 251, looked down 251, rolled his eyes 252, pointed glance 253, eyes darted 253, sly glance 254, holding my gaze 256, eyes appraised me 261, raised one eyebrow 261, examined my face 261, stared cautiously 262, looking down 263, eyes gleamed 275, gold eyes grew soft 275, gold eyes forgiving 275, rolled eyes 276, gazing at me 276, turning away eyes 277, eyes were back on me 277, stared into my eyes 278, long exasperated look 284, looked casually 285, looked thoughtfully 286, followed my gaze 287, watched me carefully 289, watching me 294, eyes intent 296, staring at my face 296, eyes were serious 296, stared into space 297, peculiar eyes 300, eyes dissected 301, raising his eyebrows 300, eyes bright 300, rolled his eyes 305, eyes on my back 305, eyes solemn 306, disbelieving look 314, watching me intensely 316, humor in eyes 316, stared at me incredulously 318, eyes grew eager/bright 321, eyes zeroed in 326, eyes on the road 333, hard look 334, stared 334, stared at me 336, squeezed eyes shut 336, glared at me 337, eyes always roving 342, saw the panic 346, stared blackly 346, looked away 350, glorious eyes burning 352, eyes went blank/dead 352, staring at me in pain 397, doubtful eyes blazed 397, looked away 401, did not return gaze 401, raised eyes to ceiling 401, stared at me 402, hurt touched his eyes 402, wide eyes earnest 403, speculative look in eyes 403, frowned 403, eyes flashed 405, eyes narrowed 409, eyes wide/serious 410, held my gaze 410, eyes dark/black 410, haunted look in eyes 411, eyes tightened 412, eyes flat black 412, stared intently 413, glared at me 413, eyes grew speculative 413, he frowned 414, closing his eyes 414, opened surprised eyes 414, rolled his eyes 415, eyes black 415, stared at each other 415, eyeing the button 415, met my gaze 417, looked in surprise 419, eyes narrowed 421, "full force of his golden scorching eyes" 422, eyes melting my fury 422, stared 422, glared 424, staring 425, looking at me intently 426, frowned 429, frown deepened 430, eyes troubled 430, smile did not touch eyes 431, glancing down 431, brows pulled together over eyes 432, pain in eyes 432, eyes probing 433, "examined my face for a long moment" 433, eyebrows rose 433, he frowned 434.

Total Score = 335

Of this total, "gold/en eyes" were mentioned 16 times (5%).

Data Excluded – Facial expressions that were too ambiguous to code accurately, e.g. "he looked puzzled" and "he still looked confused" (159) were not counted because it not clear if eyes were used. Edward may have used other body language such as "shrugging shoulders", "flared nostrils", or "shaking his head" to convey his message and emotions.

Voice/Speech References (with page numbers)

low attractive voice 23, quiet musical voice 37, kind tone 41, agreed dryly 42, murmured smugly 42, muttered quietly 42, sounded amused 43, low/frantic voice 48, voice suppressed laughter 48, soft voice 49, musical voice 52, sounding annoyed 54, resentment in his voice 54, cutting tone 54, questioning tone 55, voice held edge 55, familiar voice 63, sounded sincere 63, quite/velvet/muted voice 70, low voice cold 70, voice smoldering 72, hard edge crept into voice 75, voice inaudible 80, a different voice 83, sounded upset 83, voice right beside me 83, tone confessed weakness 85, speaking softly 87, voice like melting honey 88, smile polite 88, smiling wryly 88, voice indignant 89, voice sounded frustrated 90, tone was reproachful 91, matter of fact tone 92, he commanded 141, tone livid 141, voice tight/controlled 141, whispering 142, silken/irresistible voice 144, low/authoritative voice 144, voice alluring 145, insisted quietly 145, he ordered 147, murmured 148, voice ominous 149, voice hard 149, voice was a whisper 151, spoke in a rush 151, disbelief in voice 152, voice muffled 153, a whisper 153, voice was quiet

154, he said significantly 155, muttered 159, snapped 159, voice calm 159, voice sounded disinterested 160, tone revealing 160, hard edge to voice 161, tone was hard 161, peculiar tone 162, voice nearly audible 162, voice hard 162, asked sarcastically 162, voice bleak 162, asked flatly 162, voice skeptical 162, whispered 163, warned 163, murmured 163, voice very low 163, he sighed "yes" 164, velvety voice compelling 165, groaned quietly 165, words flowing fast 166, voice low/urgent 166, he growled 166, voice raw 166, sounded appalled 166, voice burned with regret 166, lighter tone 166, tone serious/hesitant 168, bleak voice 168, "tomorrow" he sighed 168, uncertainty in voice 173, voice guarded 173, voice was low 173, he accused 174, voice irresistible 175, murmured 175, voice was amused 180, asked condescendingly 181, voice husky 182, voice rough 182, murmured 183, voice velvet soft 183, "I know" he sighed brooding 187, voice off-hand 188, tone disinterred 188, said lightly 189, voice cutting 189, he murmured 192, voice dark 192, didn't sound repentant 195, muttered 195, he sighed "will you forgive me" 195, spoke slowly 197, low/rough voice 197, voice more even 197, voice silky 199, quiet probing questions 203, murmured 204, voice thoughtful 204, appealing voice 212, serious tone 212, voice turned sharp 213, voice was aloof 216, he mocked 217, "smile in his voice" 222, asked impatiently 223, he snapped 223, he demanded 223, voice angry 223, he muttered 223, speaking so quickly 223, said quietly 224, pain in voice 224, voice gentle 225, "bell-like echoes" 226, asked playfully 229, soft voice 229, he sighed 229, whispered 230, whispered intently 230, murmured 232, velvet voice 232, whispered 232, asked tenderly 232, "long ago" he sighed 233, voice harsher 233, "warmth" he sighed 234, sounded ashamed 237, stared off 238, closed eyes 238, pronounced carefully 239, "agreed with a laugh" 240, murmured 240, murmured 241, whispered 241, said with satisfaction 242, whispered 243, "a smile in his voice" 244, muttered 245, voice high/excited 245, asked anxiously 245, laughed quietly 246, said quietly 246, he said pleased 248, laughed aloud 248, "your best day" he teased 248, soft voice 252, respect in his voice 252, murmured 253, spoke matter-of-factly 256, "on" he urged 256, he pleaded 257, whispered 257, quiet laughing 259, smiling hugely 259, murmured 262, voice teasing 262, "not easy" he sighed 263, he whispered 263, voice pained 263, quiet/musical laugh 264, words flowed swiftly 264, whispered 265, voice abrupt 266, he hissed 267, whispered 267, whispered 268, voice had promise 270, voice persuasive 270, "it is" he threatened darkly 270, pleading voice 270, voice became a soft murmur 271, voice light 271, sounded satisfied 271, archangel voice 272, unruffled voice 273, murmured 274, sounded hopeful 276, voice harsh 276, said uncomfortably 277, asked innocently 277, he murmured 279, voice was alarmed 279, groaned 279, "good at everything" he sighed 279, said softly 285, said conversationally 285, sighed deeply 285, said through tight lips 286, murmured 287, voice smug 287, teasing 287, sounded worried 289, brief laugh was darker 290, voice very quiet 290, voice broke off 290, he sighed 296, he trailed off 296, voice a whisper/trailed off 298, barked/laughed loudly 299, murmured 299, said absently 300, growled/low sound 301, growled playfully 301, said with mock solemnity 303, low voice furious 304, he sighed 314, he sighed again 314, groaned 315, sighed 315, "now" he breathed 316, murmured 316, "hurt you?" his lips brushed 316, he growled 317, warned severely 317, said gently 319, low/even voice 326, hid stress in his voice 326, frustration colored his tone 326, muttered fiercely 326, voice was low 332, growling something fast 333, said grimly 333, voice cold 334, roared in frustration 334, hissed 335, "no" was absolute 335, voice blistering/furious 335, growled 335, voice worn 336, continued grimly 337, voice had hard edge 337, voice icy 338, defeat in voice 338, dangerous note in voice 339, voice very soft 339, said tensely 341, low/cheerful voice 341, voice in command 342, he warned 342, low intense voice 342, said fiercely 342, voice urgent 342, he whispered 343, said grimly 345, said conversationally 346, low voice 347, tone full of disgust 347, said with hopeless frustration 347, muttered 347, enraged roar 349, tone was deadly 350, sighed in frustration 364, voice hard 365, happy/beautiful/uplifting/ghastly sound 394, a deep/wild/ furious roar 394, sound of an angel calling 394, voice cried in horror 394, perfect voice in agony 394, broken sobs 395, howl of rage 395, voice was frightened 396, breathed in horror 396, bellowed 396, begged 396, agony in beautiful voice 397, strained/triumphant voice 398, said quietly 398, quiet sound/laugh 398, "I'll carry you" he soothed 398, shushed me 400, he whispered 400, voice tormented 400, whispered 401, voice was comforting 401, grim tone 401, regret in voice 401, darkened voice 402, voice even 402, asked anxiously 402, muttered 402, voice was a whisper 411, voice choked 411, said quietly 412, voice was soft 413, asked curtly 413, he snapped 414, he growled 415, said gently 415, sighed in frustration 416, voice beautiful/lullaby 417, whispered 417, laughed quietly 417, voice friendly on surface 421, tone changed/threatening 421, didn't sound sorry 421, demanded in horror 422, demanded in frustration 422, said gently 423, muttered 424, warned 425, whispered 425, murmured 425, snarled quietly 425, voice scathing 426, said tersely 429, clipped voice 429, said slowly 431, he agreed 431, objected 431, sighed deeply 432, murmured 432, said sadly 433, he whispered 433, mocking tone 433, exhaled a growl 434.

Total Score = 330

Smiling References (with page numbers)

crooked smile so beautiful 38, smiled widely flashing perfect ultra-white teeth 43, flashing his brilliant teeth 52, chuckle/patronizing smile 53, lips twitched/fighting a smile 63, snickered 70, smiled briefly 72, smiling crookedly 74, smiling 75, still smiling 75, smiled again 75, breathtakingly crooked smile 76, warning behind the smile 76, chuckled 77, shockingly tempting smile 77, snickered 77, lips pressed together to keep from laughing 78, smiled playfully 79, smiled up at me 80, grinning 83, chuckled 83, snicker 84, faint trace of a smile 92, smile vanished 92, smile returned 92, he smiled 92, grinned 93, smile playing 93, smiled crookedly 93, still smiling 94, corner of mouth twitched 142, smiled slightly 143, gleaming smile 145, chuckled 146, perfect crooked smile 146, coy smile 147, faint/mocking smile 148, smirk 149, smiled wryly 150, almost smiled, grinned amused 157, smile crookedly 158, grinned 158, lips curled up 165, smiled ruefully 165, he smiled 167, grinned 168, heard him chuckle 169, smirk 174, impish smile 175, favorite uneven smile 176, grinning wickedly 176, he grimaced 181, chuckled blackly 184, devastating smile 185, chuckled 185, smiled teasingly 188, smiled at some joke 188, snickered 189, "he flashed his bright teeth in a brief threatening smile" 189, chuckled 189, smile was brilliant 194, smile condescending 196, slight smile 196, faint smile 197, smiling/relaxed 199, chuckled 200, smiled crookedly 200, smiled 203, smiled wistfully 204, smile amused 212, he grinned 212, smirked 213, restrained a smile 213, smiled 214, he smiled 216, wry smile 216, he grinned 216, still grinned 216, smiling his crooked smile 217, chuckled 221, mocking smile 224, smiled 225, smiled 226, smirked 226, smirk grew pronounced 226, smiled wider/teeth flashed 229, smiled in apology 231, smile mocking 231, laughed bitterly 231, said gently 231, smile was dazzling 232, smiled/ashamed 232, smiled/mood shifting 234, smiled ruefully 234, smiled swiftly 235, smiled/glinted 240, smiled again 240, half-smiled 243, crooked smile 244, laughed "louder" 244, mused 246, chuckled 246, smiled 247, impish grin 248, tight grin 248, chuckle 249, grinning 249, chagrin 256, ghostly chuckle 257, smiled 263, smiling 263, gentle smile 264, smiled 264, grimaced 264, chuckled 265, teeth gleamed 266, chuckled 267, chuckled 268, smirked 276, smiled 276, smiled 277, heart-breaking smile 277, patient smile 277, chuckled 288, smiled 290, smile widened 391, chuckled darkly 295, smiled a half-smile 296, smiling 296, chuckled 297, gentle angel's smile 298, chuckled

300, smiling slightly 300, wide/wicked smile 301, chuckled 301, chuckling quietly 302, grin 305, smiled 305, grinned widely 305, crooked smile 305, grinned 315, smiled hugely 315, a smile 316, chuckled 318, smiled wistfully 320, wide grin visible 323, flashed his special crooked smile 325, smiled 340, smiled a little 346, smile was bleak 346, half a smile 401, chuckled 403, grinning 404, smiled 404, a wide grin flashed 408, almost smiled 409, chuckled humorlessly 415, crooked smile 416, mocking smile 419, grinned again 419, grin spread 420, huge smirk 421, grinned 423, chuckled 423, smiled 424, half-smiled 429, smiled briefly 431, smile 431, grinning 431, still grinning 432, smile fading 432, he smiled 433, chuckled darkly 433, smiling 434.

Total Score = 174

Data Excluded – Smiling behavior that was 1) ambiguous; 2) suggested strong "laughter" rather than "smiling"; 3) did not provide clear enough information about facial expressions (e.g. "I felt his quiet laughter shake the bed", *Twilight*, p 260) was not counted.

Appendix 2

New Moon References to Bella's Hole/Empty Chest (with page numbers)

1 "a huge hole had been punched through my chest" (118)
2 "aching around the edges of the hole in my chest" (123)
3 Edward's words *"It will be as if I never existed"* (123) "ripped the hole wide open" (124)
4 "what if this hole never got better?" (124)
5 "I felt hideously empty" (162)
6 "the hole came back" (193)
7 "my chest ached with emptiness" (195)
8 "my arms clutching my chest to hold it together" (198)
9 "I waited for the memory to hit – to open the gaping hole" (214)
10 "I was an empty shell" (216)
11 "a vacant house – condemned" (216) – Bella sees herself as a run-down house
12 "my empty chest… I had been broken beyond repair" (219)
13 "the hole in my chest was worse than ever" (228)
14 "the stupid hole in my chest" (233)
15 "there was no way I could have disguised the abyss I was plunging into now" (234)
16 "I had to curl into a ball to keep the empty hole from tearing me apart" (234–225)
17 "the raw edges of my wound throbbing" (237)
18 Edward's name "tore against my unhealed wounds like a serrated edge" (240)
19 "Another tear though my chest" (240)
20 "a ragged hole in the center of my chest" (241)
21 "the pain twisted… the jagged hole ripping me open from

the inside out" (267)

22 "I'd thought Jake had been healing the hole in me" (273)

23 Jacob had "just been carving out his own hole" (273)

24 "the hole – holes now – were already aching" (276)

25 Jacob's "harsh rejection had punched a painful new hole in... my chest" (280)

26 Bella cares so much about Edward and Jacob that it "tear big chunks right out of my chest" (294)

27 "I wrapped my arms around my chest, fighting the hole" (298)

28 When Jacob hugs Bella "there was no need for me to clutch at the hole – he kept me in one piece" (314)

29 "I squeezed my midsection, trying to ignore the throbbing around the edges of my chest" (320)

30 "I twitched as the pain lashed around the edges of the hole" (347)

31 "The whole had been festering lately" (356)

32 Bella refers to herself as "an empty box" (366)

33 Charlie describes Bella as "empty" (396)

34 When Bella hugs Edward again, she says "the hole in my chest" feels whole (452)

35 "I could feel the ghost of the hole, waiting to rip itself wide again" (507)

36 Bella explains that when Edward left "lots of piece went missing" inside and she felt "hollow" just like Edward (515)

Data Excluded:

- When Edward calls the Cullens "bloodsuckers", it makes her think about Edward, so she "pulled one arm surreptitiously around her torso" (318). This suggests that Bella feels the hole inside her chest.
- "It hurts to think about them... it's like... I'm breaking into pieces" (349).

References

Abyss. http://en.wikipedia.org/wiki/Abyss_(religion) (Viewed November 1, 2011)

Allan, T; Vitebsky, P (1998) *Triumph of the Hero: Greek and Roman Myth*. Amsterdam: Time-Life Books

Alchemy Dictionary. http://nysticorax.tripod.com/terms.html (Accessed 19/09/2009)

Aleiss, Angela. "Mormon imagery runs deep in *Twilight*." *Religious News Service* (June 25, 2010) School of Film and Religion, University of California, Los Angeles. www.freerepublic.com/focus/f-religion/ 2540912/posts (Viewed December 1, 2011)

American Psychological Association (2000) *The Diagnostic and Statistical Manual for Mental Disorders. Fourth Edition, Text Revised (DSM-IV-TR)*. Washington: American Psychiatric Association

Andréa, Hans (2004-2009) Alchemy. Harry Potter for Seekers Website. http://www.harrypotterforseekers.com/alchemy /alchemy.php (Viewed November 14, 2011)

Apple symbolism. http://wiki.answers.com/Q/ What_is_a_ symbolism_from_Twilight_by_Stephenie_Meyer#ixzz1YCpF Wmwc

Asphodel Meadows. en.wikipedia.org/wiki/Asphodel_Meadows (Viewed October 31, 2011)

Archetypes. http://www.scribd.com/doc/18171537/Arch ... y-analysis (Viewed Nov 21, 2011)

Auden, WH (1940) "O, Unicorn, among the cedars" *New Year Letter* (1940). Cited in http://www.unicornlady.net/ poetry/poetry4.html (Viewed September 21, 2011)

Bacon, S. "Vampires: Myths of the Past and the Future". Proposed Conference November 2–4, 2011, University of London. http://www.conferencealerts.com/seeconf.mv?q=ca

16i63i (Viewed April 5, 2011)
Bee Mythology. In http://en.wikipedia.org/wiki/Bee_(mythology) (Viewed September 21, 2011)
Bennett-Goleman, T (2001) *Emotional Alchemy*. London: Rider
Birds in Alchemy http://albertyonathan.blogspot.com/2008/11/meaning-of-birds-symbol.html (Accessed June 1, 2011)
Bowes, S (1999) *Life Magic: The Power of Positive Witchcraft*. Glastonbury: The Speaking Tree
Burns, GW (2005) *101 Healing Stories for Kids and Teens: Using Metaphors in Therapy*. New Jersey: John Wiley and Sons
Byron, Lord. *The Giaour* (1813) http://www.simplysupernatural-vampire.com/vampire-poem-the-giaour-byron.html (Viewed September 21, 2011)
Carpathian Mountains. http://en.wikipedia.org/wiki/Carpathian_Mountains (Viewed November 11, 2011)
Carroll, L (1865) *Alice in Wonderland*. Cited in: www.alice-in-wonderland.net › Resources › Chapters & script (Viewed November 27, 2011)
Carroll, L (2011) *Alice's Adventures in Wonderland – The Original Classic Edition*: Emereo Pty Ltd
Citrinitas/Xanthosis in Alchemy. en.wikipedia.org/wiki/ Alchemy (Viewed May 1, 2011)
Character Names. Behind the Names: The etymology and history of first names. http://www.behindthename.com/name/ (Viewed September 29, 2011)
Chubai, Hryhoriy. "When I am half a breath from you…" poem. Ukrainian Poetica. http://poetry.uazone.net/english.html (Viewed September 21, 2011). This website is the most complete Internet library of Ukrainian poetry and songs.
Coleridge, M (1896) "The Shield". In Ward, TH (Ed.) (1919) *The English Poets*. London: Macmillan and Company Ltd
Colin, D (2000) *Dictionary of Symbols, Myths and Legends*. London: Hachette
Cyclopes. http://www.gods-heros-myth.com/godpages/cyclopes

.html (Viewed November 17, 2011)

Cyclopes. http://www.mythencyclopedia.com/Cr-Dr/Cyclopes.html (Viewed November 17, 2011)

"Did Elizabeth Taylor own the Hope Diamond?" http://wiki.answers.com/Q/Did_Elizabeth_Taylor_own_the_hope_diamond (Accessed November 11, 2011)

Day, Ed (Ed) (2010) *Llewellyn's Sabbats Almanac: Samhain 2010 to Mabon 2011.* Llewellyn Worldwide Ltd. Woodbury, MN (USA). "Samhain: The Old Ways: Pomona's Day" by Elizabeth Barrette, pp 25–28

De Vore, D. Archetypes in the Gothic Novel. Wikipedia: The Free Encyclopedia. en.wikipedia.org/wiki/Gothic_fiction (Viewed Nov 27, 2011)

Dickinson, Emily (1830–1886) *A Wounded Deer Leaps Highest.* http://www.theromantic.com/poetryclassic/awoundeddeer.htm (Viewed September 21, 2011)

Eason, C (2002) *Ancient Wisdom: Magic from Around the World.* Bath: Parragon Books

Eleazar. http://en.wikipedia.org/wiki/Eleazar (Viewed September 19, 2011)

Enneagram Institute (1998–2011) *The Enneagram: Your Basic Personality Type.* http://www.enneagraminstitute.com/intro.asp (Viewed November 17, 2011)

Fir Tree. http://en.wikipedia.org/wiki/Fir (Viewed November 17, 2011)

Fir Tree. http://www.whats-your-sign.com/celtic-meaning-fir-tree.html (Viewed November 17, 2011)

Folklore of Seagulls: Myths and Old Stories. http://www.suite101.com/content/folklore-of-seagulls-myths-and-old-stories-a133385 (Viewed October 31, 2011)

Forks, Washington. http://en.wikipedia.org/wiki/Forks,_Washington (Viewed November 3, 2011)

Forks, Washington. http://twilightsaga.wikia.com/wiki/Forks (Viewed November 4, 2011)

Freud, S. Death Drive. Wikipedia: The Free Encyclopedia. http://en.wikipedia.org/wiki/Death_drive (Accessed August 3, 2011)

Freud, S. "The conscious mind... which it rises." http://www.brainyquote.com/quotes/keywords/sun.html#ixzz1EmwmNf4R (Accessed August 3, 2011)

Galbreth, J. Spirit of Samhain, poster-related text. http://fairiesandfantasy.com/catalog.php?item=2121 (Accessed Sep 2, 2011)

Genesis of the word 'Vampire'. http://vampirologist.blogspot.com/2009/01/genesis-of-word-vampire.html

Glikin-Gusinsky, Andrew. "The Slavic Origins of Vampire Myth."

http://www.suite101.com/content/the-slavic-origins-of-vampire-myth-a306789 (Accessed Nov 9, 2010)

Gothic Fiction. http://en.wikipedia.org/wiki/Gothic_fiction (Viewed September 29, 2011)

Granstrom, SL (1985) "Spiritual nursing care of oncology patients." *Topics in Clinical Nursing*. April 7 (1), 39–45

Graves, R (1968) *New Larousse Encyclopedia of Mythology*. Octopus Publishing Group

Hanna JL. "The power of dance: health and healing." *J Altern Complement Med*. 1995;1:323–331

Harissis, Haralampos V; Harissis, Anastasios V. *Apiculture in the Prehistoric Aegean. Minoan and Mycenaean Symbols Revisited.* 2009. British Archaeological Reports S1958, ISBN 9781407304540

Hartford, John. "The whole universe..." http://www.quotesarchive.com/authors/h/john-hartford/quotes/the-whole-universe-is-based-on-rhythms (Viewed August 11, 2011)

Hemlock Tree. http://www.thefreedictionary.com/madrone (Viewed November 4, 2011)

Hemlock Tree. The Spiritual Elements of Trees. Written by Lotus © July 29, 2004

http://spiritlodge.yuku.com/topic/1073 (Viewed November 4, 2011)

The Hope Diamond. http://www.diamonds-are-forever.org.uk/famous-diamonds.htm (Viewed September 19, 2011)

The Hope Diamond – legend, myth and color
http://www.diamond-legend.info/diamonds/hope.html (Viewed December 8, 2011)

The Hope Diamond: Jewelry and Gemstone Legends and Lore. http://www.streetdirectory.com/travel_guide/34962/jewelry/jewelry_and_gemstone_legends_and_lore.html (Viewed September 19, 2011)

IMHO (2009) "I love the symbolism in the story...I don't know if Stephenie Meyer did it intentionally, but there is a lot to be learned from *Twilight*, I think." Post by IMHO, February 22, 2009. http://www.experienceproject.com/stories/Love-The-Twilight-Saga/464685/ (Accessed Sep 13, 2011)

Jacksonville, Florida. http://twilightsaga.wikia.com/wiki/Jacksonville,_Florida (Viewed Nov 3, 2011)

Janko, Richard. "The Shield of Heracles and the Legend of Cycnus". *The Classical Quarterly* New Series, 36.1 (1986), pp 38–59

Johnson, James W. "That Neo-Classical Bee." *Journal of the History of Ideas* 22.2 (April 1961), pp 262–266

Koch, SC; Morlinghaus, K; Fuchs, T (2007) "The joy of dance: Specific effects of a single dance intervention on psychiatric patients with depression." *The Arts in Psychotherapy*, 34, 340–349

La Push, Washington. http://twilightsaga.wikia.com/wiki/La_Push,_Washington (Accessed November 4, 2011)

Loch Ness Monster. The Legend of Nessie the Ultimate Loch Ness Monster Site. http://www.nessie.co.uk/ (Viewed December 8, 2011)

Loch Ness Monster. http://en.wikipedia.org/wiki/Loch_Ness_Monster (Viewed December 8, 2011)

Lowell, Amy. *Apples of Hesperides*. http://www.love-poems.me.uk/lowell_apples_of_hesperides.htm (Viewed September 29,

2011)

Macaulay, TB (1800–1859). "Mad, Bad, and Dangerous To Know: Beyond Byron – Other Bad Boys" http://my-ecoach.com/project.php?id=15712&project_step=63159 (Viewed October 31, 2011)

Madrone Tree. http://www.merriam-webster.com/dictionary/madrone (Viewed November 4, 2011)

Madrone Tree. http://stacienaczelnik.hubpages.com/hub/Sacred-Trees-of-the-Pacific-Northwest (Viewed November 4, 2011)

Maple Tree. http://stacienaczelnik.hubpages.com/hub/Sacred-Trees-of-the-Pacific-Northwest (Viewed November 4, 2011)

Marcus. http://absoluteshakespeare.com/guides/caesar/characters/characters.htm (Viewed September 19, 2011)

McLellyn, Gadfly. "We Are Our Own Worst Enemy." www.harry-potterforseekers.com/articles/worstenemy.php (Viewed November 30, 2011)

Meredith, George. *The Lark Ascending*

http://allpoetry.com/poem/8475727-The_Lark_Ascending-by-George_Meredith

Meyer, S (2005) "*Twilight* began as a very vivid dream... with everyone." http://www.hachettebookgroup.com/Stephenie_Meyer_(1070099)_Article(1).aspx (Viewed Dec 1, 2011)

Meyer, S (2006) *Twilight*. London: Atom Books

Meyer, S (2007) *New Moon*. London: Atom Books

Meyer, S (2007) *Eclipse*. London: Atom Books

Meyer, S (2008) *Breaking Dawn*. London: Atom Books

Meyer, S. "Stephenie Meyer's '*Twilight*' Zone", by Gregory Kirschling (July 5, 2008) http://www.ew.com/ew/article/0,,20049578,00.html (Viewed December 1, 2011)

Meyer, S. "In my dream... " In Newkey-Burden, C (2010) *Stephenie Meyer Queen of Twilight: The Biography* (pp 54, 56) London: John Blake

Meyer, Stephenie (April 2011) "Frequently Asked Questions". *The Twilight Saga: The Official Illustrated Guide*. Little, Brown and Company

Meyer, S. "Why did you pick the title *Twilight?*" http://www.stepheniemeyer.com/twilight_faq.html_(Viewed November 11, 2011)

Milton, John. "Paradise Lost: A Brief Overview" (1999). *Paradise Lost Study Guide*. New Arts Library. Web. 5 Nov. 2009. http://www.paradiselost.org/5-overview.html (Viewed September 29, 2011)

Milton, John. Paradise Lost. http://en.wikipedia.org/wiki /Paradise_Lost (Viewed September 29, 2011)

Midnight Definition. http://www.thefreedictionary.com/mid night mid·night *n.* (Viewed Sep 22, 2011)

Neruda, Pablo. Love Sonnet XXXII. "You – The One… your white energy". http://plagiarist.com/poetry/393/ Accessed October 30, 2011)

Neruda, Pablo (1904–1973). "There was thirst and hunger, and you were the fruit." Excerpt from *A Song of Despair*. http://famouspoetsandpoems.com/poets/pablo_neruda/poem s/15712 (Viewed Oct 31, 2011)

Nozedar, A (2008) *The Element Encyclopedia of Secret Signs and Symbols: The Ultimate A–Z Guide from Alchemy to the Zodiac*. HarperCollins Publishers

Olympic Peninsula. http://en.wikipedia.org/wiki/Olympic_ Peninsula (Viewed September 22, 2011)

Pacatte, R; Rupprecht, H (July 28, 2010) "The *Twilight Saga*". In *National Catholic Reporter*. http://ncronline.org/print/19426 (Viewed September 22, 2011)

Palm Tree. http://en.wikipedia.org/wiki/Palm_branch_(symbol) (Viewed November 4, 2011)

Palm Tree Symbolism. http://www.whats-your-sign.com/palm-tree-symbolism.html (Viewed November 4, 2011)

Paris and the Apple. http://en.wikipedia.org/wiki/Judg ement_of_Paris (Viewed September 22, 2011)

Pearson, C (1998) *The Hero Within: Six Archetypes We Live By*.

HarperCollins Publishers

Petersen, LR; Roy, A (1985) "Religiosity, anxiety, and meaning and purpose: religion's consequences for psychological well-being." *Review of Religious Research*, 27, 49–62

Phillips, C; Kerrigan, M (1999) *Forests of the Vampire: Slavic Myth*. London: Duncan Baird Publishers

Phoenix, Arizona. http://twilightsaga.wikia.com/wiki/Phoenix (Accessed November 3, 2011)

Phoenix, Arizona http://en.wikipedia.org/wiki/Phoenix,_Arizona (Accessed November 3, 2011)

Port Angeles, Washington. http://twilightsaga.wikia.com/wiki/Port_Angeles,_Washington (Viewed November 4, 2011)

Quileute Indian Fact Sheet. http://www.bigorrin.org/quileute_kids.htm (Viewed November 4, 2011)

Quileute Tribe. http://twilightsaga.wikia.com/wiki/Quileute_tribe (Viewed November 4, 2011)

Rijkenborgh, Jan Van. *The Alchemical Wedding of Christian Rosycross* (1616)

http://harrypotterforseekers.com/books/alchemicalwedding.php (Accessed January 12, 2012)

Redish, L; Lewis, O. Native Languages of the Americas. Quileute Indian Fact Sheet http://www.bigorrin.org/quileute_kids.htm (Viewed November 1, 2011)

Rowling, JK (1998) *Harry Potter and the Chamber of Secrets*. London: Bloomsbury

Rowling, JK (1997) *Harry Potter and the Philosopher's Stone*. London: Bloomsbury

Sandel, SL; Judge, JO; Landry, N; Faria, L; Ouellette, R; Majczak, M. "Dance and movement program improves quality-of-life measures in breast cancer survivors." *Cancer Nurse*. 2005;28:301–9

Seattle, Washington. http://en.wikipedia.org/wiki/Seattle (Viewed November 4, 2011)

Seattle, Washington. http://twilightsaga.wikia.com/wiki/Port_

Angeles,_Washington (Viewed November 4, 2011)

Scheinberg, Susan 1979. "The Bee Maidens of the Homeric Hymn to Hermes." *Harvard Studies in Classical Philology* 83(1979), pp 1–28

Shapiro, H. "Herakles and Kyknos", *American Journal of Archaeology* 88 (1984), pp 523–39)

The Shield of Heracles. http://en.wikipedia.org/wiki/The_Shield_of_Heracles (Viewed Sep 21, 2011)

Shmoop Editorial Team. (November 11, 2008). *Twilight*. http://www.shmoop.com/twilight

(Accessed August 17, 2011)

Shmoop Editioral Team. (November 11, 2008). *Twilight* Theme of Family. http://www.shmoop.com/twilight/family-theme.html (Viewed December 8, 2011)

Sitka Spruce. http://www.ehow.com/about_6388561_interesting-spruce-trees.html (Viewed Nov 4, 2011)

Sitka Spruce. http://www.shgresources.com/ak/symbols/tree/ (November 4, 2011)

The Slavic Origins of Vampire Myth. http://andrew-glikin-gusinsky.suite101.com/the-slavic-origins-of-vampire-myth-a306789 (Viewed September 21, 2011)

Slavic Vampire Myth. http://en.wikipedia.org/wiki/Vampire_folklore_by_region (Viewed Sep 21, 2011)

Slideshare (2011) "Gothic Fiction: Byronic Hero".www.slide share.net/darlingtom/gothic-fiction-byronic-hero (Viewed November 27, 2011)

Song of Songs. In "Sumerian Songs". http://www.humanistictexts.org/sumerlove.htm (Viewed November 11, 2011)

Spindler, Audrey. Cited in http://www.harrypotterforseekers.com/articles/journeytogold.php (Accessed November 7, 2011)

Steinman, Jim. *Total Eclipse Of The Heart* lyrics. http://www.elyrics.net/read/b/bonnie-tyler-lyrics/total-eclipse-of-the-heart-lyrics.html (Viewed September 2, 2011)"Subtext of hunger… grown-up bite" *Washington Post* Article. Cited in:

"*Twilight* Theme of Sex". www.shmoop.com/twilight/sex-theme.html (Viewed November 11, 2011)

Swedenborg, E (1688–1772) "Love in its essence is spiritual fire". Swedish Naturalist, Mathematician, Scientist, Theologian. http://www.yuni.com/quotes/love_quotes.html (Viewed December 8, 2011)

Symbolism. en.wikipedia.org; www.symbolism.org (Viewed November 1, 2011)

Teaching *Twilight*: Edward as Byronic Hero. http://teachingtwilight.wordpress.com/about/ (Viewed December 1, 2011)

Tennyson, Lord Alfred. The Eagle. http://www.allgreatquotes.com/bird_quotes3.shtml (Viewed September 19, 2011)

Time-Life Books (2003) *Forests of the Vampires: Slavic Myth*. Sterling Publishing

Time Magazine Department. "10 Questions for Stephenie Meyer". Thursday, August 21, 2008. http://www.time.com/time/magazine/article/0,9171,1834663,00.html#ixzz1VLrbONdC (Accessed August 17, 2011)

TwilightMOMS. Symbolism in *Twilight* Series Thread. Posts by Shimmerskin, whome. http://forum.twilightmoms.com/archive/index.php/t-58499.html (Viewed August 17, 2011)

TwilightMOMS. *Twilight* Saga General Discussion Forum. Post by LynnL, February 3, 2009 http://forum.twilightmoms.com/archive/index.php/t-42614.html (Viewed August 17, 2011)

TwilightMOMS. *Twilight* Books General Discussion Forum. TwilightMOMS post, Maria, May 9, 2008. http://forum.twilightmoms.com/archive/index.php/t-33594.html (Viewed November 11, 2011)

TwilightMOMS. *Twilight* Books General Discussion Forum. TwilightMOMS post, sheacox January 1, 2009. http://forum.twilightmoms.com/archive/index.php/t-33594.html (Viewed November 11, 2011)

TwilightMOMS. *Twilight* Books General Discussion Forum > The Cullen Home. Posted by scoundrel March 15, 2011.

http://forum.twilightmoms.com/archive/index.php/t-39356.html (Viewed Nov 11, 2011)

TwilightMOMS. *Twilight* Books General Discussion Forum > The Cullen Home. Posted by scoundrel, March 20, 2011. http://forum.twilightmoms.com/archive/index.php/t-39356.html (Viewed Nov 11, 2011)

TwilightMOMS. Mythology and *Twilight* style vampires [Archive] – TwilightMOMS Forums http://forum.twilight moms.com/archive/index.php/t-58499.html Pygmalion's Tale posted by Shimmerskin June 17, 2011 (Viewed November 11, 2011)

TwilightMOMS. *Twilight* Books General Discussion Forum > Mythology and *Twilight* style vampires. http://forum .twilightmoms.com/archive/index.php/t-58499.html Asphodel Meadows posted by whome, March 2, 2010 (Viewed November 11, 2011)

TwilightMOMS. Symbolism in the *Twilight* Series [Archive] – TwilightMOMS Forums, TwilightMOMS, posted by Blushingmommy November 18, 2008. http://forum. twilightmoms.com/archive/index.php/t-45310.html (Viewed November 11, 2011)

TwilightMOMS. *Twilight* Books General Discussion Forum > The Cullen Home. Posted by scoundrel March 31, 2011. http://forum.twilightmoms.com/archive/index.php/t-39356.html (Viewed Nov 11, 2011)

TwilightMOMS. *Twilight* Books General Discussion Forum. http://forum.twilightmoms.com/archive/index.php/t-58937.html Diamond Ring Effect posted by Ava1981 on November 10, 2009 (Viewed November 11, 2011)

TwilightMOMS. *Twilight* Books General Discussion Forum > Mythology and *Twilight* style vampires. http:// forum.twilightmoms.com/archive/index.php/t-58499.html Carlisle-Prometheus Link, post by perkysue, Feb 13, 2010

TwilightMOMS. Symbolism in *Twilight* Series. http:/

forum.twilightmoms.com/showthread.php?45310-Symbolism-in-the-Twilight-Series post by Ava1989, December 30, 2009 (Viewed Nov 11, 2011)

TwilightMOMS. Symbolism in the *Twilight* Series. Post by Joanna Maria, April 6, 2010. http://forum.twilightmoms.com/showthread.php?45310-Symbolism-in (Viewed December 8, 2011)

TwilightMOMS. Symbolism in the *Twilight* Series. Post by Ava1981, December 30, 2009. http://forum.twilightmoms.com/archive/index.php/t-45310.html (Viewed December 8, 2011)

TwilightMOMS. First Beach vs The Meadow [Archive]. Post by Immortal Diamond, October 29, 2009) http://forum.twilightmoms.com/archive/index.php/t-58937.html (Viewed December 8, 2011)

Vampire. http://www.encyclopedia.com/topic/Vampires.aspx. *Encyclopedia of Occultism and Parapsychology,* 2001 (Accessed August 3, 2011)

Vampires: Myths of the Past and the Future. http://www.h-net.org/announce/show.cgi?ID=177736

(Accessed April 30, 2011)

Volterra, Italy. http://twilightsaga.wikia.com/wiki/Volterra,_Italy (Accessed November 3, 2011)

"Was the Hope Diamond on the Titanic?" http://www.diamond-trade.com/basics/famous.cfm (Accessed November 11, 2011)

White, TH (1939) *The Sword in the Stone*. New York: Putman

Wikipedia: The Free Encyclopedia. Number 13. http://en.wikipedia.org/wiki/13_ (number)

Witching hour. http://en.wikipedia.org/wiki/Witching_hour (Accessed January 1, 2011)

"Yea, though I walk through the valley of the shadow of death, I will fear no evil: for thou art with me". Psalm 23:4. http://library.thinkquest.org/16665/allquote.htm (Viewed January 1, 2011)

The Wolf Man (1941) http://en.wikipedia.org/wiki/The_Wolf_Man_(1941_film). Director/Producer: George Waggner. Written by: Curt Siodmak. Distributed by: Universal Pictures. Release date: December 12, 1941. (Viewed September 19, 2011)

Yew Tree. http://spiritlodge.yuku.com/topic/1073 (Viewed November 4, 2011)

Zeus Publications. http://www.zeus-publications.com/zeusgod.htm (Viewed November 10, 2011)

Zombie. http://en.wikipedia.org/wiki/Zombie (Viewed November 4, 2011)

Meet the Author

Dr. Julie-Anne Sykley is full-blood Ukrainian – a descendant of the dark, wild places of East Europe. Hey, that's *vampire* country! Traditional vampire myths originate in Slavic folklore for the winters are long and cold here, and the landscape raw and rugged. In fact, the word *vampire* derives from the Slavic root *pi*, which means to 'drink' or 'drain'.

Julie-Anne is also a fully qualified Australian Psychologist with more than 20 years professional experience helping people. From inner city Sydney to the remote Territory outback, she has assisted young people, adults, offenders, prisoners, and traditional Aboriginal people to deal with a wide range of mental health issues. Julie-Anne is keen to promote mental health skills and increase people's power to relax, solve problems, and develop positive coping strategies. This is why she wrote this book for you!

Julie-Anne currently resides in the Northern Territory where she lives with cyclones, crocodiles, her partner Steffanko (a Croatian vampire) and a bright red parrot named Ruby.

Beware! If Julie-Anne was ever turned into a *Twilight*-style vampire, her 'gift' would be a non-stop crazy 'super-humor'.

What does the cover design mean?

The *apple* – a symbol of 'knowledge', 'immortality' and 'temptation' used in *The Twilight Saga* – is set on fire. This image is trying to let readers know just how 'hot' symbols really are. Symbols have the power to chill and thrill, frighten and brighten, teach and stimulate, stir and agitate, guide and motivate, and set your inner world on fire. This book explores powerful symbols in the *Twilight* books and looks at how these symbols can work for you in real life. But beware. You may find some symbols so hypnotic, irresistible, and dazzling that they will make you burn for more, so to speak.

Thank You!

I really hope this book helps you, empowers you or inspires you somehow. If you really liked something in this book or didn't like things in this book, do share your thoughts online and recommend the book to others. *Your* comments are important and will assist other people on a quest for truth, knowledge, a positive learning experience, and an enriching emotional adventure.

If you think something in this book really helps you or will really benefit others, feel free to share it and Like, Tweet or Digg it.

Please leave comments or feedback on Amazon.com.

OUR STREET
BOOKS

Our Street Books for children of all ages, deliver a potent mix of fantastic, rip-roaring adventure and fantasy stories to excite the imagination; spiritual fiction to help the mind and the heart grow; humorous stories to make the funny bone grow; historical tales to evolve interest; and all manner of subjects that stretch imagination, grab attention, inform, inspire and keep the pages turning. Our subjects include Non-fiction and Fiction, Fantasy and Science Fiction, Religious, Spiritual, Historical, Adventure, Social Issues, Humour, Folk Tales and more.